CBT: Science Into Practice

Series Editor

Nikolaos Kazantzis, Cognitive Behavior Therapy Research Unit
Melbourne, VIC, Australia

This series addresses topics that reflect current thinking in the field of cognitive behavior therapy, the most widely accepted form of therapy across mental health disciplines. Despite the consensus that CBT is an effective treatment modality, much of the existing clinical literature focuses on single facets, such as specific disorders or populations. Mostly it does not take into account the latest evidence for transdiagnostic change mechanisms and processes. This series provides guidance on how the latest evidence can be translated into practice. Volumes focus on enhancing flexibility in both the selection and delivery of techniques tailored to individual clients. Each provides clinical insights enhanced by case studies and vignettes to ensure relevance for the practicing professional.

Elizabeth M. Goetter
Editor

Optimizing Treatment Engagement Processes in CBT for Anxiety and Related Disorders

Springer

Editor
Elizabeth M. Goetter
Department of Psychology
La Salle University
Philadelphia, PA, USA

Department of Psychiatry
Massachusetts General Hospital
Boston, MA, USA

ISSN 2946-5419 ISSN 2946-5427 (electronic)
CBT: Science Into Practice
ISBN 978-3-031-91438-6 ISBN 978-3-031-91439-3 (eBook)
https://doi.org/10.1007/978-3-031-91439-3

This Springer imprint is published by the registered company Springer Nature Switzerland AG
The registered company address is: Gewerbestrasse 11, 6330 Cham, Switzerland

Foreword

Cognitive behavior therapy (CBT) has undergone significant evolution over the past several decades, refining both its theoretical foundation and clinical application. One of the most pressing challenges in the field remains optimizing patient engagement—ensuring that individuals not only begin but also remain committed to treatment. *Optimizing Treatment Engagement Processes in CBT for Anxiety and Related Disorders*, edited by Dr. Elizabeth Goetter, provides a vital resource for clinicians and researchers seeking to enhance engagement across various treatment modalities and patient populations. This volume, as part of the **CBT: Science into Practice** series, synthesizes cutting-edge empirical findings with practical strategies for promoting adherence and engagement in CBT for anxiety and related disorders.

Dr. Goetter, an Associate Professor in the Department of Psychology at La Salle University, has dedicated her work to understanding and addressing barriers to engagement in evidence-based treatments. She has brought together an esteemed group of scholars and clinicians to provide a comprehensive examination of treatment engagement across different levels of intervention.

This book is structured into two main sections, each offering a targeted perspective on treatment engagement:

Strategies and Considerations for Promoting Engagement. This section addresses core processes influencing engagement, beginning with the therapeutic alliance and its role in fostering adherence. The contributors examine how outcome expectancy, treatment credibility, and self-efficacy shape patient participation. Motivational Interviewing (MI) is also explored as a method to enhance patient readiness for treatment, particularly in cases where ambivalence presents a barrier. Additionally, this section highlights engagement challenges specific to exposure therapy, outlining therapist strategies to enhance adherence and avoid common pitfalls. Furthermore, emerging technological approaches, including videoconferencing and virtual reality, are discussed in the context of improving access and engagement in exposure-based treatments.

As CBT continues to be implemented across diverse populations, cultural competence is essential for maximizing treatment engagement. This section also provides guidance on culturally responsive assessment and case conceptualization, emphasizing how clinicians can adapt CBT to align with patients' cultural backgrounds and lived experiences. A key chapter explores how fostering a positive racial and ethnic identity can support engagement, reinforcing the need for clinicians to approach treatment with cultural humility and responsiveness.

Engagement with Specific Populations. The second section of the book delves into engagement strategies tailored to specific clinical populations. Individual chapters address engagement challenges in social anxiety disorder (SAD), generalized anxiety disorder (GAD), panic disorder, obsessive-compulsive disorder (OCD), and posttraumatic stress disorder (PTSD). Additionally, specialized considerations for working with youth and families, as well as older adults, are presented, ensuring that engagement strategies are adapted to developmental and contextual needs.

Several contributions in this volume stand out as particularly valuable. The discussion on integrating MI into CBT provides a structured approach to addressing ambivalence, thereby reducing dropout rates and fostering long-term engagement. Equally important is the focus on exposure therapy adherence—an area where both patient and therapist challenges can lead to suboptimal treatment outcomes. By leveraging principles from inhibitory learning theory and motivational strategies, the book offers solutions to optimize exposure-based interventions.

Furthermore, the examination of videoconferencing and virtual reality highlights how digital advancements are reshaping engagement strategies, particularly in an era of increasing telehealth implementation. The emphasis on cultural responsiveness ensures that CBT remains adaptable and relevant to a broad range of individuals, acknowledging the role of identity and systemic barriers in shaping engagement.

The insights in this volume are essential reading for clinicians across disciplines—including psychologists, psychiatrists, clinical social workers, and trainees—who are committed to optimizing engagement in evidence-based interventions. By drawing upon the latest research and integrating practical applications, Dr. Goetter and her collaborators have created a resource that advances both the science and practice of CBT.

This book makes a significant contribution to our understanding of treatment engagement, offering both a conceptual framework and actionable strategies for clinicians. By emphasizing the therapeutic alliance within the broader framework of collaborative empiricism, integrating MI principles, and addressing process barriers, this volume stands as a crucial guide for those working to enhance the efficacy of CBT in real-world practice.

Conflicts of Interest

I have to disclose royalties from New Harbinger Publications, Inc. (The Anxiety Skills Workbook) and Springer Nature (Prolonged Exposure for PTSD: Innovations to Improve Access, Engagement, and Outcomes (CBT: Science Into Practice)). Kazantzis disclosed his royalties from the Guilford Press (Therapeutic Relationship in Cognitive Behavior Therapy; Cognitive and Behavior Theories in Clinical

Practice), Routledge (Using Homework Assignments in Cognitive Behavior Therapy); SpringerNature publishers (CBT: Science into Practice Book Series; Handbook of Homework Assignments in Psychotherapy: Research, Practice, & Prevention). He also disclosed editor stipend from the Association for Behavioral and Cognitive Therapies for his role as Editor-in-Chief for Cognitive and Behavioral Practice (Elsevier).

Nikolaos Kazantzis, Ph.D.
Book Series Editor, **CBT: Science into Practice**

Cognitive Behavior Therapy Research Unit
Melbourne, VIC, Australia
Beck Institute for Cognitive
Behavior Therapy
Philadelphia, PA, USA

Nikolaos Kazantzis

Contents

Chapter 1
Introduction

Elizabeth M. Goetter

Anxiety disorders are the most prevalent category of mental health disorders. In the United States, approximately one in three adults will meet diagnostic criteria for an anxiety disorder at some point in their life (Kessler et al., 2005). Anxiety disorders typically develop early in life (Kessler et al., 2007) and are associated with reduced quality of life (Cramer et al., 2005; Balayan et al., 2014). Comorbidity (Jacobi et al., 2004) and recurrence (Scholten et al., 2013) are common, likely contributing to the reasons why anxiety disorders are one of the leading causes of global disability (Baxter et al., 2014). Although no longer classified as anxiety disorders, obsessive compulsive disorder (OCD) and posttraumatic stress disorder (PTSD) are reflected in these figures, and are worth studying alongside the anxiety disorders (panic disorder [PD], social anxiety disorder [SAD], generalized anxiety disorder [GAD], and specific phobia) given the typically shared presence of maladaptive fear-based cognitions (e.g., overestimation of threat), physiological responses, and avoidance behaviors. Moreover, OCD and PTSD commonly co-occur with other anxiety disorders (e.g., Ginzburg et al., 2010; Ruscio et al., 2008). Additionally, individuals with anxiety disorders, OCD, and PTSD, have increased mortality relative to those without these conditions (Meier et al., 2016).

Despite the prevalence and detrimental impact of anxiety and related disorders, a large percentage will likely not receive adequate treatment for their condition (Wang et al., 2005). This is typically referred to as a "treatment gap," and can be defined as the percentage of individuals with an anxiety disorder or related condition who do not receive mental health treatment (Kohn et al., 2004). Although estimated prevalence rates of treatment gaps vary due to differences in study sample

E. M. Goetter (✉)
Department of Psychology, La Salle University, Philadelphia, PA, USA

Department of Psychiatry, Massachusetts General Hospital, Boston, MA, USA
e-mail: goetter@lasalle.edu

E. M. Goetter (ed.), *Optimizing Treatment Engagement Processes in CBT for Anxiety and Related Disorders*, CBT: Science Into Practice,
https://doi.org/10.1007/978-3-031-91439-3_1

characteristics, methodological approaches, timeframe parameters used when examining receipt of treatment, and definitions of what constitutes a treatment, it is unquestionable that the unmet need for anxiety disorders is substantial. For instance, one study of a nationally representative sample in the United States found that among individuals with PTSD, over 40% indicated a current unmet need for mental health treatment (Nobles et al., 2016). In a review study of over 35 community epidemiological surveys of adults, the estimated current treatment gap for those with OCD was greater than 50% (Kohn et al., 2004). In a study of individuals with panic disorder and social anxiety in Canada, where there is a nationalized healthcare system, nearly 70% of participants endorsed having a period of unmet need in their lifetime (Chartier-Otis et al., 2010). Furthermore, there is evidence that rates of unmet need are higher among marginalized individuals, such as those with minoritized racial and ethnic identities (e.g., Nobles et al., 2016).

The rates of unmet need are discouraging because anxiety and related conditions are highly treatable. Chiefly among evidence-based treatments is cognitive behavioral therapy (CBT), a short-term, skills-based intervention that targets maladaptive thoughts and behaviors that maintain dysfunctional anxiety responses. Although the specific skills taught may vary across disorders, most CBTs for anxiety include psychoeducation, reappraisal and modification of overly-generalized and often catastrophic fear-based cognitions, exposure to conditioned fear stimuli, skills practice, and relapse prevention. Decades of evidence have accrued in support of CBT as the front-line psychotherapy treatment for anxiety and related conditions. For instance, CBT for anxiety is associated with large within-treatment effect sizes (Otte, 2011), outperforms inactive control conditions (e.g., Butler et al., 2006), and is adaptable to telehealth-mediated forms of delivery (e.g., Berryhill et al., 2019; Rees & Maclaine, 2015). Corresponding treatment guidelines reflect the strong evidence base and CBT is strongly recommended as a first-line treatment of anxiety disorders (e.g., Tolin et al., 2015), OCD (e.g., NICE, 2013), and PTSD (e.g., VA/DOD, 2023).

There are numerous barriers to treatment and they exist on several levels. On an individual level, people have difficulty identifying anxiety disorders (Coles & Coleman, 2010) and lack knowledge about their treatability (Marques et al., 2010; Sareen et al., 2007). General health practitioners also have difficulty identifying anxiety disorders, representing a potential lost opportunity for diagnosis and referral (Olariu et al., 2015). Treatment access may be further impeded by stigma (Goetter et al., 2020), negative beliefs about treatments or desire to handle problems on one's own (Heinig et al., 2021), or the symptoms of the disorders themselves needing treatment, i.e. avoidance (Chartier-Otis et al., 2010). On a systems level, many people face logistical barriers, such as cost, insurance coverage concerns, and wait times (e.g., Chartier-Otis et al., 2010). Specialized providers can be difficult to access for people in underserved or rural areas (Gamm et al., 2010) and unfortunately dissemination efforts and sufficient training of providers in these front-line, evidence-based treatments cannot keep up with need (Gunter & Whittal, 2010). Systemic racism, discrimination, and health inequities contribute to unmet need and may be disproportionately salient among individuals with minoritized racial and ethnic identities, socially and economically oppressed groups (including rural populations), and other marginalized groups of people, such as gender and sexual minorities (e.g., Goetter et al., 2020; Nobles et al., 2016; Morales et al., 2020; Williams et al., 2012). Unfortunately, there is also evidence to suggest that the severity of one's anxiety disorder is associated with increased unmet need (e.g., Chartier-Otis et al., 2010) and perceived barriers to care (e.g., Goetter et al., 2020).

Once individuals decide to seek treatment, there are additional concerns related to treatment engagement. For instance, some patients receive non-evidence-based treatments for their condition (Marques et al., 2010). Among those who do successfully access an evidence-based treatment, a substantial number will receive less than adequate amounts of treatment (Wang et al., 2005). Dropout, or attrition, from CBT for anxiety and related conditions is a considerable concern (e.g., Bentley et al., 2021; Hans & Hiller, 2013). For example, in a large meta-analytic review, dropout rate estimates from CBT for anxiety ranged between 14% and 29% depending on the disorder (see Swift & Greenberg, 2014). Precise estimates are difficult to determine due to varying definitions of attrition, heterogeneity with respect to setting and institutional variables, as well as whether the treatment was delivered as part of a randomized trial or in a naturalistic setting, but clinicians and researchers note that dropout is problematic. Further compounding the problem is the reality that dropout is difficult to predict, and studies that aim to identify who is at risk for dropout have been frustratingly inconclusive (Taylor et al., 2012).

Reasons for dropout are myriad and cannot always be ascertained. Although it is sometimes due to improvement (e.g., Bados et al., 2007; Szafranski et al., 2017) less benign reasons may include issues of low motivation, low treatment expectations, dissatisfaction or preference for other treatments, insurmountable logistical inconveniences, and problems in the therapeutic alliance, including cultural misattunement (Gaztambide, 2012; Taylor et al., 2012). Dropout is problematic because it seems most common early in treatment (Bentley et al., 2021), meaning individuals have not had a full course of treatment and presumably remain symptomatic. Indeed, dropout appears to be associated with unremitted symptoms (Zieve et al., 2019) and dissatisfaction in treatment (Bentley et al., 2021), which may potentially deter future treatment-seeking. Managing issues of patient dropout can also be associated with costly mental health systems inefficiencies (see Barrett et al., 2008 for a review).

Although dropout is perhaps the most extreme manifestation of underengagement, subtler forms of underengagement are likely more prevalent. For example, patients may arrive late for or miss sessions, not adhere to between-session exercises or homework, or engage in avoidance behaviors that undermine treatment success and impede symptom improvement. Supporting engagement in treatment is essential because it optimizes outcomes for patients. For example, homework adherence predicts outcomes in CBT for anxiety disorders (e.g., LeBeau et al., 2013) and is associated with higher quality psychotherapy (Kazantzis et al., 2010). Engagement in treatment remains a central consideration, even after utilization barriers have been overcome. Given the significant unmet need and numerous barriers to care, including those faced by patients already accessing treatment, it is crucially important to understand how best to support treatment engagement once patients access care. This is the impetus for the current book.

This book brings together experts on issues of treatment engagement for anxiety and related disorders to help clinicians support patient engagement and foster optimal treatment outcomes in CBT. Part I of the book focuses on topics of theoretical centrality to issues of the psychotherapy treatment engagement process, including the role of the therapeutic alliance; patient beliefs and expectancies; motivational processes; adherence considerations in exposure therapy, including therapist pitfalls and institutional barriers; cultural, diversity, and identity considerations; and technology applications. Part II of the book reviews the evidence of treatment access and utilization within specific anxious populations as well as key considerations for optimizing CBT engagement processes for these unique populations. Clinical case examples are included throughout to enhance applicability of the material and strategies discussed. In recognition of the increasingly diverse identities of those who seek psychotherapy, I am pleased to see how the authors showcase diverse case examples to illustrate issues of engagement and related teaching points. Each chapter also includes 3–6 clinical summary points and recommendations to distill information and underscore key learning points.

As editor of the text, my hope is this book offers knowledge and understanding of the myriad factors that can impede treatment engagement for individuals with anxiety and related disorders. This text aims to provide tangible and implementable strategies to clinicians who are working to support their patients' engagement in CBT and other evidence-based treatments. Anxiety disorders are highly prevalent and characterized by symptoms (e.g., behavioral avoidance, fear-based cognitions, interpersonal anxiety, and difficulty tolerating uncertainty) that despite the intentions of patients and their clinicians, can undermine engagement in CBT. May readers of this text be encouraged and inspired by the wisdom and knowledge shared from the authors featured within, to optimally support the patients in their care.

References

Bados, A., Balaguer, G., & Saldaña, C. (2007). The efficacy of cognitive–behavioral therapy and the problem of drop-out. *Journal of Clinical Psychology, 63*(6), 585–592.

Balayan, S., Cramer, A. J., & Van Minnen, J. (2014). Quality of life in anxiety disorders: A systematic review and meta-analysis. *Journal of Affective Disorders, 167*, 1–11.

Barrett, M. S., Chua, W. J., Crits-Christoph, P., Gibbons, M. B., & Thompson, D. (2008). Early withdrawal from mental health treatment: Implications for psychotherapy practice. *Psychotherapy: Theory, Research, Practice, Training, 45*(2), 247.

Baxter, A. J., Vos, T., Lee, A. Y., Flaxman, A. D., Gobel, B. P., Murray, C. J. L., & Whiteford, H. A. (2014). Global burden of mental disorders and other disorders affecting health: Findings from the global burden of disease study 2010. *The Lancet, 384*(1000), 1503–1517.

Bentley, K. H., Cohen, Z. D., Kim, T., Bullis, J. R., Nauphal, M., Cassiello-Robbins, C., et al. (2021). The nature, timing, and symptom trajectories of dropout from transdiagnostic and single-diagnosis cognitive-behavioral therapy for anxiety disorders. *Behavior Therapy, 52*(6), 1364–1376.

Berryhill, M. B., Halli-Tierney, A., Culmer, N., Williams, N., Betancourt, A., King, M., & Ruggles, H. (2019). Videoconferencing psychological therapy and anxiety: A systematic review. *Family Practice, 36*(1), 53–63. https://doi.org/10.1093/fampra/cmy072

Butler, A. C., Chapman, J. E., Forman, E. M., & Beck, A. T. (2006). The empirical status of cognitive-behavioral therapy: A review of meta-analyses. *Clinical Psychology Review, 26*(1), 17–31. https://doi.org/10.1016/j.cpr.2005.07.003

Chartier-Otis, M., Perreault, M., & Bélanger, C. (2010). Determinants of barriers to treatment for anxiety disorders. *Psychiatric Quarterly, 81*, 127–138.

Coles, M. E., & Coleman, S. L. (2010). Barriers to treatment seeking for anxiety disorders: Initial data on the role of mental health literacy. *Depression and Anxiety, 27*(1), 63–71. https://doi.org/10.1002/da.20620

Cramer, A. J., Van Minnen, J., & Spinhoven, P. (2005). Quality of life in anxiety disorders: A review. *Journal of Affective Disorders, 86*(2–3), 119–130.

Gamm, L., Stone, S., & Pittman, S. (2010). Mental health and mental disorders—A rural challenge: A literature review. *Rural healthy people, 2*(1), 97–114.

Gaztambide, D. J. (2012). Addressing cultural impasses with rupture resolution strategies: A proposal and recommendations. *Professional Psychology: Research and Practice, 43*(3), 183.

Ginzburg, K. N., Weiss, D. S., & Siegle, G. J. (2010). Comorbidity of anxiety disorders: A review of findings from the national comorbidity survey replication. *Clinical Psychology Review, 30*(7), 888–898.

Goetter, E. M., Frumkin, M. R., Palitz, S. A., Swee, M. B., Baker, A. W., Bui, E., & Simon, N. M. (2020). Barriers to mental health treatment among individuals with social anxiety disorder and generalized anxiety disorder. *Psychological Services, 17*(1), 5–12. https://doi.org/10.1037/ser0000254

Gunter, R. W., & Whittal, M. L. (2010). Dissemination of cognitive-behavioral treatments for anxiety disorders: Overcoming barriers and improving patient access. *Clinical Psychology Review, 30*(2), 194–202.

Hans, E., & Hiller, W. (2013). A meta-analysis of nonrandomized effectiveness studies on outpatient cognitive behavioral therapy for adult anxiety disorders. *Clinical Psychology Review, 33*(8), 954–964.

Heinig, I., Wittchen, H. U., & Knappe, S. (2021). Help-seeking behavior and treatment barriers in anxiety disorders: Results from a representative German community survey. *Community Mental Health Journal, 57*(8), 1505–1517. https://doi.org/10.1007/s10597-020-00767-5

Jacobi, F., Freyberger, H. J., & Lieb, R. (2004). Comorbidity of anxiety disorders: A review. *Journal of Psychiatric Research, 38*(2), 97–108.

Kazantzis, N., Whittington, C., & Dattilio, F. (2010). Meta-analysis of homework effects in cognitive and behavioral therapy: A replication and extension. *Clinical Psychology: Science and Practice, 17*(2), 144.

Kessler, R. C., Berglund, P., Demler, O., Jin, R., Merikangas, K. R., & Walters, E. E. (2005). Lifetime prevalence and age-of-onset distributions of DSM-IV disorders in the national comorbidity survey replication. *Archives of General Psychiatry, 62*(6), 593–602.

Kessler, R. C., Chiu, W. T., Demler, O., Merikangas, K. R., & Walters, E. E. (2007). Age-of-onset of mental disorders: A review of recent evidence from the national comorbidity survey replication adolescent supplement. *Journal of the American Academy of Child & Adolescent Psychiatry, 46*(8), 1009–1022.

Kohn, R., Saxena, S., Levav, I., & Saraceno, B. (2004). The treatment gap in mental health care. *Bulletin of the World Health Organization, 82*(11), 858–866.

LeBeau, R. T., Davies, C. D., Culver, N. C., & Craske, M. G. (2013). Homework compliance counts in cognitive-behavioral therapy. *Cognitive Behaviour Therapy, 42*(3), 171–179.

Marques, L., LeBlanc, N. J., Weingarden, H. M., Timpano, K. R., Jenike, M., & Wilhelm, S. (2010). Barriers to treatment and service utilization in an internet sample of individuals with obsessive-compulsive symptoms. *Depression and Anxiety, 27*(5), 470–475. https://doi.org/10.1002/da.20694

Meier, B. J., Osborn, C. Y., & Blazer, D. G. (2016). Mortality in adults with anxiety disorders: A systematic review and meta-analysis. *JAMA Psychiatry, 73*(7), 650–658.

Morales, D. A., Barksdale, C. L., & Beckel-Mitchener, A. C. (2020). A call to action to address rural mental health disparities. *Journal of Clinical and Translational Science, 4*(5), 463–467.

NICE (2013). *Obsessive-compulsive disorder: Evidence update September 2013.* NICE clinical guideline 31. Available at https://www.nice.org.uk/guidance/cg31/evidence/evidence-update-194847085

Nobles, C. J., Valentine, S. E., Gerber, M. W., Shtasel, D. L., & Marques, L. (2016). Predictors of treatment utilization and unmet treatment need among individuals with posttraumatic stress disorder from a national sample. *General Hospital Psychiatry, 43*, 38–45.

Olariu, E., Forero, C. G., Castro-Rodriguez, J. I., Rodrigo-Calvo, M. T., Álvarez, P., Martín-López, L. M., Sánchez-Toto, A., Adroher, N. D., Blasco-Cubedo, M. J., Vilagut, G., Fullana, M. A., & Alonso, J. (2015). Detection of anxiety disorders in primary care: A meta-analysis of assisted and unassisted diagnoses. *Depression and Anxiety, 32*(7), 471–484. https://doi.org/10.1002/da.22360

Otte, C. (2011). Cognitive behavioral therapy in anxiety disorders: Current state of the evidence. *Dialogues in Clinical Neuroscience, 13*(4), 413–421. https://doi.org/10.31887/DCNS.2011.13.4/cotte

Rees, C. S., & Maclaine, E. (2015). A systematic review of videoconference-delivered psychological treatment for anxiety disorders. *Australian Psychologist, 50*(4), 259–264. https://doi.org/10.1111/ap.12122

Ruscio, A. M., Stein, M. B., & Chiu, W. T. (2008). Comorbidity of anxiety and mood disorders. *Journal of Clinical Psychiatry, 69*(Suppl 9), 2–10.

Sareen, J., Jagdeo, A., Cox, B. J., Clara, I., ten Have, M., Belik, S. L., de Graaf, R., & Stein, M. B. (2007). Perceived barriers to mental health service utilization in the United States, Ontario, and The Netherlands. Psychiatric services (), 58(3), 357–364. doi:https://doi.org/10.1176/ps.2007.58.3.357

Scholten, R. F., de Graaf, R., & Spinhoven, P. (2013). Recurrence of anxiety disorders: A systematic review and meta-analysis. *Clinical Psychology Review, 33*(2), 126–139.

Swift, J. K., & Greenberg, R. P. (2014). A treatment by disorder meta-analysis of dropout from psychotherapy. *Journal of Psychotherapy Integration, 24*(3), 193.

Szafranski, D. D., Smith, B. N., Gros, D. F., & Resick, P. A. (2017). High rates of PTSD treatment dropout: A possible red herring? *Journal of Anxiety Disorders, 47*, 91–98.

Taylor, S., Abramowitz, J. S., & McKay, D. (2012). Non-adherence and non-response in the treatment of anxiety disorders. *Journal of Anxiety Disorders, 26*(5), 583–589.

Tolin, D. F., McKay, D., Forman, E. M., Klonsky, E. D., & Thombs, B. D. (2015). Empirically supported treatment: Recommendations for a new model. *Clinical Psychology: Science and Practice, 22*(4), 317–338. https://doi.org/10.1037/h0101729

VA/DoD Clinical Practice Guideline. (2023). *Management of posttraumatic stress disorder and acute stress disorder work group*. U.S. Government Printing Office.

Wang, P. S., Lane, M., Olfson, M., Pincus, H. A., Wells, K. B., & Kessler, R. C. (2005). Twelve-month use of mental health services in the United States: Results from the national comorbidity survey replication. *Archives of General Psychiatry, 62*(6), 629–640.

Williams, M. T., Domanico, J., Marques, L., Leblanc, N. J., & Turkheimer, E. (2012). Barriers to treatment among African Americans with obsessive-compulsive disorder. *Journal of Anxiety Disorders, 26*(4), 555–563.

Zieve, G. G., Persons, J. B., & Yu, L. A. D. (2019). The relationship between dropout and outcome in naturalistic cognitive behavior therapy. *Behavior Therapy, 50*(1), 189–199.

Part I
Strategies and Considerations for Promoting Engagement

Chapter 2
Attending to the Therapeutic Alliance

Allison L. Baier, Shannon M. Kehle-Forbes, and Tara Galovski

Introduction

The therapeutic alliance is a critical factor contributing to the success of cognitive behavioral therapy (CBT) for anxiety and related disorders with specific texts dedicated to cultivating a positive and productive therapeutic relationship (Castonguay et al., 2010; Kazantzis et al., 2017). The importance of the therapist–patient relationship was recognized from the inception of CBT (Beck et al., 1979; Goldfried & Davison, 1974). Mounting evidence supports the association between a stronger alliance and better treatment engagement, both within sessions (e.g., attendance, active participation; Hara et al., 2015; Murphy et al., 2022) and between sessions (e.g., homework adherence; Hara et al., 2017). Research on the therapeutic process in CBT has proliferated in the past decade highlighting the importance of the alliance to the delivery and efficacy of CBT for anxiety and related disorders (e.g., Buchholz & Abramowitz, 2020; Luong et al., 2020).

A. L. Baier (✉) · T. Galovski
National Center for PTSD Women's Health Sciences Division at VA Boston Healthcare System, Boston, MA, USA

Boston University Chobanian & Avedisian School of Medicine, Boston, MA, USA
e-mail: Allison.Baier@va.gov; Tara.Galovski@va.gov

S. M. Kehle-Forbes
National Center for PTSD Women's Health Sciences Division at VA Boston Healthcare System, Boston, MA, USA

Center for Care Delivery & Outcomes Research, Minneapolis VA Healthcare System, Minneapolis, MN, USA

Department of Medicine, University of Minnesota, Minneapolis, MN, USA
e-mail: Shannon.Kehle-Forbes@va.gov

E. M. Goetter (ed.), *Optimizing Treatment Engagement Processes in CBT for Anxiety and Related Disorders*, CBT: Science Into Practice,
https://doi.org/10.1007/978-3-031-91439-3_2

Definition of Alliance in CBT

Writings from early cognitive and behaviorally oriented theorists acknowledged the importance of relational factors on treatment success highlighting specific relational qualities such as warmth, empathy, genuineness, and trust and described the need for a strong therapeutic alliance in CBT as similar to other therapies (Beck et al., 1979; Brady et al., 1980; Goldfried & Davison, 1974). Bordin's (1979) seminal work helped form contemporary, pantheoretical definitions of the alliance as a collaborative relationship between therapist and patient fostered by three essential components: agreement on therapeutic goals, consensus on therapeutic tasks that make up therapy, and a mutually supportive and respectful bond between patient and therapist (Bordin, 1994). To this end, the therapeutic alliance is a dyadic process and perspectives on the nature and quality of the relationship may differ between therapist and patient.

Although definitionally the therapeutic alliance is similar across psychotherapies, the theoretical contribution of alliance as a therapy element differs in CBT than from other therapies in meaningful ways. CBT assumes that the therapeutic alliance fosters engagement in the specific cognitive and behavioral techniques of CBT, such as cognitive restructuring or exposure exercises, but does not serve as a specific change mechanism itself. Thus, the therapeutic alliance in CBT is generally theorized as a critical component necessary for successful therapy and treatment engagement but not sufficient alone to cause clinical improvement (Castonguay et al., 2010). Further, CBT emphasizes collaborative empiricism, a concept that first emerged from cognitive theory (Beck et al., 1979). Working as a team, patient and therapist utilize the scientific method to iteratively identify and address problems collaboratively. For example, in more cognitively-oriented therapies, therapists often use Socratic dialogue wherein the therapist purposefully avoids the role of "expert" and instead relies on principles of inductive reasoning and reflection to help both the therapist and patient together identify and examine the issues that brought the patient to therapy (Dobson, 2022). Below we briefly review empirical research on alliance in CBT and then discuss clinical strategies for optimizing the relationship.

Historical Debate about the Nature and Role of Alliance in CBT

The historical empirical focus on orientation-specific techniques rather than relational variables in CBT fueled common clinical concerns that CBT is too rigid with little room for relationship building resulting in a presumed detrimental effect on the therapeutic alliance (Addis & Krasnow, 2000; Lilienfeld et al., 2013). Such concerns appear to be particularly prominent for exposure-based techniques (Meyer et al., 2014). Furthermore, concerns that CBT is more of a "cookie-cutter approach" proliferated in the mid-90 s (Garfield, 1996) and continue to persist decades later (Gnaulati, 2022). Specifically, in applying a manualized approach to complicated clinical presentations, academicians and clinicians alike feared that the nuances of the therapeutic process that can only be revealed in the presence of a strong alliance would be lost despite evidence of the contrary (Lilienfeld et al., 2013). However, the importance of the therapeutic alliance is evidenced by multiple meta-analyses and empirical reviews consistently demonstrating a modest, positive correlation between good alliance and symptom reduction irrespective of psychotherapy type or diagnosis (Fluckiger et al., 2018; Horvath et al., 2011). Thus, despite the historical debates surrounding CBT, the importance of the therapeutic alliance to treatment is less arguable; perspectives differ most across theoretical orientations on the ability of the treatment approach to yield a strong alliance and the reliance on the therapeutic relationship as a critical mechanism of action in fostering change.

Empirical Study of Alliance in CBT

Efforts to understand the relative contribution of the alliance in CBT have increasingly focused on testing three hypotheses regarding the nature of the alliance–outcome relationship in CBT: The alliance may directly influence symptom reduction, symptom reduction may lead to improvements in alliance, or the relationship observed between the alliance and outcome may be spurious and the result of third variables (Pfeifer & Strunk, 2015). This research is challenging as therapy process variables must be studied longitudinally in order to establish temporal precedence (Kazdin, 2007). Furthermore, this type of study requires the difficult task of disentangling the trait-like (reflecting individual differences; between-patient effect) and state-like (reflecting a potential causal process; within-patient effect) components of alliance (Zilcha-Mano & Ben David-Sela, 2022). Although both trait-like and state-like components appear to play a role in treatment outcome (Zilcha-Mano, 2017), the latter reflects the presumed malleable, treatment-related component of alliance. To date, most research examining the alliance–outcome relationship does not adequately disentangle these alliance components and research has predominantly focused on depression with less attention specifically on CBT for anxiety and related disorders (Baier et al., 2020).

In a study investigating longitudinal changes in alliance in CBT delivered weekly for social anxiety, disaggregated multilevel models revealed the state-like alliance component assessed pre-session predicted subsequent decreases in social anxiety at the following session suggesting alliance may drive symptom change or facilitate other processes driving symptom improvement (Kivity et al., 2021). Similarly, for veterans completing an intensive treatment for PTSD that included receiving daily cognitive processing therapy (a CBT treatment for PTSD), alliance ratings increased over the course of treatment and improvements in the state-like alliance component predicted subsequent reductions in PTSD symptoms over time (Held et al., 2022). Furthermore, Rubel et al. (2019) found that better state-like alliance component scores in one session were followed by fewer anxiety symptoms in the next session in a sample of GAD patients treated with CBT. Taken together, this research lends support for the alliance as a precursor of symptom change, theoretically via greater patient engagement in, and benefit from, cognitive and behavioral tasks. Indeed, research suggests a stronger alliance may be associated with better treatment engagement, including lower risk of dropout (Moshe-Cohen et al., 2024) and better homework adherence (Hara et al., 2017).

However, other studies suggest the alliance–outcome relationship may be driven more by stable patient characteristics (the trait-like alliance component) rather than the state-like components (which reflect potential causal processes). For example, Baier et al. (2024) examined the temporal relationships between change in negative posttraumatic cognitions and alliance among a PTSD sample receiving prolonged exposure or sertraline. They initially found a robust temporal relationship between alliance and subsequent cognition change; however, after disentangling effects, the relation observed was entirely accounted for by the between-patient variability in alliance. These findings suggested that stable patient traits (e.g., presumed demographic variables, interpersonal pathology) drove the alliance–outcome relationship initially observed, highlighting the potential role of patient characteristics on therapy process and the need for additional study (Baier et al., 2024). Additional research is needed to understand if and how stable patient traits may impact the development of the alliance and subsequent engagement in treatment.

Some researchers have further hypothesized that the bond, goal, and task components of alliance (Bordin, 1994) may differentially contribute to outcome in meaningful ways for anxiety disorders. For example, in a study of exposure and response prevention (ERP) for OCD, Wheaton et al. (2016) found that although the overall strength of the alliance did not predict outcomes, higher task alliance scores, but not goal or bond scores, were associated with lower posttreatment symptom severity, a finding mediated by patient adherence to homework, an indicator of treatment engagement. In another study of ERP for OCD, higher task and goal alliance scores, but not bond scores, were associated with treatment outcome (Hagen et al., 2017). However, in both studies, the authors reported on the alliance at only one time point (session 3) and did not adequately disentangle the alliance components thus limiting findings. In a study investigating prolonged exposure for PTSD, stronger within-patient task and bond scores, but not goal scores, were associated with larger decreases in symptoms over the course of treatment (Hoffart et al., 2013). Despite the variability in these findings, this evidence suggests patient and therapist agreement on the tasks of treatment, i.e., the methods used to achieve symptom reduction, may be particularly important in CBT, supporting the theoretical importance of the collaborative relationship in CBT. See Luong et al. (2020) and Buchholz and Abramowitz (2020) for comprehensive reviews of the alliance–outcome relationship in CBT and exposure therapy for anxiety and related disorders.

Considering the dyadic nature of the therapeutic alliance, concordance among patient and therapist alliance ratings may also be particularly relevant (Kazantzis & Dobson, 2024). For example, convergence in patient–therapist alliance ratings was associated with greater reductions in worry and distress among patients receiving

CBT for generalized anxiety disorder (Coyne et al., 2018). And in a sample of patients receiving CBT for panic disorder, higher combined alliance ratings predicted lower attrition rates and greater symptom improvements (Moshe-Cohen et al., 2024). Alliance ratings may be influenced by individual patient and therapist factors. Buchholz and Abramowitz (2020) proposed the possibility that the therapeutic alliance may be particularly important for individuals with certain diagnoses such as OCD and PTSD compared to other anxiety and fear-based disorders due to the common feelings of guilt and shame that may impact patient disclosure, treatment engagement, and buy-in until a strong relationship is built. However, the authors noted that more research across anxiety and related disorders is needed to further evaluate this possibility.

Therapist factors likely also impact the therapeutic alliance though explicit empirical research examining the role of therapist factors on the alliance in CBT is limited. Although not specific to CBT, two reviews found that therapist personal qualities and attributes (e.g., being warm, honest, respectful, and trustworthy) were associated with more positive alliance ratings (Ackerman & Hilsenroth, 2003), whereas the opposite qualities and attributes (e.g., being uncertain, critical, and rigid) were associated with more negative ratings (Ackerman & Hilsenroth, 2001). The therapeutic alliance may also be related to therapist competence and adherence to treatment in CBT. In a longitudinal analysis pooling data from three studies that examined CBT for social anxiety, illness anxiety, and depression, Weck et al. (2015) found the therapeutic alliance significantly predicted therapist adherence and competence but the reverse relationships were not found suggesting alliance may be an important foundation for the adherent and competent application of therapy techniques. Furthermore, the importance of therapist cultural competency in building a strong therapeutic alliance (Asnaani & Hofmann, 2012) and knowledge of social determinants of health has also been emphasized (Williams et al., 2022).

Understanding the precise nature of the alliance–outcome relationship is complex. Recent methodological and statistical advances have helped to better understand and differentiate the influences of stable trait-like and malleable state-like components of alliance on outcome though more research is needed. Nonetheless, the studies highlighted here suggest the therapeutic alliance is an important component of treatment engagement in CBT. The remainder of this chapter focuses on clinical strategies for optimizing the alliance in CBT.

Putting Research into Practice

CBT for anxiety and related disorders targets cognitions and behaviors that maintain anxiety. Successful therapy requires patients to be vulnerable and open with their emotions and thoughts, and be willing to work with their therapist to learn new ways of thinking and behaving. Thus, the effective use of therapeutic techniques in CBT, and patient engagement in CBT, is only possible within the context of a strong therapeutic alliance. In order to illustrate the clinical strategies introduced, we present two case studies.

Clinical Case Examples

Case 1

Rosie is a 33-year-old, married, cis-gender, Black woman with one toddler aged daughter. She meets DSM-5 criteria for OCD. She has several obsessions related to inflicting harm and violence on loved ones, especially her toddler such as drowning her child in the bathtub or pushing her child out the second story window. As a result, she engages in several compulsive rituals to "cleanse" her thoughts such as praying, washing, and seeking reassurance from others. Growing up, her parents spoke poorly of those with mental health difficulties which has resulted in internalized stigma around help-seeking. She also reports low mood and relationship difficulties with her spouse. Rosie has no prior experience with psychotherapy and has agreed to engage in Exposure and Response Prevention (ERP) in an outpatient anxiety clinic.

Case 2

Bobby is a 48-year-old, twice divorced man who served 10 years in the Army as an infantryman including 1 year-long combat tour in Baghdad, Iraq. He enlisted at 18 to escape an abusive home and since separating from service has struggled with an increase in PTSD symptoms predominantly related to childhood sexual abuse and characterized by extreme feelings of shame, nightmares, difficulty sustaining healthy relationships, and difficulty managing anger. He is chronically unemployed, lives in subsidized housing in a high-crime neighborhood, has been hospitalized six times for acute alcohol intoxication resulting in detox, and has completed multiple brief residential programs to address his substance use disorder. Bobby has agreed to Prolonged Exposure (PE) therapy and is being seen in the VA where he also participates in a weekly relapse prevention group.

Clinical Strategies for Optimizing Alliance

Convey Confidence in the CBT Approach and Utilize Foundational Clinical Skills

Treating anxiety is hard work—both for patient and therapist. Despite the volume of evidence supporting the efficacy and effectiveness of CBT for anxiety (Carpenter et al., 2018), therapists may express weariness about the treatment, especially the use of exposure citing concerns that exposure is dangerous and even unethical (Deacon et al., 2013; Meyer et al., 2020). Therapists may also wish to delay initiating CBT for anxiety in favor of spending time building the alliance and developing "readiness" for treatment despite evidence that such delays in care negatively impact patients (Cook et al., 2017). Thus, it is critical that therapists understand the theoretical underpinnings of CBT and the rationale for the techniques employed in treatment. Conveying confidence in the therapy is an important factor in establishing trust with patients and thus the therapeutic alliance. We encourage clinicians to reflect on their concerns about CBT and connect with both research-oriented and practice-oriented clinicians to address these concerns and regularly engage in discussions with colleagues to help dispel misapprehensions and improve confidence in CBT (Gallo & Barlow, 2012; Lilienfeld et al., 2013).

Core foundational clinical skills (e.g., empathy and warmth) from the outset of treatment is important for creating a space in which patients feel respected, valued, and safe to disclose their thoughts and emotions. Patients are often comforted by learning that their experiences are not uncommon and that their therapist is not "shocked" by what the patient shares and are often comforted when therapists express hope, optimism, and confidence in treatment. Additionally, remaining curious about your patient's experiences and maintaining a warm interpersonal style will help you to develop a robust case conceptualization, select and adapt the appropriate CBT techniques for your patient, promote treatment engagement, and address challenges as they arise. To illustrate some of these skills, consider Rosie who struggles during the intake to disclose the nature of her obsessive intrusive thoughts, particularly given the internalized stigma and shame she has around her mental health difficulties:

Therapist: Can you tell me more about these upsetting thoughts triggering anxiety?

Patient: Um. Yeah, I just get a little stressed when I'm alone with my daughter. Like, I worry about various things like her safety. Not that she's unsafe with me! I'd never hurt her! It's just stressful to think some of these things… You know, I'm not sure we need to talk about this. I'm just anxious. That's all I want to say about it. (Patient crosses her arms and looks away.)

Therapist (leaning in): I hear how important your daughter is to you and appreciate how upsetting it is to think about her being harmed. Based on what we've talked about, can I guess that you have thoughts of hurting your daughter and that you're ashamed of these thoughts and are finding it difficult to talk about it with me?

Patient (after a pause): Yeah, this is hard.

Therapist: I appreciate you saying so. I know it is hard to talk about those kinds of thoughts. It's important for you to know that everyone has intrusive thoughts like yours at times, including people without clinical levels of anxiety. You may not realize this because we usually don't share these unwanted, unpleasant thoughts with others, and sometimes our families and communities don't talk about them, but the majority of the population experiences such thoughts from time to time and often, these thoughts pertain to topics that are personally important. I want you to know that as strange or scary as you think your thoughts are, they are just thoughts and completely normal.

Patient (kind of laughs): If you say so.

Therapist: Why do you say that?

Patient: Well, I guarantee you my parents have never had these thoughts. They'd be so ashamed if they knew. My father always talks shit about "crazy" people.

Therapist: It sounds like you really value how your parents see you and from what you shared earlier, you really respect them. It also sounds like you may not have had much exposure to mental health information before now. Is that right?

Patient: Yeah.

Therapist: Well, let me share with you that I think it incredibly brave what you've done, seeking out care. And, I'm optimistic that we can work together to help you feel better. Would it be okay if I shared some more about what we know about obsessive thoughts like yours and effective treatment options?

Patient: Yes, I'd like that.

In the above example, the therapist watches the patient closely and uses validation, reflective statements, and gentle questions to surmise how difficult this conversation is for the patient and to solicit the general nature of her obsessive thoughts. The process of collaboratively engaging a patient in assessment (and then CBT) is presumed to build the relationship and thus there is no need for the therapist to delay the assessment of Rosie's obsessive thoughts in favor of some other standalone, nondirective alliance-building approach. However, the therapist capitalizes on the inherent flexibility of CBT and incorporates knowledge of various patient factors (e.g., internalized stigma and low mental health literacy) into their approach to the assessment and utilizes basic counseling skills (e.g., warmth and empathy), validation, cultural attunement, and psychoeducation to build hope and engagement in treatment.

Develop, Share, and Reinforce the Conceptualization and Treatment Plan

We begin to better understand our patients through diagnostic and functional assessment procedures and by soliciting patient goals for treatment. Patients will often respond with vague desires (e.g., "I want to feel less anxious") and although this is a reasonable desire, this is not a specific goal. We encourage therapists to take the time to help patients identify and develop "SMART" goals that are specific, measurable, attainable, realistic, and timely (Doran, 1981). The process of developing such goals presents an opportunity for therapists to potentially modify patient expectations and ensures patient and therapist are in agreement on what the targets of treatment will be, thereby promoting engagement in therapy. Consider Bobby's goals:

Therapist: Bobby, we've gone over a lot of information today about your traumatic experiences and how these memories are currently affecting you. Let's talk a little bit more about therapy. What would you like to see happen as a result of treatment?

Patient: I would like to not feel this fear anymore. I would never be anxious.

Therapist: Mmhmm. Let me ask you something. Based on our conversations about emotions and anxiety, and fear in particular, how reasonable would you say it is that you will never feel fear or anxiety again following treatment?

Patient (chuckling): Okay, I hear ya. Yeah, I'm sure there will be moments when I'm a bit anxious but, I'd like to not be anxious all the time. I'm so exhausted.

Therapist: That makes sense to me. So, if I'm hearing you correctly, it sounds like you'd like to reduce the frequency and intensity of these emotions.

Patient: Yeah.

Therapist: Okay, and if you were less anxious, what would that look like for you?

Patient: I'm not sure I understand what you mean.

Therapist: Let me rephrase that question. How would your life be different if therapy were to be helpful to you? What would you be doing (or not doing)?

Patient: Well, I'd be able to sleep through the night.

Therapist: Ah, so sleep would improve. What else?

Patient: I'd love to maybe start dating again without having to worry about going to a crowded restaurant or backing away from intimacy. I'd like to not fly off the handle in anger and I'd like to try and steer clear of alcohol. I'm afraid diving into this trauma stuff is going to lead me to drink again.

Therapist: Those sound like really important goals. Let's dive into them a bit further….

The therapist works to help Bobby understand that having "no anxiety" as a result of treatment is an unrealistic expectation and instead helps the patient identify, behaviorally, how he would like his life to be different following successful treatment. Additional conversations about the role of emotions may be helpful. Psychoeducation both about the nature and treatment of anxiety is important though therapists must be wary of lecturing the patient. Instead, therapists are encouraged to invite the patient to participate in the discussion, using Socratic questioning, and culturally appropriate metaphors and analogies, which will also foster treatment engagement.

As you collaborate with patients on the specifics of their treatment plan, drawing in the information you know about their goals will help cater treatment to target anxiety maintaining behaviors and explicitly work toward the patient's behavioral goals. Returning to these goals and relying on a strong therapeutic relationship can help with patient buy-in to treatment rationale during challenging moments. For example, consider how Bobby's therapist helps him work through the anticipatory anxiety prior to engaging in his first imaginal exposure after discussing the rationale for the imaginal and providing the necessary instructions.

Therapist: Okay, when you're ready start at the beginning.
Patient (after a long pause): I can't do this. I feel like I'm going to pass out.
Therapist: I believe you can do this. I'm right here with you. So you're in your room, tell me what happens next.
Patient (tearfully): Please don't make me do this… I can't do this.
Therapist (leaning forward and using a soft, confident voice): Bobby, I know this hard and, as we've talked about, I will never make you do anything. This is your therapy and the decision to engage in this imaginal exposure is yours, and yours only. We are also a team, you and I. And, as your coach *(referring to analogy previously used with patient)*, my job is to challenge you in the service of your goals. I'm encouraging you to do this imaginal exposure so that you get the most out of treatment.
Patient: I'm nervous.
Therapist: Mmhmm. What part feels hard?
Patient: Everything. I don't know… getting started I guess.
Therapist: Do you remember how you were feeling before your first in-vivo exercise?
Patient: Yeah, I was really scared. I felt like I couldn't breathe. Kind of like now!
Therapist: And what happened during that in-vivo?
Patient: It got easier as I stayed in the exercise.
Therapist: And what did you learn?
Patient: That my mind made it seem worse than it actually was.
Therapist: Yes. So I'm noticing similarities between how you were feeling before your first in-vivo and how you are feeling now. What do you make of this? How can we draw from your experience during the in-vivo to this moment right now?
Patient: That I can do this even though I'm anxious. The hardest part of the in-vivo was just getting started.
Therapist: Right. I think you may have a similar experience here—the hardest part being getting started. What do you say, shall we try it out?
Patient: Okay.

In this dialogue, the therapist uses their knowledge and confidence in the treatment to remain calm in the face of Bobby's increasing display of anxiety. The therapist also explicitly emphasizes the therapeutic relationship and the connection between therapeutic tasks (imaginal exposure) and reaching Bobby's specific goals. Sensing Bobby's trepidation, the therapist then engages Bobby in a brief conversation using Socratic questioning to draw parallels from the imaginal exposure to a previous exposure exercise in which Bobby experienced success.

Emphasize the Collaborative Nature of CBT

As a CBT therapist, you have an important responsibility to invite patients to become an active partner in their care, which will foster engagement in treatment and facilitate more positive outcomes. Many therapists may use a "coaching" metaphor to illustrate the collaborative nature of treatment and the therapist's role in guiding the patient outside their comfort zone so they can get the most out of therapy. You might consider communicating to your patient that, while you have specific expertise in treating anxiety, they (your patient) are the expert on themselves. Highlighting this fact validates patients' experiences and communicates the important role they have as an active, rather than passive, participant in therapy which helps patients build intrinsic motivation to change (Norouzian et al., 2021) and enhances treatment engagement (Kazantzis, 2024). Furthermore, helping patients develop self-efficacy and "become their own therapist" is also an important goal of CBT and sets the stage for continued gains post therapy.

The collaborative nature of treatment can be emphasized through the use of Socratic dialogue and collaborative empiricism yet both techniques may encounter resistance that impacts the relationship. Patients may hold on tightly to their beliefs for a number of reasons and any kind of questioning may feel unsetting or even seem threatening. As articulated by others (Galovski et al., 2020), the Socratic questioning process can be thought of as a dance—an opportunity to join together as a team to explore and evaluate the accuracy of thoughts and synthesize evidence gathered together from exposures or behavioral exercises. Additionally, therapists often play an important role in conducting therapeutic exposures with patients both in and outside of the office environment. In the following dialogue, the therapist works on an exposure with Rosie who has unwanted intrusive thoughts related to harming others. For the in-session exposure exercise, the therapist and patient collaboratively agree to conduct an exposure to a fear cue (i.e., a knife) associated with her intrusive thoughts and the therapist uses their easy rapport to facilitate the exercise.

Therapist: Okay, Rosie. You've had this knife in your hand for 2 min now. How are you feeling?

Patient: Anxious. I'm sweating, can't you tell?! I don't want to hurt you. My SUDS are like 90!

Therapist: Okay, I know this is difficult. You said, "I don't want to hurt you." Is your mind telling you something scary?

Patient: Yeah, it's a mix between thinking and seeing myself hurting you. Also I think I'm going to pass out. God, I can't believe you're trusting me to do this right now. Like, I've literally told you I have all these thoughts about hurting you.

Therapist: Ah, okay so you're having intrusive thoughts about hurting me and your brain is also telling you, "I am going to pass out."

Patient: Yeah.

Therapist: I can stick with this longer, and I think you can stick with this longer. I propose we let some more time pass and see if those things actually happen. What do you think?

Patient: If you trust me, I guess maybe I can trust myself. We can keep going.
Therapist: (after another 2 min). Are you hurting me?
Patient: No.
Therapist: Are you passing out?
Patient: No. I'm still with you.
Therapist: So your brain was telling you these bad things were going to happen but are they really happening?
Patient: No… my anxiety is.
Therapist: Right, and before we started, I asked you to predict how long you thought you could tolerate holding the knife. Do you remember what you said?
Patient: Yeah, I said 2 min.
Therapist: 2 min, that's right. It's been nearly 5 min! Your SUDS are high and you haven't done anything to hurt me. What do you make of all this?
Patient: Well this really sucks but I guess what I thought would happen hasn't. I worried that if I didn't complete the positive affirmation mantra to neutralize the bad thoughts, the bad things would happen. But they haven't happened. I haven't hurt you.
Therapist: Right! It sounds like you're learning something new.

In CBT, we often follow a specific treatment manual. While fidelity to the treatment is critical to success, it is also important to be flexible and research supports the efficacy of personalizing treatments (Galovski, 2024). Sticking to the manual at the expense of considering individual factors will undoubtedly impact the therapeutic relationship. In the following dialogue, consider how the therapists engages the patient in shared decision making to move forward with their treatment session.

Therapist: Rosie, is there anything else you'd like to add to our agenda today?
Patient (tearing up): Well, um, a friend—Sarah—was in a car accident earlier this week and she… she passed away 2 days ago.
Therapist: Oh, Rosie. I'm so sorry to hear about your loss. (pauses). What is going through your mind right now?
Patient (crying): Just how unfair the world is sometimes. I really cared about her but we hadn't connected in some time… It's hitting me really hard for some reason and I haven't been able to stop crying since I found out she died.
Therapist: Thank you for sharing with me. Learning about the death of someone you care is so painful and difficult and grief is a mix of many emotions. I'm aware of our agenda and our exposure practice for today. That said, it's also ok if we shift plans. We could continue with our exposure practice or save that for next session and instead spend some time talking about your loss. What would be most helpful for you today?
Patient: Really? Okay, yeah, I think I'd really like to talk about Sarah.
Therapist: Okay, then that's what we'll do. Let's save some time at the end of our session to briefly review homework from the past week and identify a plan for the coming week. Would that be ok?
Patient: Yeah, that sounds good.

In the above example, the therapist and patient collaboratively set the agenda. Upon learning about the patient's loss, the therapist was careful to not make assumptions and instead inquired about the patient's automatic thoughts in the moment and used that information to help the patient make a decision regarding how to move forward with the session. In doing so, the therapist was attentive to the patient's immediate needs and thus the alliance. Research suggests that adding emergency sessions and additional treatment sessions do not negatively impact treatment and may even lead to better outcomes (Galovski et al., 2012). Furthermore, the therapist and patient agreed to return to the protocol at the end of session to review homework completed in the previous week and explore the patient's openness to completing homework for the upcoming week helping to facilitate a return to the protocol at the following session.

Seek Feedback

Soliciting feedback from patients demonstrates your interest in their progress and clearly communicates that you value their input and the collaborative nature of therapy. Regularly seeking feedback provides an opportunity to identify potential therapeutic ruptures or stuck points in therapy. Informal methods of requesting feedback include protecting time at the end of each session to check in such as by saying, "how did our session go today?" or "How are you feeling about this treatment?" Be observant for changes in your patient's attitude, tone of voice, and body posture. Sudden changes may warrant investigation (e.g., "I noticed you seemed to shut down just now. I'm wondering if something I said didn't sit well with you"). Additionally, consider that there are many formal methods for assessing the strength of the therapeutic alliance including those that elicit patient, therapist, and independent observer perspectives. We recommend three of the most commonly used measures which have all demonstrated good psychometric properties: the Working Alliance Inventory (WAI; Horvath & Greenberg, 1989), the Helping Alliance Questionnaire (Haq; Luborsky et al., 1996), and the California Psychotherapy Alliance Scale (CALPAS; Marmar et al., 1989). Be curious and genuine, model openness with your body language and voice, and express appreciation for their willingness to provide the feedback. You can also communicate explicitly what you plan to do with the feedback. For example, you might state, "I appreciate you sharing this with me. My homework for the week is going to be to think about how to incorporate that feedback into our work to make sure you get the most out of treatment." During homework review at the following session, the therapist should share their thoughts on how the treatment might be adjusted or modified to reflect the patient's concerns and invite the patient to collaboratively discuss how they would like to move forward and what adjustments (if any) are needed. Regular solicitation of feedback will theoretically make it more likely that the therapist will receive candid feedback from patients and thus, more readily address alliance concerns, in turn optimizing patient outcomes.

Repair Ruptures

Therapeutic ruptures refer to points in therapy when the therapeutic relationship is strained due to disagreement about treatment goals, the tasks of therapy, or strain on the affective therapist–patient bond (Safran & Muran, 2000). Repairing ruptures is essential for optimizing and sustaining treatment engagement. Repaired ruptures refer to subsequent improvements in the alliance and may provide opportunity for further growth and clinical gains, whereas unrepaired ruptures are significant predictors of poorer outcome and dropout (Eubanks et al., 2018). You may become aware of a rupture through soliciting feedback from a patient, a patient volunteering their displeasure or frustration, or you may suspect through observation that there is newfound tension or strain in the relationship that warrants further investigation. Therapeutic ruptures range from more minor infractions or tensions in the relationship (e.g., a therapist jumps to Socratic questioning before the patient feels validated and heard) to difficulties that result in premature termination of therapy.

Ruptures may reflect a patient problem or symptom (e.g., an inaccurate belief that is impacting engagement in treatment) or reflect a need to collaboratively re-evaluate the case conceptualization and treatment plan. Irrespective of the reason for therapeutic rupture, it is important that therapists acknowledge their own contribution to the rupture. Research highlights the importance of repairing (Eubanks et al., 2018) and specific practice guides provide detailed suggestions for repairing ruptures in CBT (Impala et al., 2023). In addition to employing important relational elements of psychotherapy (e.g., non-defensive stance, patient validation), CBT therapists also utilize collaborative empiricism and Socratic dialogue in repairing ruptures (Okamoto & Kazantzis, 2021). Okamoto and Kazantzis recommend employing eight, nonsequential and potentially overlapping strategies when addressing ruptures in CBT: (1) identify and acknowledge the rupture; (2) validate the patient's experience; (3) collaboratively explore what led to the rupture; (4) engage in shared decision making regarding how to proceed with the resolution process; (5) seek and incorporate the patient's direct experience into the resolution process; (6) use Socratic questions to explore the situation, shift perspectives or synthesize viewpoints; (7) invite and demonstrate responsiveness to feedback; and (8) engage in personal self-reflection, self-practice, and mindfulness to better consider how therapists' personal beliefs and cultural factors impact the relationship with patients. Consider the following exchange with Bobby wherein the therapist tries to instill confidence in the patient's ability to engage in an exposure exercise but inadvertently invalidates the patient's feelings:

Patient: I just don't think I can do this.

Therapist: I hear your concerns, but I don't think it will be as bad as you worry. A lot of veterans tell me it's easier than they thought it would be. I'm confident you can do this!

Patient (crossing arms and looking away): Mmm.

Therapist (pauses): Can you tell me what's going through your mind right now?

Patient: Lots of things.

Therapist (pauses): It would be helpful for me to hear your thoughts. I would like to understand what you are thinking and feeling right now.

Patient: I know that someone who hasn't been through what I have been through wouldn't get it. You don't really understand how hard this is for me and what thinking about this will do to me. I don't know, maybe those other veterans are stronger than me. Maybe I'm more messed up than they were. I just know that this is going to be really bad.

Therapist (pauses): Thank you for sharing what's on your mind. I'm so sorry. I did not mean to discount your emotions or suggest that engaging in this exposure would be easy. What you are doing is so challenging. I shared my experience working with others in an effort to normalize the anxiety you're feeling and convey my confidence in you. However, I can see how this was invalidating and did not mean to minimize the difficulty of this exposure. I apologize.

Patient: This is really hard and I'm scared.

Therapist: I understand. I'm wondering what would be helpful in this moment?

Patient (shrugs): I don't know.

Therapist: I wonder if starting the imaginal exposure with your eyes open may feel more doable to you.

Patient: Ok. Yeah, that might help.

In the above example, the patient's beliefs about their ability to engage in the exposure led to hesitation which they communicated to the therapist. The therapist minimized the difficulty of the exposure with the goal of convincing the patient to engage; however, this resulted in invalidating the patient. Using foundational clinical skills, the therapist noticed a change in the patient's behavior (e.g., crossed arms and short responses) cuing the therapist to the rupture. Rather than persist with the session agenda, the therapist worked with the patient to acknowledge the tension and better understand the rupture before then working toward repairing the relationship by apologizing, sharing their intensions, acknowledging that this was not effective and validating the patient. The dyad then collaboratively decided how to move forward. They agreed to slightly adapt the exposure exercise in a way that allowed the veteran to still engage in the task but also feel heard and that their concerns were taken seriously thereby repairing the rupture.

Conclusion

In summary, research points to the therapeutic alliance as an important treatment factor that fosters engagement in the cognitive and behavioral techniques of CBT that contribute to successful therapy outcomes. Building and maintaining a strong therapeutic alliance in CBT requires clinicians to consistently use foundational clinical skills and convey confidence in the CBT approach. Furthermore, maintaining a collaborative approach to treatment and regularly seeking feedback about the alliance is critical for repairing any therapeutic ruptures and optimizing treatment outcomes.

Clinical Summary Points and Recommendations

- The therapeutic alliance is a collaborative relationship between therapist and patient fostered by three essential components: agreement on therapeutic goals, consensus on therapeutic tasks that make up therapy, and a mutually supportive and respectful bond.
- A large body of evidence highlights the important contribution of the therapeutic alliance to treatment engagement and outcomes in CBT for anxiety and related disorders through supporting and facilitating the use of and adherence to cognitive and behavioral strategies.
- Patient and therapist agreement on the tasks of therapy (i.e., cognitive and behavioral strategies) may be particularly important for engagement in CBT for anxiety and related disorders.
- Research suggests patient and therapist ratings of alliance may not always match and that concordance in ratings is an important predictor of treatment outcomes.
- The therapeutic alliance, and thus treatment engagement and outcomes, may be optimized by the following: Conveying confidence in the CBT approach, utilizing foundational clinical skills, developing and sharing case conceptualization and treatment plans, emphasizing the collaborative nature, regularly seeking feedback, and taking steps to identify and repair therapeutic ruptures.

References

Ackerman, S. J., & Hilsenroth, M. J. (2001). A review of therapist characteristics and techniques negatively impacting the therapeutic alliance. *Psychotherapy: Theory, Research, Practice Training, 38*(2), 171–185. https://doi.org/10.1037/0033-3204.38.2.171

Ackerman, S. J., & Hilsenroth, M. J. (2003). A review of therapist characteristics and techniques positively impacting the therapeutic alliance. *Clinical Psychology Review, 23*(1), 1–33. https://doi.org/10.1016/S0272-7358(02)00146-0

Addis, M. E., & Krasnow, A. D. (2000). A national survey of practicing psychologists' attitudes toward psychotherapy treatment manuals. *Journal of Consulting and Clinical Psychology, 68*(2), 331–339. https://doi.org/10.1037/0022-006x.68.2.331

Asnaani, A., & Hofmann, S. G. (2012). Collaboration in multicultural therapy: Establishing a strong therapeutic Alliance across cultural lines. *Journal of Clinical Psychology, 68*(2), 187–197. https://doi.org/10.1002/jclp.21829

Baier, A. L., Feeny, N. C., Coyne, A. E., & Zoellner, L. A. (2024). Temporal sequencing of change in trauma-related beliefs and therapeutic alliance during prolonged exposure and sertraline for chronic PTSD. *Psychotherapy Research, 34*(1), 17–27. https://doi.org/10.1080/10503307.2023.2184733

Baier, A. L., Kline, A. C., & Feeny, N. C. (2020). Therapeutic alliance as a mediator of change: A systematic review and evaluation of research. *Clinical Psychology Review, 82*, 101921. https://doi.org/10.1016/j.cpr.2020.101921

Beck, A. T., Rush, J. J., Shaw, B. F., & Emergy, G. (1979). *Cognitive therapy of depression.* Guilford Press.

Bordin, E. S. (1979). The generalizability of the psychoanalytic concept of the working alliance. *Psychotherapy: Theory, Research & Practice, 16*(3), 252.

Bordin, E. S. (1994). Theory and research on the therapeutic working alliance: New directions. In *The working alliance: Theory, research, and practice* (pp. 13–37). John Wiley & Sons.

Brady, J. P., Davison, G. C., Dewald, P. A., Egan, G., Fadiman, J., Frank, J. D., & al., e. (1980). Some views on effective principles of psychotherapy. *Cognitive Therapy and Research, 4,* 271–306. https://doi.org/10.1007/BF01371318

Buchholz, J. L., & Abramowitz, J. S. (2020). The therapeutic alliance in exposure therapy for anxiety-related disorders: A critical review. *Journal of Anxiety Disorders, 70,* 102194. https://doi.org/10.1016/j.janxdis.2020.102194

Carpenter, J. K., Andrews, L. A., Witcraft, S. M., Powers, M. B., Smits, J. A. J., & Hofmann, S. G. (2018). Cognitive behavioral therapy for anxiety and related disorders: A meta-analysis of randomized placebo-controlled trials. *Depression and Anxiety, 35*(6), 502–514. https://doi.org/10.1002/da.22728

Castonguay, L. G., Constantino, M. J., McAleavey, A. A., & Goldfried, M. R. (2010). The therapeutic alliance in cognitive-behavioral therapy. In *The therapeutic alliance: An evidence-based guide to practice* (pp. 150–171).

Cook, J. M., Simiola, V., Hamblen, J. L., Bernardy, N., & Schnurr, P. P. (2017). The influence of patient readiness on implementation of evidence-based PTSD treatments in veterans affairs residential programs. *Psychological Trauma: Theory, Research, Practice, and Policy, 9*(Suppl 1), 51–58. https://doi.org/10.1037/tra0000162

Coyne, A. E., Constantino, M. J., Laws, H. B., Westra, H. A., & Antony, M. M. (2018). Patient–therapist convergence in alliance ratings as a predictor of outcome in psychotherapy for generalized anxiety disorder. *Psychotherapy Research, 28*(6), 969–984. https://doi.org/10.1080/10503307.2017.1303209

Deacon, B. J., Farrell, N. R., Kemp, J. J., Dixon, L. J., Sy, J. T., Zhang, A. R., & McGrath, P. B. (2013). Assessing therapist reservations about exposure therapy for anxiety disorders: The therapist beliefs about exposure scale. *Journal of Anxiety Disorders, 27*(8), 772–780. https://doi.org/10.1016/j.janxdis.2013.04.006

Dobson, K. S. (2022). Therapeutic relationship. *Cognitive and Behavioral Practice, 29*(3), 541–544. https://doi.org/10.1016/j.cbpra.2022.02.006

Doran, G. T. (1981). There's a SMART way to write management's goals and objectives. *Management Review, 70,* 35–36.

Eubanks, C. F., Muran, J. C., & Safran, J. D. (2018). Alliance rupture repair: A meta-analysis. *Psychotherapy (Chic), 55*(4), 508–519. https://doi.org/10.1037/pst0000185

Fluckiger, C., Del Re, A. C., Wampold, B. E., & Horvath, A. O. (2018). The alliance in adult psychotherapy: *A metaanalytic synthesis. Psychotherapy, 55*(4), 316–340. https://doi.org/10.1037/pst0000172

Gallo, K. P., & Barlow, D. H. (2012). Factors involved in clinician adoption and nonadoption of evidence-based interventions in mental health. *Clinical Psychology: Science and Practice, 19*(1), 93–106. https://doi.org/10.1111/j.1468-2850.2012.01276.x

Galovski, T. (2024). *Walking the line between fidelity and flexibility: A conceptual review of personalized approaches to manualized treatments for PTSD. Journal of Trauma Stress, 37*(5), 768–774. https://doi.org/10.1002/jts.23073

Galovski, T., Nixon, R., & Kaysen, D. (2020). Chapter 7–navigating rough waters: Managing common challenges across the four cornerstones of CPT. In T. Galovski, R. Nixon, & D. Kaysen (Eds.), *Flexible applications of cognitive processing therapy* (pp. 123–159). Academic Press. https://doi.org/10.1016/B978-0-12-816715-1.00007-8

Galovski, T. E., Blain, L. M., Mott, J. M., Elwood, L., & Houle, T. (2012). Manualized therapy for PTSD: Flexing the structure of cognitive processing therapy. *Journal of Consulting and Clinical Psychology, 80*(6), 968–981. https://doi.org/10.1037/a0030600

Garfield, S. L. (1996). Some problems associated with" validated" forms of psychotherapy. *Clinical Psychology: Science and Practice, 3*(3), 218.

Gnaulati, E. (2022). Overlooked ethical problems associated with the research and practice of evidence-based treatments. *Journal of Humanistic Psychology, 62*(5), 653–668. https://doi.org/10.1177/0022167818800219

Goldfried, M. R., & Davison, G. C. (1974). *Clinical behavior therapy*. Holt, Rinehart & Winston.

Hagen, K., Solem, S., Opstad, H. B., Vogel, P. A., Kennair, L. E. O., Kvale, G., & Hansen, B. S. S. (2017). Therapist variability in the task/goal dimension of the early working alliance predicts outcome in exposure and response prevention treatment for obsessive-compulsive disorder.

Hara, K. M., Aviram, A., Constantino, M. J., Westra, H. A., & Antony, M. M. (2017). Therapist empathy, homework compliance, and outcome in cognitive behavioral therapy for generalized anxiety disorder: Partitioning within- and between-therapist effects. *Cognitive Behaviour Therapy, 46*(5), 375–390. https://doi.org/10.1080/16506073.2016.1253605

Hara, K. M., Westra, H. A., Aviram, A., Button, M. L., Constantino, M. J., & Antony, M. M. (2015). Therapist awareness of client resistance in cognitive-behavioral therapy for generalized anxiety disorder. *Cognitive Behaviour Therapy, 44*(2), 162–174. https://doi.org/10.1080/16506073.2014.998705

Held, P., Meade, E. A., Kovacevic, M., Smith, D. L., Pridgen, S., Coleman, J. A., & Klassen, B. J. (2022). Building strong therapeutic relationships quickly: The effect of the perceived working alliance on veterans' intensive PTSD treatment outcomes. *Psychotherapy (Chicago, Ill.), 59*(3), 470–480. https://doi.org/10.1037/pst0000447

Hoffart, A., Oktedalen, T., Langkaas, T. F., & Wampold, B. E. (2013). Alliance and outcome in varying imagery procedures for PTSD: A study of within-person processes. *Journal of Counseling Psychology, 60*(4), 471–482. https://doi.org/10.1037/a0033604

Horvath, A. O., & Greenberg, L. S. (1989). Development and validation of the working Alliance inventory. *Journal of Counseling Psychology, 36*(2), 223–233. https://doi.org/10.1037/0022-0167.36.2.223

Horvath, A. O., Del Re, A. C., Flückiger, C., & Symonds, D. (2011). Alliance in individual psychotherapy. *Psychotherapy, 48*(1), 9–16. https://doi.org/10.1037/a0022186

Impala, T., Okamoto, A., & Kazantzis, N. (2023). Alliance rupture and repair in cognitive behavior therapy. In C. F. Eubanks, L. W. Samstag, & J. C. Muran (Eds.), *Rupture and repair in psychotherapy: A critical process for change* (pp. 119–139). American Psychological Association. https://doi.org/10.1037/0000306-006

Kazantzis, N. (2024). Cognitive behavioral therapy: Strategies for enhancing treatment engagement. *The Psychiatric Clinics of North America, 47*(2), 301–310. https://doi.org/10.1016/j.psc.2024.03.002

Kazantzis, N., Dattilio, F. M., & Dobson, K. S. (2017). *The therapeutic relationship in cognitive-behavioral therapy: A clinician's guide*. Guilford Publications.

Kazantzis, N., & Dobson, K. S. (2024). Therapeutic relationships in cognitive behavioral therapy: Agreement in alliance, client factors, therapist factors, and CBT specific processes. *Psychotherapy Research: Journal of the Society for Psychotherapy Research*, 1–3.

Kazdin, A. E. (2007). Mediators and mechanisms of change in psychotherapy research. *Annual Review of Clinical Psychology, 3*, 1–27. https://doi.org/10.1146/annurev.clinpsy.3.022806.091432

Kivity, Y., Strauss, A. Y., Elizur, J., Weiss, M., Cohen, L., & Huppert, J. D. (2021). The alliance mediates outcome in cognitive-behavioral therapy for social anxiety disorder, but not in attention bias modification. *Psychotherapy Research, 31*(5), 589–603. https://doi.org/10.1080/10503307.2020.1836423

Lilienfeld, S. O., Ritschel, L. A., Lynn, S. J., Cautin, R. L., & Latzman, R. D. (2013). Why many clinical psychologists are resistant to evidence-based practice: Root causes and constructive remedies. *Clinical Psychology Review, 33*(7), 883–900. https://doi.org/10.1016/j.cpr.2012.09.008

Luborsky, L., Barber, J. P., Siqueland, L., Johnson, S., Najavits, L. M., Frank, A., & Daley, D. (1996). The revised helping Alliance questionnaire (HAq-II): Psychometric properties. *The Journal of Psychotherapy Practice and Research, 5*(3), 260–271.

Luong, H. K., Drummond, S. P. A., & Norton, P. J. (2020). Elements of the therapeutic relationship in CBT for anxiety disorders: A systematic review. *Journal of Anxiety Disorders, 76*, 102322. https://doi.org/10.1016/j.janxdis.2020.102322

Marmar, C. R., Weiss, D. S., & Gaston, L. (1989). Toward the validation of the California therapeutic Alliance rating system. *Psychological Assessment, 1*, 46–52.

Meyer, J. M., Farrell, N. R., Kemp, J. J., Blakey, S. M., & Deacon, B. J. (2014). Why do clinicians exclude anxious clients from exposure therapy? *Behaviour Research and Therapy, 54*, 49–53. https://doi.org/10.1016/j.brat.2014.01.004

Meyer, J. M., Kelly, P. J., & Deacon, B. J. (2020). Therapist beliefs about exposure therapy implementation. *The Cognitive Behaviour Therapist, 13*. https://doi.org/10.1017/S1754470X20000112

Moshe-Cohen, R., Kivity, Y., Huppert, J. D., Barlow, D. H., Gorman, J. M., Shear, K., & Woods, S. W. (2024). Agreement in patient-therapist alliance ratings and its relation to dropout and outcome in a large sample of cognitive behavioral therapy for panic disorder. *Psychotherapy Research, 34*(1), 28–40. https://doi.org/10.1080/10503307.2022.2124131

Murphy, S. T., Garcia, R. A., Cheavens, J. S., & Strunk, D. R. (2022). The therapeutic alliance and dropout in cognitive behavioral therapy of depression. *Psychotherapy Research, 32*, 995. https://doi.org/10.1080/10503307.2021.2025277

Norouzian, N., Westra, H. A., Button, M. L., Constantino, M. J., & Antony, M. M. (2021). Ambivalence and the working alliance in variants of cognitive-behavioural therapy for generalised anxiety disorder. *Counselling & Psychotherapy Research, 21*(3), 587–596. https://doi.org/10.1002/capr.12332

Okamoto, A., & Kazantzis, N. (2021). Alliance ruptures in cognitive-behavioral therapy: A cognitive conceptualization. *Journal of Clinical Psychology, 77*(2), 384–397. https://doi.org/10.1002/jclp.23116

Pfeifer, B. J., & Strunk, D. R. (2015). A Primer on Psychotherapy Process Research: A Review of Cognitive Therapy of Depression. *Australian Psychologist, 50*(6), 411–415. https://doi.org/10.1111/ap.12147

Rubel, J. A., Hilpert, P., Wolfer, C., Held, J., Vîslă, A., & Flückiger, C. (2019). The working alliance in manualized CBT for generalized anxiety disorder: Does it lead to change and does the effect vary depending on manual implementation flexibility? *Journal of Consulting and Clinical Psychology, 87*, 989. https://doi.org/10.1037/ccp0000433

Safran, J. D., & Muran, J. C. (2000). *Negotiating the therapeutic alliance: A relational treatment guide*. Guilford Press.

Weck, F., Grikscheit, F., Jakob, M., Höfling, V., & Stangier, U. (2015). Treatment failure in cognitive-behavioural therapy: Therapeutic alliance as a precondition for an adherent and competent implementation of techniques. *The British Journal of Clinical Psychology, 54*(1), 91–108. https://doi.org/10.1111/bjc.12063

Wheaton, M. G., Huppert, J. D., Foa, E. B., & Simpson, H. B. (2016). How important is the therapeutic alliance in treating obsessive-compulsive disorder with exposure and response prevention? An empirical report. *Clin Neuropsychiatry, 13*(6), 88–93.

Williams, A. M., Baier, A. L., Woolley, M. G., & Galovski, T. E. (2022). Integrating social determinants of health within cognitive therapy. *Current Treatment Options in Psychiatry, 9*(3), 215–228. https://doi.org/10.1007/s40501-022-00268-0

Zilcha-Mano, S. (2017). Is the alliance really therapeutic? Revisiting this question in light of recent methodological advances. *American Psychologist, 72*(4), 311–325. https://doi.org/10.1037/a0040435

Zilcha-Mano, S., & Ben David-Sela, T. (2022). Is alliance therapeutic in itself? It depends. *J Couns Psychol, 69*(6), 786–793. https://doi.org/10.1037/cou0000627

Chapter 3
Leveraging Beliefs in Treatment: Outcome Expectancy, Treatment Credibility, and Self-Efficacy

Nora Brier, Lily A. Brown, and Jeremy Tyler

Introduction

In the health behavior literature broadly, beliefs about one's ability to engage in a behavior as well as expected outcomes from those behaviors dictate whether a person will follow a treatment recommendation (Zhou et al., 2021; Bandura, 1977). Treatment engagement proxies—homework adherence, treatment attendance, and commitment to treatment—each impacts treatment outcomes for individuals being treated with cognitive behavioral therapy (CBT) for anxiety disorders (Glenn et al., 2013). Anxiety-related disorders, including obsessive compulsive disorder (OCD) and posttraumatic stress disorder (PTSD), have the highest overall prevalence rate among psychiatric diagnoses in the United States, including a 12-month rate of 18.1% and a lifetime rate of 28.8% (Kessler et al., 2005a, 2005b; Olatunji et al., 2007; Bandelow & Michaelis, 2015). Therefore, it is essential to better understand how to encourage patients to complete the recommended components of their treatments, and mechanisms to achieve this goal may include targeting their beliefs about the ability to do the treatment, their beliefs that the treatment will reduce their anxiety, and their sense of support in the therapeutic relationship while conquering their fears.

N. Brier (✉) · L. A. Brown · J. Tyler
University of Pennsylvania, Philadelphia, PA, USA
e-mail: nora.brier@pennmedicine.upenn.edu; lilybr@pennmedicine.upenn.edu; jeremyty@pennmedicine.upenn.edu

E. M. Goetter (ed.), *Optimizing Treatment Engagement Processes in CBT for Anxiety and Related Disorders*, CBT: Science Into Practice,
https://doi.org/10.1007/978-3-031-91439-3_3

Defining and Measuring Self-efficacy and Outcome Expectancy

Self-efficacy (SE) is the perception that an individual can perform a specific behavior or set of behaviors that are necessary to achieve an outcome (Bandura, 1977; Gallagher et al., 2020). Considered a transdiagnostic mechanism of change for psychological treatments, SE is thought to be increased through mastery experiences, such as increased self-confidence upon facing a feared scenario or completing behavioral activation activities for individuals with low mood (Gallagher et al., 2020). Examples of how SE can be assessed include using the General Self-Efficacy Scale (GSE) and the Self-Efficacy Survey (SES) (Schwarzer & Jerusalem, 1995; Panc et al., 2012).

Outcome expectancy (OE) is the belief that a given behavior will or will not lead to a specific outcome (e.g., confronting feared situations will reduce anxiety) and is associated with a significant increase in an intention to perform a behavior (Maddux et al., 1982). Prior anxiety disorder research on OE suggests that early treatment OE predicts treatment outcome, however it can fluctuate, and often changes throughout treatment (Constantino et al., 2018; Brown et al., 2014; Vîslă et al., 2021). An example of a measure that can be used to assess OE is the **Stanford Expectations of Treatment Scale (SETS) (Younger et al.,** 2012**).** The working alliance, or the agreement on certain goals, tasks, and the therapeutic bond between the patient and therapist, which will be addressed in Chap. 1 (Bordin, 1979), may be a mediator between treatment OE and actual treatment outcome, however more research is needed in this area (Sauer-Zavala et al., 2018). In general, treatment outcome, SE, and working alliance are correlated but distinct constructs that benefit from different therapeutic techniques to promote engagement in and optimize the efficacy of CBT.

Moderating Factors of the Influence of Self-efficacy and Outcome Expectancy on Treatment Outcome

Demographic and clinical factors, such as educational level, gender, age, symptom severity, and comorbid symptoms may play a role in SE, OE, and working alliance. Being older or a woman is associated with more positive pretreatment OE in some studies (Collins & Hyer, 1986; Tsai et al., 2014). On the other hand, higher global symptom severity and multiple mental health comorbidities are associated with lower levels of pretreatment OE (Connolly Gibbons et al., 2003). From research conducted with individuals with depression, a study on group CBT for depression suggested that less severe depression at intake, greater amounts of hope during treatment, greater interpersonal problem reduction, and higher self-reported OE at session one predicted stronger posttreatment outcome (Constantino et al., 2016). In consideration of therapist-related, nonspecific therapeutic factors, research suggests that greater observer-rated therapist competence is associated with more favorable pretreatment OE in individuals receiving CBT (Westra et al., 2011; Ametrano et al., 2017; Ahmed & Westra, 2009).

In a study of CBT for generalized anxiety disorder (GAD), higher depression severity at intake was associated with lower pretreatment OE (Vîslă et al., 2021). In a study on panic disorder (PD) and social anxiety disorder (SAD) patients receiving CBT, higher therapist competence, defined as sticking to and being capable in delivering treatment in accordance with the specified theoretical and technical model, and adherence to purported treatment, was associated with better outcomes for PD patients. Low competence/adherence was associated with dropout for SAD patients. Lastly, exposure to traumatic events can reduce SE beliefs about one's ability to successfully overcome obstacles and adapt to changes (Chung et al., 2017; Solomon et al., 2005), which might affect a patient's perceptions of their ability to do what is necessary in CBT.

Self-Efficacy, Outcome Expectancy, and Treatment Outcome

SE and OE each independently predicts treatment outcome in CBT for anxiety-related disorders (Brown et al., 2014; Haug et al., 2016; Baier et al., 2020). Higher treatment OE and greater perceived SE beliefs prior to starting CBT for anxiety disorders predicted improved treatment outcome, specifically for GAD and PD (Jakubovski & Bloch, 2016). In a transdiagnostic sample with anxiety-related disorders, SE and OE each independently predicted improvements in anxiety symptoms, and a steeper rate of change in SE and OE each predicted faster improvement in outcome (Brown et al., 2014). Additionally, research with individuals with SAD has suggested that within-treatment improvements in SE predict improved treatment outcomes as patients may feel more responsible for treatment improvements, which increases their motivation to continue engaging in healthy behaviors (Delsignore 2008). Thus, for those seeking treatment for anxiety disorders, SE, and OE are meaningful mechanisms of treatment success (Gallagher et al., 2020; Rubel et al., 2019).

Self-Efficacy, Outcome Expectancy, and Treatment Engagement

SE and OE both predict treatment engagement. For instance, higher reported pretreatment OE predicts more homework assignment adherence in transdiagnostic treatment for anxiety, a key part of CBT treatment (Glenn et al., 2013). This may contribute to overall treatment progress and symptom reduction compared to individuals with low OE beliefs during CBT for depression and anxiety treatment, although study results are mixed (Greenberg et al., 2006; Detweiler & Whisman, 1999). In a study of CBT for SAD, higher OE was associated with greater homework completion rates (Peters et al., 2019). Thus, if a patient is more engaged with treatment, they may be more likely to complete homework assignments, experience symptom reduction, and feel inclined to believe that the treatment works (Chambless et al., 1997; Westra et al., 2007). Research on individuals with OCD suggests that OE may be influenced by belief in a biopsychosocial model of the disorder versus purely a biological outlook (Gershkovich et al., 2018). This suggests that if an individual believes in their ability to positively impact treatment, they may work hard in treatment to achieve reduced symptoms. Similarly, individuals undergoing treatment for PTSD who endorsed positive OE displayed post trauma resilience (Gallagher et al., 2020). As SE and OE fluctuate from pre to post treatment (Brown et al., 2014), accounting for and implementing interventions to enhance both are warranted.

Interventions to Promote Self-efficacy and Outcome Expectancy

There are a variety of interventions that can be used to target SE and OE. Several of these interventions are inspired by principles from Motivational Interviewing (MI). MI may supplement anxiety disorder treatment and improve self-efficacy and outcome expectancy (Miller & Rollnick, 2013) (See Chap. 3).

Motivational Interviewing

MI is an intervention that focuses on building a collaborative communication style between provider and patient to strengthen an individual's motivation and commitment towards behavior change (Miller & Rollnick, 2013). Motivation plays a key role in a patient's willingness to engage with principles of treatment, including psychoeducation about CBT, homework compliance, and one's belief that he or she can accomplish treatment outcomes and reduce symptoms (Dozois, 2010). In a 2018 metanalysis, MI as an adjunct for CBT for anxiety disorders was investigated, with MI used as a prelude to CBT (Marker & Norton, 2018). The combination of MI and CBT had a moderate effect size improvement on anxiety symptom reduction compared to CBT alone (Marker & Norton, 2018). MI has been associated with improved expectancy for change as well as improved homework adherence and outcome expectancy in CBT for anxiety (Westra & Dozois, 2006; Westra et al., 2007).

In instances where patients are reluctant to engage in CBT for anxiety, MI skills that may be helpful for increasing SE beliefs during CBT therapy begin with eliciting information from patients about why they are in treatment, and "rolling with any resistance" that occurs (Miller & Rollnick, 2013). In other words, instead of the therapist making arguments for why exposure therapy for OCD works, the patient could be tasked with elucidating these reasons during early sessions after the therapist provides initial psychoeducation on CBT (Miller & Rollnick, 2013). Resistance can take many forms throughout therapy, including homework nonadherence, disagreeing, debating therapy content, avoiding cognitively or behaviorally, withdrawing or stalling, or balking at assignments (Westra & Norouzian, 2018). These nonadherence behaviors may suggest a patient is ambivalent about adhering to treatment recommendations due to fear, which keeps clients trapped in the status quo (Westra & Norouzian, 2018). Therapists can listen closely to the patients' communication to reveal where they are in terms of their stage of change (i.e., precontemplation, contemplation, preparation, and action) and not assume clients are in a stage of preparation or action at the time of therapy initiation (Miller & Rollnick, 2013). This can include listening for patients' concerns about change (e.g., fears about fully participating in exposure therapy and completing homework and *why* they fear it), which may help patients believe their own behaviors can be efficacious when they are ready to adhere to treatment recommendations (Miller & Rollnick, 2013). The DARN CAT is an MI technique that assess commitment to change, the ability to change, and taking steps in that direction (Westra & Norouzian, 2018). To support engagement, the therapist can ask the patient to elucidate their **d**esires to change, **a**bility to change, **r**easons for change, and **n**eed for change (i.e., the "why" in practical terms), and foster **c**ommitment to change, **a**ctuation or statements about willingness for change, and **t**aking steps toward change (i.e., the "how"). Once a patient has the reasons and commitment-level identified, the individual may feel increased self-efficacy beliefs in the ability to complete treatment.

Returning to the Rationale

Some patients may benefit from returning to the rationale for treatment as a strategy to build OE or SE. This may be especially helpful when patients become overwhelmed by anxiety and lose sight of why it might be important to engage in distressing tasks, such as exposure practice. To promote collaboration and engagement, the therapist can return to the rationale and normalize the patient's trepidation about completing an emotionally challenging therapy, while also helping them gain perspective that if CBT has helped many prior patients, it may also be possible for them to do it (SE) and it may also benefit them (OE).

Problem-Solving

Motivation and commitment to adhering to change-oriented behaviors is critical for patient's success in treatment. Yet, it is challenging and perhaps especially so for patients with anxiety, who may still struggle with practical problem-solving skills, making them more prone to experiencing anxiety and depression (Nezu et al., 2013; D'Zurilla & Nezu, 2006) and remaining engaged in treatment. Problem-solving therapy was designed as a short-term psychotherapy approach designed to involve a step-by-step assessment of recent challenges that a patient has encountered (Zhang et al., 2018). There are 14 modules in problem- solving therapy to assist patients with fostering an orientation wherein they see problems as challenges instead of insurmountable obstacles. This is called having a positive problem orientation

(D'Zurilla & Nezu, 2006). Subsequently, individuals learn how to address and assess problems, including recognition and generation of alternatives and solution implementation. It is noteworthy that one module addresses fostering SE as a key component of treatment success (D'Zurilla & Nezu, 2006). Specifically, this includes visualization of a problem being done successfully (D'Zurilla & Nezu, 2006). By helping a patient to envision successfully overcoming a difficult challenge, they may become inspired to consider and enact new solutions to solving problems and may become more confident in their ability to break large dilemmas into smaller challenges to accomplish one at a time. Visualization includes having a patient close their eyes and imagine themselves successfully solving a problem (i.e., parking at a difficult lot on a busy day without an accident). This can build confidence in one's problem-solving ability.

If a therapist decides to incorporate MI and Problem Solving Therapy (PST) components, they can be delivered in tandem with a CBT treatment. For example, a therapist might add MI techniques during the initial session of treatment and further assess whether a patient requires additional assistance with these techniques midway through treatment. The same strategy applies for using PST in conjunction with CBT. The therapist might incorporate psychoeducation during the initial session and assist the patient in identifying their problem orientation (e.g., negative problem orientation or positive problem orientation) as part of that discussion. As some research suggests that level of SE is predicted by problem-solving, it is important to ensure individuals have effective problem-solving tools (Çam et al., 2020). Before incorporating these techniques, and to be sure that doing so is done in an efficient and targeted manner, it is important for the therapist to have a clear understanding of the behavior (s) and/or belief(s) that are hypothesized to be reflecting low OE and/or SE and thus undermining the patient's engagement in treatment (e.g., homework nonadherence, trepidation around exposure, difficulty attending sessions, and avoidance). Further, to optimize collaboration, the therapist is encouraged to share their understanding and suggestions for overcoming these barriers with the patient, much as one does with the primary anxiety intervention.

Additional Theory-Based Applications for Promoting Self-efficacy and Outcome Expectancy

Expectation Violation

A core goal of exposures is to create new learning about safety and threat, which is achieved when a patient experiences a discrepancy between what they expected to occur during an exposure and what actually occurred, also known as expectation violation (Craske et al., 2012). Some exposures can promote learning about a patient's own competence, such as about their ability to tolerate distress when they had previously predicted that they would have to escape from a situation due to anxiety. In processing exposure exercises, therapists can use expectation violation to promote SE and OE.

To promote SE, a therapist might ask: "What does it mean about you that you were able to stay in a really stressful situation, even when you wanted to leave? What does that mean about your abilities in general?" Processing of the exposure practice might focus on building the patient's confidence to do exposures in general, in the hope that this will generalize to increased confidence in the patient's ability to conduct exposures independently, and then eventually to increased confidence about other areas in their life.

To promote OE, a therapist might ask "Given that what you expected to happen did not occur, what does this mean about exposure practice in general? Given that your anxiety actually decreased, rather than increased, what does it mean about how exposure works for you?" and "How do you see this helping you in the future?"

Intolerance of Uncertainty

Intolerance of uncertainty is a central factor in multiple anxiety disorders and is closely related to SE (Gu et al., 2020). Intolerance of uncertainty is the way an individual responds to or perceives ambiguous or uncertain information in everyday situations that leads to a set of cognitive, emotional, and behavioral responses (Birrell et al., 2011). Intolerance of anxiety is relevant to all anxiety disorders but especially salient in OCD and SAD, and most prominent in GAD (Wilson et al., 2023). Patients with higher intolerance of uncertainty may struggle with lower confidence that they can engage in treatment (SE), lower confidence that treatment will work (OE), and even lower trust in their therapist (working alliance) because of low trust in themselves. In studies of anxiety disorders such as OCD and GAD, individuals with higher levels of intolerance of uncertainty were more likely to believe they may not have adequate coping skills to handle stressful situations (Holaway et al., 2006). Conversely, higher levels of SE were associated with a greater tolerance of uncertainty (Jones et al., 2023; Fetherston et al., 2018).

Clinical Case Example

The following case example details how MI and PST can be applied to increase SE, OE, and working alliance for a patient receiving exposure and response prevention (EX/RP) for OCD at an outpatient clinic. Consider the case of "Roberto" (a pseudonym with identifying information changed to protect patient identity) is a 28-year-old cisgender Latino man. He presented with symptoms of OCD and no prior psychotherapy treatment. Roberto's obsessions included fears of harming others and of being contaminated. Specific harm obsessions included intrusive cognitions about hitting pedestrians with his vehicle, spreading illness to others, and poisoning family members. Contamination obsessions included fears of consuming spoiled meat as well as pervasive feelings of disgust. Core compulsive behaviors included seeking reassurance from others, reassuring himself, checking in relation to feared objects, and extensive online searches. Avoidance behaviors included limiting media usage to prevent compulsions, avoiding specific driving routes, isolating within the home, and following a restrictive diet plan.

At the time of the intake evaluation, Roberto was unmarried, lived alone, and sought treatment due to significantly impaired occupational and interpersonal functioning. He entered treatment with severe symptoms of OCD. He stated that symptoms were present for approximately 10 years and noted symptoms worsened over the course of the previous month before treatment began due to occupational stress.

Roberto reported having one younger sibling and married parents who were employed at a local school district. He noted that his parents' values included self-reliance, hard work, and their Christian faith. Roberto stated that for most of his life he believed that accepting help meant he was "weak" or "inferior." Additionally, he explained that his childhood upbringing and Christian faith influenced him to worry he was morally inferior, or a "bad person." Roberto reported his coping strategies throughout his life included speaking with friends and family, attending church, and engaging in "good deeds" (e.g., volunteering at a soup kitchen and confessing sins to a priest). He noted that he often assumed, "If I'm not trying my best to be a good person, that means I am a sinner and a bad person." Roberto's pervasive intrusive thoughts developed from the core fear that he was a bad person. Compulsive behaviors maintained these obsessions through repeated checks that he did not cause harm to others or contaminate himself. Roberto also completed pretreatment measures of SE and OE, which indicated he believed that treatment would help him, but was somewhat uncertain of his own ability to be successful with the treatment.

Elicitation of Self-efficacy and Outcome Expectancy about Treatment

The following is an example dialogue between Roberto and his therapist who implements components of MI and PST interventions alongside EX/RP after reviewing his pretreatment measures:

Provider: "You mentioned that you heard about our treatment for OCD, exposure and response prevention, through your cousin. Can you say more about that?"

Roberto: "Yeah. I'm close with her, we pretty much grew up together. She's a counselor or something. But she told me that this therapy is like, really helpful for what I have, for OCD. She knows because she studied it and because her friend went through this treatment. So, I thought about it for a while, about attending therapy, but I wasn't ready because I was so busy at work."

Provider: "So you know about the therapy from her and think this could work for you because of what she has told you and what you learned about it?"

Roberto: "I guess so, yes, and I know it works, but it's tough."

Provider: "That makes sense, you know it works, but it requires a lot of effort. Did your cousin explain how it works?"

Roberto: "She said it's basically doing things that scare you, but like, its broken down into smaller parts with the therapist, and you can work together on it then practice it."

Provider: "That's right, that's the premise of exposure therapy. Can I tell you a bit more about it now?"

Roberto: Absolutely.

Provider: "EX/RP for OCD is designed to help you approach your obsessions and things you fear collaboratively and gradually, without doing any compulsive behavior. This is done in two ways: by confronting things you fear in real life (in vivo exposure) and in your imagination (imaginal) in order to confront the core of your worry. We know from lots of research that OCD can only be treated when we take away the compulsions, so as you and I collaboratively confront the things you are afraid of, we will work really hard to stop all of your compulsions. By doing this, you will realize that you are way more capable of confronting your fears than you think you are, and that either the bad outcome does not happen, or that you can handle it if it does. How does that sound to you?"

Roberto: "That makes a lot of sense, and I'm still nervous. Like, will I have to, I don't know, hurt people or eat bad food? I can't do any of that, I refuse. I don't think I could stand it."

Provider: "I can see why you would be fearful of approaching your fears through exposure, in fact most people are. However, it will be a collaborative process where we will approach your fears gradually. I will explain more when we review how exposure works in a bit. First, I want to ask, what are some ways your life would be better if you didn't have to worry about harming others or feeling disgusted so frequently?"

Roberto: "I think I really would have so much more peace of mind and freedom to live my life. I really want to not to be afraid anymore, period (***Therapist makes note of this as an example of DARN CAT-DESIRE***). I am afraid now of hurting people or myself all the time, and even when I'm not afraid of that, I still feel bad."

Provider: "You're not enjoying life like you would like to, and OCD is one of the reasons for that."

Roberto: "I would say it's the main reason and I really want it to be gone totally. I also need it to go away, because I'm starting to be late for work because of re-driving routes to see if I hit anyone, and spending time checking Twitter to make sure a hit-and-run wasn't reported in the mornings and at night. I also want to not be like this for the rest of my life or else I'm never going to date anyone or have a life (***Therapist makes note of this as an example of DARN CAT-REASONS***)."

Provider: "There are a lot of reasons you want this to go away, and it's motivating you to be here today."

Roberto: "It is. It was really hard to get here, and I still feel like I want to leave, to be honest. I am very anxious. But I also know I need to stay, and I think I can do this therapy (***Therapist makes note of this as an example of DARN CAT-***

ABILITY). I started to try to not re-drive my routes the other day, and even tried to cook a burger for myself the other day, but I think it was too hard."

Roberto: "It was maybe a bit more than you felt like you could handle, and I think at the same time, it's great that you are thinking that way and adopting a mindset of changing your beliefs and behaviors. That is the first step. You also mentioned being committed to EX/RP treatment. Could you say more about that?"

Roberto: "Sure. I talked with my parents and a few close friends about going into the therapy, so they can like, help hold me accountable. I also made sure I had reserved time in my calendar for twice weekly visits and stuff." (***Therapist makes note of this as an example of DARN CAT-COMMITMENT***).

Provider: "You've made a lot of changes to purposely help support your treatment in advance, which is wonderful. That also leads me to wonder about whether there are any unique challenges that might make attending therapy or practicing homework difficult (***Therapist draws on PST- evaluating barriers***)?"

Roberto: "Maybe there are more than these, but I think when I'm stressed at work, I can sometimes see my schedule and everything as so overwhelming that it's just another thing I can't handle…I think it made me sometimes miss appointments, like doctor's appointments, in the past or caused me to reschedule. Because it's just like, I can only do one problem at a time."

Provider: "When work is busy, it feels like everything becomes more intense for you, and appointments are problems that you need to maybe, put off in order to feel better or get work done?"

Roberto: "Exactly. And I don't know how other people can balance all this stuff."

Provider: "It feels like more of a burden to you than other people. That makes sense. I'm wondering if we can talk about how you view work stressors when they arise for a moment?"

Roberto: "Of course."

Provider: "Frequently when people experience dilemmas or problems, it can feel overwhelming. The way we think about a problem, your 'problem orientation', plays a role in how we overcome it. We know that if someone views problems as threatening obstacles that are too difficult to handle, they think pessimistically about their problem (***Therapist draws on PST-psychoeducation on problem orientation***)."

Roberto: "This makes a lot of sense. I've wondered why it seems so easy for some people to deal with things that come up, and I guess how they think about it is does matter."

Provider: You're exactly right. And good news: there is a lot of research to support the idea that you can be taught ways to think differently about your problems. This is called having a positive problem orientation or thinking of problem as challenges to overcome rather than obstacles or road blocks. This means that if you view a problem as something you can overcome, it will be more likely that you come up with a successful solution. There is more to it, but this is just the first part. Does that make sense?"

Roberto: "Totally. How do I get better at it though?"

Provider: "Excellent question. One thing we know is that practicing problem-solving is key. The first step would be to generate a bunch of possible solutions, no matter how far-fetched they may seem, for a problem you are currently facing. A good practice may be if you can give me an example of a recent problem you had (***Therapist draws on PST-generating alternatives***)."

Roberto: "Hm, ok. I wasn't sure if I should stay in and do work one night or go meet my friends for a drink. The issue was that I was busy at work, so I needed to work, but also that I was afraid of hitting someone with my car and didn't know if I had it in me that night."

Provider: "How did you deal with the situation?"

Roberto: "I just ran out of time! They were like, almost done and I was like 'Ok, I guess I missed it'."

Provider: "I see. So not making a decision turned out to be a choice (therapist pauses). It makes sense that you weren't satisfied fully with how it happened. The next time a potential problem comes up, I want you to try something different. I'd like you to pause for a moment and quickly list all of the ways you could respond to the problem. There is no strategy too outlandish! Anything that comes to mind is great for brainstorming."

Roberto: "Ok, I can do that. Is that all I need to do?"

Provider: "Yes. Just list everything and bring it back to me in session and we can discuss it. Does that sound good?"

Roberto: "It does."

Provider: "Okay, great, and we can go from there. Before we begin talking about the next steps for EX/RP treatment, I wanted to ask you your thoughts on the treatment and its outcome. Do you think you can get better by completing EX/RP here with me?"

Roberto: "I'm half-and-half. I think so because I'm here and my cousin made it seem like her friend's life is so much better now because of the treatment. Her friend wasn't working or seeing people socially, and now she is. So, I want that too. So that's why I'm here, but I'm also thinking how could it get that much better? I have had this for so long. So, I guess I still have my doubts."

Teaching Points

In the above dialogue, the patient demonstrated ambivalence in his ability to tolerate and follow-though with exposure therapy. For example, he said "I'm half-and-half [in terms of whether I can do it]," "I wasn't ready," I don't think I can stand that," etc. This kind of ambivalence, commonly expressed by patients, suggests negative beliefs about the patient's SE beliefs. Notice that the therapist used DARN-CAT statements and probes to elicit opportunities for the patient to challenge his negative beliefs about SE. For example, the therapist asked, "Can you think of ways in which OCD prevents you from enjoying your life?" to help the patient identify reasons to reduce OCD symptoms despite the patient's perceived lack of ability to handle it.

Furthermore, the therapist used validating statements frequently to strengthen the working alliance in service of challenging and strengthening the client's SE beliefs. For example, the therapist said "that makes sense," "you're exactly right," which validates the client's contributions to the plan and further emphasizes collaboration between the client and the provider. By strengthening the working alliance through validating statements, the provider is reinforcing the client's belief that the client possesses the ability to manage their symptoms through treatment. This is one way establishment of a strong working alliance can encourage the client to consider positive alternative beliefs about their SE.

The patient's beliefs about OE appeared more optimistic that his SE beliefs, but in this case, the patient still had some mixed information. For example, the patient said: "I know it works, but it's tough," "I have had this for long," and "I still have my doubts," etc. The therapists used DARN-CAT questions to assess the patient's beliefs about OE (e.g., "Do you think you can get better by completing EX/RP here with me?"). Given the patient was distressed and therapy naïve, it was important for the therapist to understand the patient's beliefs about the expected outcome. The provider hypothesized that the patient's positive beliefs about his expected outcome would encourage commitment to completing behavioral assignments and adhering to treatment protocol. Simultaneous to this, the therapist also remains aware that the patient's high frequency, intensity, and duration of symptoms over time appeared to contribute to an ambivalent pretreatment self-efficacy mindset, and that this ambivalence could create a barrier to future treatment commitment and effectiveness.

In addition to regular administration of OE and SE assessment measures throughout treatment, therapeutic interventions included the following: repetition of rationale, motivational interviewing, and problem-solving therapy components. Specifically, motivational interviewing techniques included DARN CAT: assess desire, action, reasons, and need for change, commitment, activation, and taking steps (Marker & Norton, 2018). Problem-solving therapy (Nezu et al., 2013) techniques included identifying the problem orientation and teaching the patient to use brainstorming as part of solution-generation.

Elicitation of Self-efficacy and Outcome Expectancy about Exposure

In this section, we will describe the details of a specific exposure during a later stage of therapy (session 8 of EX/RP) related to contamination fears and highlight moments that demonstrate the role of SE and OE in the outcome of that exposure task, while retaining a strong working alliance.

Provider: "So we are up to our next planned *in vivo* contamination exposure, cooking a hamburger for yourself and your family (SUDS 90). How are you feeling about completing this exposure today?"

Roberto: "Not going to lie, I'm really nervous! I have been thinking about this one for a while, as we have been building up to it. I'm really anxious but I know I can do it. I've been able to do everything else so far."

Provider: "That's a good point, you've been surprised that you were able to accomplish all the other exposures and repeat them for homework, and they were not as challenging as you thought they would be!"

Roberto: "Exactly. Don't get me wrong, they were scary, but mostly it was the worst before I did the exposures. So I guess that's helping me today."

Provider: "You remember it was more the anticipation of the exposure than the exposure itself that was scary."

Roberto: "Yeah. Plus, cooking for myself and my family has been so hard for me but also a goal, so I want to be able to do it. I really do."

Provider: "It's been really important for you for a long time to do this exposure. I wonder what impact do you think this will have on your treatment progress?"

Roberto: "I don't know I think it will help this go away because if I can get over cooking and doing the exposure and repeating it, then that is my most challenging exposure and other stuff will be easier."

Teaching Points

In the above dialogue the patient demonstrated enhanced SE (i.e., "I'm really anxious but I know I can do it. I've been able to do everything else so far.") and more confident beliefs in his expected outcome (i.e., "Don't get me wrong, they were scary, but mostly it was the worst before I did the exposures."). In this example the patient was open about his anxious emotions and perceived difficulty of the planned exposure, and this honesty suggests a positive working alliance between the patient and therapist. Although anxious about a challenging exposure, the patient references past experiences of completing challenging exposures as evidence of his ability to handle this new exposure practice. Of note, the therapist highlighted the patient's statement about past experiences during which the patient's feared expectations were violated (i.e., "you've been surprised that you were able to accomplish all the other exposures...they were not as challenging as you thought they would be."). The therapist's reinforcement of past positive experience with changes in OE directly prompted the patient to feel enhanced SE and confidence in completing the planned exposure. The therapist maintained a positive working alliance by prompting the patient to further reflect on ways in which succeeding in treatment serves the patient values and derives meaning in his life.

Addressing Intolerance of Uncertainty to Build Self-efficacy and Outcome Expectancy

The following dialogue with Roberto highlights the therapist's role in asking and clarifying uncertainty levels while treating to build skills of SE and OE through the working alliance:

Provider: "I'm wondering how you're feeling about treatment working now that we are more than halfway through our exposure therapy work together."

Roberto: "Yeah, that's a question I've actually been thinking about, because I know you said that this was time limited therapy. I think it's been really helpful so far because I can eat things that may not be perfectly cooked and make mistakes and stuff, way easier than I used to, and I check a lot less. So, I think it will get better the more I practice the exposures. I think that I'm also worried about the future—practicing on my own without you there, like what if it gets worse."

Provider: "It's good to hear that you are noticing progress. It's also tough because you are worried about the future and not sure how it will work out, is that right?"

Roberto: "Yeah, exactly. I think I feel confident now that the treatment will work and that I can do it, but I think a lot of it was that I relied on seeing you every week to help."

Provider: "That makes sense, but remember that the work you've put in will not go away even when we stop meeting weekly. Towards the end of treatment, we can make a relapse prevention plan for what to do when you're doing exposures on your own without my direct help. If we were to try to create a relapse prevention plan now (for current exposure items), what do you think would be critical to include?

Roberto: "I would like that; it helps to remind me of how we discussed things and how you remind me that I can do the exposures even when they are tough. I think I would need to have on the list to remind myself to that I can do hard things, like creating my own exposures sometimes."

Teaching Points

Add a few points here to summarize take-aways from above excerpt—otherwise consider deleting this last illustration about tolerating uncertainty to save space

Conclusion

SE and OE beliefs play an important role in treatment engagement and outcomes in CBT for anxiety disorders. SE and OE each independently predicts treatment outcome in CBT for anxiety-related disorders (Brown et al., 2014; Haug et al., 2016;

Baier et al., 2020). Higher treatment OE and greater perceived self-efficacy beliefs prior to starting CBT for anxiety disorders predict improved treatment outcome, specifically for GAD and PD (Jakubovski & Bloch, 2016). Despite this, gaps in the literature remain, as to how to bridge the gap between these constructs and skills to use to help foster SE and OE in treatment. Clinicians working with individuals with anxiety or depressive disorders may encounter individuals struggling with low motivation, excessive fear, and hopeless. Practicing clinicians can consider implementing evidence-based principles alongside CBT to foster SE and PE. For example, practical application of MI skills can greatly enhance treatment engagement. Clinicians should follow the principles of DARN CAT: assess desire, action, reasons, and need for change, commitment, activation, and taking steps. These steps will help clinicians to assess whether a client can create their own reasons for change. Additionally, by assessing motivation for change, clinicians can assess whether there is a skills deficit that the clinician can assist with by teaching PST. PST, or the orientation of the client to how to cope with problems, can greatly assist patients in building a framework to think about problem-solving. If a patient can increase their problem-solving ability, they may be more likely to increase their SE and OE beliefs, however more research is needed in this area. Additionally, SE and OE can be enhanced by targeting intolerance of uncertainty and strategic processing of expectancy violations in exposure therapy. Future research should continue to explore the relationship between beliefs about treatment outcome, beliefs about the self and ability in relation to treatment engagement and outcome, and the ways that evidenced-based skills can assist in optimizing CBT for individuals with anxiety disorders.

Clinical Summary Points and Recommendations

- SE and OE each independently predicts treatment outcome in CBT for anxiety-related disorders.
- CBT and exposure-based therapies for anxiety disorders may be improved by incorporating MI and PST to help improve outcome expectancy and self-efficacy beliefs.
- SE and OE can be enhanced by targeting intolerance of uncertainty and strategically processing expectancy violations in exposure therapy.
- More research is necessary to identify optimal use of evidence-based strategies to improve outcome expectancy and self-efficacy and understand their connection to engagement and outcomes across anxiety disorders.

References

Ahmed, M., & Westra, H. A. (2009). Impact of a treatment rationale on expectancy and engagement in cognitive behavioral therapy for social anxiety. *Cognitive Therapy and Research, 33*(3), 314–322. https://doi.org/10.1007/s10608-008-9182-1

Ametrano, R. M., Constantino, M. J., & Nalven, T. (2017). The influence of expectancy persuasion techniques on socially anxious analogue patients' treatment beliefs and therapeutic actions. *International Journal of Cognitive Therapy, 10*(3), 187–205. https://doi.org/10.1521/ijct.2017.10.3.187

Bandura, A. (1977). Self-efficacy: Toward a unifying theory of behavioral change. *Psychological Review, 84*(2), 191–215.

Bandelow, B., & Michaelis, S. (2015). Epidemiology of anxiety disorders in the 21st century. *Dialogues in Clinical Neuroscience, 17*(3), 327–335.

Baier, A. L., Kline, A. C., & Feeny, N. C. (2020). Therapeutic alliance as a mediator of change: A systematic review and evaluation of research. *Clinical Psychology Review, 82*, 101921.

Birrell, J., Meares, K., Wilkinson, A., & Freeston, M. (2011). Toward a definition of intolerance of uncertainty: A review of factor analytical studies of the intolerance of uncertainty scale. *Clinical Psychology Review, 31*(7), 1198–1208.

Bordin, E. S. (1979). The generalizability of the psychoanalytic concept of the working alliance. *Psychotherapy, 16*(3), 252–260. https://doi.org/10.1037/h0085885

Brown, L. A., Wiley, J. F., Wolitzky-Taylor, K., Roy-Byrne, P., Sherbourne, C., Stein, M. B., Sullivan, G., Rose, R. D., Bystritsky, A., & Craske, M. G. (2014). Changes in self-efficacy and outcome expectancy as predictors of anxiety outcomes from the CALM study. *Depression and Anxiety, 31*(8), 678–689. https://doi.org/10.1002/da.22256

Çam, Z., Eşkisu, M., Kardaş, F., Saatçioğlu, Ö., & Gelibolu, S. (2020). The mediating role of self-efficacy in the relationship between problem solving and hope. *Participatory Educational Research, 7*(1), 47–58.

Chambless, D. L., Tran, G. Q., & Glass, C. R. (1997). Predictors of response to cognitive-behavioral group therapy for social phobia. *Journal of Anxiety Disorders, 11*(3), 221–240. https://doi.org/10.1016/S0887-6185(97)00008-X

Chung, M. C., AlQarni, N., Al Muhairi, S., & Mitchell, B. (2017). The relationship between trauma centrality, selfefficacy, posttraumatic stress and psychiatric co-morbidity among Syrian refugees: Is gender a moderator? *Journal of Psychiatric Research, 94*, 107–115.

Collins, J., & Hyer, L. (1986). Treatment expectancy among psychiatric inpatients. *Journal of Clinical Psychology, 42*(4), 562–569.

Connolly Gibbons, M., Crits-Christoph, P., de la Cruz, C., Barber, J. P., Siqueland, L., & Gladis, M. (2003). Pretreatment expectations, interpersonal functioning, and symptoms in the prediction of the therapeutic alliance across supportive-expressive psychotherapy and cognitive therapy. *Psychotherapy Research, 13*(1), 59–76. https://doi.org/10.1093/ptr/kpg007

Constantino, M. J., Vîslă, A., Coyne, A. E., & Boswell, J. F. (2018). A meta-analysis of the association between patients' early treatment outcome expectation and their posttreatment outcomes. *Psychotherapy, 55*(4), 473–485. https://doi.org/10.1037/pst0000169

Constantino, M. J., Vîslă, A., Ogrodniczuk, J. S., Coyne, A. E., & Söchting, I. (2016). Forward thinking: Correlates of posttreatment outcome expectation among depressed outpatients/ Pensamiento prospectivo: Correlatos de las expectativas de resultados post-tratamiento de pacientes ambulatorios que sufren depresión. *Estudios de Psicología, 37*(2–3), 282–310. https://doi.org/10.1080/02109395.2016.1189205

D'Zurilla, T. J., & Nezu, A. M. (2006). *Problem-solving therapy: A positive approach to clinical intervention* (3rd ed.). Springer.

Craske, M. G., Liao, B., Brown, L., & Vervliet, B. (2012). Role of inhibition in exposure therapy. *Journal of Experimental Psychopathology, 3*(3), 322–345. https://doi.org/10.5127/jep.026511

Detweiler, J. B., & Whisman, M. A. (1999). The role of homework assignments in cognitive therapy for depression: Potential methods for enhancing adherence. *Clinical Psychology: Science and Practice, 6*(3), 267.

Dozois, D. J. A. (2010). Understanding and enhancing the effects of homework in cognitive-behavioral therapy. *Clinical Psychology: Science and Practice, 17*(2), 157–161.
Delsignore, A. (2008). Does prior psychotherapy experience affect the course of cognitive-behavioural group therapy for social anxiety disorder?. *The Canadian Journal of Psychiatry, 53*(8), 509–516.
Fetherston, M., Cherney, M. R., & Bunton, T. E. (2018). Uncertainty, technology use, and career preparation self-efficacy. *Western Journal of Communication, 82*(3), 276–295. https://doi.org/10.1080/10570314.2017.1294704
Gallagher, M. W., Long, L. J., & Phillips, C. A. (2020). Hope, optimism, self-efficacy, and post-traumatic stress disorder: A meta-analytic review of the protective effects of positive expectancies. *Journal of Clinical Psychology, 76*(3), 329–355.
Gershkovich, M., Deacon, B. J., & Wheaton, M. G. (2018). Biomedical causal attributions for obsessive-compulsive disorder: Associations with patient perceptions of prognosis and treatment expectancy. *Journal of Obsessive-Compulsive and Related Disorders, 18*, 81–85.
Glenn, D., Golinelli, D., Rose, R. D., Roy-Byrne, P., Stein, M. B., Sullivan, G., Bystritksy, A., Sherbourne, C., & Craske, M. G. (2013). Who gets the most out of cognitive behavioral therapy for anxiety disorders? The role of treatment dose and patient engagement. *Journal of Consulting and Clinical Psychology, 81*(4), 639.
Greenberg, R. P., Constantino, M. J., & Bruce, N. (2006). Are patient expectations still relevant for psychotherapy process and outcome?. *Clinical psychology review, 26*(6), 657–678.
Gu, Y., Gu, S., Lei, Y., & Li, H. (2020). From uncertainty to anxiety: How uncertainty fuels anxiety in a process mediated by intolerance of uncertainty. *Stress Induced Neuroplasticity and Mental Disorders., 2020*. https://doi.org/10.1155/2020/8866386
Haug, T., Nordgreen, T., Öst, L. G., Tangen, T., Kvale, G., Hovland, O. J., et al. (2016). Working alliance and competence as predictors of outcome in cognitive behavioral therapy for social anxiety and panic disorder in adults. *Behaviour Research and Therapy, 77*, 40–51.
Holaway, R. M., Heimberg, R. G., & Coles, M. E. (2006). A comparison of intolerance of uncertainty in analogue obsessive-compulsive disorder and generalized anxiety disorder. *Journal of Anxiety Disorders, 20*(2), 158–174. https://doi.org/10.1016/j.janxdis.2005.01.00
Jakubovski, E., Bloch, M.H. (2016). Anxiety disorder-specific predictors of treatment outcome in the coordinated anxiety learning and management (CALM) trial. *Psychiatry Q, 87*, 445–464. https://doi.org/10.1007/s11126-015-9399-6
Jones, D., McCalla, M., & Beverly, E. A. (2023). Measuring grit, self-efficacy, curiosity, and intolerance of uncertainty in first-generation college and first-generation osteopathic medical students. *BMC medical education, 23*(1), 190.
Kessler, R. C., Berglund, P., Demler, O., Jin, R., Merikangas, K. R., & Walters, E. E. (2005a). Lifetime prevalence and age-of-onset distributions of DSM-IV disorders in the National Comorbidity Survey Replication. *Archives of General Psychiatry, 62*(6), 593–602.
Kessler, R. C., Chiu, W. T., Demler, O., & Walters, E. E. (2005b). Prevalence, severity, and comorbidity of 12-month DSM-IV disorders in the national comorbidity survey replication. *Archives of General Psychiatry, 62*(6), 617–627.
Maddux, J. E., Sherer, M., & Rogers, R. W. (1982). Self-efficacy expectancy and outcome expectancy: Their relationship and their effects on behavioral intentions. *Cognitive Therapy and Research, 6*(2), 207–211.
Marker, I., & Norton, P. J. (2018). The efficacy of incorporating motivational interviewing to cognitive behavior therapy for anxiety disorders: A review and meta-analysis. *Clinical Psychology Review, 62*, 1–10. https://doi.org/10.1016/j.cpr.2018.04.004
Miller, W. R., & Rollnick, S. (2013). *Motivational interviewing: Helping people change* (3rd ed.). Guilford Press.
Nezu, A. M., Maguth Nezu, C., & D'Zurilla, T. J. (2013). *Problem-solving therapy: A treatment manual*. Springer.
Olatunji, B. O., Cisler, J. M., & Tolin, D. F. (2007). Quality of life in the anxiety disorders: A meta-analytic review. *Clinical Psychology Review, 27*(5), 572–581. https://doi.org/10.1016/j.cpr.2007.01.015

Panc, T., Mihalcea, A., & Panc, I. (2012). Self-efficacy survey: A new assessment tool. *Procedia–Social and Behavioral Sciences, 33*, 880–884.
Peters, L., Romano, M., Byrow, Y., Gregory, B., McLellan, L. F., Brockveld, K., Baillie, A., Gaston, J., & Rapee, R. M. (2019). Motivational interviewing prior to cognitive behavioural treatment for social anxiety disorder: A randomised controlled trial. *Journal of Affective Disorders, 256*(1), 70–78. https://doi.org/10.1016/j.jad.2019.05.042
Rubel, J. A., Hilpert, P., Wolfer, C., Held, J., Vîslă, A., & Flückiger, C. (2019). The working alliance in manualized CBT for generalized anxiety disorder: Does it lead to change and does the effect vary depending on manual implementation flexibility? *Journal of Consulting and Clinical Psychology, 87*(11), 989.
Sauer-Zavala, S., Boswell, J. F., Bentley, K. H., Thompson-Hollands, J., Farchione, T. J., & Barlow, D. H. (2018). Expectancies, working alliance, and outcome in transdiagnostic and single diagnosis treatment for anxiety disorders: An investigation of mediation. *Cognitive Therapy and Research, 42*, 135–145.
Schwarzer, R., & Jerusalem, M. (1995). *General self-efficacy scale (GSE)* [Database record]. APA PsycTests. https://doi.org/10.1037/t00393-000
Solomon, Z., Gelkopf, M., & Bleich, A. (2005). Is terror gender-blind? Gender differences in reaction to terror events. *Social Psychiatry and Psychiatric Epidemiology, 40*, 947–954. https://doi.org/10.1007/s00127-005-0973-3
Tsai, M., Ogrodniczuk, J. S., Sochting, I., & Mirmiran, J. (2014). Forecasting success: Patients' expectations for improvement and their relations to baseline, process, and outcome variables in group cognitive-behavioural therapy for depression. *Clinical Psychology & Psychotherapy, 21*(2), 97–107.
Vîslă, A., Constantino, M. J., & Flückiger, C. (2021). Predictors of change in patient treatment outcome expectation during cognitive-behavioral psychotherapy for generalized anxiety disorder. *Psychotherapy, 58*(2), 219–229. https://doi.org/10.1037/pst0000371
Westra, H. A., Constantino, M. J., & Aviram, A. (2011). The impact of alliance ruptures on client outcome expectations in cognitive behavioral therapy. *Psychotherapy Research, 21*(4), 472–481. https://doi.org/10.1080/10503307.2011.581708
Westra, H. A., & Dozois, D. J. A. (2006). Preparing clients for cognitive behavioral therapy: A randomized pilot study of motivational interviewing for anxiety. *Cognitive Therapy and Research, 30*(4), 481–498.
Westra, H. A., Dozois, D. J. A., & Marcus, M. (2007). Early improvement, expectancy for change, homework compliance, and outcome in cognitive behavioral therapy for anxiety. *Journal of Consulting and Clinical Psychology, 75*(3), 363–373.
Westra, H. A., & Norouzian, N. (2018). Using motivational interviewing to manage process markers of ambivalence and resistance in cognitive behavioral therapy. *Cognitive Therapy and Research, 42*(2), 193–203. https://doi.org/10.1007/s10608-017-9857-6
Wilson, E. J., Abbott, M. J., & Norton, A. R. (2023). The impact of psychological treatment on intolerance of uncertainty in generalized anxiety disorder: A systemic review and meta-analysis. *Journal of Anxiety Disorders, 97*, 102729. https://doi.org/10.1016/j.janxdis.2023.102729
Younger, J., Gandhi, V., Hubbard, E., & Mackey, S. (2012). Development of the Stanford expectations of treatment scale (SETS): A tool for measuring patient outcome expectancy in clinical trials. *Clinical Trials., 9*(6), 767–776. https://doi.org/10.1177/1740774512465064
Zhang, A., Park, S., Sullivan, J. E., & Jing, S. (2018). The effectiveness of problem-solving therapy for primary care patients' depressive and/or anxiety disorders: A systematic review and meta-analysis. *The Journal of the American Board of Family Medicine, 31*(1), 139–150.
Zhou, C., Yue, X. D., Zhang, X., Shangguan, F., & Zhang, X. Y. (2021). Self-efficacy and mental health problems during COVID-19 pandemic: A multiple mediation model based on the health belief model. *Personality and Individual Differences, 179*, 110893.

Chapter 4
Integrating Motivational Interviewing into the Treatment of Anxiety and Related Disorders

Peter J. Norton and Isabella Marker

Introduction

Motivational Interviewing (MI) is a client-centered therapeutic style, designed to motivate an individual to overcome ambivalence and facilitate client choice in changing problematic behaviors. MI first emerged in the treatment of alcohol use disorders (see Miller, 1983) and has been successful in this area (e.g., Hettema et al., 2005). More recently, MI has been explored as an adjunct or sole therapy for numerous other disorders. For anxiety disorders, MI has been suggested as an adjunct to Cognitive Behavior Therapy (CBT) due to the ambivalence that often accompanies anxiety presentations (Westra, 2012). Despite the impairments resulting from anxiety disorders, ambivalence about change is common and clients may hold both positive and negative beliefs about their anxiety and their necessity to change (Westra, 2012). Research suggests clients may be conflicted about changing: Although anxiety symptoms are debilitating, they are simultaneously regarded as helpful or protective (Borkovec et al., 1999; Engle & Arkowitz, 2008).

The most evidence-supported (Kaczkurkin & Foa, 2015) and clinically recommended (Australian Psychological Society, 2015; National Institute of Health and Clinical Excellence, 2011) psychotherapy for anxiety disorder is cognitive behavior therapy (CBT). CBT is a proactive therapy requiring the client to take active steps toward reaching therapy goals. Alongside the specified time-commitment, CBT asks clients to challenge current belief systems and change unhelpful and avoidant behaviors. Furthermore, CBT for anxiety disorders requires clients to directly face

P. J. Norton (✉)
Cairnmillar Institute, Hawthorn, VIC, Australia
e-mail: peter.norton@cairnmillar.edu.au

I. Marker
Private Practice, Prahran, VIC, Australia

E. M. Goetter (ed.), *Optimizing Treatment Engagement Processes in CBT for Anxiety and Related Disorders*, CBT: Science Into Practice,
https://doi.org/10.1007/978-3-031-91439-3_4

their fears, a component of treatment that is highly distressing for many clients (Westra, 2012). For example, in a study of individuals awaiting CBT for anxiety disorders (Purdon et al., 2004), 94% expressed fears and concerns about commencing CBT. These fears included the possibility of a worsening in anxiety symptoms due to exposure components, uncertainty about their ability to cope with treatment demands and their capacity for change, as well as worries about the stigma of receiving treatment and judgement from therapists. The process of changing cognitive and behavioral habits is not straightforward and requires a degree of motivation on the part of the client. A client's motivation is therefore an important aspect of treatment, both to overcome ambivalence about symptoms and to cope with the requirements of CBT.

Client Motivation

Client motivation is recognized as a common factor across therapies, and its relevance for therapeutic issues such as drop out, compliance, and maintenance of change is well established (Pelletier et al., 1997). Client motivation has been defined in terms of both *energy* and *direction of action* and is more commonly understood as the intrinsic drive, willingness, and desire for change exhibited by a client (Ryan et al., 2010). Motivation impacts treatment beyond initial entrance, and may prove more critical during therapy, when obstacles relating to behavioral change must be overcome, and behavioral change maintained (Ryan et al., 2010).

Client motivation is described as a fluctuating construct, and one that can be considered to fall along a series of stages (Miller, 1985). The transtheoretical model (Prochaska & DiClemente, 1982) describes five stages of change: pre-contemplation, contemplation, preparation, action, and maintenance (see Table 4.1).

Upon entering therapy, clients may align with any one of these five stages and thus present with varying levels of willingness (De Nadai et al., 2014). Although low treatment motivation may appear illogical, particularly for anxiety disorders

Table 4.1 The five stages of change

Stage	Description
Pre-contemplation	Individuals are not yet thinking about changing their behaviors. They may not see their behaviors as problematic, or the costs of change outweigh the positives
Contemplation	Individuals are ambivalent about change. They acknowledge problematic behaviors and their consequences but also find positive aspects of the behavior
Preparation	Individuals understand that the pros of changing outweigh the cons and believe change is necessary. They may be making small steps or preparing to make change
Action	Individuals actively take steps toward change
Maintenance	Individuals have sustained behavioral change and intend to maintain new behavioral patterns

characterized by significant levels of psychological distress, many clients enter treatment with low motivation (Greenberg, 2004). In fact, research suggests that up to 80% of individuals entering treatment are not at action-oriented stages of change and thus not ready to engage in treatment planning and initiation (Prochaska et al., 2013). Early treatment ambivalence can have lasting effects throughout therapy, with studies indicating that low pre-treatment motivation has detrimental effects on anxiety outcomes in CBT (Huppert et al., 2006; Lombardi et al., 2014). Rather than being viewed as an individual difference characteristic (i.e., trait), motivation is considered a client state, and it is the task of both the client and therapist to facilitate change (Ryan & Deci, 2008). Research exploring ways to increase motivation for CBT has flourished in previous years, with much of the literature drawing upon principles of Motivational Interviewing (MI).

Motivational Interviewing

MI is a client-centered therapy, which first emerged as a treatment for alcohol use disorders (see Miller, 1983). It is designed to help individuals overcome ambivalence and change problematic behaviors. Many of the underlying assumptions of MI are based on the transtheoretical model, and MI can be conceptualized as a therapy intended to guide individuals through the stages of change. MI has been proven to be an effective treatment in the area of alcohol use disorders (e.g., Hettema et al., 2005) and has now gained popularity as an adjunct or sole therapy to many other disorders, including anxiety disorders (Arkowitz & Miller, 2008).

Theory and Development

MI was originally developed by Miller (1983), who saw in many of his clients with alcohol use disorders, degrees of ambivalence in changing drinking behaviors. For example, an individual may recognize that their habits are causing harm to family and employment, yet they also enjoy drinking alcohol as a way of socializing, numbing cravings, and a means of escaping painful thoughts and feelings. Miller noted that clients often “get stuck,” during the contemplative stages of change, when they are able to acknowledge both positive and negative aspects of change (Miller & Rollnick, 2012). He further identified that during the contemplative stage, clients did not respond well to judgement, criticism, or receiving excessive education about reasons for changing their behavior. Indeed, when therapists tried to convince clients of changing through these mechanisms, ambivalent clients appeared to exhibit greater resistance. Thus, MI first emerged as a way of intentionally discussing ambivalence in therapy, without fear of negative judgement.

The Spirit of MI

Although there are numerous MI manuals and different MI techniques, what is considered the most important element of MI is its fundamental spirit. Rather than being viewed as a technique, MI is considered a way of being and relating to a client by having a coherent understanding of human nature and the process of change (Miller & Rollnick, 2002). The spirit of MI consists of four integrated elements: partnership, acceptance, compassion, and evocation (Miller & Rollnick, 2012).

Partnership. The therapeutic alliance is crucial to the spirit of MI, and the relationship between therapist and client is seen as a partnership, one that is collaborative, where both parties contribute to the process. An MI therapist takes the role of a guide, rather than the expert with superior knowledge. The client is considered an expert on oneself, and the therapist's task is not to pressure, persuade, or argue with the client but instead to understand the client's perspective through exploration, openness, and curiosity. This environment, while conducive to change, is not coercive. For behavioral change to occur, a client must initially have intention to change behavior, and importantly also believe in their ability to change behavior (Montaño & Kasprzyk, 2008). Thus, the aim of the therapeutic relationship is to activate the role of expert in the client and foster a state of self-efficacy.

Acceptance. Based on Rogerian principles, an MI therapist must harvest an attitude of acceptance toward the client. This means having an inherent understanding of the absolute worth of all people. Acceptance does not mean approving of all behavior, but accepting the person for who they are. To practice acceptance, an MI therapist must express accurate empathy, support autonomy, provide affirmations and acknowledgements of a client's efforts, and have an inherent understanding of a client's worth. This creates a safe, comforting, and supportive environment where the client feels understood. MI suggests that without such an environment, trust cannot be established and change cannot occur (Miller & Rollnick, 2012).

Compassion. An MI therapist must act for the welfare of one's clients. In the context of MI, compassion means to be in the service of others, and does not refer to the emotional experience of personalization or sympathy. Compassion is not pitying the client or seeing them as helpless, as this would undermine the notion of "client as expert." In MI, compassion refers to working with the client to understand the nature of the problem in a non-judgmental, non-blaming, and non-shaming manner (Hall & McMaster, 2016). Compassion is seen as crucial to the MI spirit and entails having "your heart in the right place so that the trust you engender will be deserved" (Miller & Rollnick, 2012, p. 29).

Evocation. The final element that forms the MI spirit is the inherent understanding that a client brings with them experience, wisdom, and knowledge. A client is not viewed as flawed or lacking in some way, rather they are considered to already possess all that is required for change to occur. It is not the role of the MI therapist to provide skills, motivation, or insight, but rather to evoke what is needed from within the client. The focus of MI is building upon strengths and resources already present. In relation to ambivalence, evocation also entails exploring clients' unique reasons for change. The basis of ambivalence is that clients have reasons both for and against change, meaning they are aware of their motivations for changing. The role of the MI therapist is therefore not to provide their own arguments for change, but to evoke the motivations already present within the client. The aim is for the client, not the therapist, to be the advocate of change (Wheaton et al., 2016).

The Four Processes of MI

The practice of MI involves four processes: (1) engaging, (2) focusing, (3) evoking, and (4) planning (Miller & Rollnick, 2012). These processes are not to be viewed as strictly sequential, but understood to align with a client's stage of change, which may alter both during the process of treatment and within a single session.

Engaging. The first MI process relates to engaging the client, by creating an environment that is therapeutic, supportive, and understanding. The working relationship between therapist and client is considered the foundation by which all other processes occur, and without it change cannot transpire. To appropriately engage with a client, an MI therapist must understand why the client has sought therapy and what unique values and goals lie behind treatment. A therapist must understand a client's frame of reference, rather than using their own or others' ideals (e.g., "What makes you feel like *now* is the ideal time to start working on your anxiety?"). It is therefore important for a therapist to ask open-ended questions, listen, reflect, and provide summaries of what a client has said to fully understand their frame of mind.

Focusing. This is the technique used by therapists to clarify the direction of therapy; that is, the goals the client would like to reach by the end of treatment (e.g., "How would you like things to be for you at the end of treatment? How would things be different for you?"). This process is necessary so that therapist and client are "on the same page," and that both have a clear understanding of a clients' hopes, expectations, and fears. Focusing goes above setting an agenda for session or a plan for treatment, it is the ongoing collaborative process between client and therapist of finding direction and prioritizing goals.

Evoking. This process prepares clients for change and increases motivation; however, it requires the foundation of the working alliance and the mutual understanding of direction in therapy to be effective. It is through the first two processes of engaging and focusing that an exploration of ambivalence can occur. Rather than ignoring ambivalence, an MI therapist encourages a discussion of the pros and cons of change, as ambivalence is considered a normal part of the pre-contemplative and contemplative stage of change (DiClemente & Velasquez, 2002). Evoking requires a therapist to be able to identify clients' change talk (CT) and counter-change talk (CCT). CT is any statement a client says which provides a reason, desire, ability, need, and commitment toward change (e.g., "I want to stop feeling so tense all the time"). CCT, on the other hand is a statement that includes a reason, desire, ability, need, or commitment against change (e.g., "doing the homework is a waste of time"). An MI therapist must identify and appropriately respond to both by using MI techniques of reflecting and affirming. Evoking also allows for the empathic discussion of discrepancies between a clients' current behavior and their desire to change. As part of this process, it is important for a client to recognize that they are their own agent of change. Motivation is formed not only by a desire for change but also a belief in one's ability to carry out the change. Thus, it is important for an MI therapist to build self-efficacy within a client. If a client believes that change came from outside forces, such as due to therapist expertise, they are unlikely to maintain lasting behavioral change after therapy has terminated (Markland et al., 2005).

Planning. The final process of MI is that of planning, which occurs only after clear indications of client readiness occur. Such indications include a decrease in CCT, and an increase in CT, particularly in a client's use of commitment and action-oriented language. A client and therapist collaboratively plan for change and MI techniques are used to strengthen commitment and support the process of change (e.g., "I've noticed that you are sounding much more resolved in your desire to begin getting out of the house more. You said that you were 'ready,' and I think you are ready, too. How do you think we should proceed?").

These four processes rely on the ability of an MI therapist to appropriately use OARS (Open-ended questions, Affirming, Reflecting, and Summarizing), the acronym given to what are considered the core skills of MI. These four skills are used throughout the engaging, focusing, evoking, and planning process. An MI therapist asks questions in a way in which allows the client to think before responding. An MI therapist responds to a client with affirmations, reflections, and summaries to portray understanding, empathy, and the acknowledgement of a clients' innate worth (Table 4.2).

Table 4.2 Open-ended questions, affirming, reflecting, and summarizing (OARS)

Open-ended questions allow the therapist to understand their clients' values and goals. It can help clarify a clients' motivation	**Example:** Can you tell me a bit more about how your anxiety is interfering with your life? Why is making this change important to you?
Affirmations are statements made by therapists that highlight a clients' strengths and efforts	**Example:** I can see how difficult it was to come to session today. Thank you for making the effort. You completed your homework. Well done!
Reflections allow a therapist to reinforce specific parts of a client's dialogue	**Example:** It sounds like the exposure task was really difficult, but when you finished it, you felt a sense of accomplishment
Summaries are usually completed at the end of a dialogue. Therapists use them to highlight ambivalence. It is often best to end a summary by highlighting the positive elements of change	**Example:** You mentioned that you have tried therapy several times and you have not noticed lasting improvements in your anxiety. However, you also feel like you are in a different headspace than you were previously and are more hopeful than you have been in the past

Motivational Interviewing as an Adjunct to CBT for Anxiety Disorders

Due to its focus on resolving ambivalence, increasing motivation, and building client self-efficacy, MI has been suggested as an adjunct to CBT for anxiety disorders (Westra, 2012). MI was initially proposed as a pre-treatment condition, with the purpose of improving motivation prior to entering action-oriented therapies such as CBT (Miller & Rollnick, 2012), as clients with high motivation at baseline have better post-treatment outcomes (Lombardi et al., 2014). More recently, however, MI strategies have been suggested at other stages of treatment. For instance, MI may be used as needed, such as when resistance occurs in session (Aviram et al., 2016), and as an integrated approach to create a more effective behavioral therapy, rather than using the treatments individually or consecutively (Naar & Safren, 2017).

In 2004, the first published study emerged describing a series of three case studies which incorporated MI into CBT for anxiety disorders (Westra, 2004). These case studies presented a basis for ongoing research in the area by showing that the inclusion of MI as a prelude to CBT is feasible and may provide therapeutic benefit by increasing engagement and motivation. From this time, numerous case studies, open trials, and randomized controlled trials (RCTs) have been completed across a wide range of anxiety and anxiety-related disorders, including generalized anxiety disorder (GAD), obsessive-compulsive disorder (OCD), posttraumatic stress disorder (PTSD), social anxiety disorder (SAD), and illness anxiety disorder (IAD). The adjunct of pre-treatment MI to standard CBT for anxiety disorders has shown promising results, but with considerable variability. Randomized controlled trials (RCTs) have shown that in comparison to psychoeducation and waitlist controls, MI as an adjunct to CBT has been shown to a) increase treatment seeking amongst individuals with SAD and OCD (Buckner & Schmidt, 2009; Maltby & Tolin, 2005); b) increase attendance in group CBT treatment for PTSD (Murphy et al., 2009); c) enhance openness to particular treatment components in OCD (McCabe et al., 2008); d) reduce anxiety, stress, and nonproductive coping strategies in anxiety for traumatic brain injury (Hsieh et al., 2012); and e) reduce treatment resistance in GAD (Aviram & Westra, 2011). Furthermore three (Westra & Dozois, 2006; Yang & Strodl, 2011) and four (Westra et al., 2009) sessions of MI prior to CBT for anxiety appear to improve treatment response and outcome. Although these results are promising, other conflicting literature has found little or no added benefit of including MI (Blain, 2013; Coffey et al., 2016; Maltby & Tolin, 2005; Simpson et al., 2010). Furthermore, several studies have found that the effectiveness of a single pre-treatment session of MI subsides over time (Barrera et al., 2016; Yang & Strodl, 2011). Another study found that, while brief MI intermittently integrated at key timepoints throughout CBT improved outcomes compared to a CBT-only intervention, but had no effect on attrition (Marker et al., 2020). Meta-analytic findings from a study of 12 published trials, dated between 2006 and 2016, and encompassing 609 individuals also suggested that overall, MI and CBT, in comparison to CBT-only, had a moderate effect on treatment outcome, that was not seemingly moderated by the dose of MI or the specific anxiety diagnosis (Marker & Norton, 2018).

Integrating MI and CBT

Various ways of integrating MI and CBT have been suggested. The most common approach utilizes MI as a pre-treatment component, followed by CBT. As a pre-treatment condition, MI can strengthen initial motivation, help a client to resolve ambivalence, and focus on meaningful reasons for changing behavior. This approach has been favored in the literature, likely due to the relative ease of delivering MI and CBT in this manner. A key advantage of pre-treatment MI is that two different therapists can deliver the two treatments; this means expertise is required in only one treatment. Furthermore, conceptual differences leading to difficulties integrating the two treatments can be avoided. Although CBT and MI share many common characteristics—for example, both place heightened importance on the therapeutic relationship, the collaborative nature of goal setting and planning, providing and eliciting reflection and feedback, and using guided discovery techniques—there are also some key differences, particularly when considering CBT in its traditional form.

Traditionally CBT was viewed as a structured, manualized, and directive form of therapy where the therapist was placed in the role of expert, akin to a doctor-patient relationship. Emphasis was placed on CBT skills rather than the therapeutic relationship (Balán et al., 2016). Although this understanding of CBT is dated, and numerous studies exist testifying to the important role of therapist expression of empathy, warmth, genuineness, and positive regard on treatment outcome (Keijsers et al., 2000), some therapists struggle balancing the equivocal importance of techniques and relational factors (Balán et al., 2016). For example, in a study integrating MI and CBT for OCD, therapists rated as competent in delivering MI during pure-MI sessions, received low competency ratings during subsequent CBT sessions (Simpson et al., 2010). Studies have also shown that therapists have difficulty understanding when MI and CBT should be used based on client presentation (Moyers & Houck, 2011; Simpson et al., 2010).

Despite these challenges, researchers have suggested a move toward more integrated approaches (e.g., Balán et al., 2016; Naar & Safren, 2017), with the aim of better supporting clients as they progress through the demands of therapy. A concern of MI as solely a pre-treatment condition is that it assumes motivation will remain stable after completing MI and moving into CBT. However, conceptualizations of motivation consider motivation a client state, rather than client trait, and one that is likely to change in direction and intensity throughout treatment (Miller & Rollnick, 2012). This conceptualization supports transtheoretical models of change, which highlight that individuals rarely move through the five stages of change in a purely linear fashion (Prochaska et al., 2013). Furthermore, research by Marker et al. (2019) provided evidence that patterns of motivation differ over the course of group transdiagnostic CBT for anxiety disorders. It also found that depending on the stage of therapy, motivation was predictive of several outcome variables, even in latter therapy sessions, further supporting the integration of MI throughout the course of CBT. For example, both greater verbalizations of reasons for change and fewer verbalizations of reasons to not change predicted slope of improvement earlier sessions. In later sessions, only fewer verbalizations of reasons to not change was predictive of poorer treatment outcomes, while greater verbalizations of reasons for change predicted client attendance and less treatment drop out. Relatedly, several studies now indicate that the effectiveness of MI subsides over time. For example, a study utilizing a single one-hour MI session prior to CBT found that although MI showed preliminary treatment improvements in comparison to a control group, these later became on par with the CBT-only comparison group (Barrera et al., 2016).

Integration of MI within CBT also has the advantage that MI techniques can be used beyond their role of resolving early treatment ambivalence. For example, in a study of individuals with GAD, research indicated that using MI strategies during active signs of resistance was associated with greater symptom reduction at post-treatment (Aviram et al., 2016). Resistance and disharmony in the therapeutic relationship has been shown to worsen treatment outcome (Button et al., 2014) and CBT therapists may have difficulty identifying when resistance or ruptures in alliance occur (Hara et al., 2015). The detrimental effects of resistance can be mitigated when therapists respond using MI consistent techniques (Aviram et al., 2016).

MI techniques can also be utilized to build self-efficacy in the client (Westra & Dozois, 2006). Self-efficacy is the belief that one can effectively accomplish the behavior required for the desired outcome (Bandura, 1977). The construct has already received much attention as a transdiagnostic mechanism of change thought to impact both the development and treatment of anxiety disorders (Gallagher et al., 2013). Self-efficacy is shown to be predictive of symptom severity (Richards et al., 2002) and changes in self-efficacy during CBT have been found to predict post-treatment outcomes in anxiety disorders (Brown et al., 2014; Gallagher et al., 2013; Goldin et al., 2012) (See Chap. 2). MI specifically targets client beliefs about their ability to change. In fact, prior conceptualizations of MI recognized two distinct phases of MI (see Table 4.3). Phase 1 is used in pre-treatment MI and focuses on exploring and resolving ambivalence about change. Phase 2 rather, aims to foster self-efficacy within the individual by elaborating commitment language, exploring past and current instances of change, and attuning to client strengths (Westra & Dozois, 2003). This latter Phase is often overlooked when MI is delivered only as a pre-treatment condition. Building self-efficacy not only facilitates post-treatment symptom relief but is also thought to lead to better long-term outcomes. In their review of integrated MI and CBT for depression, Arkowitz and Burke (2008) describe the ability of integrated MI to increase self-efficacy, which in turn yields longer lasting post-treatment improvements, due to the change being attributed to the client's own ability, rather than due to the therapist's proficiency. Thus, integrated MI and CBT approaches have the further advantage of decreasing resistance in therapy and increasing self-efficacy.

Table 4.3 Core elements in phases 1 and 2 of motivational interviewing

Phase 1	Phase 2
1. Continue cost–benefit analysis Continue to add pros and cons for staying the same and for change **2. Looking forward exercise** Asking clients to project into future, e.g. "*how would things be different if you made this change?*" **3. Identifying values** Asking clients what is most important to them, what they want their life to stand for **4. Developing discrepancies** Bringing the pros and cons together as well as discussing discrepancy between values and actions **5. Role-plays** *1. Devil's advocate:* The therapist plays the role of articulating the "good reasons" for the problem (i.e., the pros of the problem as identified in the CBA). The client is instructed to respond to these arguments by making forceful counter-arguments. *2. Ambivalence resolution:* The client plays both sides of the ambivalence in order to wrestle with the approach/avoidance dilemma. This role-play is a version of the empty chair technique	If a client brings in examples of changes they have made... **1. Use reflections** e.g., "*this sounds like a change for you?*" **2. Stay value free** Responding, "*that's great that you got a job*" would assume that it is a positive development and the client may perceive that you have a change agenda. Rather, ask, "*How are you feeling about this change*?" **3. Support self-efficacy** "*What does the fact that you did something different here say about you?*" **4. Explore previous experiences of change** "*Have there been other times when you were reluctant to make a change but you succeeded in making it anyway?*" If a client does not bring examples of changes they have made… **1. Hypothetical client exercise** Invite the client to imagine that you and they are co-therapists treating someone who is exactly like the client. The exercise is making a list of the advice that we would offer to someone in this position. **2. Enhancing self-efficacy with questions** "*What makes you think that you could change if your wanted to?*"

Note: CBA: Cost–benefit analysis

Although conceptually advantageous, few integrated approaches have been empirically examined in the literature. Of the 12 studies in Marker & Norton's, 2018 meta-analysis, only three attempted to integrate MI and CBT. Two methods of integrating MI and CBT were identified. Though all studies used MI at pre-treatment, two studies (Blain, 2013; Simpson et al., 2010) allowed for additional MI strategies to be used when resistance occurred in therapy. Although prior research indicates that MI improves treatment outcomes when used as a tool for addressing resistance in CBT for anxiety disorders (Aviram et al., 2016), neither study found post-treatment advantages of including MI. However, these studies failed to report if and how often MI strategies were used during CBT. Prior research indicates therapists often have difficulty identifying and responding to resistance (Hara et al., 2015) and thus opportunities for MI may have been missed during CBT. The third study used MI as an integrative framework where the "spirit of MI" formed the basis of the delivery of CBT (Aviram et al., 2016). This study found no post-treatment advantages of MI over CBT alone; however, greater improvements and maintenance were found at follow-up when MI was included. This study provides preliminary evidence of the value of integrated approaches. A concern with the method used by Aviram et al., (2016) is that extensive training is required of therapists, as generally CBT therapists have difficulty knowing when and how to integrate MI strategies into CBT, and MI therapists have difficulty implementing CBT strategies (Simpson et al., 2010). Furthermore, both approaches (responding to resistance and the integrative framework) make quantifying findings difficult, as individuals received varying amounts of MI. A different mode of integrating MI and CBT is to use an intermittent approach. This has previously been trialed by Merlo et al. (2010) in a trial for adolescents with OCD. The protocol included 20–30 min of MI prior to sessions 1, 4, and 8. Preliminary findings were encouraging, indicating that symptom reduction was significantly greater for the group receiving the MI protocol and fewer sessions were required to reach clinically significant levels of improvement.

More recently, Marker, Corbett, Drummond, and Norton (2020; also see Marker & Norton, 2019) conducted a randomized controlled trial of integrated MI and transdiagnostic CBT in comparison to CBT-only among 36 participants with a principal anxiety disorder diagnosis. In the integrated condition, approximately 15 min of MI was delivered at the start of sessions 1, 3, 8, and 10 in a 12-session protocol, with the therapist selecting Phase 1 or Phase 2 approaches in sessions 3, 8, and 10 based on client scores on the Change Questionnaire (Miller & Johnson, 2008), which was administered immediately prior to session. Fifteen minutes of psychoeducation was administered at the start of the same sessions for participants allocated to CBT-only. Those allocated to integrated MI and CBT showed superior outcomes to those in CBT-only on self-report measures and clinician-rated severity, although no differences were observed between conditions on change in the severity of the principal anxiety diagnosis or premature termination.

Conclusions

Although some studies (e.g., Blain, 2013; Coffey et al., 2016; Maltby & Tolin, 2005; Simpson et al., 2010) have little or no shown benefit of adding MI to CBT for anxiety disorders, the majority of studies, including case studies (Westra, 2004), randomized clinical trials (e.g., Buckner & Schmidt, 2009; Marker et al., 2020; Westra et al., 2009), and a meta-analysis (Marker & Norton, 2018), have found positive effects of adding MI to CBT, although it remains unclear whether MI should be applied globally or only when resistance is encountered. Dose of MI appears to impact outcomes as studies using only a single session of MI (e.g., Barrera et al.,

2016; Yang & Strodl, 2011) showing poorer effects than those incorporating three or four sessions of MI (Westra et al., 2009; Westra & Dozois, 2006). Finally, although additional larger trials are required, integration of MI throughout the course of CBT, as opposed to MI delivered only at pre-treatment, shows promise (Blain, 2013; Marker et al., 2020; Simpson et al., 2010).

Case Example

The following case study is derived from a client seen by one of the authors (IM) and involved an integrated approach to MI and CBT loosely based on the protocol used in Marker et al. (2020). Given the treating psychologist's experience with MI, however, MI strategies were adopted as needed as opposed to the structured delivery schedule used in Marker et al. (2020). CBT was based on the transdiagnostic CBT protocol described by Norton (2012). The case study has been heavily anonymized per recommendations of Clifft (1986).

"Jake" was a 24-year-old medical student, living in a share house. He was referred via his local GP for anxiety and depression. Jake was seen for an initial assessment session. He described symptoms consistent with generalized anxiety disorder (GAD), social anxiety disorder (SAD), and major depressive disorder. During the initial assessment session, a strong focus was placed on the first process of MI, i.e., engagement. In MI, engaging the client means to have a sound understanding of not just the client's symptoms, but how they impact functioning and more importantly what personal values and goals are impeded due to a client's symptoms.

Jake's primary fear was that he was a burden on other people and feared annoying others. This fear extended to both acquaintances and strangers. Jake reported that when he was driving and stationed in the left-hand lane at traffic lights, he would turn left with a green arrow, if someone behind him needed to turn, despite him needing to continue straight. Jake reported that he would often be late to events due to this and scheduled in an extra 20 min to his drives. Jake also disclosed that during a telehealth GP appointment, he urinated onto his chair, as he felt rude disrupting the appointment to use the bathroom.

Jake was the youngest of three brothers. Jake reported that he idolized his older twin brothers growing up even though they consistently teased him for being annoying. Consequently, he always felt left out at home. He also described a history of bullying during middle and high school. Jake's primary therapy goal was to improve his confidence. He reported that he felt behind his peers due to low self-esteem. Jake performed well academically, though struggled with the practical elements of his medical degree. He had difficulty speaking up, and his performance deteriorated in tasks where he was being observed. His days in the hospital left him depleted and he had little time for socializing.

During Jake's first therapy session, he reported that he was highly motivated to make changes because he feared he could not continue his medical degree without addressing his anxiety. In this session, he and his therapist completed a cost-benefit analysis to understand the pros and cons for making changes (see Table 4.4). Jake was able to list benefits of making changes as well as costs to staying the same, though had greater difficulty articulating costs to making changes. An eagerness to please the therapist was evident, and numerous lines of questioning had to be completed to draw out the challenges of making changes.

Therapist: It sounds like you are very clear on why you want to make changes.
Jake: Yes, I just can't keep going this way. I think my supervisors are fed up with me because I keep making mistakes. I'm probably going to fail my placements.
Therapist: Why is being a doctor is important to you?
Jake: I've always wanted to be a doctor. When I was about 10, my mum was hospitalized for a few weeks. We visited her in hospital most nights and she always said, "the doctors are looking after me." I wanted to be able to look after people too.
Therapist: That's sweet. It sounds like supporting others is a personal value of yours.
Jake: It is. I've always wanted to help people. But the anxiety just gets in the way.
Therapist: How so?
Jake: At Uni obviously. But because I'm shy, I think people view me as standoffish.
Therapist: It stops people from seeing the real you?
Jake: Yeah. Like I think I'm a pretty nice guy, but I come across as awkward and weird.
Therapist: How would you like people to see you?
Jake: I want to be seen as nice, as confident, and competent.
Therapist: And if we were able to treat the anxiety, do you think you would be able to live these values of kindness, confidence, and competence?
Jake: Yeah, I think so.
Therapist: Is there anything that is holding you back? Can you think of any benefits to remaining how you are?
Jake: No. There's nothing good about being an anxious mess.
Therapist: What's stopped you from making changes earlier?

Table 4.4 Jake's cost–benefit analysis

	Cost	Benefit
Staying the same	– Might fail medical degree. – Low self-esteem. – Lonely. – Come across as incompetent. – Come across as standoffish.	– Easier.
Making changes	– Hard. – Therapy is time consuming and expensive.	– Pass medical degree to become a doctor. – Find it easier to make friends. – Be able to ask out girls. – Be perceived as friendly and confident. – Able to live value of being kind and supportive.

Jake: I don't know, it's hard, I guess. I always tell myself, tomorrow will be different. Tomorrow I'll be the first to raise my hand and answer a question, but I never do.

Therapist: So, it's difficult to overcome the anxiety?

Jake: Yeah, I just often feel frozen in place. Like I know the answer, or I know what to do. I'm just so afraid that I might be wrong, and everyone will think I'm an idiot.

Therapist: How do you think you come across by not saying anything?

Jake: Like an idiot! [laughs]. I just think that they all think I'm incompetent.

The assessment session and first therapy session utilized the two first processes of MI: engagement and focusing. The therapist attempted to understand why making changes is important to Jake, but also to understand what has made making changes hard up until this point. A cost-benefit analysis can highlight the ambivalence that often accompanies anxiety presentations and validate how difficult it is to engage in exposure work. It allows the client to be compassionate toward themself for not having made changes in the past. It also allows them to understand how their lives might be different once change is made. The therapist asked Jake to take a photo of the cost-benefit analysis and make it his phone's background image. This allowed him to keep the information on hand and served as a constant reminder about the importance of engaging in therapeutic work outside sessions.

The first few sessions with Jake were spent engaging in thought monitoring and thought challenging. Jake was meticulous with completing his homework tasks. He completed thought diaries and was able to challenge unhelpful thoughts. He recognized that he had a prominent fear of appearing incompetent and annoying other people. Throughout these sessions, the therapist asked Jake about his motivation for treatment, and he reported high motivation at each session.

In session four, Jake was introduced to exposure therapy and exposure hierarchies (see below). He understood the rational for exposure therapy but reported hesitation about changing behaviors (Table 4.5).

Therapist: Looking at this list we can see that there are some activities that make you very anxious and your motivation to do them is low.

Table 4.5 Jake's exposure hierarchy

Task	SUDS (0–10)	Motivation (0–10)
1. Answer supervisor question.	6	7
2. Don't turn at traffic light when someone is behind me.	5	5
3. Ask housemate to contribute to chores/cleaning.	9	5
4. Ask out a girl.	10	6
5. Ask peer to get coffee after Uni.	8	6
6. Ask friends for help doing something (e.g., pick up).	8	4
7. Go to a club.	9	3
8. "Annoy someone," e.g. arrive late, forget to bring something.	9	3

Note. *SUDS* subjective units of distress

Jake: It's not that I don't want to. I just don't think I can. Like I've tried and just can't seem to do it.

Therapist: I remember from our cost-benefit analysis, you wrote down that making changes would be challenging.

Jake: Yeah, I just wished I didn't have anxiety!

Therapist: Me too! [both laugh] How do you think we might make that wish a reality?

Jake: Probably by doing this stuff.

Therapist: Are there some things on the list you'd be willing to try?

Jake: Yeah, maybe the first two.

Therapist: Okay, that would be a great start. How do you feel about setting these two for homework?

Jake: I'll try.

Therapist: That's great. Now for the first one, you've put quite a high motivation score. What made you choose a 7, and not a 5?

Jake: Well… I guess I can really see the benefit. Usually, I do know the answer and I would like to show my supervisors that I am capable.

Therapist: Ahh so this relates back to wanting to pass your medical degree?

Jake: Yeah, it's important.

Therapist: What about the second one? Not turning at traffic lights?

Jake: It's stupid. Particularly in our traffic, sometimes it adds so much time to my drives.

Therapist: I bet! You've rated your motivation a bit lower here, why is that?

Jake: I really hate inconveniencing people, like it makes me so anxious. I can just imagine them sitting behind me and thinking that I'm making them late and that I should have been in the other lane.

Therapist: So, you're predicting they would be thinking negative thoughts about you?

Jake: Yeah.

Therapist: How bad would that be?

Jake: I don't know…bad. Like how annoying is that?

Therapist: Have you ever been stuck behind someone wanting to turn?

Jake: Yeah, all the time.

Therapist: And what do you think about?

Jake: I don't know… I don't really mind.

Therapist: Do you ever get a little annoyed.

Jake: Maybe a little… if I'm running late to something.

Therapist: For how long?

Jake: Like a few seconds.

Therapist: So, it sounds like the worst that happens is that you might annoy someone for a few seconds?

Jake: Yeah, I guess. I know it doesn't seem bad, in my head it just feels bad.

Therapist: Let's think about this a little though. You mentioned that you're often adding 20 min to your drives, so you are inconvenienced by 20 min vs. the stranger who might be inconvenienced for a few seconds.

Jake: When you put it like that…

MI encourages a collaborative approach between client and therapist. Hence, it is useful to allow the client to determine which homework exercises they would like to practice. When exposure tasks are introduced, it is important to integrate the MI process of evocation. As therapists, we want to correctly identify change and counter-change talk, as well as further evoke change talk within a client. Remember change talk is expressing a reason, desire, ability, need, and commitment toward change (Table 4.6).

Jake cancelled his next two therapy sessions due to university exams. When he attended his next session, he began by describing the events of his last 3 weeks and detailing a conflict he was having with his father. When asked whether he wanted to spend this session receiving supportive counseling about the conflict, Jake stated that he would. At Jake's next session, he again began detailing his week.

Therapist: I have noticed that we have fallen into a habit of talking about your week and forgetting to review your homework.
Jake: What homework?
Therapist: A few weeks ago, we created an exposure hierarchy and you wanted to try the first two things on that list.
Jake: Oh yeah, I have been trying to speak up a little more.
Therapist: That's fantastic, can you tell me a bit more about that?
Jake: Um, I guess just at Uni, I've been trying to talk to people.
Therapist: What was that experience like for you?
Jake: It's fine.
Therapist: I wonder whether we could spend a little time having a look at this hierarchy again. One of the goals was to answer a supervisor question and the other was to turn at traffic lights. Did you give that a go?
Jake: Not really.
Therapist: What got in the way?
Jake: I guess I just forgot, I was so stressed about exams I didn't think about it.
Therapist: That's understandable. Were there any times you did remember?

Table 4.6 Questions which evoke change talk

Strategy	Example question
1. Rate motivation	You rated your motivation a 6, why did you choose 6 and not a 3?
2. Ask about readiness and willingness	What would you be willing to try? Do you need anything else in order to try this?
3. Look into the future	If we could look 5 years ahead and you have successfully completed CBT therapy, what might your life look like? If you were to quit therapy now, what would life look like 5 years from now?
4. Look at the past	What was your life like before you had this problem? What has life been like with this problem?
5. Elicit extremes	What are the best and worst case scenarios about making/not making this change?
6. Elaborate on existing change talk	When change talk emerges, ask clients to elaborate or provide explicit examples

Jake: No, it really slipped my mind.
Therapist: What might help you remember next time?
Jake: I think now that my exams are over, I can focus on this again.
Therapist: That's great. Do you think your motivation levels are the same as when we first rated these?
Jake: Maybe a bit lower?
Therapist: What's changed?
Jake: I don't know… will doing this stuff actually make me less anxious? It seems so silly.
Therapist: It might, it might not. It sounds like you have some doubts about the process.
Jake: No, I think I understand the process, it just seems so far off. I don't know if I'll be able to see it through.
Therapist: You're doubting your ability?
Jake: Yeah.
Therapist: I wonder Jake, have you ever doubted your ability in the past?
Jake: What do you mean?
Therapist: Throughout your life, have there been times when you have doubted yourself?
Jake: Yeah, all the time.
Therapist: What was that like for you?
Jake: I guess it's just always having this little voice in my head saying that I can't do it, that I'm a failure.
Therapist: That sounds really challenging. I understand why it's difficult to believe in yourself when there is a voice always telling you that you can't. Have you ever been able to prove that voice wrong?
Jake: Yeah, I never thought I would get into medical school, but I did.
Therapist: What do you think helped you get in?
Jake: I guess just trying to remain focused. I always just focused on the next thing I needed to do.
Therapist: Do you think we could try that here?
Jake: Yeah, I think so.

One element of incorporating MI into CBT, is rolling with resistance when it arises in therapy. It is important to not immediately challenge counter-change talk, but to allow for an exploration of ambivalence. A common misstep in therapy is to get into arguments with clients, where the therapist argues for change, while the client argues against change. This is often observed with a client answering "yes, but" to therapist suggestions. Rather than arguing for change, we want to understand why a client might be experiencing ambivalence. Low self-efficacy is a common reason for ambivalence and resistance in therapy. MI therapists will support self-efficacy by identifying strengths that clients already possess and enquiring about past successes.

Over the next several sessions, Jake started to engage in exposure exercises with some success. At each session the therapist placed a strong emphasis on understanding Jake's SUDs and level of motivation for each task. To foster self-efficacy, the therapist often highlighted Jake's courage in completing tasks, despite feeling high levels of anxiety. Although Jake's motivation continued to fluctuate, motivation generally increased throughout the exposure sessions as he experienced success in tacking increasingly anxiety-provoking exposures.

As should be apparent from this case study, despite clients typically reporting high motivation to change, and both limited costs to changing and benefits of staying the same, actual willingness to engage in challenging aspects of CBT can fluctuate considerably throughout the course of treatment. Through integrating a MI stance and principals, these fluctuations can be explored and processed to maintain client engagement.

Clinical Summary Points and Recommendations

- Some degree of ambivalence toward change is highly common, even among treatment-seeking individuals with anxiety disorders.
- Motivation and ambivalence can fluctuate throughout treatment, so therapists should be mindful of change talk and counter-change talk during sessions.
- The flexible incorporation of MI principles into CBT for anxiety disorders can help resolve ambivalence and promote motivation to engage in treatment.

References

Arkowitz, H., & Burke, B. L. (2008). Motivational interviewing as an integrative framework for the treatment of depression. In H. Arkowitz, H. A. Westra, W. R. Miller, & S. Rollnick (Eds.), *Motivational interviewing in the treatment of psychological problems* (pp. 145–172). Guilford Publications.

Arkowitz, H., & Miller, W. R. (2008). Learning, applying, and extending motivational interviewing. In H. Arkowitz, H. A. Westra, W. R. Miller, & S. Rollnick (Eds.), *Motivational interviewing in the treatment of psychological problems* (pp. 1–25). Guilford Publications.

Australian Psychological Society (2015). *Evidence-based psychological interventions in the treatment of mental disorders: A review of the literature*. Retrieved from: https://www.psychology.org.au

Aviram, A., & Westra, H. A. (2011). The impact of motivational interviewing on resistance in cognitive behavioural therapy for generalized anxiety disorder. *Psychotherapy Research, 21*(6), 698–708. https://doi.org/10.1080/10503307.2011.610832

Aviram, A., Westra, H. A., Constantino, M. J., & Antony, M. M. (2016). Responsive management of early resistance in cognitive–behavioral therapy for generalized anxiety disorder. *Journal of Consulting and Clinical Psychology, 84*(9), 783–794. https://doi.org/10.1037/ccp0000100

Balán, I. C., Lejuez, C. W., Hoffer, M., & Blanco, C. (2016). Integrating motivational interviewing and brief behavioral activation therapy: Theoretical and practical considerations. *Cognitive and Behavioral Practice, 23*(2), 205–220. https://doi.org/10.1016/j.cbpra.2015.07.001

Bandura, A. (1977). Self-efficacy: Toward a unifying theory of behavioral change. *Psychological Review, 84*(2), 191–215. https://doi.org/10.1037/0033-295x.84.2.191

Barrera, T. L., Smith, A. H., & Norton, P. J. (2016). Motivational interviewing as an adjunct to cognitive behavioral therapy for anxiety. *Journal of Clinical Psychology, 72*(1), 5–14. https://doi.org/10.1002/jclp.22239

Blain, L. M. (2013). Motivational interviewing as an augmentation to increase effectiveness in cognitive processing therapy for PTSD: An Initial Trial (Dissertation). 295. Retrieved from http://irl.umsl.edu/dissertation/295

Borkovec, T. D., Hazlett-Stevens, H., & Diaz, M. L. (1999). The role of positive beliefs about worry in generalized anxiety disorder and its treatment. *Clinical Psychology & Psychotherapy: An International Journal of Theory & Practice, 6*(2), 126–138. https://doi.org/10.1002/(SICI)1099-0879(199905)6:2<126::AID-CPP193>3.0.CO;2-M

Brown, L. A., Wiley, J. F., Wolitzky-Taylor, K., Roy-Byrne, P., Sherbourne, C., Stein, M. B., et al. (2014). Changes in self-efficacy and outcome expectancy as predictors of anxiety outcomes from the CALM study. *Depression and Anxiety, 31*(8), 678–689. https://doi.org/10.1002/da.22256

Buckner, J. D., & Schmidt, N. B. (2009). A randomized pilot study of motivation enhancement therapy to increase utilization of cognitive–behavioral therapy for social anxiety. *Behaviour Research and Therapy, 47*(8), 710–715. https://doi.org/10.1016/j.brat.2009.04.009

Button, M. L., Westra, H. A., Hara, K. M., & Aviram, A. (2014). Disentangling the impact of resistance and ambivalence on therapy outcomes in cognitive behavioural therapy for generalized anxiety disorder. *Cognitive Behaviour Therapy, 44*(1), 44–53. https://doi.org/10.1080/16506073.2014.959038

Coffey, S. F., Schumacher, J. A., Nosen, E., Littlefield, A. K., Henslee, A. M., Lappen, A., & Stasiewicz, P. R. (2016). Trauma-focused exposure therapy for chronic posttraumatic stress disorder in alcohol and drug dependent patients: A randomized controlled trial. *Psychology of Addictive Behaviors, 30*(7), 778. https://doi.org/10.1037/adb0000201

DiClemente, C. C., & Velasquez, M. M. (2002). Motivational interviewing and the stages of change. In W. R. Miller & S. Rollnick (Eds.), *Motivational interviewing: Preparing people for change*. Guildford Press.

Engle, D., & Arkowitz, H. (2008). Viewing resistance as ambivalence: Integrative strategies for working with resistant ambivalence. *Journal of Humanistic Psychology, 48*, 389–412. https://doi.org/10.1177/0022167807310917

Gallagher, M. W., Payne, L. A., White, K. S., Shear, K. M., Woods, S. W., Gorman, J. M., & Barlow, D. H. (2013). Mechanisms of change in cognitive behavioral therapy for panic disorder: The unique effects of self-efficacy and anxiety sensitivity. *Behaviour Research and Therapy, 51*(11), 767–777. https://doi.org/10.1016/j.brat.2013.09.001

Goldin, P. R., Ziv, M., Jazaieri, H., Werner, K., Kraemer, H., Heimberg, R. G., & Gross, J. J. (2012). Cognitive reappraisal self-efficacy mediates the effects of individual cognitive-behavioral therapy for social anxiety disorder. *Journal of Consulting and Clinical Psychology, 80*(6), 1034–1040. https://doi.org/10.1037/a0028555

Greenberg, R. P. (2004). Essential ingredients for successful psychotherapy: Effects of common actors. In M. J. Dewan, B. N. Steenbarger, & R. P. Greenberg (Eds.), *The art and science of brief psychotherapies* (pp. 231–242). APPI.

Hall, S. & McMaster, K. (2016). *The spirit of motivational interviewing*. Retrieved from: hma.co.nz

Hara, K. M., Westra, H. A., Aviram, A., Button, M. L., Constantino, M. J., & Antony, M. M. (2015). Therapist awareness of client resistance in cognitive-behavioral therapy for generalized anxiety disorder. *Cognitive Behaviour Therapy, 44*, 162–174. https://doi.org/10.1080/16506073.2014.998705

Hettema, J., Steele, J., & Miller, W. R. (2005). Motivational interviewing. *Annual Review of Clinical Psychology, 1*(1), 91–111. https://doi.org/10.1146/annurev.clinpsy.1.102803.143833

Hsieh, M.-Y., Ponsford, J., Wong, D., Schönberger, M., Taffe, J., & Mckay, A. (2012). Motivational interviewing and cognitive behaviour therapy for anxiety following traumatic brain injury: A pilot randomised controlled trial. *Neuropsychological Rehabilitation, 22*(4), 585–608. https://doi.org/10.1080/09602011.2012.678860

Huppert, J. D., Barlow, D. H., Gorman, J. M., Shear, M. K., & Woods, S. W. (2006). The interaction of motivation and therapist adherence predicts outcome in cognitive behavioral therapy for panic disorder: Preliminary findings. *Cognitive and Behavioral Practice, 13*(3), 198–204. https://doi.org/10.1016/j.cbpra.2005.10.001

Kaczkurkin, A. N., & Foa, E. B. (2015). Cognitive-behavioral therapy for anxiety disorders: An update on the empirical evidence. *Dialogues in Clinical Neuroscience, 17*(3), 337. Retrieved from https://www.ncbi.nlm.nih.gov

Keijsers, G. P. J., Schaap, C. P. D. R., & Hoogduin, C. A. L. (2000). The impact of interpersonal patient and therapist behavior on outcome in cognitive-behavior therapy. *Behavior Modification, 24*(2), 264–297. https://doi.org/10.1177/0145445500242006

Lombardi, D. R., Button, M. L., & Westra, H. A. (2014). Measuring motivation: Change talk and counter-change talk in cognitive behavioral therapy for generalized anxiety. *Cognitive Behaviour Therapy, 43*, 12–21. https://doi.org/10.1080/16506073.2013.846400

Maltby, N., & Tolin, D. F. (2005). A brief motivational intervention for treatment-refusing OCD patients. *Cognitive Behaviour Therapy, 34*(3), 176–184. https://doi.org/10.1080/16506070510043741

Marker, I., & Norton, P. J. (2018). The efficacy of incorporating motivational interviewing to cognitive behavior therapy for anxiety disorders: A review and meta-analysis. *Clinical Psychology Review, 62*, 1–10. https://doi.org/10.1016/j.cpr.2018.04.004

Marker, I., Corbett, B. E., Drummond, S. P., & Norton, P. J. (2020). Intermittent motivational interviewing and transdiagnostic CBT for anxiety: A randomized controlled trial. *Journal of Anxiety Disorders, 75*, 102276.

Marker, I., Salvaris, C. A., Thompson, E. M., Tolliday, T., & Norton, P. J. (2019). Client motivation and engagement in Transdiagnostic group cognitive behavioral therapy for anxiety disorders: Predictors and outcomes. *Cognitive Therapy and Research*. Advanced Online Publication, *43*, 819. https://doi.org/10.1007/s10608-019-10014-1

Markland, D., Ryan, R. M., Tobin, V. J., & Rollnick, S. (2005). Motivational interviewing and self–determination theory. *Journal of Social and Clinical Psychology, 24*(6), 811–831. https://doi.org/10.1521/jscp.2005.24.6.811

McCabe, R. E., Rowa, K., Antony, M. M., Young, L., & Swinson, R. P. (2008). *Using motivational enhancement to augment treatment outcome following exposure and response prevention for obsessive-compulsive disorder: Preliminary findings*. Paper presented at the Annual Meeting of the Association for Behavioral and Cognitive Therapies (Orlando, FL, November 13–16).

Merlo, L. J., Storch, E. A., Lehmkuhl, H. D., Jacob, M. L., Murphy, T. K., Goodman, W. K., & Geffken, G. R. (2010). Cognitive behavioral therapy plus motivational interviewing improves outcome for pediatric obsessive–compulsive disorder: A preliminary study. *Cognitive Behaviour Therapy, 39*(1), 24–27. https://doi.org/10.1080/16506070902831773

Miller, W. R. (1983). Motivational interviewing with problem drinkers. *Behavioural Psychotherapy, 11*(02), 147. https://doi.org/10.1017/s0141347300006583

Miller, W. R. (1985). Motivation for treatment: A review with special emphasis on alcoholism. *Psychological Bulletin, 98*(1), 84–107. https://doi.org/10.1037/0033-2909.98.1.84

Miller, W. R., & Johnson, W. R. (2008). A natural language screening measure for motivation to change. *Addictive Behaviors, 33*(9), 1177–1182. https://doi.org/10.1016/j.addbeh.2008.04.018

Miller, W. R., & Rollnick, S. (2002). *Motivational interviewing: Preparing people for change*. Guilford Press.

Miller, W. R., & Rollnick, S. (2012). *Motivational interviewing: Helping people change*. Guilford press.

Montaño, D. E., & Kasprzyk, D. (2008). Theory of reasoned action, theory of planned behavior, and the integrated behavioral model. In K. Glanz, B. K. Rimer, & K. Viswanath (Eds.),

Health behavior and health education: Theory, research, and practice (4th ed., pp. 67–96). Jossey-Bass.

Moyers, T. B., & Houck, J. (2011). Combining motivational interviewing with cognitive-behavioral treatments for substance abuse: Lessons from the COMBINE research project. *Cognitive and Behavioral Practice, 18*(1), 38–45. https://doi.org/10.1016/j.cbpra.2009.09.005

Murphy, R. T., Thompson, K. E., Murray, M., Rainey, Q., & Uddo, M. M. (2009). Effect of a motivation enhancement intervention on veterans' engagement in PTSD treatment. *Psychological Services, 6*(4), 264–278. https://doi.org/10.1037/a0017577

Naar, S., & Safren, S. A. (2017). *Motivational interviewing and CBT: Combining strategies for maximum effectiveness*. Guilford Press.

De Nadai, A. S., King, M. A., Karver, M. S., & Storch, E. A. (2014). Addressing patient motivation, therapeutic alliance, and treatment expectancies in interventions for anxiety disorders. In P. Emmelkamp & T. Ehring (Eds.), *The Wiley handbook of anxiety disorders* (pp. 1215–1227). John Wiley & Sons.

National Institute of Health and Clinical Excellence. (2011). *Common mental health disorders: Identification and pathways to care*. National Institute for Health and Clinical Excellence. Retrieved from: www.nice.org.uk

Norton, P. J. (2012). *Group cognitive-behavioral therapy of anxiety: A transdiagnostic treatment manual*. The Guilford Press.

Pelletier, L. G., Tuson, K. M., & Haddad, N. K. (1997). Client motivation for therapy scale: A measure of intrinsic motivation, extrinsic motivation, and amotivation for therapy. *Journal of Personality Assessment, 68*(2), 414–435. https://doi.org/10.1207/s15327752jpa6802_11

Prochaska, J. O., & DiClemente, C. C. (1982). Transtheoretical therapy: Toward a more integrative model of change. *Psychotherapy: Theory, Research & Practice, 19*(3), 276–288. https://doi.org/10.1037/h0088437

Prochaska, J. O., Norcross, J. C., & DiClemente, C. C. (2013). Applying the stages of change. In G. P. Koocher, J. C. Norcross, & B. A. Greene (Eds.), *Psychologists' desk reference* (3rd ed., pp. 177–181). Oxford University Press.

Purdon, C., Rowa, K., & Antony, M. M. (2004). *Treatment fears in individuals awaiting treatment of OCD*. Paper presented at the meeting of the Association for Advancement of behavior therapy.

Richards, J. C., Richardson, V., & Pier, C. (2002). The relative contributions of negative cognitions and self-efficacy to severity of panic attacks in panic disorder. *Behaviour Change, 19*(2), 102–111. https://doi.org/10.1375/bech.19.2.102

Ryan, R. M., & Deci, E. L. (2008). A self-determination theory approach to psychotherapy: The motivational basis for effective change. *Canadian Psychology, 49*(3), 186–193. https://doi.org/10.1037/a0012753

Ryan, R. M., Lynch, M. F., Vansteenkiste, M., & Deci, E. L. (2010). Motivation and autonomy in counseling, psychotherapy, and behavior change: A look at theory and practice 1ψ7. *The Counseling Psychologist, 39*(2), 193–260. https://doi.org/10.1177/0011000009359313

Simpson, H. B., Zuckoff, A. M., Maher, M. J., Page, J. R., Franklin, M. E., Foa, E. B., et al. (2010). Challenges using motivational interviewing as an adjunct to exposure therapy for obsessive-compulsive disorder. *Behaviour Research and Therapy, 48*(10), 941–948. https://doi.org/10.1016/j.brat.2010.05.026

Westra, H. (2004). Managing resistance in cognitive behavioural therapy: The application of motivational interviewing in mixed anxiety and depression. *Cognitive Behaviour Therapy, 33*(4), 161–175. https://doi.org/10.1080/16506070410026426

Westra, H. A. (2012). *Motivational interviewing in the treatment of anxiety*. Guilford Press.

Westra, H. A., Arkowitz, H., & Dozois, D. J. A. (2009). Adding a motivational interviewing pretreatment to cognitive behavioral therapy for generalized anxiety disorder: A preliminary randomized controlled trial. *Journal of Anxiety Disorders, 23*(8), 1106–1117. https://doi.org/10.1016/j.janxdis.2009.07.014

Westra, H. A., & Dozois, D. J. A. (2003). *Motivational interviewing adapted for anxiety.* Unpublished treatment manual.

Westra, H. A., & Dozois, D. J. A. (2006). Preparing clients for cognitive behavioral therapy: A randomized pilot study of motivational interviewing for anxiety. *Cognitive Therapy and Research, 30*(4), 481–498. https://doi.org/10.1007/s10608-006-9016-y

Wheaton, M. G., Puliafico, A. C., Zuckoff, A., & Simpson, H. B. (2016). Treatment of an adult with obsessive-compulsive disorder with limited treatment motivation. In E. A. Storch & A. B. Lewin (Eds.), *Clinical handbook of obsessive-compulsive and related disorders (pp. 385–397).* https://doi.org/10.1007/978-3-319-17139-5_26

Yang, W., & Strodl, E. (2011). Motivational interviewing changes the treatment trajectory of group cognitive-behavioral therapy for anxiety. In S. Boag & N. Tiliopoulos (Eds.), *Personality and individual differences: Theory, assessment, & application* (pp. 237–248). Nova Science Publishers, Inc.

Chapter 5
Promoting Adherence to Exposure Therapy

David Yusko and Shannon Murphy

Introduction

The curative power of exposure-based therapies for those struggling with anxiety disorders broadly speaking (e.g., social anxiety disorder [SAD], generalized anxiety disorder [GAD], panic disorder, and specific phobias), as well as obsessive compulsive disorders (OCD) and trauma disorders such as posttraumatic stress disorder (PTSD), is well established. This is reflected in a variety of clinical practice guidelines (e.g., APA, 2017; U.S. Department of Veterans Affairs, 2023; Society of Clinical Psychology, APA Division 12, 2017) that all strongly recommend exposure-based therapy as one of the most evidenced-based treatments for this class of disorders. While the essence of exposure therapy is fairly simple, the skillful delivery of it, as well as maintaining adherence to its principles, can prove to be more challenging.

Adherence as a predictive variable in exposure therapy is related to the degree to which a client follows the treatment plan (e.g., regularly attending sessions at the prescribed dose, actively participating in session, and completing homework assignments as prescribed by the therapist). The existing research, albeit mostly in the OCD treatment population, suggests greater treatment adherence to the prescribed elements of exposure therapy (such as homework completion between sessions) is a robust predictor of reduced symptom pathology (Simpson et al., 2011; Wheaton et al., 2016; Ojalehto et al., 2020). Therefore, as therapists look to maximize the curative power of exposure therapy with their clients, strategies that promote treatment adherence are promising for increasing positive treatment outcomes.

D. Yusko (✉) · S. Murphy
Center for Anxiety & Behavior Therapy, Bryn Mawr, PA, USA
e-mail: davidyusko@centerabt.com

E. M. Goetter (ed.), *Optimizing Treatment Engagement Processes in CBT for Anxiety and Related Disorders*, CBT: Science Into Practice,
https://doi.org/10.1007/978-3-031-91439-3_5

Part 1: Adherence Begins with Therapist Commitment to a Theoretical Model of Exposure

Improving treatment adherence to exposure therapy requires a therapist to go beyond the technique of exposure and commit to a deeper transdiagnostic case conceptualization within an exposure-based theoretical framework. By deepening our understanding of how exposure works, therapists will be better prepared to help their clients adhere to that model of therapy. Using this as our starting point, we have divided this chapter into three sections: (1) introduction to the two main theories of exposure therapy—emotional processing theory and inhibitory learning theory; (2) how theory can practically improve process variables associated with exposure therapy (e.g., therapeutic alliance) and exposure technique (e.g., exposure processing); and (3) common barriers therapists encounter with exposure treatments (e.g., low distress tolerance, low willingness to take risks, and poor insight) and strategies to overcome these barriers to support the client's treatment engagement in exposure therapy.

For most people who feel afraid, the instinctual behavioral response is to withdraw from whatever prompt is activating that fear. Fear induces quick learning (LeDoux, 2014), so regardless of whether the fear-based prompt is rational, one quickly learns what activates fear and what behaviors can be used to protect oneself. The essence of exposure therapy is about developing new learning by spending time in the proximity of prompts that are perceived and experienced as frightening to determine if that prompt warrants efforts at protection. Therefore, in order to apply exposure therapy techniques with greater fidelity and adherence, therapists would benefit from enhancing their knowledge and understanding of foundational theories underlying how exposure therapy leads to new learning about what is, and what may not be, dangerous. Negative reinforcement learning is a critical mechanism in the development and maintenance of anxiety disorders that forms the foundation of both emotional processing theory (EPT; Foa & Kozak, 1986; Foa et al., 2006) and inhibitory learning theory (ILT; Craske et al., 2014; Craske et al., 2008). While the premise for exposure therapy is quite simple, getting a person to stick with an approach that intentionally activates uncomfortable emotions is more complicated.

Negative Reinforcement

Negative reinforcement learning was first described by B.F. Skinner as a principle associated with his theory of operant conditioning (Skinner, 1963). The "negative" aspect of the term means that an aversive experience has been *removed*; while the "reinforcement" part of the term (associated with learning) reflects that the behavior responsible for removing the aversive experience *increases* in frequency. Negative reinforcement applies to a developing anxiety disorder through learning that a person can actually do certain things (behaviorally and cognitively) to accomplish at least two goals: (1) protect themselves from a perceived threat they either are, or anticipate, experiencing and (2) prevent, lessen, or eliminate the experience of physiological and emotional distress that comes with fear activation.

Consider a person with germ-driven, contamination-based OCD and imagine how early on in this process a person touches a doorknob, believes they have just been contaminated by something, experiences a spike in distress, and then has the thought that they should wash their hands. Regardless of whether washing is necessary, the resulting outcome is one of relief—an almost immediate removal of the distress they were just experiencing, as well as the elimination of their concern about potential contamination related consequences. The next time this person encounters a similar feeling of being contaminated they remember that washing makes it better. It is easy to see how this learning can quickly generalize—any prompt that activates contamination fears can be immediately remedied with certain behavioral responses (washing). While this is an OCD example, negative reinforcement learning is essentially how all fear-based psychopathologies are hypothesized to develop and maintain over time. Both EPT and ILT rely on these learning principles to explain how exposure therapy can remedy a malfunctioning anxiety system.

Emotional Processing Theory

Emotional processing theory (EPT) stipulates two essential conditions that must be present in order to modify a pathologically operating fear structure (defined as an organized network of information in the brain that includes representations of feared stimuli, the person's responses to those stimuli, and the meanings attached to both; Foa & Kozak, 1986): (1) adequate activation of emotion and (2) the availability and incorporation of new information that is incompatible with the information currently informing that fear structure (Foa & Kozak, 1986). Consider a person with a dog phobia. Once fear is activated, the dog phobic has a behavioral response choice to make—either withdraw for safety or remain to see what happens. If the person chooses to withdraw from the dog (i.e., avoid), the experience results in negative reinforcement learning: "Phew!! Lucky I left when I did because that dog may have bitten me and now I am safe." Even though the prompt activated the fear structure, the behavioral response provided no access to new information, leaving the meaning of that exposure intact—dogs are dangerous. However, if this person chooses to stay near the dog, now there is an opportunity to access new information that can be incorporated into the fear structure: "This dog didn't bite me. Why? Is it possible that dogs aren't always as dangerous as I thought they were?" Therefore, activation of emotion, when paired with a different behavioral response, provides access to new information and new learning—it is possible to feel afraid, to perceive danger, even though a realistic threat is not occurring.

Additionally, EPT emphasizes two additional concepts that are important to modifying a maladaptively functioning fear structure—duration and repetition. Duration of an exposure is related to the amount of time clients are asked to remain in the proximity of an activating prompt. Let's go back to our dog phobic. If a dog stimulus is presented to a client that activates the fear structure, and is then quickly withdrawn, that experience mimics the typical avoidant response a dog phobic—to avoid. A brief exposure like this will likely add to negative reinforcement learning—"Phew! Lucky that dog was taken away because who knows what could have happened and now I feel better." By prolonging the duration of an exposure, more opportunity is given to the client to learn that this dog may not be the threat it is perceived to be. The beginning of new learning is established and a client has to make meaning with this new, valuable information—"How could all dogs be dangerous if I just spent 20 min with this one and nothing bad happened?" Therefore, adherently-delivered exposure treatment must take duration of an exposure into account for access to, and incorporation of, contradictory information that can modify a fear structure.

Repetition is the second key concept that helps strengthen new learning. The idea of repetition in learning is not a novel idea and applies to the learning needed to modify a fear structure (Clark et al., 1960). A dog phobic can easily reason that luck contributed to the dog not biting that one time, but that reasoning is easily challenged by the 20th time they practice being with a dog and observe they still have not been bitten. Repetition supports the modification of the fear structure by facilitating the incorporation of newly learned contradictory information. This new learning is demonstrated by a client who can now stay in the presence of an activating prompt because they are better able to access from memory what was learned from previous exposure trials.

Inhibitory Learning Theory

Inhibitory learning theory (ILT) offers an alternative hypothesis for how exposure therapy helps correct anxiety-based psychopathologies. ILT approaches fear extinction—the process by which a fear response no longer occurs—through the lens of inhibiting a learned fear response with a newly learned non-fear-based response. A fear-based learning pathway becomes heavily over-learned through hundreds, if not thousands, of experiences that teach a person about what activates fear, how to interpret that fear, and what to do in order to reduce distress and increase the perception of safety. Given how over-practiced the fear-based learning is, it can easily suffocate any other competing response a person may wish to rely on once confronted by fear activation. Think of the OCD client who tells you they know their obsessions don't make sense, and they know they don't really need to do their compulsions, but they also can't break free from the overly learned "super highway" that is guiding them through life. ILT suggests that exposure therapy is akin to building a new "super highway" that can ultimately compete with the fear-based one.

Importantly within an ILT context, old learning is never fully extinguished. This idea suggests that the learning associated with the acquisition of fear is never eliminated or fully replaced by fear inhibitory learning. The new learning from exposure therapy may atrophy the "super highway" of fear-based learning, but exposure therapy does not erase, eliminate, or otherwise eradicate the old learning. The implication of this idea of competing learning pathways (versus elimination and replacement of the learned fear response), is that relapse is always possible since the fear-based learning is never extinguished. If a person is confronted by a fear inducing prompt, and resorts to responding to that prompt based on fear-based learning principles, then that fear pathway begins to grow stronger again and starts to compete with the fragile, newly learned fear inhibiting pathway. If a person resorts back to primarily relying on the fear-based response pathway, then the anxiety disorder returns.

Finally, ILT offers a unique emphasis on how to most effectively maximize the learning and development of a fear inhibiting pathway. ILT suggests that a hierarchical approach to exposure does not match the real-life experiences of clients. The implication is that, in order to better mimic the chaotic and unpredictable nature of the real world, therapists must ensure that the exposures practiced in therapy resemble the unpredictable exposures of real life. Therefore, ILT emphasizes helping clients learn to tolerate the presence of distress in order to also learn that the presence of distress is not always a reliable signal of danger or threat. Therapists relying on ILT attempt to teach clients to accept that an objectively safe stimulus can produce physiological and emotional distress while still being technically safe. The learning associated with this apparent contradiction is critical to our client's ability to inhibit the fear response.

Part 2: Using Theory to Enhance Treatment Adherence

The value of increased treatment adherence is directly related to the robust relationship between exposure therapy and treatment outcome for anxiety disorders. Treatment adherence is much less of an issue when a client is progressing in treatment. However, as a person demonstrates less progress from treatment the need to address and increase treatment adherence becomes more important. In all likelihood, treatment adherence becomes more of a therapeutic concern in cases that are more complicated. Thus, increased complexity of the case, drives the need for a therapist to have a deeper theoretical understanding of exposure therapy concepts so that the therapist can make idiosyncratic, but theory consistent adjustments to the treatment. Therapists can be confident in predicting improvement in anxious clients ***if*** they can apply these interventions in theoretically informed ways. To help therapists faithfully deliver exposure-based treatments in a manner that maximizes patient engagement, we outline the following key considerations: therapeutic alliance, treatment rationale, the importance of the first exposure, and the importance of effective processing alongside exposure implementation.

Therapeutic Alliance

Bordin (1979) conceptualized the therapeutic alliance as having three distinct elements. *Bond alliance*, the quality of the connection between therapist and client, is what is most commonly thought of as defining the therapeutic alliance. However, the other two components of the therapeutic alliance, *goal alliance* and *task alliance*, is where greater investment could help with exposure therapy adherence throughout the treatment process. Goal alliance is the degree to which therapist and client are in agreement on the goals of treatment. Task alliance is the degree to which therapist and client agree on the tasks, strategies, and interventions that will be used to accomplish these goals. There are a few studies that suggest that task alliance, compared to bond and goal alliance, has the strongest impact on symptom reduction (Blakey & Abramowitz, 2016). Additional research supports the idea that the therapeutic alliance is associated with treatment adherence (Simpson et al., 2011; Wheaton et al., 2016). In consideration of optimizing treatment engagement, this research supports the hypothesis that deepening task alliance specifically could uniquely impact treatment adherence. Therefore, given the unique value of task alliance, coupled with how therapeutic alliance and treatment adherence are associated, we suggest broadening the treatment rationale to include strategies that specifically target and strengthen task alliance.

Exposure Treatment Rationale

Literature on the treatment rationale highlights a few relevant ideas to this ongoing hypothesis that attending to the therapeutic alliance within treatment rationales could also increase treatment adherence. Söchting et al. (1998) reported that in vivo exposure and improvement of panic symptoms were equal whether or not a cognitive or deconditioning rationale was delivered. Similarly, Arch et al. (2015) reported that an acceptance and commitment therapy/ILT based rationale was no better than a traditional CBT rationale in fostering greater exposure treatment credibility. Lastly, Ahmed and Westra (2009) reported that a CBT rationale for social anxiety produced greater self-efficacy for change, more confidence in doing exposure, and increased perceived helpfulness of exposure from pre to post rationale delivery. These studies suggest that providing an exposure rationale that is guided by a given theoretical orientation is less relevant than simply providing a thorough, coherent, and understandable rationale that increases treatment credibility. Whether or not the rationale is informed by EPT, or ILT, or both could be less important to the client versus providing the client with a treatment rationale that both the therapist and the client understand, agree with, and fits with their treatment goals.

Generally speaking, the goals of exposure rationales are: (A) to increase the client's understanding of how their disorder developed and describe how exposure will help produce change and (B) increase client's perception of treatment credibility and thereby also enhance treatment agreement, commitment and buy-in. The task for therapists seeking to increase treatment adherence is to build on these foundational rationale ideas to include the therapeutic alliance—with a specific focus on task alliance. As examples, the exposure treatment rationales for OCD and PTSD do discuss the therapeutic alliance—but really only bond alliance (Foa et al., 2019; Foa et al., 2012). Therefore, we suggest adding theoretically consistent ideas into the rationale and ensure ability to flexibly explain it. Knowing theory allows the therapist to guide a more ambivalent client to a better understanding of how (i.e., task alliance) exposure therapy is going to help them reach their treatment goals. As a client demonstrates difficulty with adherence to the treatment model (whether in the very beginning of treatment or at any future point of the therapy), that is a sign for the therapist to revisit the rationale (goal and task alliance specifically) in order to help the client better commit to adhering to the treatment tasks, hopefully fostering treatment engagement. Therapists with a strong foundational knowledge of theory can do this throughout treatment with greater flexibility via theoretically adherent *and* individually tailored analogies, metaphors, examples from media and/or pop culture, personal client examples, and other client examples from the clinician's history.

Increasing task alliance should be driven by the needs of the individual client struggling with treatment adherence. As an example, consider the common treatment goal of breaking the cycle of negative reinforcement always discussed in a traditional rationale. This is also an opportunity to attend to bond and goal alliance by having the therapist ensure that the client: (1) truly grasps the concept of negative reinforcement; (2) agrees that breaking the habit of negative reinforcement is a goal they want from therapy; and (3) understands what tasks will be used in therapy to accomplish this goal of breaking the habit of negative reinforcement learning. The clinician remains genuinely open, curious, and interested throughout the rationale process—not assuming the client understands and agrees with the rationale just because it was delivered. Clinician techniques could include helping the client: (a) explore challenges to the ideas of the rationale, (b) observe any discomfort with the rationale and to articulate concerns, (c) consider how the rationale does or does not fit with their treatment goals, and (d) imagine if the therapy tasks are really things the client is open to doing. Negative reinforcement is just one example, and every point within the rationale is an opportunity for the therapist to similarly attend to goal and task alliance using these techniques.

Importance of the First Exposure

The first exposure is another moment in the therapy to pay close attention as a therapist when thinking about future treatment adherence. A successful first exposure is one that allows the client to experience the ideas of the rationale in order to deepen the client's understanding of how being adherent to this model will help them reach their treatment goals. Therefore, it is critical for the therapist to be thinking about how this first exposure can maximize the likelihood of demonstrating as many of the rationale points as possible. Intellectual understanding of the rationale gets the client to this point. Experiential learning can either nudge the client forward with added motivation and curiosity or add doubt about the treatment, and thus undermine engagement. As such, the first exposure is usually best when it is highly predictable, repeatable, and able to adhere to the concept of duration.

Predictability is incredibly important as clients begin developing the skill of exposure. Examples of highly predictable exposure prompts are things like a picture, an object, a video, a smell, and/or something to read. The idea is that the prompt will always be the same when the client practices exposure (in session or for homework). Examples of less predictable exposures include going places, or interacting with people, because we really don't know what conditions will be at a place when a client visits, nor do we know how people will act or respond to the client. Alternately, a picture, video, story, or object will always be the same stimulus each time a client engages with it. This maximizes the likelihood that the client will learn what the exposure is designed to teach while minimizing surprises during early exposure practice.

In addition to predictability, the first exposure should also be easily repeatable. Some exposures are more amenable to repetition than others. Consider a client who has the goal of attending religious services but due to panic disorder has not been able to go. It is unlikely that the therapist will suggest going to services as the first exposure for a number of reasons, chiefly among them though is that services are typically once per week. This makes repeating this exposure difficult (not to mention it is also highly unpredictable). The inability to repeat exposure frequently decreases the learning value around breaking negative reinforcement, disconfirming feared consequences, experiencing habituation, and/or learning to tolerate the presence of distress. Essentially all of the core concepts of the rationale are more easily learned when repetition is possible.

Similarly, duration of the exposure is also helpful early in treatment. The common analogy used here is that the anxiety system operates on a battery for just about everyone. The longer that battery is left on the more likely that battery will run out. Duration of the exposure provides a client with their best chance of experiencing the rationale point of habituation, and while there is debate about whether habituation is necessary for clinical improvement, there is little doubt that habituation helps motivate clients to adhere to and engage with the exposure process. Therefore, ensuring the first exposure, and to some extent all early exposures, has sufficient duration is important for clients to truly experience the treatment rationale. Returning to the idea of a dog phobic, a first exposure could be looking at a picture of a dog for 20 min. It is a predictable prompt, easily repeatable, and nicely accommodates duration. On the other hand, for a social phobic, making eye contact may not be the best first exposure since it is less predictable, given it involves other people. Moreover, while it is amenable to repetition, eye contact isn't a great exposure for duration.

The exposure elements of predictability, repetition, and duration are all points of emphasis for the first exposure to help the client experientially learn what has been intellectually understood to this point. As the client deepens their experiential understanding of how the task of exposure is helping them reach their goals, more difficult exposures that also lack predictability, repetition, and duration can be incorporated into the treatment plan.

Processing of Exposure

While exposure therapy falls under the larger umbrella of CBT, it is often true that formal cognitive restructuring is deemphasized. Processing an exposure is not cognitive restructuring per se, but it is a semi-structured dialogue that intends to help create, change, and/or reinforce new learning from an exposure. Processing is the technique in exposure therapy that guides the assimilation of new learning obtained from an exposure exercise. While we have very little research on processing—how to do it most effectively and if it has any value as a mechanism of change—we do see processing as an opportunity to further invest in the therapeutic alliance and to contribute to better treatment adherence and engagement.

Specific anxiety disorders often have their own unique cognitive biases, as well as a shared list of common cognitive distortions. For example, in OCD there is magical thinking, over importance on thoughts, and overestimation of threat. In PTSD there are predictable changes in thinking around the self, others, and the world that serve to support and maintain PTSD symptoms. SAD is defined by cognitions that include misappraisals of others negatively evaluating the self. The idea that our client's thoughts support the development and maintenance of anxiety disorders is not new. What seems underappreciated in exposure therapy is how processing can enhance treatment outcomes. For example, research findings suggest that reductions in PTSD symptoms are preceded by, and driven by, changes in trauma related cognitions and not vice versa (Zalta et al., 2014). Therefore, focused processing of the exposure experience can help with treatment adherence and engagement by altering unhelpful thoughts and beliefs that support avoidance and unhelpful safety behaviors. Exposure, by itself, is an incredibly important behavioral change that often leads to emotional change (feeling less afraid/anxious), and processing is the last key ingredient for cognitive change.

Processing is a dialogue between the clinician and client that often follows a given exposure exercise. Since it is a dialogue, the therapist's stance is one of asking open-ended questions that are designed to lead a client to the new learning associated with an exposure. Good processing is a conversation between therapist and client that raises discrepancies between the client's current unhelpful beliefs and their experience during an exposure that hopefully challenges those beliefs. Processing typically focuses on three themes—habituation, disconfirmation, and mastery. These processing themes directly parallel the themes of the treatment rationale; therefore, processing these topics is also related to goal and task alliance and ideally contributes to better treatment adherence and engagement. Consider these kinds of open-ended questions a therapist can use when processing exposure within these three themes:

Habituation: Why do you think your anxiety went from a 60 to a 30? Did your anxiety respond the way you thought it would during this exposure? What's your theory about why your anxiety didn't respond the way you thought it would?

Disconfirmation: Did this go the way you said it would? Why not? What did you learn about the risk of [*client's feared outcome*] when you don't avoid/do a safety behavior or compulsion? How come you didn't die/hurt others/go crazy/get sick because of doing this exposure? Did anything surprise you about what happened?

Mastery: How do you feel about yourself now that exposure is done? What did you learn about yourself from doing this tough exposure? What does it say about you that you were able to do this exposure today? What did you learn about how well you can tolerate your anxiety?

These processing questions, and subsequent dialogue, are focused on the client achieving the goals they want from the therapy and adds structure to the assimilation of new information that is now available from doing the task of exposure therapy.

Part 3: Factors Most Likely to Challenge Exposure Treatments

Understanding relevant client factors that can make their adherence to exposure more difficult can help clinicians anticipate and prepare for engagement challenges. To date, research findings in this area have not offered a clear or consistent picture regarding client-related variables that reliably predict poorer treatment outcomes in exposure therapy (Taylor et al., 2012). However, suggestive evidence coupled with clinical experience points to several factors that are more likely to challenge engagement in exposure treatment.

Readiness for Change

Exposure therapy asks a lot of a client. The treatment necessitates a willingness to take risks, to deliberately confront fear, to fully experience anxiety and uncertainty, and to engage in this process again and again. On top of this, there is a significant time commitment in attending therapy sessions and completing the daily home practice that is so critical to progress in treatment. Given all of this, it's understandable that clients might experience ambivalence regarding exposure treatment. For some clients, ambivalence is more easily addressed, especially when there is buy-in with the treatment rationale and successful experiences early on in exposure lend credibility to the model and increase confidence in one's capacity for change. However, for other clients, low motivation to change may need to be directly targeted in treatment, as it can significantly impact engagement and progress in exposure therapy. In such cases, clinicians may benefit from utilization of motivational interviewing (MI) strategies, which aim to help clients explore and resolve ambivalence about behavior change and desired treatment goals while minimizing resistance (Marker & Norton, 2018; Miller & Rollnick, 2013; Randall & McNeil, 2017). Integrating MI techniques into practice hinges on an empathic, collaborative, and compassionate style, in which the clinician utilizes four core skills: open-ended questions, reflective listening, affirmation, and summary statements. These skills, in combination with other strategies, can assist therapists in eliciting, amplifying, and properly reflecting "change talk" (statements that favor making changes) (see Chap. 3).

Safety Behaviors

Safety behaviors are defined as strategies designed to reduce the likelihood of perceived threat, negative outcome, or anxiety. Ongoing reliance on safety behaviors and behavioral avoidance as a primary means of coping with anxiety will impede progress and detrimentally impact exposure-based treatments (Salkovskis, 1991). Utilization of safety behaviors prevents clients from accessing opportunities for critical new learning about themselves, their anxiety, and the situations, things, people, ideas and/or activities which elicit threat. In particular, use of safety behaviors interferes with our clients' ability to test predictions about the likelihood and severity of the occurrence of their feared outcomes. As a result, new learning about the relative safety or tolerability of anxiety-provoking stimuli cannot be achieved and, worse, is often attributed to use of one's safety behaviors.

Further, safety behaviors undermine clients' self-confidence as they reinforce unhelpful beliefs about the one's inability to tolerate or cope with feared stimuli and the presence of anxiety. In this way, safety behaviors serve as a crutch and can be easily pointed to by our clients as the explanation for why their feared outcomes did not occur (i.e., the crutch was effective, not the client). Additionally, reliance on safety behaviors prevents the clients from learning that they can, in fact, face their fears and cope better than they expected even while experiencing intense and distressing thoughts, feelings, and physical sensations. For example, an individual with social anxiety, who uses a beta-blocker to manage physiological arousal during an important presentation, can easily attribute "success" to use of the medication rather than their capacity for managing distress.

Paradoxically, the use of safety behaviors can exacerbate anxiety problems by magnifying the intensity of the feared stimuli and potentially even increase the likelihood of the very feared outcomes that they are intended to prevent. Such is the case in contamination OCD where excessive washing due to fear of illness can lead to raw or cracked skin that may increase the likelihood of infection. Similarly, someone with health anxiety who is worried about developing lymphoma may engage in excessive checking of their lymph nodes leading to discovery of new "abnormalities" that then amplifies their preoccupation and worry regarding health.

Clients may also infer threat from their own behavior, such as when individuals with PTSD engage in hypervigilance and monitoring of their surroundings. For instance, repeated scanning of others for signs of danger (e.g., concealed weapons, unusual or erratic behavior) while out to dinner at a restaurant can communicate and reinforce beliefs regarding the presence and likelihood of threat even when nothing threatening occurs.

For all these reasons and more, targeting and working to eliminate safety behaviors in the context of exposure-based treatment is critical. Supporting clients in this work requires compiling a comprehensive list of the various strategies the client utilizes to reduce anxiety and/or increase their sense of safety and certainty in response to anxiety-provoking triggers. This includes assessment of both overt safety behaviors and covert (mental) safety behaviors, more subtle strategies a client may use to manage anxiety (e.g., in the case of social anxiety, mentally rehearsing what to say when speaking with someone new). Additionally, this includes assessment of safety signals, such as people (e.g., therapist, loved ones) or objects (e.g., medication, cell phone, water) whose presence alone falsely communicates to the client that they are "safe."

Habitual use of safety behaviors can make it difficult for clients, at first, to recognize and identify their use and function in daily life. Assignment of self-monitoring early in treatment can help increase clients' awareness of and engagement in these behaviors and the types of situations or stimuli that commonly trigger their use. Given that clients may not be aware of their use of these behaviors, it is important for the therapist to ask targeted questions and make specific inquiries about commonly used safety behaviors in order to help clients gain insight in this area. Use of safety behavior self-report measures, such as the Social Behavior Questionnaire (SBQ; Clark, 2005) or the Safety Behavior Assessment Form (SBAF; Goodson et al., 2016), can also be valuable in helping identify reliance on specific strategies.

Assessment and identification of safety behaviors inform case conceptualization and delivery of psychoeducation and treatment rationale. Specifically, it is incorporated into discussion regarding the importance of safety behavior elimination for progress in treatment. Clients are generally encouraged to eliminate all of their safety behaviors at once, although some clients are unwilling or unable to do this successfully and rigidly insisting on their full elimination could threaten treatment engagement. When complete safety behavior elimination is not feasible, working with clients to gradually phase their safety behaviors is a helpful and necessary alternative (Blakey & Abramowitz, 2016). This approach will require identifying with your client which safety behaviors they are most willing or able to work on resisting. Often, this will include addressing the "lowest hanging fruit," the safety behaviors clients rely on frequently, but may only anticipate mild to moderate anxiety should they work on resisting use. Additionally, safety behaviors that contribute to high levels of distress or impairment may warrant more immediate attention and, if improved, stand to increase clients' buy-in and motivation for addressing other safety behaviors in treatment. Devising and implementing exposures that specifically target removal of safety behaviors in a step-wise fashion can also be helpful in creating structure and approachability for clients who otherwise may be overwhelmed by the prospect of total safety behavior elimination.

Such an approach is illustrated in the treatment of Evelyn, a 40-year-old financial advisor with panic disorder circumscribed to driving on highways. Specifically, Evelyn feared "losing control" during a panic attack such that she would become immobilized while driving, leading to a catastrophic car accident. At the onset of treatment, Evelyn avoided driving on almost all highways or roads in which the speed limit was greater than 40 MPH (i.e., speeds at which losing control due to panic could lead to a serious accident). If Evelyn did have to drive on a highway, which happened rarely, she would remain in the slow lane with a support person on the phone "just in case" of an emergency. On the roads that Evelyn would drive more consistently, she still utilized numerous safety behaviors to reduce the likelihood of panic, including persistent adjustment of temperature settings in her car, frequent drinking of her water bottle, and distraction with a classical music radio station.

A core component of treatment with Evelyn focused on completion of both interoceptive and in vivo exposures. In working with Evelyn, it was quickly discovered that interoceptive exposures on their own were minimally anxiety-provoking, as the sensations were experienced as non-threatening outside of the context of driving. In creating Evelyn's exposure hierarchy, multiple anxiety-provoking highways were identified and rated from least anxiety provoking to most anxiety provoking. In vivo exposure first targeted driving on the roads that Evelyn regularly frequented, but without the use of safety behaviors to manage physiological arousal. Evelyn found these exposures to be anxiety-provoking, but tolerable and was even willing to engage in compound exposures (e.g., the addition of an interoceptive exposure, such as voluntary hyperventilation, to an in vivo exposure) while driving on these roads.

However, as Evelyn progressed up the hierarchy and approached more anxiety-provoking roads, especially those that had been avoided for months, she was resistant to the idea of driving without the use of safety behaviors. Helping Evelyn approach such roads required judicious use of safety behaviors, including the presence of the therapist in the car and driving in the slow lane. As Evelyn approached each new road, a plan was made to gradually phase out both of these safety behaviors. In relation to the therapist, exposures were initially conducted with the therapist in the front seat of the car, followed by the therapist in the backseat of the car, followed by the therapist driving closely behind in a separate car, then following at a distance in a separate car, and finally with the Evelyn driving entirely independently. Similarly, Evelyn progressively worked from slow lane to fast lane over the course of the exposures. As Evelyn gained confidence, interoceptive exposures were added to her in vivo driving to further foster learning. Although phasing safety behaviors in this way likely extended Evelyn's course of treatment, this approach supported treatment engagement: It fostered willingness and created tolerable enough conditions for Evelyn to confront her fears, which otherwise might not have been possible if strict safety behavior elimination was enforced.

Experiential Avoidance

Experiential avoidance, a concept closely related to and overlapping with safety behaviors, is broadly defined as attempts to avoid or escape aversive internal experiences (e.g., thoughts, emotions, physical sensations, images, memories) due to a general unwillingness to remain in contact with such experiences (Hayes et al., 1996). In many instances, exposure learning naturally addresses these issues, but for some clients, especially those who continue to rely on avoidance and safety behaviors, they need to be more explicitly addressed. Helping our clients reduce experiential avoidance requires addressing the "spirit" of exposure, so that clients are operating from a perspective of "bring it on" rather than trying to make their anxiety "go away." In such cases, incorporating principles from Acceptance and Commitment Therapy (ACT) can be a valuable adjunct to the exposure process. In exposure-based treatment, the importance of acceptance and willingness to experience one's anxiety tends to be implied. For clients that struggle specifically with how to achieve this objective, ACT offers a variety of experiential exercises and metaphors for illustrating this process and providing a shared language between clinician and client about acceptance and willingness during exposure (Hayes et al., 2012; Thompson et al., 2023). Cultivation of acceptance-based skills in ACT can be achieved through multiple interrelated channels, including, but not limited to, engendering a state of creative hopelessness (i.e., helping clients see the "unworkability" of their attempts to control or avoid their inner experience), use of mindfulness skills to foster non-judgmental contact with one's present moment experience, and implementation of cognitive defusion to help clients gain distance from, rather than entanglement with, their thoughts.

Comorbid Conditions

The presence of comorbidities, although common in anxiety disorders with estimates of lifetime comorbidity as high as 60%, can impact the extent to which an individual can successfully engage in exposure-based treatment (Goldstein-Piekarski et al., 2016). Determining appropriateness for exposure therapy hinges not only on the accurate diagnosis of a primary anxiety disorder, but also on identification of comorbidities and contextual factors (e.g., significant stressors, logistical constraints) that may serve as barriers to treatment. Important to consider with comorbidities is the extent to which they will need to be addressed prior to engagement with exposure therapy. When treatment planning, it is important that the therapist and client agree about the prioritization of treatment targets (i.e., goal alliance). Most often, priority level is determined by the severity of each concern and its impact on the client's functioning. Patient safety concerns, such as imminent risk of suicide, self-injurious behavior, severe mood instability, and high-risk substance use, will almost always take precedence above other treatment targets and will need to be addressed prior to engagement in exposure therapy. If and when the determination is ultimately made to move forward with exposure therapy, at minimum, careful monitoring of comorbid conditions is warranted. This can be accomplished in multiple ways during treatment, including routine use of symptom-specific self-report measures, self-monitoring of problematic behaviors, and prompt response to adherence challenges related to comorbid conditions.

Severe depression is one such comorbid condition that has been shown to lead to poorer treatment outcomes in exposure therapy (Abramowitz et al., 2000; Ledley et al., 2005). Extreme levels of hopelessness, lethargy, and anhedonia can understandably interfere with clients' motivation and beliefs about their ability to improve in treatment. Interventions that specifically target depressive symptoms, such as behavioral activation, cognitive therapy, and psychotropic medications, may be needed, especially when depressed clients persistently struggle to engage in treatment, as evidenced by inconsistent attendance, poor adherence with home practice, and difficulty participating in sessions. Importantly, severe depression may have distinct adherence challenges in exposure therapy compared to milder forms of depression. In less severe cases of depression, reduction in anxiety symptoms may also lead to improvements in depression, especially when symptoms are a result of the suffering and restrictions anxiety has placed on a client's life. Still, incorporating behavioral activation items on client exposure hierarchies may be helpful in encouraging symptom reduction in depressed clients even when symptoms are less severe.

Substance use problems also commonly co-occur in individuals with anxiety disorders and can lead to poorer engagement and progress in treatment (Bedard-Gilligan et al., 2018). Severe substance use problems may need to be addressed prior to engagement in exposure therapy. However, emerging research suggests that an integrated approach for substance use disorder (SUD) and anxiety may be more beneficial than sequential treatment or treatment of SUD alone (Wolitzky Taylor, 2023). For mild to moderate substance use problems, consideration and discussion of the function of the substance use, especially if used as an anxiety management strategy, is important to address at the outset of treatment. In this way, substance use functions, at least in part, as a safety behavior and impedes learning via the exposure process. Addressing with clients their ability and willingness to abstain from use or encouraging use in a more controlled or reduced manner prior to and during engagement in exposure therapy is critical. If a client is unable to completely abstain from use, it will also be necessary to address limits around use before, during, and after exposure practice and therapy appointments in conjunction with a physician.

Distress Intolerance

Distress intolerance refers to a person's perception that they are unable to cope with negative emotional experiences, which leads to greater efforts to avoid or escape from these emotions. Ideally, exposure therapy helps clients build greater distress tolerance by highlighting the client's capability to tolerate uncomfortable thoughts, feelings, and sensations without having to respond in ways that make their anxiety "go away." Designing exposures that allow clients to specifically test and violate expectancies regarding their own anxiety tolerance is important for helping clients build these skills and adjust distress intolerant beliefs. This will require operationalizing with your client their specific predictions regarding the nature and consequences of distress if they were to confront their fears.

For example, addressing distress tolerance was a critical component of treatment with Hector, a 20-year-old college student with "just right" OCD. While Hector was initially enthusiastic regarding treatment, he struggled to progress up his exposure hierarchy, frequently setting limits around what exposures he was willing to do. Exploration with Hector regarding the barriers to moving on to more anxiety-provoking exposures (i.e., task alliance) led to identification and discussion of his distress intolerant beliefs ("I just won't be able to handle it"). This led to defining with Hector his specific predictions about distress intolerance in the context of the exposure next on his hierarchy (disordering items in his kitchen cabinets). This included predictions related to: his anticipated level of distress during/after the exposure (80/100); the persistence of that distress following the exposure (until he was able to fall asleep that evening); how long he would be able to resist engagement in safety behaviors to cope with the distress (he would need to change his cabinets back by the next morning); and the functional impact associated with the distress (it would interfere with his ability to focus on school work and fall asleep that evening). Although, initially, Hector remained reluctant to engage in further exposures, the "testability" of this specific framing appealed to Hector. Operationalizing Hector's distress intolerance in this way created multiple avenues for disconfirming feedback, which challenged his beliefs regarding his capacity for coping with discomfort and increased his willingness to confront more challenging exposures on his hierarchy. Critical to this work was the centering and reinforcing of this new learning in post-exposure processing conversations and in the review of home practice learning at the start of each session.

Conclusion

Treatment adherence, defined as the degree a given patient follows the prescribed treatment advice of a healthcare provider (Chakrabarti, 2014), is known to be a robust predictor of treatment outcomes in exposure therapy (Simpson et al., 2011; Wheaton et al., 2016; Ojalehto et al., 2020). Exposure therapy has a tremendous capacity to transform the lives of those struggling with a variety of anxiety disorders and related conditions like PTSD and OCD. Typically, the biggest barrier to exposure therapy is access to a provider, but even once a course of exposure therapy begins, difficulties around maintaining fidelity and adherence to the exposure therapy model can limit therapeutic outcomes. Remaining adherent to the principles of exposure therapy is often complicated by a client's readiness for change and oscillations in motivation, complicated comorbid presentations, client difficulties tolerating distress, and a client's reliance on avoidance. In this chapter, we have focused on strategies to help therapists increase treatment adherence and engagement in care by primarily deepening a therapist's commitment and expertise around the theoretical ideas behind exposure therapy—EPT and ILT. Furthermore, by giving more attention to elements of the therapeutic alliance, in particular goal and task alliance, therapists may be able to increase treatment engagement and adherence. Lastly, there is nothing more reinforcing than success; providing clients with early opportunities to experientially learn the benefits of exposure can significantly increase engagement and adherence throughout treatment.

Clinical Summary Points and Recommendations

- Treatment adherence is a significant predictor of treatment outcomes, therefore increasing treatment adherence likely improves treatment results for clients.
- Therapists can deepen their knowledge of how to use exposure theory to increase treatment flexibility without sacrificing treatment fidelity.
- Investing in the therapeutic alliance, specifically goal and task alliance, can also increase treatment engagement and adherence.
- Early success with exposure can provide the experiential learning to help clients better understand the importance of adherence to treatment plan.
- Predictable barriers to engagement with and adherence to exposure include readiness to change, ongoing reliance on avoidant coping, comorbidity, and difficulty tolerating distressing emotions. Therapists must monitor for the presence of these throughout treatment to foster engagement in care and optimize treatment outcomes.

References

Abramowitz, J. S., Franklin, M. E., Street, G. P., Kozak, M. J., & Foa, E. B. (2000). Effects of comorbid depression on response to treatment for obsessive-compulsive disorder. *Behavior Therapy, 31*(3), 517–528.

Ahmed, M., & Westra, H. A. (2009). Impact of a treatment rationale on expectancy and engagement in cognitive behavioral therapy for social anxiety. *Cognitive Therapy and Research, 33*, 314–322.

American Psychological Association. (2017). *Clinical practice guideline for the treatment of posttraumatic stress disorder (PTSD) in adults*. https://www.apa.org/ptsd-guideline

Arch, J. J., Twohig, M. P., Deacon, B. J., Landy, L. N., & Bluett, E. J. (2015). The credibility of exposure therapy: Does the theoretical rationale matter? *Behaviour Research and Therapy, 72*, 81–92.

Bedard-Gilligan, M., Garcia, N., Zoellner, L. A., & Feeny, N. C. (2018). Alcohol, cannabis, and other drug use: Engagement and outcome in PTSD treatment. *Psychology of Addictive Behaviors, 32*(3), 277.

Blakey, S. M., & Abramowitz, J. S. (2016). The effects of safety behaviors during exposure therapy for anxiety: Critical analysis from an inhibitory learning perspective. *Clinical Psychology Review, 49*(1-15).

Bordin, E. S. (1979). The generalizability of the psychoanalytic concept of the working alliance. Psychotherapy: *Theory, research & practice, 16*(3), 252.

Clark, D. M. (2005). *Three questionnaires for measuring central constructs in the cognitive model of social Phobia*. King's College London.

Chakrabarti, S. (2014). What's in a name? Compliance, adherence and concordance in chronic psychiatric disorders. *World journal of psychiatry, 4*(2), 30.

Clark, L. L., Lansford, T. G., & Dallenbach, K. M. (1960). Repetition and associative learning. *The American Journal of Psychology, 73*(1), 22–40.

Craske, M. G., Kircanski, K., Zelikowsky, M., Mystkowski, J., Chowdhury, N., & Baker, A. (2008). Optimizing inhibitory learning during exposure therapy. *Behaviour Research and Therapy, 46*(1), 5–27.

Craske, M. G., Treanor, M., Conway, C. C., Zbozinek, T., & Vervliet, B. (2014). Maximizing exposure therapy: An inhibitory learning approach. *Behaviour Research and Therapy, 58*, 10–23.

Foa, E. B., Hembree, E. A., Rothbaum, B. O., & Rauch, S. A. M. (2019). *Prolonged exposure therapy for PTSD: Emotional processing of traumatic experiences: Therapist guide* (2nd ed.). Oxford University Press.

Foa, E. B., Huppert, J. D., & Cahill, S. P. (2006). Emotional processing theory: An update.

Foa, E. B., & Kozak, M. J. (1986). Emotional processing of fear: Exposure to corrective information. *Psychological Bulletin, 99*(1), 20.

Foa, E. B., Yadin, E., & Lichner, T. K. (2012). *Exposure and response (ritual) prevention for obsessive-compulsive disorder: Therapist guide* (2nd ed.). Oxford University Press.

Goldstein-Piekarski, A. N., Williams, L. M., & Humphreys, K. (2016). A trans-diagnostic review of anxiety disorder comorbidity and the impact of multiple exclusion criteria on studying clinical outcomes in anxiety disorders. *Translational Psychiatry, 6*(6).

Goodson, J. T., Haeffel, G. J., Raush, D. A., & Hershenberg, R. (2016). The safety behavior assessment form: Development and validation. *Journal of Clinical Psychology, 72*(10), 1099–1111. https://doi.org/10.1002/jclp.22325. Epub 2016 May 26.

Hayes, S. C., Wilson, K. G., Gifford, E. V., Follette, V. M., & Strosahl, K. (1996 Dec). Experimental avoidance and behavioral disorders: a functional dimensional approach to diagnosis and treatment. *Journal of Consulting and Clinical Psychology, 64*(6), 1152–1168. https://doi.org/10.1037/0022-006x.64.6.1152

Hayes, S. C., Strosahl, K. D., & Wilson, K. G. (2012). *Acceptance and commitment therapy: The process and practice of mindful change* (2nd ed.). Guilford Press.

Ledley, D. R., Huppert, J. D., Foa, E. B., Davidson, J. R., Keefe, F. J., & Potts, N. L. (2005). Impact of depressive symptoms on the treatment of generalized social anxiety disorder. *Depression and Anxiety, 22*(4), 161–167.

LeDoux, J. E. (2014). Coming to terms with fear. *Proceedings of the National Academy of Sciences, 111*(8), 2871–2878.

Marker, I., & Norton, P. J. (2018). The efficacy of incorporating motivational interviewing to cognitive behavior therapy for anxiety disorders: A review and meta-analysis. *Clinical Psychology Review, 62*, 1–10.

Miller, W. R., & Rollnick, S. (2013). *Motivational interviewing: Helping people change (3rd edition)*. Guilford Press.

Ojalehto, H. J., Abramowitz, J. S., Hellberg, S. N., Buchholz, J. L., & Twohig, M. P. (2020). Adherence to exposure and response prevention as a predictor of improvement in obsessive-compulsive symptom dimensions. *Journal of anxiety disorders, 72*, 102210.

Randall, C. L., & McNeil, D. W. (2017 Aug). Motivational Interviewing as an Adjunct to Cognitive Behavior Therapy for Anxiety Disorders: A Critical Review of the Literature. *Cognitive and Behavioral Practice, 24*(3), 296–311.

Salkovskis, P. M. (1991). The importance of behaviour in the maintenance of anxiety and panic: A cognitive account. *Behavioural Psychotherapy, 19*, 6–19.

Simpson, H. B., Maher, M. J., Wang, Y., Bao, Y., Foa, E. B., & Franklin, M. (2011). Patient adherence predicts outcome from cognitive behavioral therapy in obsessive-compulsive disorder. *Journal of consulting and clinical psychology, 79*(2), 247.

Society of Clinical Psychology, APA Division 12. (2017). *Psychological treatments for obsessive-compulsive disorder*. https://www.div12.org/psychological-treatments/disorders/obsessive-compulsive-disorder/

Skinner, B. F. (1963). Operant behavior. *American Psychologist, 18*(8), 503–515. https://doi.org/10.1037/h0045185

Söchting, I., Taylor, S., Freeman, W., De Koning, E., Segerstrom, S., & Thordarson, D. (1998). In vivo exposure for panic disorder and agoraphobia: Does a cognitive rationale enhance treatment efficacy? In *Behavior and cognitive therapy today* (pp. 279–288). Pergamon.

Taylor, S., Abramowitz, J. S., & McKay, D. (2012). Non-adherence and non-response in the treatment of anxiety disorders. *Journal of Anxiety Disorders, 26*(5), 583–589. https://doi.org/10.1016/j.janxdis.2012.02.010. Epub 2012 Feb 13.

Thompson, B. L., Pilecki, B. C., & Chan, J. C. (2023). *ACT-informed exposure for anxiety: Creating effective, innovative, and values-based exposures using acceptance and commitment therapy*. New Harbinger Publications/Context Press.

U.S. Department of Veterans Affairs. (2023). *VA/DoD clinical practice guideline for the management of posttraumatic stress disorder and acute stress disorder*. https://www.healthquality.va.gov/guidelines/MH/ptsd/

Wheaton, M. G., Galfalvy, H., Steinman, S. A., Wall, M. M., Foa, E. B., & Simpson, H. B. (2016). Patient adherence and treatment outcome with exposure and response prevention for OCD: Which components of adherence matter and who becomes well?. *Behaviour research and therapy, 85*, 6–12.

Wolitzky-Taylor, K. (2023). Integrated behavioral treatments for comorbid anxiety and substance use disorders: A model for understanding integrated treatment approaches and meta-analysis to evaluate their efficacy. *Drug Alcohol Depend., 253*, 110990.

Zalta, A. K., Gillihan, S. J., Fisher, A. J., Mintz, J., McLean, C. P., Yehuda, R., & Foa, E. B. (2014). Change in negative cognitions associated with PTSD predicts symptom reduction in prolonged exposure. *Journal of Consulting and Clinical Psychology, 82*(1), 171.

Chapter 6
The Role of the Therapist and Treatment Setting: Common Pitfalls that Undermine Patient Engagement in Exposure Therapy

David Yusko

> *"If there is no struggle, there is no progress."*
>
> *Frederick Douglass*

Introduction

Any discussion about the underutilization of exposure-based interventions must eventually turn to us, the clinicians in the room who are typically the ones making decisions about how to treat a given client. Therefore, much of this chapter may require a trigger warning—we, clinicians, might be the biggest barrier that mental health consumers have to accessing one of mental health's most effective treatments, exposure therapy. Much of the research on treatment engagement centers on the role of the client's beliefs, motivation, and adherence to treatment. However, client variables related to treatment engagement only become relevant if an exposure-based treatment plan is offered. Therefore, it is essential to understand the potential attitudes and biases that providers hold about exposure therapy that could significantly limit access to this highly effective, evidenced-based mental health care.

Exposure interventions are core to cognitive behavioral therapy (CBT), but there is generally poor utilization and implementation of exposure-based interventions despite an abundance of opportunity to use it. For example, exposure-based interventions are identified as first-line treatments in every national and international publication of treatment guidelines for all of the anxiety disorders (including panic disorder, agoraphobia, social phobia, specific phobia and generalized anxiety disorder), and for PTSD and OCD (e.g., Bandelow, Lichte, Rudolf, Wiltink, & Beutel, 2014; Clark, 2011; Katzman et al., 2014). When taken together, in any given year, about one in nine people will experience one of these conditions in which exposure

D. Yusko (✉)
Center for Anxiety & Behavior Therapy, Bryn Mawr, PA, USA
e-mail: davidyusko@centerabt.com

E. M. Goetter (ed.), *Optimizing Treatment Engagement Processes in CBT for Anxiety and Related Disorders*, CBT: Science Into Practice,
https://doi.org/10.1007/978-3-031-91439-3_6

therapy would be the ideal treatment (11.6%; Baxter et al., 2013). Given the prevalence of these conditions, along with the overwhelming evidence supporting the effectiveness of exposure therapy to treat these conditions, one would imagine exposure therapy is a core staple of the mental health field. And yet, research in the United States found that 87% of mental health professionals reported that they did not use exposure treatments at all, or minimally, with their clients (Cook et al., 2010). In a more focused study of mental health professional's use of exposure therapy when the presenting problem is an anxiety disorder, less than half (46.8%) reported using any exposure-based interventions (Pittig et al., 2019). Unfortunately, even when clinicians did utilize exposure interventions when treating anxiety disorders, they often did so in a non-adherent way as prescribed by research-driven treatment protocols (e.g., over using safety behaviors and/or relaxation techniques during exposure; Hipol & Deacon, 2013).

To summarize, the available literature consistently highlights that most clinicians do not utilize exposure techniques to treat mental health disorders where our professional treatment guidelines suggest exposure as a first-line treatment option. Even in a sample of clinicians where 71% identified CBT as their clinical orientation, only 12–38% of them used exposure to treat anxiety disorders (Freiheit et al., 2004). The underutilization of evidenced-based treatments like exposure therapy is not only present across the continuum of mental health professionals, but also significantly limited within clinician populations (i.e., CBT therapists) where knowledge, training, and awareness of exposure techniques are supposedly higher (Simmons et al., 2008). Despite the effectiveness of exposure therapy, it is underused by most clinicians, and when it is used, it is often modified and/or adapted in a way that reduces its effectiveness.

Therapist Barriers to Exposure Therapy

Negative Beliefs about Exposure Therapy

Consider having a medical condition and when you seek treatment your health care professional offers you a variety of interventions but none of them are recognized as the most effective treatments options for your condition. Maybe it is the litigious nature of healthcare but it is almost unfathomable to think that medical providers could get away with this level of suboptimal care. And yet, in mental healthcare, we have a system where up to a third of the population will develop a disorder in their lifetime (anxiety disorder, PTSD, OCD, etc.) that could be effectively treated by a given treatment (exposure therapy) but the providers of healthcare in that system rarely offer the most effective treatment for those disorders. The potential impact of underutilizing exposure therapy, as well as the inadequate delivery of exposure therapy, includes longer courses of illness, larger costs associated with untreated illness, added stigma to mental health disorders being different from medical healthcare, and diminished trust from the public in the mental healthcare system. Therefore, given these potential risks for withholding effective treatment options, why do so many mental health professionals resist offering exposure treatments? Despite solid evidence for the efficacy of exposure therapy, clinicians maintain persistent negative beliefs about exposure that appear to be a major reason behind why exposure treatments aren't more commonly utilized.

It is difficult to find another example like this in healthcare—where providers have these negative beliefs about one of their most robust and effective treatments and ultimately choose to not utilize the treatment that professional guidelines suggest as a first-line intervention. There is a substantive, replicated body of research that identifies a host of therapist negative beliefs about exposure therapy and the impact of those therapist beliefs on the use of exposure treatments, as well as how exposure treatments are delivered.

Researchers have been exploring reasons behind the underutilization of exposure therapy for several decades, but with the development of the Therapist Beliefs about Exposure Scale (TBES; Deacon et al., 2013a) a more consistent, reliable, and replicable literature has emerged detailing how therapist beliefs have influenced the utilization, and delivery, of exposure interventions. The TBES is a 21-item questionnaire that allows for the reliable and valid assessment of negative therapist beliefs about the use of exposure therapy, including that it is intolerable, aversive, unethical, unacceptable, harmful, traumatizing, and inhumane. The research using the TBES tells a consistent story about frequently held negative therapist beliefs about exposure therapy related to two domains: (1) the use of exposure therapy and (2) the practice of exposure therapy protocols. Lastly, research that examines the impact of systemic and institutional barriers on therapist negative beliefs about exposure therapy suggest they also limit therapist use of this highly effective mental health treatment.

Impact on Clients

Some of the early research examining how negative therapist beliefs impact the use of exposure therapy began to develop several common themes that research using the TBES was able to further refine and replicate. Early research revealed that therapists were concerned about exposure therapy being inconsiderate to the needs of the individual client (Feeny et al., 2003), that exposure treatments would cause harm to their clients (Becker et al., 2004), that it would worsen symptoms (Cook et al., 2004), increase client drop out from therapy (van Minnen et al., 2010), harm the therapist via vicarious traumatization (Zoellner et al., 2011), and therapist beliefs that clients just won't agree to exposure treatments (Zoellner et al., 2011). Similar beliefs about exposure being not safe or tolerable have been discussed for the treatment of PTSD using prolonged exposure therapy (Cahill et al., 2006). Pittig et al. (2019) looked to build on research that was using the TBES in order to examine barriers to the dissemination of exposure therapy in Germany. Beginning with the therapist negative beliefs about exposure, 23% to 52% of the therapists agreed or strongly agreed with the ideas that exposure therapy is either too distressing for the patient or exposure therapy is limited to superficial effects of symptom reduction. Examples of exposure therapy being too distressing for patients included patients would have to manage and tolerate the distress activated by exposure, therefore patients are at risk for becoming emotionally overwhelmed, and/or decompensating from exposure treatment, and even potentially being traumatized or retraumatized by exposure therapy techniques. With regards to the superficial impact of exposure therapy, therapists endorsed beliefs such as exposure therapy works poorly in complex case presentations, is only useful for reducing anxiety symptoms, and/or exposure only superficially addresses symptoms. Interestingly, four of the top five agreed-upon therapist beliefs identified by Pittig et al. (2019) overlapped with the top beliefs identified by Deacon et al. (2013a). Overall, therapist negative beliefs about exposure therapy were linked to its reduced use in all 14 studies that used the TBES (De Jong et al., 2020; Deacon et al., 2013a; Kannis-Dymand et al., 2022; Keleher et al., 2020; Kline et al., 2021; Meyer et al., 2014, 2020; Pittig et al., 2019; Reid et al., 2018; Rowe & Kangas, 2020; Sars & van Minnen, 2015; Schumacher et al., 2018, 2019; Whiteside et al., 2016). Taken together, these research findings describe a consistent, longstanding history of negative therapist beliefs toward exposure therapy. Not only does the research replicate these negative beliefs among therapists, but some of these studies were conducted in different health care systems. Thus, the common negative beliefs of exposure therapy being potentially harmful for the patient and superficial in its effects may be universally held by clinicians across cultures and health care systems (Pittig et al., 2019).

Impact on Therapists

Another category of therapist's negative beliefs about exposure therapy is related to the impact of exposure on the therapist themself. Returning to the study by Pittig et al. (2019), they found that 37% of therapists either agreed or strongly agreed that conducting exposure is difficult due to the practice being strenuous for the therapist. Schumacher et al. (2015) also reported findings where therapists stated exposure therapy was stressful to implement and this was a reason that led therapists to choose interventions such as progressive muscle relaxation or breathing exercises over the use of exposure therapy (Deacon et al., 2013b). Additionally, 10%–15% of clinicians agreed or strongly agreed that they limit the use of exposure because they are unsure if the patient is ready for exposure, they had a bad prior experience with a failed exposure intervention, or cannot do exposure due to their own anxiety (Pittig et al., 2019). In fact, five additional studies also found that therapists with higher anxiety themselves were less likely to use exposure therapy (Levita et al., 2016; Meyer et al., 2014; Pittig et al., 2019; Scherr et al., 2015; Parker & Waller, 2019). Furthermore, 25% of clinicians agreed with the idea that sessions taking place outside of the office, in the "real" world (a common delivery format of exposure therapy), posed concerns related to patient privacy and confidentiality. Similar research also found that therapists had concerns that the intentional activation of anxiety in exposure therapy is unethical (Olatunji et al., 2009) and potentially increases risk for malpractice litigation (Cook et al., 2004).

Delivery of Exposure Therapy

So far we have been discussing the impact of negative therapist beliefs about exposure therapy and how they work against optimal treatment engagement by creating significant barriers to the implementation of exposure interventions. Therapist beliefs about exposure therapy not only impact whether or not exposure is even used, but these beliefs also impact the way exposure interventions are delivered and can lead a therapist to drift from adhering to the front-line, evidence-based exposure treatment protocols. Therefore, in addition to lowering the overall use of exposure in practice, therapist's negative beliefs have also been linked to a more cautious and suboptimal delivery of exposure-based interventions (Deacon et al., 2013a, 2013b; Farrell et al., 2013). For example, two of the most strongly and commonly held therapist beliefs were related to patients not being able to tolerate the distress of exposure and being at risk for decompensation. These frequently held therapist beliefs often led therapists to modify the delivery of exposure in order to make it "easier" and "safer" for clients. Deacon et al. (2013a) reported that therapists with greater concerns about the dangers of intense and prolonged interoceptive exposure (activation of bodily sensations like heart racing, dizziness, loss of breath, etc.) for panic disorder were more likely to use controlled breathing strategies to help their clients reduce the experience of distress initiated from exposure. Additionally, therapists with higher TBES scores, i.e., more negative beliefs about exposure, delivered exposure treatment in a more cautious manner to a confederate client with OCD (Farrell et al., 2013). They reported a more cautious approach as indicated by adding less ambitious items on the exposure hierarchy, a propensity to select a less distressing exposure task, and more attempts to lessen client anxiety during exposure (Farrell et al., 2013). Anecdotally, the author has observed therapists who are new to prolonged exposure for PTSD demonstrate caution during client revisiting of traumatic memories by incorporating breathing retraining during exposure, being quick to end exposure to trauma memories, and greater reluctance to probe for more details of a traumatic memory. When clinicians who hold negative biases toward exposure therapy do implement exposure techniques, its implementation often substantially deviates from the research manual's recommendations on how to most effectively deliver exposure interventions (Deacon et al., 2013a, Freiheit et al., 2004, Hipol & Deacon, 2013). Therapists with higher TBES scores often selected lower exposure items from a hierarchy, made more frequent attempts to reduce the client's distress during exposure, and allowed client's to use more safety behaviors. The impact of increased negative beliefs about exposure are therefore two fold—limiting its overall use despite significant evidence of its effectiveness for a large proportion of mental health problems, and altering its delivery in such a way that it significantly dilutes exposure's effectiveness.

These cautious tactics in the delivery of exposure therapy are reminiscent of the way client's use safety behaviors to reduce anxiety and/or prevent feared outcomes (Deacon & Farrell, 2013; Deacon et al., 2013a). As is often the case when clients use safety behaviors, the long term impact of those behaviors is often paradoxical to the goals of the client. Therapists' cautious use of exposure has this same paradoxical effect—while trying to keep clients safe in the short term by modifying exposure techniques, in the long term this strategy results in poorer client outcomes and erroneously reinforces therapist beliefs that exposure therapy doesn't work. In circumstances such as these, well-intentioned therapists are modifying the delivery of exposure and deviating from the established protocols, in such a way that many clients will unfortunately receive suboptimal and/or such a diluted quality of exposure treatment that it is rendered ineffective. When looking at the research presented so far, therapist negative beliefs about exposure therapy result in a significant barrier to its utilization, as well as to an overly cautious and less effective manner in which exposure is delivered. Either way, clients are deprived access to one of mental health's most effective treatments. These findings implicate therapist negative beliefs about exposure therapy as a significant barrier to not just the competent delivery of this treatment but to whether or not the treatment is offered at all. In summary, these therapist-reported difficulties around the delivery of exposure supplement the research on therapist negative beliefs about exposure and highlight just how complicated the reasons are behind why exposure-based treatments are so rarely utilized. Therefore, the importance of identifying strategies that can effectively reduce therapist reservations about exposure would seem essential in order to improve the overall use, as well as the competent use, of exposure in mental health care.Overcoming Negative Therapist Beliefs About Exposure Therapy

The development of the TBES has helped us better understand the significant impact of therapist beliefs on the use of exposure therapy. Additionally, the research literature outlines a longstanding history of negative therapist beliefs about exposure and the persistence of these beliefs across the mental health field (e.g., doctoral therapists, masters level therapists, across all theoretical orientations, as well as across cultures and mental health systems) despite treatment research and clinical practice guidelines that contradict these beliefs. For example, prolonged exposure therapy (PE) for PTSD is a demanding therapy given it asks clients to approach trauma reminders via two forms of exposure—external trauma reminders via in vivo exposure and the memories of traumatic experiences via imaginal exposure. Despite the demands of PE on clients, it was preferred by people diagnosed with PTSD (Becker et al., 2007) and determined to be more acceptable and effective compared to pharmacotherapy (Deacon & Abramowitz, 2005).

Recognizing Bias Against Exposure

The difficulty of challenging therapist negative beliefs about client acceptance of exposure therapy is the dilemma of the self-fulfilling prophecy. When therapists already hold negative beliefs about exposure, it influences the way therapists talk about exposure therapy with clients, potentially nudging them away from agreeing to exposure treatment. That result reinforces the negative bias within the therapist since it is more evidence that clients don't want to do exposure. That being said, the right preparation and psychoeducation about the process of exposure therapy can significantly enhance client acceptance. When clients know what to expect and understand the purpose of the therapy, they are more likely to commit to it (Beck & Dozois, 2011).

Reviewing the Empirical Findings and Treatment Guidelines

Some persistent beliefs about exposure therapy include: "Exposure is limited to the reduction of superficial symptoms," "Exposure is ineffective with more complex case presentations," and "Exposure leads to higher dropout from treatment." Yet, empirical research does not support these therapist beliefs either. PE is another great example of this, because PTSD is a notoriously complicated disorder that is comprised of difficult emotions (anxiety, fear, sadness, anger, guilt, shame, embarrassment) as well as prevalent complex diagnostic comorbidity with other disorders such as depression, anxiety disorders, substance use disorders, borderline personality disorder, and/or psychosis. And, yet due to the accumulation of evidence, PE is consistently given the strongest recommendation across every published treatment guideline that is available, including the American Psychological Association, American Psychiatric Association, Veterans Administration/Department of Defense, International Society for Traumatic Stress Studies, National Institute for Clinical Excellence (NICE) in the United Kingdom, Canadian Psychiatric Association, and the World Health Organization. The existing treatment literature on the effectiveness of PE with comorbid substance use disorder (Berenz & Coffey, 2012), borderline personality disorder (Slotema et al., 2020), and comorbid psychosis (de Bont et al., 2013) all contradict therapist beliefs about exposure therapy being ineffective with complex client presentations. In terms of treatment dropout rates, studies that have examined this in PE and exposure and response prevention therapy (ERP) for OCD suggest exposure treatments have no greater dropout than other treatment modalities (Hembree et al., 2003; Ong et al., 2016). As for the therapist's concern about harming clients by doing exposure, literature reviews just do not support that idea (e.g., Olatunji et al., 2009). Nor is there any reliable or consistent information available that practicing exposure therapy is a risk for the therapist. There is not one example of therapist ethical misconduct or case law as it pertains to the delivery of exposure therapy. There is no evidence of a therapist being sued for practicing exposure therapy or any other probable liable risk to a therapist's license. It is also very reasonable to believe that clinical practice guidelines that give exposure therapy their strongest recommendation would absolutely not do so if there was consistent, reliable evidence that exposure treatments harmed clients, harmed therapists, placed therapists in ethical and/or legal risk, or any of the other areas where therapists have expressed concerns related to exposure therapy. In fact, one might debate the opposite side of this argument—by not providing one of the strongest recommended treatments to one's clients, the therapist is at risk for harming their client via them not improving and/or being sued for not using a treatment recommended for a given mental health disorder.

Taken together, the research on negative therapist beliefs about exposure therapy is almost entirely contradicted by a variety of clinical practice guidelines and the supporting treatment research literature. While there are individual cases that can support the identified therapist concerns associated with exposure therapy, those idiosyncratic examples disappear when research looks at the averages across larger sample sizes.

Challenging Emotional Reasoning

The reasons driving such a baffling discrepancy between therapist beliefs about exposure and available scientific information on the topic remain elusive and certainly difficult to change. One hypothesis about why this discrepancy exists between clinical practice and clinical practice guidelines is that empathy and emotion are more influential variables (than scientific reasoning) when it comes to making treatment planning decisions. Research from the TBES has identified certain therapist demographic variables that predicted more or less negative beliefs toward exposure therapy. One of the most influential factors predicting high TBES scores was the baseline anxiety level of the therapist. The more a therapist was prone to be anxious themselves, the more likely that therapist was to have negative beliefs about exposure therapy and to be less likely to use it (Farrell et al., 2013). When you look closely at the most commonly held negative beliefs about exposure, they have an underlying current of anxiety—primary concerns of causing harm to the client, along with a similar concern of harming themselves (the therapists). The hypothesis is that therapists who are predisposed to being more anxious, and possibly also more empathic to the anxious client's experience, are more likely to have these strong emotional negative beliefs about exposure therapy. Furthermore, these emotional beliefs are also supported by what appear to be more rational, logic driven beliefs such as exposure is for simple case presentations or the simple/superficial reduction of anxiety symptoms, most clients refuse the treatment, and/or it causes greater dropout. The point is that the primary beliefs related to exposure therapy potentially harming a client or the therapist may be highly supported by strong emotional reasoning strategies that are not easily refuted by scientific research studies. The hypothesis extends further to suggest that the best technique to challenge these negative beliefs would be an experiential one—exposure to the use of exposure. The ability of exposure to ultimately increase positive beliefs about exposure therapy by first lessening the anxiety the therapist experiences with doing exposure therapy may enable the therapist to learn how to do exposure better, see clients improve, and feel more confident about using exposure, which ideally leads a therapist to use exposure more. However, the paradox of anxiety and safety presents itself again—one of the more effective ways of addressing therapists' negative beliefs about exposure therapy is doing exposure themselves, and because they have such negative beliefs about it, they may be less likely to utilize it and therefore less likely to change their negative beliefs.

The Role of Training and Consultative Support

Modifying therapist negative beliefs about exposure is essential and, compared to institutional barriers, may prove to be more malleable. In fact, there are evidence-based strategies that may reduce therapist negative beliefs. For example, more experience with exposure-based interventions during the educational training years is associated with more frequent use of exposure later in a therapists' career (Broicher et al., 2017; Pittig et al., 2017). Additionally, specific exposure training for licensed therapists has been found to increase therapist's sense of competency to actually use the interventions taught in the training (e.g., Sholomskas et al., 2005). Similarly, Deacon et al., (2013a) found that the negative beliefs about exposure in a group of community therapists were significantly reduced after a 1-day workshop on the theory and practice of exposure therapy. While these initial findings are promising, challenging therapist negative beliefs about exposure later in a therapist's career could remain a significant challenge. Some research suggests that despite exposure therapy training, a sizable number of therapists do not incorporate exposure into their practice (Becker et al., 2004), and another study suggested that exposure-based interventions in particular were the least likely to be carried over into practice following training (Hoyer et al., 2017).

In sum, the earlier in their career a therapist can be trained in exposure therapy the more likely they are to keep using it. Even though training in exposure can help reduce negative beliefs right after a workshop, there is no research indicating the lasting nature of that change. This could help explain why after a workshop there is an immediate change in beliefs, but over time, without accompanying behavior change, therapists ultimately return to their pre-training beliefs and practices. Therefore, increasing the use of exposure therapy may require initial trainings and then assisting therapists with implementation of exposure therapy through post-workshop consultation to support therapists to implement what they learned from a workshop (e.g., Charney et al., 2019). When providers get consultative support, they may feel more confident in trying a new therapeutic skill and be encouraged by seeing their clients engage and improve. When providers believe a treatment is effective, they are more likely to deliver it with fidelity, their clients adhere to the treatment better, and overall treatment outcomes are also better (Bystritsky et al., 2005).

Adopting a Beginner's Mindset

A "beginner's mindset" is a concept rooted in Zen Buddhism and refers to approaching experiences with a sense of openness, curiosity, and a lack of preconceived notions or judgments (Kabat-Zinn, 1990). Once committed to a beginner's mindset, then take a deep dive into understanding why clinical practice guidelines repeatedly suggest exposure therapy as the gold-standard mental health treatment for a variety of disorders. Review and understand the evidence that supports those guidelines as a strategy to also increase confidence of using exposure in practice. Additionally, learn how and why exposure therapy works as well as it does—understand how the mechanisms of adherently delivered exposure treatment work—emotional processing, inhibitory learning, habituation, extinction learning, etc.

As a therapist works on a beginner's mindset to what exposure therapy can offer clients, the value of consultation or supervision cannot be over-stated. This can be accomplished by watching videos of experts doing exposure, observing colleagues with their clients, listening to podcasts, and attending professional conferences and workshops. Negative beliefs about exposure cultivate avoidance—therapists limit their experience using it and/or modify exposure techniques. Experience using exposure will ultimately be the best way to challenge inaccurate, negative beliefs about exposure. Exposure works for clients and it will work for therapists in this context as well. Be patient with yourself, expect discomfort during this process and start small. Therapists might consider developing a list of the kinds of clients that would raise concern if one were to use exposure with them. Take that list and then turn it into a hierarchy; start at the bottom and work up.

Lastly, the therapist might find it to be beneficial to incorporate strategies to assess, monitor, and track themself as they challenge beliefs about exposure therapy. Fill out the TBES to provide some objective measurement of the beliefs being worked on. There is also the Exposure Implementation Beliefs Scale (EIBS) which can help therapists assess the potential use of unnecessary safety behaviors when implementing exposure therapy with clients (Meyer et al., 2020). Using this information can help identify important areas of challenging avoidance behaviors while also utilizing peer support, supervision, and/or consultation aid the therapist in confronting challenge beliefs. Finally, therapists must remain compassionate with themselves during this process, just as one would with a client who is struggling to make a difficult change. Therapists should be validated with respect to the difficulty of the process. Therapists are encouraged to have empathy for themself, remind themself why they are working on challenging beliefs, and bring what they learn to the exposure work they do with their clients.

Systemic and Institutional Barriers to Exposure Therapy

In addition to negative therapist beliefs, there are also substantive institutional and systemic barriers standing in the way of therapists who do want to provide exposure treatments as they are most effectively designed. These barriers encompass healthcare systems, organizational structures, training availability, and resource limitations that hinder the consistent and effective implementation of exposure therapy, thus preventing optimal patient engagement in care.

High Caseloads and Limited Session Time

A significant systemic barrier stems from the logistical constraints within many mental health organizations—high caseloads and limited session time create an environment where evidence-based practices like exposure therapy may be seen as impractical. Exposure therapy can require a more intensive and structured approach than other forms of therapy. Successful exposure-based interventions often necessitate planning and time for in-session exposure exercises, which can be challenging to implement within standard 45- to 50-min therapy sessions, especially if the exposure has to be done outside the office. In one study, therapists reported that exposure treatments often require more time, planning, and effort from the clinician while the financial payoff is the same despite the additional efforts of the clinician (Pittig et al., 2019). Additionally, due to clinicians often having high caseloads, the increased time needed to plan for and implement exposure interventions, forces clinicians to make difficult decisions about session frequency and duration which are often contraindicated by exposure treatment protocols that ask for weekly, extended sessions. In this context, the perceived complexity or time-consuming nature of exposure therapy may push therapists toward other forms of therapy, even if less effective for anxiety disorders.

Insurance and Reimbursement Challenges

Financial and systemic pressures from insurance companies and reimbursement policies also present significant barriers to the implementation of exposure therapy. In many healthcare systems, including the United States, mental health services are subject to constraints imposed by insurance reimbursement. Adherent delivery of exposure interventions often requires weekly, prolonged sessions—60–90 min. Seeing clients for 90-min sessions is almost impossible for the vast majority of therapists practicing in community mental health or if clients are relying on health insurance reimbursement since most health insurance plans rarely pay for 90-min sessions. In fact, the system for billing medical appointments uses Current Procedural Terminology (CPT) codes and there is currently no CPT code a licensed clinician can use to bill for a 90-min session. That is a significant systemic barrier to a therapist's ability to offer gold-standard exposure therapy to consumers in an adherent manner.

Insufficient Training and Supervision

A critical systemic barrier to the implementation of exposure therapy is the insufficient availability of proper training and supervision. Exposure therapy requires specialized knowledge and skills, yet many mental health professionals receive only limited or superficial training in evidence-based practices, including exposure techniques, during their graduate programs (Weissman et al., 2006). In many cases, clinical training curricula prioritize a broad approach to therapy over in-depth, specialized training in evidence-based treatments for anxiety disorders. As a result, therapists may graduate without the confidence or competence needed to effectively deliver exposure therapy.

Additionally, post-graduate training opportunities, such as workshops, continuing education, or supervision by experienced clinicians, may be inaccessible to many therapists (Beidas & Kendall, 2010). These training resources often require time and financial investment making it difficult for therapists to access them. Without ongoing supervision or mentorship, therapists may feel isolated in their practice, increasing the likelihood of using less effective, more comfortable treatment methods instead of exposure therapy.

Organizational Culture and Resistance to Change

The organizational environment in which a therapist works can influence the use of this treatment. Many mental health organizations face systemic inertia, where longstanding practices and institutional culture resist the adoption of new or evidence-based treatments. Clinics and hospitals may rely on familiar therapeutic modalities, such as CBT without the exposure component or psychodynamic therapy, that align with the preferences of clinical leadership. In organizations where exposure therapy is not promoted or prioritized, therapists may lack the encouragement or support to integrate it into their practice. In addition, fear of liability or concerns over client distress may lead administrators to discourage therapists from using exposure techniques, as exposure therapy involves confronting feared stimuli, which may be perceived as risky or harmful. Similarly, many mental health organizations restrict therapists from doing any work outside of the office. This prevents a therapist from leaving the office with a client and, for instance, doing a driving exposure with a panic client, a home visit for a client with OCD, or social phobia exposures in public. Therefore, even if therapists wanted to provide adherent exposure therapy to their clients, systemic and institutional barriers such as these stand firmly in the way of therapists offering the treatment recommended by practice guidelines.

Overcoming Systemic Barriers to Exposure Adoption and Engagement

The breadth of individual, organizational, and systemic barriers to the use of exposure is substantive, therefore, it will require a multilevel approach to break through them all (see also Pittig et al., 2017). In addition to the tips around challenging the individual therapist barriers to using exposure therapy, below are some ideas related to addressing systemic barriers to exposure therapy.

Improved Training

Organizational systems can contribute to increasing engagement in exposure therapy by facilitating access to specialized training, education, and support for clinicians. One barrier to the individual therapist obtaining this on their own is the cost. Employers can invest in the professional development of its staff, and the overall wellbeing of their clientele, by increasing the organization's capacity to deliver safe and effective evidence-based treatments like exposure. One such organizational space where this can be done is in graduate school training programs. Requiring educational settings to teach the treatments that are recommended by our clinical practice guidelines would be a great start. Similarly, mental health employers can continue to invest in the professional development of clinicians by further supporting training, education, and consultation and supervision for the most effective mental health interventions. All of this will require leadership that champions evidence-based treatments. Even if clinicians are better trained in exposure therapy, institutional leaders will also need to alter the way clinics operate by providing more time for clinicians to prepare for exposure sessions, giving clinicians permission to do out of office exposures, setting the expectation for staff that evidence-based treatments are to be utilized, and setting up caseloads in a way where clinicians can see clients more often.

Professional and Organizational Advocacy

Professional organizations can also help by increasing awareness, among both the lay public and mental health professionals, about the strong evidence base for exposure therapy to treat anxiety disorders, PTSD, and OCD. A media promotional campaign could assist by informing the public about how effective and safe exposure therapy is, while normalizing the experience of discomfort as part of the healing process. For example, pharmaceutical companies have the resources to advertise medications for mental health disorders that are often far less effective and have many more side effects, than behavioral treatments but there is currently no comparable advertising campaign promoting the most effective and safest treatment for anxiety, i.e. exposure therapy.

Promoting Research-Driven Solutions

Lastly, strategies that can increase access to and practical application of exposure therapy are essential. For example, researchers could look to develop treatments that are more readily transferable to the real world of mental health care. It is great that exposure therapy is so effective, but if it has to be delivered over a 90-min session and mental health appointments are typically 45 min, then that intervention is not very practical. More research on group therapy interventions would be welcomed by clinicians who have to carry high caseloads. Increasing advocacy—both in practice and in graduate training programs—may also be key. For instance, increasing the activism around insurance reimbursement for the time it takes to provide exposure treatments would significantly reduce the cost of evidence-based care and increase access to evidenced based treatments. Mental health clinics can offer more support and incentives for clinicians to follow treatment guidelines, challenge systemic biases around the risks of exposure, and alleviate the realistic barriers therapists face when wanting to use exposure-based treatments. By dismantling these systemic barriers, more clients with anxiety disorders can receive the full benefit of this powerful therapeutic approach.

Conclusion

The combination of therapist negative beliefs about exposure, with the reality of institutional and systemic barriers to implementing exposure therapy with adherence to the model, together create a significant mountain to overcome if the field of mental health is to enhance engagement in one of our most effective treatments. Overcoming these barriers to using exposure therapy requires a multifaceted approach that targets individual misconceptions, institutional practices, and broader systemic challenges. At the therapist level, common barriers include fears of harming clients, discomfort with eliciting anxiety, and limited training or confidence in using exposure therapy. These challenges can be addressed through comprehensive education, supervision, and mentorship to build therapists' competence and comfort. Encouraging therapists to adopt a beginner's mind, normalize client discomfort, and focus on the strong evidence base for exposure therapy can also help mitigate resistance.

Systemic and institutional barriers, such as high caseloads, lack of organizational support, and insufficient resources, often prevent the widespread implementation of exposure therapy. Addressing these barriers involves integrating exposure therapy into graduate training curricula and ensuring that it is prioritized and supported within clinical settings. Leadership and advocacy is critical for allocating time, resources, and policies that enable clients to engage in evidence-based treatments. Increasing accessibility for clients through reduced financial barriers can also enhance the reach of exposure therapy. By addressing both therapist-level and systemic challenges, the field can promote the consistent and effective delivery of exposure therapy, ultimately improving treatment outcomes for clients with anxiety disorders, PTSD, and OCD.

> ***Clinical Summary Points and Recommendations***
>
> - Despite the high prevalence of anxiety and related disorders (like OCD and PTSD), and overwhelming evidence supporting the efficacy and effectiveness of exposure therapy in the treatment of these conditions, most therapists do not utilize exposure therapy interventions as designed.
> - Common therapist-level barriers to a patient's engagement in exposure therapy include fear of harming clients, discomfort with eliciting anxiety, and limited training or confidence in the use of these techniques.
> - Systemic and institutional barriers, such as high caseloads, lack of organizational support, and insufficient resources, also hinder wider implementation practices and thus, patient engagement in exposure therapy.
> - Strategies to overcome therapist- and institution-level barriers to engagement in exposure therapy must be multifaceted and include education, training, better integration of evidence with clinical practice, leadership, advocacy, and policy change.

References

Bandelow, B., Lichte, T., Rudolf, S., Wiltink, J., & Beutel, E. M. (2014). The diagnosis of and treatment recommendations for anxiety disorders. Deutsches Ärzteblatt International, 111(27–28), 473.

Baxter, A. J., Scott, K. M., Vos, T., & Whiteford, H. A. (2013). Global prevalence of anxiety disorders: A systematic review and meta-regression. *Psychological Medicine, 43*(5), 897–910.

Beck, J. S., & Dozois, D. J. A. (2011). *Cognitive therapy: Basics and beyond* (2nd ed.). Guilford Press.

Becker, C. B., Darius, E., & Schaumberg, K. (2007). An analog study of patient preferences for exposure versus alternative treatments for posttraumatic stress disorder. *Behaviour Research and Therapy, 45*(12), 2861–2873.

Becker, C. B., Zayfert, C., & Anderson, E. (2004). A survey of psychologists' attitudes towards and utilization of exposure therapy for PTSD. *Behaviour Research and Therapy, 42*(3), 277–292.

Beidas, R. S., & Kendall, P. C. (2010). Training therapists in evidence-based practice: A critical review of studies from a systems-contextual perspective. *Clinical Psychology: Science and Practice, 17*(1), 1–30. https://doi.org/10.1111/j.1468-2850.2009.01187.x

Berenz, E. C., & Coffey, S. F. (2012). Treatment of co-occurring posttraumatic stress disorder and substance use disorders. *Current Psychiatry Reports, 14*, 469–477.

Broicher, T., Gerlach, A. L., & Neudeck, P. (2017). Relevance of psychotherapy training on the later use of exposure in psychotherapeutic practice. *Zeitschrift für Klinische Psychologie und Psychotherapie, 46*(2), 107–117.

Bystritsky, A., Khalsa, S. S., Cameron, M. E., & Schiffman, J. (2005). Current diagnosis and treatment of anxiety disorders. *Pharmacy and Therapeutics, 30*(5), 282–291.

Cahill, S. P., Foa, E. B., Hembree, E. A., Marshall, R. D., & Nacash, N. (2006). Dissemination of exposure therapy in the treatment of posttraumatic stress disorder. *Journal of Traumatic Stress: Official Publication of The International Society for Traumatic Stress Studies, 19*(5), 597–610.

Charney, M. E., Chow, L., Jakubovic, R. J., Federico, L. E., Goetter, E. M., Baier, A. L., Riggs, D., Phillips, J., Bui, E., & Simon, N. M. (2019). Training community providers in evidence-based treatment for PTSD: Outcomes of a novel consultation program. *Psychological Trauma: Theory, Research, Practice, and Policy, 11*(7), 793–801. https://doi.org/10.1037/tra0000427

Clark, D. M. (2011). Implementing NICE guidelines for the psychological treatment of depression and anxiety disorders: The IAPT experience. *International Review of Psychiatry, 23*(4), 318–327.

Cook, J. M., Biyanova, T., Elhai, J., Schnurr, P. P., & Coyne, J. C. (2010). What do psychotherapists really do in practice? An internet study of over 2,000 practitioners. *Psychotherapy: Theory, Research, Practice, Training, 47*(2), 260.

Cook, J. M., Schnurr, P. P., & Foa, E. B. (2004). Bridging the gap between posttraumatic stress disorder research and clinical practice: The example of exposure therapy. *Psychotherapy: Theory, Research, Practice, Training, 41*(4), 374–387. https://doi.org/10.1037/0033-3204.41.4.374

Deacon, B. J., & Abramowitz, J. S. (2005). Patients' perceptions of pharmacological and cognitive-behavioral treatments for anxiety disorders. *Behavior Therapy, 36*(2), 139–145.

Deacon, B. J., & Farrell, N. R. (2013). Therapist barriers to the dissemination of exposure therapy. In Handbook of treating variants and complications in anxiety disorders (pp. 363–373). New York, NY: Springer New York.

Deacon, B. J., Farrell, N. R., Kemp, J. J., Dixon, L. J., Sy, J. T., Zhang, A. R., & McGrath, P. B. (2013a). Assessing therapist reservations about exposure therapy for anxiety disorders: The therapist beliefs about exposure scale. *Journal of Anxiety Disorders, 27*(8), 772–780.

Deacon, B. J., Lickel, J. J., Farrell, N. R., Kemp, J. J., & Hipol, L. J. (2013b). Therapist perceptions and delivery of interoceptive exposure for panic disorder. *Journal of Anxiety Disorders, 27*(2), 259–264.

de Jong, R., Lommen, M. J., van Hout, W. J., de Jong, P. J., & Nauta, M. H. (2020). Therapists' characteristics associated with the (non-) use of exposure in the treatment of anxiety disorders in youth: A survey among Dutch-speaking mental health practitioners. *Journal of Anxiety Disorders, 73*, 102230.

de Bont, P. A., van Minnen, A., & de Jongh, A. (2013). Treating PTSD in patients with psychosis: A within-group controlled feasibility study examining the efficacy and safety of evidence-based PE and EMDR protocols. *Behavior Therapy, 44*(4), 717–730.

Freiheit, S. R., Vye, C., Swan, R., & Cady, M. (2004). Cognitive-behavioral therapy for anxiety: Is dissemination working? *The Behavior Therapist.*

Farrell, N. R., Deacon, B. J., Kemp, J. J., Dixon, L. J., & Sy, J. T. (2013). Do negative beliefs about exposure therapy cause its suboptimal delivery? An experimental investigation. *Journal of Anxiety Disorders, 27*(8), 763–771.

Feeny, N. C., Hembree, E. A., & Zoellner, L. A. (2003). Myths regarding exposure therapy for PTSD. *Cognitive and Behavioral Practice, 10*(1), 85–90.

Hembree, E. A., Foa, E. B., Dorfan, N. M., Street, G. P., Kowalski, J., & Tu, X. (2003). Do patients drop out prematurely from exposure therapy for PTSD? *Journal of Traumatic Stress, 16*, 555–562.

Hipol, L. J., & Deacon, B. J. (2013). Dissemination of evidence-based practices for anxiety disorders in Wyoming: A survey of practicing psychotherapists. *Behavior Modification, 37*(2), 170–188.

Hoyer, J., Čolić, J., Pittig, A., Crawcour, S., Moeser, M., Ginzburg, D., et al. (2017). Manualized cognitive therapy versus cognitive-behavioral treatment-as-usual for social anxiety disorder in routine practice: A cluster-randomized controlled trial. *Behaviour Research and Therapy, 95*, 87–98.

Kabat-Zinn, J. (1990). *Full catastrophe living: Using the wisdom of your body and mind to face stress, pain, and illness*. Delacorte Press.

Kannis-Dymand, L., Grace, E., McDonald, L., & Chambers, R. (2022). Australian and New Zealand psychologists' perceptions and use of therapist-guided exposure for panic disorder. *Clinical Psychologist, 26*(1), 11–22.

Katzman, M. A., Bleau, P., Blier, P., Chokka, P., Kjernisted, K., Van Ameringen, M., & Canadian Anxiety Guidelines Initiative Group on behalf of the Anxiety Disorders Association of Canada/Association Canadienne des troubles anxieux and McGill University. (2014). Canadian clinical practice guidelines for the management of anxiety, posttraumatic stress and obsessive-compulsive disorders. *BMC Psychiatry, 14*, 1–83.

Keleher, J., Jassi, A., & Krebs, G. (2020). Clinician-reported barriers to using exposure with response prevention in the treatment of paediatric obsessive-compulsive disorder. *Journal of Obsessive-Compulsive and Related Disorders, 24*, 100498.

Kline, A. C., Klein, A. B., Bowling, A. R., & Feeny, N. C. (2021). Exposure therapy beliefs and utilization for treatment of PTSD: A survey of licensed mental health providers. *Behavior Therapy, 52*(4), 1019–1030.

Levita, L., Duhne, P. G. S., Girling, C., & Waller, G. (2016). Facets of clinicians' anxiety and the delivery of cognitive behavioral therapy. *Behaviour Research and Therapy, 77*, 157–161.

Meyer, J. M., Farrell, N. R., Kemp, J. J., Blakey, S. M., & Deacon, B. J. (2014). Why do clinicians exclude anxious clients from exposure therapy? *Behaviour Research and Therapy, 54*, 49–53.

Meyer, J. M., Kelly, P. J., & Deacon, B. J. (2020). Therapist beliefs about exposure therapy implementation. *The Cognitive Behaviour Therapist, 13*, e10.

Olatunji, B. O., Deacon, B. J., & Abramowitz, J. S. (2009). The cruelest cure? Ethical issues in the implementation of exposure-based treatments. *Cognitive and Behavioral Practice, 16*(2), 172–180.

Ong, C. W., Clyde, J. W., Bluett, E. J., Levin, M. E., & Twohig, M. P. (2016). Dropout rates in exposure with response prevention for obsessive-compulsive disorder: What do the data really say? *Journal of Anxiety Disorders, 40*, 8–17.

Parker, Z. J., & Waller, G. (2019). Psychotherapists' reports of technique use when treating anxiety disorders: Factors associated with specific technique use. *The Cognitive Behaviour Therapist, 12*, e33.

Pittig, A., Kotter, R., & Hoyer, J. (2019). The struggle of behavioral therapists with exposure: Self-reported practicability, negative beliefs, and therapist distress about exposure-based interventions. *Behavior Therapy, 50*(2), 353–366.

Reid, A. M., Guzick, A. G., Fernandez, A. G., Deacon, B., McNamara, J. P., Geffken, G. R., et al. (2018). Exposure therapy for youth with anxiety: Utilization rates and predictors of implementation in a sample of practicing clinicians from across the United States. *Journal of Anxiety Disorders, 58*, 8–17.

Rowe, C., & Kangas, M. (2020). The impact of Australian psychologists' education, beliefs, theoretical understanding, and attachment on the use and implementation of exposure therapy. *Behaviour Change, 37*(3), 151–170.

Sars, D., & van Minnen, A. (2015). On the use of exposure therapy in the treatment of anxiety disorders: A survey among cognitive behavioural therapists in The Netherlands. *BMC Psychology, 3*, 1–10.

Simmons, A. M., Milnes, S. M., & Anderson, D. A. (2008). Factors influencing the utilization of empirically supported treatments for eating disorders. *Eating Disorders, 16*(4), 342–354.

Scherr, S. R., Herbert, J. D., & Forman, E. M. (2015). The role of therapist experiential avoidance in predicting therapist preference for exposure treatment for OCD. *Journal of Contextual Behavioral Science, 4*(1), 21–29.

Schumacher, S., Miller, R., Fehm, L., Kirschbaum, C., Fydrich, T., & Ströhle, A. (2015). Therapists' and patients' stress responses during graduated versus flooding in vivo exposure in the treatment of specific phobia: A preliminary observational study. *Psychiatry Research, 230*(2), 668–675.

Schumacher, S., Weiss, D., & Knaevelsrud, C. (2018). Dissemination of exposure in the treatment of anxiety disorders and post-traumatic stress disorder among German cognitive behavioural therapists. *Clinical Psychology & Psychotherapy, 25*(6), 856–864.

Schumacher, S., Schopka, N. M., Heinrich, M., & Knaevelsrud, C. (2019). The German adaptation of the therapist beliefs about exposure scale: A validation study among licensed cognitive behavioural therapists in Germany. *Behavioural and Cognitive Psychotherapy, 47*(2), 164–180.

Sholomskas, D. E., Syracuse-Siewert, G., Rounsaville, B. J., Ball, S. A., Nuro, K. F., & Carroll, K. M. (2005). We don't train in vain: A dissemination trial of three strategies of training clinicians in cognitive-behavioral therapy. *Journal of Consulting and Clinical Psychology, 73*(1), 106.

Slotema, C. W., Wilhelmus, B., Arends, L. R., & Franken, I. H. (2020). Psychotherapy for post-traumatic stress disorder in patients with borderline personality disorder: A systematic review and meta-analysis of its efficacy and safety. *European Journal of Psychotraumatology, 11*(1), 1796188.

van Minnen, A., Hendriks, L., & Olff, M. (2010). When do trauma experts choose exposure therapy for PTSD patients? A controlled study of therapist and patient factors. *Behaviour Research and Therapy, 48*(4), 312–320.

Weissman, M. M., Verdeli, H., Gameroff, M. J., Bledsoe, S. E., Betts, K., Mufson, L., et al. (2006). National survey of psychotherapy training in psychiatry, psychology, and social work. *Archives of General Psychiatry, 63*(8), 925–934. https://doi.org/10.1001/archpsyc.63.8.925

Whiteside, S. P., Deacon, B. J., Benito, K., & Stewart, E. (2016). Factors associated with practitioners' use of exposure therapy for childhood anxiety disorders. *Journal of Anxiety Disorders, 40*, 29–36.

Zoellner, L. A., Feeny, N. C., Bittinger, J. N., Bedard-Gilligan, M. A., Slagle, D. M., Post, L. M., & Chen, J. A. (2011). Teaching trauma-focused exposure therapy for PTSD: Critical clinical lessons for novice exposure therapists. *Psychological Trauma: Theory, Research, Practice, and Policy, 3*(3), 300.

Chapter 7
Videoconference-Mediated Interventions for Anxiety and Related Disorders: Implications for Treatment Engagement

Erica K. Yuen and Elizabeth M. Goetter

Introduction

Telehealth (i.e., teleconference, and sometimes "teletherapy" or "telemental health") is one type of digital mental health intervention (DMHI) that encompasses several forms of electronic communications, including videoconference, email, text messaging, and phone (Pineda et al., 2023; Thomas et al., 2021). Specifically, videoconference enables patients to have interactive electronic meetings with their clinician using a computerized device, digital camera, and Internet. Videoconference-mediated interventions (VMIs) allow for real-time treatment interactions regardless of the patient's or clinician's physical location (Przeworski & Newman, 2006).

VMIs have the potential to reduce treatment access gaps given their flexible delivery format and the convenience for patients who can access treatment from home without the burden of transportation logistics. Videoconference may also be especially appealing to individuals with anxiety and related disorders. Anxiety disorders can be marked by fear of negative appraisals by others; hypervigilance in public settings; agoraphobia; interpersonal avoidance; intolerance of uncertainty; and generalized worries about time, logistics, and travel (Goetter & Yuen, 2024). Videoconference-based technologies may mitigate many of these worries by providing some interpersonal distance, convenience, flexibility, and an opportunity to engage in treatment on one's own terms (Yuen et al., 2012). Moreover, when treatment can be accessed without physically presenting to a mental health treatment

E. K. Yuen (✉)
Department of Psychology, University of Tampa, Tampa, FL, USA
e-mail: eyuen@ut.edu

E. M. Goetter
Department of Psychology, La Salle University, Philadelphia, PA, USA

Department of Psychiatry, Massachusetts General Hospital, Boston, MA, USA

E. M. Goetter (ed.), *Optimizing Treatment Engagement Processes in CBT for Anxiety and Related Disorders*, CBT: Science Into Practice,
https://doi.org/10.1007/978-3-031-91439-3_7

facility, VMIs may represent a viable option for those who might otherwise be deterred from seeking mental health treatment. Indeed, one study found that individuals who cite stigma as a barrier to care were especially interested in Internet-mediated treatment (Wallin et al., 2018).

Origins in Empirical Research

In one of the earliest investigations of videoconference, researchers in England reported on the success of treating a 38-year old man with mixed anxiety and depression using 12 sessions of cognitive behavioral therapy (CBT) over interactive video (Manchanda & McLaren, 1998). Later, in one of the first comparative studies, Bouchard et al. (2004) delivered CBT for panic disorder for 21 adults (11 received treatment via videoconference and 10 received treatment in-person). Group assignment was non-random and based on geographic location. Both groups showed significant improvements, and the therapeutic alliance was rated as strong and was similar between the two groups at post-treatment. In the decades since, videoconference has been studied and applied in a variety of contexts for patients with anxiety disorders, obsessive-compulsive disorder (OCD), and posttraumatic stress disorder (PTSD).

Evidence of Outcome

Systematic reviews and meta-analyses consistently report that videoconference is as effective as in-person treatment. A systematic review of studies (published between 2004 and 2014) of anxiety disorders (including PTSD and OCD) treated with videoconference demonstrated that VMIs were effective with outcomes comparable to in-person treatments (Rees & Maclaine, 2015). In a systematic review of 21 studies (published between 1991 and 2017) that included any measure of anxiety reduction as an outcome, VMIs led to improvements across most studies (Berryhill et al., 2018). Effect sizes generally ranged between medium and large (with larger between-group effects seen, unsurprisingly, in uncontrolled trials). In a systematic review and meta-analysis of telehealth (videoconference and phone) versus in-person treatment for anxiety and related disorders that included five total trials (mostly of OCD), there were no differences in symptom outcomes, functioning, therapeutic alliance, and satisfaction between telehealth and in-person formats (Krzyzaniak et al., 2024).

Panic Disorder

Some of the earliest studies of VMIs for anxiety disorders were conducted with patients with panic disorder. As noted, an early pretest-posttest design with non-equivalent groups found that CBT was associated with symptom reductions for both the videoconference and in-person treatment conditions: 81% of those in the videoconference condition were panic free at post-treatment and 91% were panic free at 6-month follow-up (Bouchard et al., 2004). More recently, a 2-arm non-inferiority study was conducted in which 71 adults with panic disorder received 12 sessions of weekly CBT via videoconference or in-person, with allocation based on region (Bouchard et al., 2020). The study found that videoconference was no less effective relative to in-person treatment on the primary outcome variable of self-reported panic and agoraphobia symptoms and gains were maintained for both conditions at 1-year follow-up.

Social Anxiety Disorder

There are currently no published randomized controlled trials (RCTs) comparing videoconference to in-person treatment for adults with social anxiety disorder (SAD), but VMIs may hold particular appeal for this population, given core fears of negative evaluation. In one of the first home-based videoconference trials, Yuen et al. (2013) examined the effects of acceptance-based behavior therapy for 24 adults with SAD. Participants demonstrated significant improvements in symptoms at post-treatment and over half no longer met criteria for SAD at post-treatment. In an uncontrolled study of an empirically supported group-based treatment, Nauphal et al. (2021) found that eight 2-h sessions of social self-reappraisal therapy were associated with improvements for 5 individuals in a naturalistic clinic setting during the COVID-19 pandemic. In a study of youth, 40 children with SAD (ages 3–8) were randomized to waitlist control or a home-based telehealth treatment program based on an adapted version of Parent Child Interaction Therapy (PCIT) (Comer et al., 2021). Using an intent-to-treat analysis, relative to waitlist, the telehealth treatment group had a higher percentage of responders (50% vs. 6%) as determined by independent assessors.

Generalized Anxiety Disorder

Studies among individuals with generalized anxiety disorder (GAD) are generally fewer, as noted by others (Rees & Maclaine, 2015). In an experimental, multiple baseline case study, 5 individuals with GAD no longer met criteria for GAD following 14 sessions of weekly CBT via videoconference and all experienced clinical and statistical improvements (Théberge-Lapointe et al., 2015). In a larger RCT, 148 adults with GAD were randomized to videoconference or face-to-face psychotherapy, comprised of 15 weekly sessions of manualized CBT, and results demonstrated that videoconference treatment was noninferior to in-person treatment (Bouchard et al., 2022).

Obsessive-Compulsive Disorder

Several uncontrolled studies found that exposure-based treatment for OCD delivered through videoconference was associated with significant reductions in symptoms for adults (Feusner et al., 2022; Fletcher et al., 2022; Goetter et al., 2014) and children (Comer et al., 2014). In addition, a RCT conducted by Vogel et al. (2014) with 30 patients found that exposure and response prevention (ERP) delivered via videoconference over 12 weeks was associated with significantly greater reductions in OCD symptoms compared to waitlist control and self-help control, with large between-group effect sizes. Another RCT conducted by Storch et al. (2011) with 31 youth found that family-based CBT for adolescents and children delivered via videoconference over 12 weeks experienced significantly greater improvements compared to a waitlist control, also with large effect sizes. However, there are a lack of published randomized trials that compare videoconference directly with in-person treatment for OCD. A randomized trial conducted by Comer et al. (2017) did compare videoconference to in-person family-based CBT for 22 children with OCD and found no significant differences in efficacy.

Posttraumatic Stress Disorder

Several recent meta-analyses found no differences in treatment outcome for RCTs that compared videoconference directly to in-person treatment for PTSD (Kelber et al., 2024; Scott et al., 2022). Almost all of the included trials were with Veterans, and a couple included mixed Veteran/active duty (Peterson et al., 2022) or Veteran/active duty/civilian participants (Morland et al., 2015). Non-inferiority was supported for a variety of evidence-based protocols delivered through videoconference, including cognitive processing therapy (CPT; e.g., Liu et al., 2020), prolonged exposure therapy (PE; e.g., Acierno et al., 2017), and combined behavioral activation with situational/imaginal exposure (Acierno et al., 2016). Implementation of videoconference treatment included both home-based telehealth, where patients attended sessions while in their own home or other chosen location (e.g., Acierno et al., 2017) as well as the "Hub and Spoke model" (also known as "office-based telehealth") where the patient attended sessions while physically located at a local satellite VA clinic while the provider was physically located at a central VA clinic (e.g., Maieritsch et al., 2016). However, there is a dearth of published randomized trials directly comparing videoconference to in-person treatment for civilians with PTSD.

Specific Phobia, Mixed Samples, and Unspecified Anxiety Symptoms

Almost no studies have examined VMIs for specific phobias, though a prior study that delivered virtual reality exposure therapy remotely (using telephone) offered encouraging results (Cherestal et al., 2021), suggesting that telehealth may be effective for this population. In two uncontrolled pilot studies, an acceptance-based group intervention delivered through videoconference was associated with improvements in public speaking anxiety (Yuen et al., 2019).

In a randomized trial comparing CBT delivered via videoconference versus in-person for a mixed anxiety and mood disorder sample, videoconference was effective and there were no significant differences in outcome by condition (Stubbings et al., 2013). In a naturalistic setting, with a nonrandomized design, 413 adult patients with anxiety disorders received group CBT either in-person (prior to the COVID-19 pandemic) or via videoconference (during the pandemic) (Milosevic et al., 2022). Results revealed a small but significant effect in favor of in-person treatment, but this only appeared to be true for patients with GAD and all between-group differences were small.

An uncontrolled study of a single-session consultation delivered via videoconference to 65 patients on an outpatient psychotherapy waitlist was associated with decreased self-reported generalized anxiety symptoms at 2-week follow-up (Sung et al., 2023). Finally, in a systematic review of controlled studies, VMIs appeared to be beneficial in reducing anxiety symptoms for individuals with various health and medical needs during the COVID-19 pandemic (Tarhan et al., 2023).

Challenges to Engagement

Videoconference-mediated CBT is clearly effective for treating anxiety and related disorders, in both research and clinical settings, but some have raised concerns about whether patients can optimally engage in these formats. Potential barriers to engagement include concerns about impaired working alliance, difficulty being present or emotionally engaged in treatment, technological disruptions, low technological literacy, competition with external distractions (particularly in home-based videoconference formats), and loss of control over the therapeutic environment.

Working Alliance

Concerns about the working alliance have been raised since VMIs were first used. In fact, in one of the earliest studies of CBT via videoconference (Manchanda & McLaren, 1998), the authors expressly examined the therapeutic alliance due to concerns that "interactive video" may weaken the therapist's attempts to display "warmth, accurate empathy and genuineness…and the development of the therapeutic relationship may be more gradual, prolonging therapy" (p. 53). These concerns have not generally materialized in studies examining this issue. In fact, the data consistently suggest that a strong working alliance can be forged in CBT delivered via videoconference for panic disorder (Bouchard et al., 2004, 2020), GAD (Watts et al., 2020), SAD (Yuen et al., 2013), OCD (Vogel et al., 2014), and PTSD (Scott et al., 2022). Even a study of a single-session VMI for individuals on a waitlist for therapy revealed positive patient-reported feelings about the alliance (Sung et al., 2023). Furthermore, when there is an in-person comparator group, the alliance appears to be roughly equivalent, and this is true across diverse clinical samples (Shaker et al., 2023; Simpson & Reid, 2014; Stubbings et al., 2013; Watts et al., 2020). Marginal differences sometimes appear, but their clinical meaning appears low. For instance, a study of GAD found alliance was higher in the videoconference condition compared to the in-person condition, but only at later sessions (Watts et al., 2020). In a review by Simpson and Reid (2014), the only studies that found an alliance effect in favor of in-person treatment were *group* treatments for non-anxiety related problems. While the evidence, particularly with respect to patient report, has not borne out any consistent problem of alliance in VMIs, therapists have persistently raised concerns about the alliance in telehealth formats. And indeed, there is evidence that therapists may rate the alliance lower than patients do in telehealth (e.g., Watts et al., 2020). Another within-subjects study of 440 therapists (with varying levels of experience) found that therapists consistently rated their ability to deliver common therapeutic skills (e.g., empathy, intentional silence, emotional expression) lower when doing treatment via videoconference compared to in-person treatment (Lin et al., 2021).

Emotional Connection and Presence

Another potential concern, as it relates to engagement in VMIs, is the possibility for diminished emotional connection and lack of sufficient telepresence, which is the perception of being in a shared environment even when the therapist is located in a different place (Berthiaume et al., 2018). Related to concerns about alliance, some have noted that it may be difficult to promote deeper emotional engagement because of impediments to noticing subtler nonverbal cues over telehealth (Wrape & McGinn, 2019) and detecting emotional states (Thomas et al., 2021). Some have raised concerns about the less personal nature of remote interaction and lack of ability to provide physical comfort and reassurance as clinicians might when conducting an in-person session (see Cowan et al., 2019). For instance, one study comparing in-person treatment to remote CBT via videoconference for combat PTSD revealed that patients in the in-person treatment group reported greater comfort with their therapist than those in the telehealth condition (Frueh et al., 2007). There are also reports that some patients may subjectively feel more comfortable discussing certain topics in person (Fletcher et al., 2022; Lindsay et al., 2017). On the other hand, some have commented that VMIs may encourage connection in ways that in-person treatments do not (Kocsis & Yellowlees, 2018) and some may find it less intimidating than in-person therapy (e.g., Fitt & Rees, 2012). Clients may even be more willing to discuss sensitive topics in VMIs (Roddy et al., 2019). Additionally, VMIs may actually facilitate communication by encouraging the participants to actively listen, slow down, and attend closely to what the other is saying (Dunstan & Tooth, 2012; Jerome & Zaylor, 2000). Furthermore, despite initial concerns about telepresence, many reports suggest that high presence can be achieved in VMIs (Ashwick et al., 2019; Bouchard et al., 2004; Goetter et al., 2014; Himle et al., 2006), including during highly emotional conversations (Bouchard et al., 2011).

Environmental Issues

When delivering VMIs, clinicians must also contend with external distractions that threaten to undermine the therapeutic environment, and thus, patient engagement. Due to the limited web camera view, clinicians may fail to detect distractions to the patient such as someone walking into the room or the patient participating in other activities, such as checking their phone, checking their email, looking at a webpage, or playing a game (Goetter et al., 2013). Furthermore, some telehealth patients may lack a quiet private room in their homes to have their sessions (Franklin et al., 2017). This can be true for anyone living with family or roommates but may be particularly problematic for those in lower socioeconomic groups where the patient may experience limitations to their physical space or simultaneous caregiving responsibilities (Falicov et al., 2020). Patients may thus feel uncomfortable discussing personal information due to the fear of a family member or roommate overhearing or entering the room (Song & Foster, 2022). The home environment may also be distracting for patients suffering from home-based and/or family trauma who feel unsafe in their own homes (Song & Foster, 2022). This lack of "safe therapeutic space" may pose a barrier to patient engagement in treatment. Due to privacy or safety concerns, the technology requirements of telehealth, or other logistical considerations, some patients may choose to have their sessions in a location other than their home, such as a work office, conference room in a public library, or even their own parked car (Storch et al., 2011; Yuen et al., 2013).

In-Session Behavioral Exercises

There are both benefits and challenges to engagement for in-session behavioral exercises during VMIs. On one hand, feasibility and treatment outcome studies suggest that in-session exposure for anxiety and related disorders can be implemented effectively during videoconferencing. In fact, several clinical trials show non-inferiority to in-person treatment for CBT interventions that have prominent in-session behavioral components, such as imaginal exposure for PTSD (e.g., Acierno et al., 2016) and interoceptive exposure for panic disorder (Bouchard et al., 2020). Furthermore, exposure-based activities do not appear to weaken the therapeutic alliance in VMIs (Germain et al., 2010). On the other hand, both clinicians and patients have reported unique challenges with respect to engagement in behavioral exercises in VMIs (Song & Foster, 2022).

For certain disorders, engagement can be enhanced by the ability of patients to participate in exposures in the home environment during a videoconference session. For example, may patients with OCD have fears and rituals that occur directly in their own homes. Several studies report that home-based exposure therapy for OCD can be successfully conducted during videoconference sessions (e.g., Goetter et al., 2013; Vogel et al., 2014). Observing patients in their natural home environment also helps therapists notice and better understand the patients' unique triggers and safety behaviors and then tailor the exposure exercises accordingly (Comer et al., 2014; Fletcher et al., 2022). Furthermore, because patients perform in-session exposures without the physical presence of the therapist, and in a "naturalistic environment" where obsessions and rituals are typically present, this can potentially foster generalization of skills to a variety of situations in the patient's domestic life (Comer et al., 2014; Fletcher et al., 2022). Home-based exposures also facilitate engagement of family members in treatment. Although many obsessions and rituals may involve family members (e.g., contamination fears, safety concerns, reassurance-seeking), it can be logistically difficult to schedule in-person sessions with family members present in the office (Goetter et al., 2013). VMIs can make it easier to involve family members in treatment, for both adult and youth patients (Storch et al., 2011).

A challenge to engagement in VMI in-session exposure exercises is that some patients may view the exposures as less realistic and thus less generalizable. This may be particularly true for patients with SAD, where exposure to conversation with strangers via videoconference may feel very different from conversing with strangers in person (Yuen et al., 2013). Thus, with videoconference, there may be missed opportunities for a variety of social situation exposures that in-person treatment would be able to provide (Song & Foster, 2022). On the other hand, mobile videoconference technology (e.g., via smartphone) provides opportunities for the patient to complete in-session exposures with real-life people outside of their home, for example, if they visit a nearby location in their community while their therapist listens in via the videoconference software program (Goetter et al., 2013; Thomas et al., 2021). Therefore, while the videoconference medium may potentially diminish engagement in social exposures in some respects, it may also facilitate engagement for community-based exposures. Overall, clinicians should consider carefully how they might adapt the videoconference modality to enhance engagement in behavioral exercises for their specific patients.

Other challenges to engagement during behavioral exercises include limits on the clinician's ability to visually discern, via the webcam, the patient's level of anxiety (Himle et al., 2006), attentiveness to feared stimuli (Goetter et al., 2013), employment of subtle safety behaviors (Goetter et al., 2013), and deficits in social skills (Yuen et al., 2013). These limits could affect the clinician's ability to give relevant feedback and work these elements into behavioral exercises tailored to the patient. In addition, the absence of the therapist's physical presence could potentially impede the patient's willingness to engage in challenging exposures. For example, during in-person treatment, a clinician can physically walk the patient to an anxiety-provoking location, but during a VMI session, the patient must walk themselves (Goetter et al., 2013). Furthermore, therapist modeling is an important component in treatment for some disorders, such as OCD, but this may be difficult to do with the therapist in a different physical location (Comer et al., 2014).

Written/Visual Collaboration

Another reported engagement challenge stems from the lack of ability to share physical materials during VMIs. For example, during in-person treatment, many clinicians rely on pen-and-paper or a whiteboard during the clinical formation process, delivery of psychoeducation, or the creation of a fear hierarchy. This promotes a collaborative experience with the patient. In addition, many patients handwrite their homework into forms given to them by their therapist. Collaboration and information exchange can feel threatened when in different physical locations and unable to utilize a shared whiteboard, write on the same paper, and/or directly read homework that is physically handed over by the patient (Fletcher et al., 2022; Song & Foster, 2022).

Technological Issues and Technological Literacy

Technological issues may undermine treatment engagement in VMIs and have been identified as a concern by both patients and clinicians (Petersen et al., 2020). Technical problems include variable Internet speeds, poor video quality, audio delays, and occasional disconnections, all of which can be disruptive to the flow of session (Lin et al., 2021; Turgoose et al., 2018). For instance, a therapist may inadvertently interrupt a patient while they are still speaking, a client may not be able to identify a therapeutic versus disrupted silence, or a session may be inadvertently ended due to poor Internet connection, which can cause frustration for both patient and therapist and threaten treatment engagement (Lin et al., 2021; McClelland et al., 2024). Technological literacy is a related concern. If patients do not feel experienced enough with the platform, they may become frustrated with the technology and disengage (McClelland et al., 2024). Moreover, if the usability of these platforms is low, i.e., the technology is cumbersome to figure out or difficult to use, then issues of technological literacy can be amplified.

Despite concerns about technological literacy, Price and Gros (2014) found that confidence and prior familiarity with videoconference technology was not related to treatment outcome in a study with Veterans with PTSD. Furthermore, the research literature suggests that encountering technical problems does not significantly reduce treatment outcome or patient satisfaction (Thomas et al., 2021; Turgoose et al., 2018). A learning curve is commonly observed, where technical difficulties decrease over time as both patients and therapists become more adept at using and managing the videoconference technology (Connolly et al., 2020; Yuen et al., 2013). For example, patients learn how to manage their microphone volume, their camera position and on/off status, and troubleshoot problematic Internet connection (Yuen et al., 2015). As digital technologies continue to grow and become more accessible, technological literacy may also increase in the population, rendering patients more adept at managing videoconference technology (Thomas et al., 2021).

Evidence of Engagement

Evidence on treatment outcomes in VMIs has exceeded research on treatment engagement processes. For instance, few randomized controlled studies have directly compared videoconference to in-person treatment for anxiety disorders, and those that have only sometimes analyzed potential differences in engagement-related variables such as dropout rates, session attendance, and homework adherence. Research comparing engagement-related variables between VMIs and in-person treatment is scarce for anxiety and related disorders. Furthermore, most published RCTs comparing VMIs with in-person treatment have occurred with Veteran participants diagnosed with PTSD. In addition, research on moderators of treatment engagement, (e.g., patient preference, technological literacy) is very limited. Below, we attempt to summarize key findings of the most reported variables reflective of treatment engagement.

Dropout

Dropout rates in VMIs are highly variable and imprecise (Berryhill et al., 2019) and definitions of dropout vary widely based on study. RCTs of Veterans with PTSD have consistently found similar dropout rates between patients who receive videoconference versus comparable in-person treatment (Turgoose et al., 2018). An exception is that Morland et al. (2020) found lower dropout rates for patients who received PE in person compared to home-based or office-based videoconference. Bouchard et al. (2020) found no significant differences in dropout rates between patients who received CBT for panic disorder in person versus through office-based videoconference. Comer et al. (2017) also found no differences in retention for family-based CBT to treat pediatric OCD through videoconference versus in-person. A small RCT with a mixed diagnostic sample (primarily anxiety/mood disorders) found similar retention rates for patients receiving CBT through videoconference versus in person (Stubbings et al., 2013). In a nonrandomized post-COVID trial in Spain, no differences in dropout rates were found between videoconference and in-person treatment in a mixed sample of patients with anxiety, depression, and/or trauma (Fernández-Regueras et al., 2023).

Attendance

RCTs with Veterans with PTSD have consistently found no significant differences in number of sessions attended between VMI and in-person treatment (e.g., Acierno et al., 2021; Liu et al., 2020; Morland et al., 2015). An exception is the Morland et al. (2020) study where in-person patients attended more PE sessions compared to office-based telehealth patients. No significant differences in attendance rates were found in the nonrandomized Fernández-Regueras et al. (2023) study of mixed patients who received videoconference or in-person treatment. Valentine et al. (2020) found that greater anxiety severity was associated with lower attendance for Veterans receiving VMIs, with some of the patients receiving home-based telehealth and others office-based telehealth. This same study also found that attendance was not correlated to demographic variables such as age, gender, race, marital status, or service era.

Homework

Most studies that analyzed homework adherence in Veterans with PTSD found no significant differences between videoconference and in-person treatment (Liu et al., 2020; Turgoose et al., 2018). An exception is that Frueh et al. (2007) found that Veterans receiving treatment via videoconference had lower homework adherence rates compared to those receiving in-person treatment. No significant differences in homework completion rates were found in the nonrandomized Fernández-Regueras et al. (2023) study of mixed-diagnosis patients.

Patient Satisfaction

VMI studies for PTSD have consistently found high levels of patient satisfaction and acceptability, with no significant differences between videoconference and in-person ratings of satisfaction (Scott et al., 2022; Thomas et al., 2021; Turgoose et al., 2018). A meta-analysis by Shaker et al. (2023) also found no differences in satisfaction between telemedicine and in-person treatments for patients with a mix of PTSD, mood, anxiety, and personality disorders. A randomized controlled trial with GAD patients also found no significant differences in patient satisfaction between those who received CBT in-person versus office-based videoconference (Bouchard et al., 2022).

Clinical Considerations

As clinicians consider the aforementioned challenges to engagement in VMIs and the supporting evidence, they may naturally wonder: *What does ideal engagement look like in this format? What can we, as clinicians, do to foster patient engagement in videoconference-mediated CBT for anxiety and related conditions?* We outline several suggestions below:

Foster Positive Expectations for Videoconference and Consider Patient Variables to Facilitate Uptake

Clinicians can encourage engagement by using positive language and presenting telehealth as an appealing option when describing the videoconference modality to potential patients (Tuerk et al., 2010). Note that some patients may be more willing to participate in VMIs as opposed to in-person treatment, which has implications for engagement. The convenience of VMIs, greater scheduling flexibility, and reductions in travel-related anxiety may increase motivation to participate in therapy for some (Song & Foster, 2022). VMIs may also reduce barriers associated with physically presenting at a clinic. For instance, some female Veterans may have hesitations receiving treatment in-person with programs that have predominantly male patients (Jaconis et al., 2017). Although VMIs have the potential to increase treatment uptake, this option may be less accessible to those with severe mental illness and populations without access to high-speed Internet and computer technology (Klee et al., 2016). Additionally, the therapist might consider how patient motivation and commitment to therapy may be affected by the videoconference modality and be sure to stress the importance of attendance and engagement with both in-session and between-session exercises (Vogel et al., 2014). When considering the appropriateness of videoconference-mediated CBT, a therapist may wish to gather information about the patient's access to private spaces, access to requisite equipment (e.g., high-speed Internet), the home environment, and any concerns related to motivation and the therapeutic alliance. Information gathered may help the therapist determine the optimal balance of videoconference to in-person care (Song & Foster, 2022).

Promote a Positive Therapeutic Alliance and Encourage Emotional Expression to Facilitate Patient Engagement

Clinicians are encouraged to actively attend to the alliance but should be reassured by the research that suggests it can be strongly developed in VMIs. There is no evidence to suggest that therapists should delay starting active treatment in VMIs in favor of specific alliance building activities. In many ways, alliance building-efforts during videoconference sessions will mimic what is done in in-person formats. However, clinicians are encouraged to be intentional about attending to patient behaviors and recognize that subtler nonverbal behaviors will be harder for therapists and patients to discern.

Clinicians should also actively work to facilitate emotional expression. Emotional disclosures appear to be associated with greater telepresence, which should facilitate engagement (Bouchard et al., 2011). To further encourage emotional connection and engagement, both clinicians and patients should position their web cameras strategically, keeping the torso and face in view, and choose a location where lighting is favorable for image transmission (Springer et al., 2025). On the clinician's screen, the patient's video image should be positioned close to the webcam so that, from the patient's perspective, the clinician appears to be making eye contact (Yuen et al., 2013). The clinician could also pan their webcam across their office at the beginning of the session (or at least upon treatment initiation), to assure patients that the session is private, and hopefully increase their comfort level in discussing personal topics. (Springer et al., 2025). Clinicians might consider assessing telepresence using established measures, such as the Telepresence in Videoconference Scale (TVS; Berthiaume et al., 2018).

Consider the Usability of the Technology and Troubleshoot Technological Issues in a Timely Manner

Clinicians who deliver treatment via videoconference will, at times, find themselves also serving in a technical support role. Clinicians must become well versed in the technology so they can prevent inevitable technical disruptions from undermining engagement. Therapists may need to provide training in the technology to patients *before* the start of the first official therapy session (e.g., Acierno et al., 2016; Goetter et al., 2014), including how to troubleshoot potential technical problems (Yuen et al., 2013). It is also important to test the patient's Internet connection to make sure it can support the bandwidth and consistency required for smooth videoconference (Goetter et al., 2013). In the face of disruptive Internet connection, workarounds can be employed, such as switching to telephone instead of video, or using an Ethernet cord instead of wireless connection (Goetter et al., 2013; Yuen et al., 2013). In Hub and Spoke models where patients travel in person to a satellite clinic to videoconference, it is helpful to have staff on hand to provide technical assistance if needed (Liu et al., 2020). In addition, patients should be encouraged to speak up and verbalize any technical problems interfering with the session so that the therapist can provide assistance and adjust the session accordingly (Yuen et al., 2012).

Leverage the Technology to Support Engagement in CBT

Although lack of physical proximity can pose some challenges, clinicians can compensate for the lack of shared physical materials by utilizing various technical features of their videoconference or other software program for collaboration or information exchange. These features include screen sharing, shared documents (digitally stored and which both parties can edit simultaneously), shared digital whiteboards, file upload/download capabilities, and chatrooms (Song & Foster, 2022; Thomas et al., 2021). Telehealth clinicians can also share handouts and receive homework via emails and attachments (Song & Foster, 2022). As such, technological features can be utilized to promote collaboration and patient engagement.

In some cases, the technology may enhance treatment engagement, if leveraged appropriately. For example, in the case of exposure therapy for SAD, behavioral experiments can be recorded via the videoconference program and then played back for the patient to evaluate the effects of employing or refraining from safety behaviors during conversation (Song & Foster, 2022). Therapists may also benefit from having a session outline on their computer screen to organize the session, maintain structure, and ensure protocol fidelity (Goetter et al., 2013).

Set up the Therapeutic Environment for Success

Therapists using VMIs must actively work to minimize distractions and ensure that sessions are being conducted in a manner that optimizes patient engagement. It is recommended that clinicians have a clear discussion with patients at the onset of therapy about potential environmental issues and distractors (Goetter et al., 2013). Boundaries and expectations should be clearly set with regard to behavior that could undermine engagement, e.g., checking phone, eating food, lying in bed, or smoking. Therapists must also consider their patient's situation and determine what locations are acceptable for sessions (e.g., in home, in car, in a private space in a public setting), being mindful of and responsive to social and economic factors that may impede the patient's ability to access remote treatment. The discussion should also include the optimal day, time, and location for the patient to have sessions, as well as how to prepare their physical space beforehand (Springer et al., 2025). For example, family members or roommates can be asked to stay away, activities can be set up for children in another room, a noise machine can be set up outside the door, a "do not disturb" sign can be affixed, and the door can be locked if possible (Springer et al., 2025). The patient should also strategically choose their location within their room so that seating is comfortable but not distracting (e.g., avoid swivel chairs and the bed if possible).

Plan Ahead for Exposures

In addition to creating a successful virtual therapeutic environment, therapists must also ensure that exposures are conducted in a strategic manner to ensure optimal effectiveness. Clinicians should consider carefully how they might adapt the videoconference modality to enhance engagement in behavioral exercises for their specific patients. Therapists will need to plan in advance to adequately prepare for in-session exposures, especially if patients are restricted to the home environment (Song & Foster, 2022). Pre-session preparation can facilitate therapist modeling of the exposure during VMIs for example, having both therapist and patient gather feared stimuli in advance, such as specific objects, chemicals, or fluids (Himle et al., 2006). Clinicians can also promote engagement by offering verbal reinforcement before, during, and after the exposures (Himle et al., 2006). Therapists must also be prepared to proactively discuss with patients how avoidance and safety behaviors may interfere with treatment engagement and effectiveness (e.g., Valentine et al., 2020).

Future Research Directions

An accumulating body of research suggests that VMIs for anxiety and related disorders are noninferior to in-person treatment formats. However, except for research on CBT for PTSD in Veteran and military samples, there have been a surprising low number of randomized controlled studies making direct comparisons between telehealth and in-person formats. Even in studies that have made direct comparisons, home-based telehealth is underrepresented for some populations (e.g., panic disorder, GAD) relative to office-based telehealth where patients must travel to a clinic to videoconference. Additionally, group therapy is underrepresented relative to individual therapy, and behavioral therapies with an exposure component may be overrepresented relative to more cognitively-focused CBTs (see Thomas et al., 2021). As such, future research must include a greater number of controlled studies across diverse formats and intervention types with patients in geographically different locations. Future research must also actively work to include underrepresented populations, including civilians with PTSD, those with minoritized racial and ethnic identities, and individuals from lower socioeconomic groups. As has been noted, many of those experiencing economic marginalization or those in rural areas (who are perhaps most in need of remote options to see to specialist providers) may experience the greatest disparities with respect to technology access (Comer et al., 2014). Relatedly, most of the VMI research to date is in higher income countries. Future research should investigate the feasibility and efficacy of these methods in globally underrepresented areas (Turgoose et al., 2018).

While controlled studies are few, even fewer studies have systematically examined dropout and other engagement proxies (e.g., attendance, homework adherence) in comparative trials. Such information would be useful to understand the nuances of videoconference with respect to the treatment engagement process. Additionally, as some have noted, such research could also consider pre-treatment patient variables (e.g., motivation, modality preference) or intervention characteristics (e.g., therapeutic alliance, intervention type) that might be associated with engagement and retention in telehealth (Valentine et al., 2020). For instance, as others have speculated, due to cognitive dissonance, patients may be less motivated to prepare for a videoconference session because the convenience requires less effort and commitment to attend, while the logistical efforts required for in-person treatment may thus have a positive impact on motivation (Vogel et al., 2014). Additionally, there are other technology features—including text messaging, supplemental mobile apps, and online peer and community support—that could be evaluated with respect to their potential for enhancing treatment engagement in VMIs (Feusner et al., 2022).

The COVID-19 pandemic was associated with a widespread uptake and normalization of telehealth communication, in both the healthcare and greater social milieu. Updated research on VMIs for anxiety and related disorders is needed in light of changes to how individuals engage with digital technology in the contemporary social and cultural context. Anecdotally, the ubiquity of videoconference technology has been associated with greater patient and provider comfort with telehealth as a method of treatment, which is consistent with prior speculation that more usage would lead to more positive attitudes (Connolly et al., 2020; Thomas et al., 2021). Additionally, for research studies that reported on videoconference treatments delivered in the midst of the COVID-19 panic, results may be confounded by the universal shared experience of a global health crisis, which may have affected how patients engaged in VMIs during this time period (Davis et al., 2024). Thus, it is necessary to have an updated understanding of the outcomes and engagement processes associated with telehealth for anxiety and related disorders for VMIs delivered during post-pandemic times. VMIs have demonstrated widespread effectiveness and acceptability, but additional research in these areas will enhance our understanding of how best to optimize this technology to encourage engagement in evidence-based treatment for anxiety and related disorders.

Clinical Summary Points and Recommendations

- Videoconference may be particularly appealing to individuals with anxiety and related disorders, particularly among those for whom stigma, fears of social evaluation, fears of uncertainty, interpersonal avoidance, hypervigilance or fears of traveling far from home may pose a specific barrier.
- Evidence suggests that videoconference-mediated CBT is effective for treating anxiety and related disorders and, in many cases, is noninferior to in-person treatment. However, research on treatment engagement proxies between in-person and videoconference-mediated CBT (e.g., dropout, homework adherence, and session attendance) is scarce, limiting firm conclusions in this regard.
- Clinicians must attend to potential engagement challenges that may arise in videoconference treatments including working alliance, difficulty being present or emotionally engaged in treatment, technological disruptions, low technological literacy, competition with external distractions (particularly in home-based videoconference formats), and loss of control over the therapeutic environment.

References

Acierno, R., Gros, D. F., Ruggiero, K. J., Hernandez-Tejada, M. A., Knapp, R. G., Lejuez, C. W., Muzzy, W., Frueh, C. B., Egede, L. E., & Tuerk, P. W. (2016). Behavioral activation and therapeutic exposure for posttraumatic stress disorder: A noninferiority trial of treatment delivered in person versus home-based telehealth. *Depression and Anxiety, 33*(5), 415–423. https://doi.org/10.1002/da.22476

Acierno, R., Jaffe, A. E., Gilmore, A. K., Birks, A., Denier, C., Muzzy, W., Lopez, C. M., Tuerk, P., & Grubaugh, A. L. (2021). A randomized clinical trial of in-person vs. home-based telemedicine delivery of prolonged exposure for PTSD in military sexual trauma survivors. *Journal of Anxiety Disorders, 83*, 102461. https://doi.org/10.1016/j.janxdis.2021.102461

Acierno, R., Knapp, R., Tuerk, P., Gilmore, A. K., Lejuez, C., Ruggiero, K., Muzzy, W., Egede, L., Hernandez-Tejada, M. A., & Foa, E. B. (2017). A non-inferiority trial of prolonged exposure for posttraumatic stress disorder: In person versus home-based telehealth. *Behaviour Research and Therapy, 89*, 57–65. https://doi.org/10.1016/j.brat.2016.11.009

Ashwick, R., Turgoose, D., & Murphy, D. (2019). Exploring the acceptability of delivering cognitive processing therapy (CPT) to UK veterans with PTSD over skype: A qualitative study. *European Journal of Psychotraumatology, 10*(1), 1573128. https://doi.org/10.1080/20008198.2019.1573128

Berryhill, M. B., Halli-Tierney, A., Culmer, N., Williams, N., Betancourt, A., King, M., & Ruggles, H. (2018). Videoconferencing psychological therapy and anxiety: A systematic review. *Family Practice, 36*(1), 53–63. https://doi.org/10.1093/fampra/cmy072

Berryhill, M. B., Halli-Tierney, A., Culmer, N., Williams, N., Betancourt, A., King, M., & Ruggles, H. (2019). Videoconferencing psychological therapy and anxiety: A systematic review. *Family Practice, 36*(1), 53–63. https://doi.org/10.1093/fampra/cmy072

Berthiaume, M., Bouchard, S., Brisebois, C., & Robillard, G. (2018). The validation of a telepresence scale for psychotherapy delivered in videoconference. *Annual Review of Cybertherapy and Telemedicine, 16*, 131–136.

Bouchard, S., Allard, M., Robillard, G., Dumoulin, S., Guitard, T., Loranger, C., Green-Demers, I., Marchand, A., Renaud, P., Cournoyer, L.-G., & Corno, G. (2020). Videoconferencing psychotherapy for panic disorder and agoraphobia: Outcome and treatment processes from a non-randomized non-inferiority trial. *Frontiers in Psychology, 11*, 2164. https://doi.org/10.3389/fpsyg.2020.02164

Bouchard, S., Dugas, M. J., Belleville, G., Langlois, F., Gosselin, P., Robillard, G., Corno, G., & Marchand, A. (2022). A multisite non-inferiority randomized controlled trial of the efficacy of cognitive-behavior therapy for generalized anxiety disorder delivered by videoconference. *Journal of Clinical Medicine, 11*(19), 5924. https://doi.org/10.3390/jcm11195924

Bouchard, S., Dumoulin, S., Michaud, M., & Gougeon, V. (2011). Telepresence experienced in videoconference varies according to emotions involved in videoconference sessions. In *Annual review of cybertherapy and telemedicine 2011* (pp. 128-132).

Bouchard, S., Paquin, B., Payeur, R., Allard, M., Rivard, V., Fournier, T., Renaud, P., & Lapierre, J. (2004). Delivering cognitive-behavior therapy for panic disorder with agoraphobia in videoconference. *Telemedicine Journal and E-Health, 10*(1), 13–25. https://doi.org/10.1089/153056204773644545

Cherestal, S., Schare, M. L., Grimaldi, S., Costello, K., & DeJesus, C. (2021). Remotely conducted versus office-based virtual reality treatment for aviophobia: Questions of feasibility and accessibility. *Translational Issues in Psychological Science, 7*(3), 218–228. https://doi.org/10.1037/tps0000303

Comer, J. S., Furr, J. M., Cooper-Vince, C. E., Kerns, C. E., Chan, P. T., Edson, A. L., Khanna, M., Franklin, M. E., Garcia, A. M., & Freeman, J. B. (2014). Internet-delivered, family-based treatment for early-onset OCD: A preliminary case series. *Journal of Clinical Child & Adolescent Psychology, 43*(1), 74–87. https://doi.org/10.1080/15374416.2013.855127

Comer, J. S., Furr, J. M., del Busto, C., Silva, K., Hong, N., Poznanski, B., Sanchez, A., Cornacchio, D., Herrera, A., Coxe, S., Miguel, E., Georgiadis, C., Conroy, K., & Puliafico, A. (2021). Therapist-led, internet-delivered treatment for early child social anxiety: A waitlist-controlled evaluation of the iCALM telehealth program. *Behavior Therapy, 52*(5), 1171–1187. https://doi.org/10.1016/j.beth.2021.01.004

Comer, J. S., Furr, J. M., Kerns, C. E., Miguel, E., Coxe, S., Elkins, R. M., Carpenter, A. L., Cornacchio, D., Cooper-Vince, C. E., DeSerisy, M., Chou, T., Sanchez, A. L., Khanna, M., Franklin, M. E., Garcia, A. M., & Freeman, J. B. (2017). Internet-delivered, family-based treatment for early-onset OCD: A pilot randomized trial. *Journal of Consulting and Clinical Psychology, 85*(2), 178–186. https://doi.org/10.1037/ccp0000155

Connolly, S. L., Miller, C. J., Lindsay, J. A., & Bauer, M. S. (2020). A systematic review of providers' attitudes toward telemental health via videoconferencing. *Clinical Psychology: Science and Practice, 27*(2), e12311. https://doi.org/10.1111/cpsp.12311

Cowan, K. E., McKean, A. J., Gentry, M. T., & Hilty, D. M. (2019). Barriers to use of telepsychiatry: Clinicians as gatekeepers. *Mayo Clinic Proceedings, 94*(12), 2510–2523. https://doi.org/10.1016/j.mayocp.2019.04.018

Davis, K. A., Zhao, F., Janis, R. A., Castonguay, L. G., Hayes, J. A., & Scofield, B. E. (2024). Therapeutic alliance and clinical outcomes in teletherapy and in-person psychotherapy: A non-inferiority study during the COVID-19 pandemic. *Psychotherapy Research, 34*(5), 589–600. https://doi.org/10.1080/10503307.2023.2229505

Dunstan, D. A., & Tooth, S. M. (2012). Treatment via videoconferencing: A pilot study of delivery by clinical psychology trainees. *Australian Journal of Rural Health, 20*(2), 88–94. https://doi.org/10.1111/j.1440-1584.2012.01260.x

Falicov, C., Nino, A., & D'Urso, S. (2020). Expanding possibilities: Flexibility and solidarity with under-resourced immigrant families during the COVID-19 pandemic. *Family Process, 59*(3), 865–882. https://doi.org/10.1111/famp.12578

Fernández-Regueras, D., Calero-Elvira, A., & Guerrero-Escagedo, M. C. (2023). Comparison of clinical indicators between face-to-face and videoconferencing psychotherapy: Success,

adherence to treatment and efficiency. *Behavioral Psychology/Psicología Conductual, 31*(3), 543–562. https://doi.org/10.51668/bp.8323306n
Feusner, J. D., Farrell, N. R., Kreyling, J., McGrath, P. B., Rhode, A., Faneuff, T., Lonsway, S., Mohideen, R., Jurich, J. E., Trusky, L., & Smith, S. M. (2022). Online video teletherapy treatment of obsessive-compulsive disorder using exposure and response prevention: Clinical outcomes from a retrospective longitudinal observational study. *Journal of Medical Internet Research, 24*(5), e36431. https://doi.org/10.2196/36431
Fitt, S., & Rees, C. (2012). Metacognitive therapy for obsessive compulsive disorder by videoconference: A preliminary study. *Behaviour Change, 29*(4), 213–229. https://doi.org/10.1017/bec.2012.21
Fletcher, T. L., Boykin, D. M., Helm, A., Dawson, D. B., Ecker, A. H., Freshour, J., Teng, E., Lindsay, J., & Hundt, N. E. (2022). A pilot open trial of video telehealth-delivered exposure and response prevention for obsessive-compulsive disorder in rural veterans. *Military Psychology, 34*(1), 83–90. https://doi.org/10.1080/08995605.2021.1970983
Franklin, C. L., Cuccurullo, L.-A., Walton, J. L., Arseneau, J. R., & Petersen, N. J. (2017). Face to face but not in the same place: A pilot study of prolonged exposure therapy. *Journal of Trauma & Dissociation, 18*(1), 116–130. https://doi.org/10.1080/15299732.2016.1205704
Frueh, B. C., Monnier, J., Yim, E., Grubaugh, A. L., Hamner, M. B., & Knapp, R. G. (2007). A randomized trial of telepsychiatry for post-traumatic stress disorder. *Journal of Telemedicine and Telecare, 13*(3), 142–147. https://doi.org/10.1258/135763307780677604
Germain, V., Marchand, A., Bouchard, S., Guay, S., & Drouin, M.-S. (2010). Assessment of the therapeutic alliance in face-to-face or videoconference treatment for posttraumatic stress disorder. *Cyberpsychology, Behavior, and Social Networking, 13*(1), 29–35. https://doi.org/10.1089/cyber.2009.013
Goetter, E. M., Herbert, J. D., Forman, E. M., Yuen, E. K., Gershkovich, M., Glassman, L. H., Rabin, S. J., & Goldstein, S. P. (2013). Delivering exposure and ritual prevention for obsessive–compulsive disorder via videoconference: Clinical considerations and recommendations. *Journal of Obsessive-Compulsive and Related Disorders, 2*(2), 137–145. https://doi.org/10.1016/j.jocrd.2013.01.003
Goetter, E. M., Herbert, J. D., Forman, E. M., Yuen, E. K., & Thomas, J. G. (2014). An open trial of videoconference-mediated exposure and ritual prevention for obsessive-compulsive disorder. *Journal of Anxiety Disorders, 28*(5), 460–462. https://doi.org/10.1016/j.janxdis.2014.05.004
Goetter, E. M., & Yuen, E. K. (2024). Technological advances in treating anxiety disorders. *Psychiatric Clinics, 47*(4), 813–827. https://doi.org/10.1016/j.psc.2024.04.020
Himle, J. A., Fischer, D. J., Muroff, J. R., Van Etten, M. L., Lokers, L. M., Abelson, J. L., & Hanna, G. L. (2006). Videoconferencing-based cognitive-behavioral therapy for obsessive-compulsive disorder. *Behaviour Research and Therapy, 44*(12), 1821–1829. https://doi.org/10.1016/j.brat.2005.12.010
Jaconis, M., Santa Ana, E. J., Killeen, T. K., Badour, C. L., & Back, S. E. (2017). Concurrent treatment of PTSD and alcohol use disorder via telehealth in a female Iraq veteran. *The American Journal on Addictions, 26*(2), 112–114. https://doi.org/10.1111/ajad.12481
Jerome, L. W., & Zaylor, C. (2000). Cyberspace: Creating a therapeutic environment for telehealth applications. *Professional Psychology: Research and Practice, 31*(5), 478. https://doi.org/10.1037/0735-7028.31.5.478
Kelber, M. S., Smolenski, D. J., Boyd, C., Shank, L. M., Bellanti, D. M., Milligan, T., Edwards-Stewart, A., Libretto, S., Parisi, K., Morgan, M. A., & Evatt, D. P. (2024). Evidence-based telehealth interventions for posttraumatic stress disorder, depression, and anxiety: A systematic review and meta-analysis. *Journal of Telemedicine and Telecare, 0*(0), 1357633X231224491. https://doi.org/10.1177/1357633x231224491
Klee, A., Stacy, M., Rosenheck, R., Harkness, L., & Tsai, J. (2016). Interest in technology-based therapies hampered by access: A survey of veterans with serious mental illnesses. *Psychiatric Rehabilitation Journal, 39*(2), 173–179. https://doi.org/10.1037/prj0000180

Kocsis, B. J., & Yellowlees, P. (2018). Telepsychotherapy and the therapeutic relationship: Principles, advantages, and case examples. *Telemedicine and e-Health, 24*(5), 329–334. https://doi.org/10.1089/tmj.2017.00

Krzyzaniak, N., Greenwood, H., Scott, A. M., Peiris, R., Cardona, M., Clark, J., & Glasziou, P. (2024). The effectiveness of telehealth versus face-to face interventions for anxiety disorders: A systematic review and meta-analysis. *Journal of Telemedicine and Telecare, 30*(2), 250–261. https://doi.org/10.1177/1357633x211053738

Lin, T., Stone, S. J., Heckman, T. G., & Anderson, T. (2021). Zoom-in to zone-out: Therapists report less therapeutic skill in telepsychology versus face-to-face therapy during the COVID-19 pandemic. *Psychotherapy, 58*(4), 449–459. https://doi.org/10.1037/pst0000398

Lindsay, J. A., Hudson, S., Martin, L., Hogan, J. B., Nessim, M., Graves, L., Gabriele, J., & White, D. (2017). Implementing video to home to increase access to evidence-based psychotherapy for rural veterans. *Journal of Technology in Behavioral Science, 2*, 140–148. https://doi.org/10.1007/s41347-017-0032-4

Liu, L., Thorp, S. R., Moreno, L., Wells, S. Y., Glassman, L. H., Busch, A. C., Zamora, T., Rodgers, C. S., Allard, C. B., Morland, L. A., & Agha, Z. (2020). Videoconferencing psychotherapy for veterans with PTSD: Results from a randomized controlled non-inferiority trial. *Journal of Telemedicine and Telecare, 26*(9), 507–519. https://doi.org/10.1177/1357633x19853947

Maieritsch, K. P., Smith, T. L., Hessinger, J. D., Ahearn, E. P., Eickhoff, J. C., & Zhao, Q. (2016). Randomized controlled equivalence trial comparing videoconference and in person delivery of cognitive processing therapy for PTSD. *Journal of Telemedicine and Telecare, 22*(4), 238–243. https://doi.org/10.1177/1357633x15596109

Manchanda, M., & McLaren, P. (1998). Cognitive behaviour therapy via interactive video. *Journal of Telemedicine and Telecare, 4*(1), 53–55. https://doi.org/10.1258/135763398193145

McClelland, B., Ponting, C., Levy, C., Mah, R., Moran, P., Sobhani, N. C., & Felder, J. (2024). Viewpoint: Challenges and strategies for engaging participants in videoconferencing appointments. *Contemporary Clinical Trials, 137*, 107425. https://doi.org/10.1016/j.cct.2023.107425

Milosevic, I., Cameron, D. H., Milanovic, M., McCabe, R. E., & Rowa, K. (2022). Face-to-face versus video teleconference group cognitive behavioural therapy for anxiety and related disorders: A preliminary comparison. *The Canadian Journal of Psychiatry, 67*(5), 391–402. https://doi.org/10.1177/07067437211027319

Morland, L. A., Mackintosh, M.-A., Glassman, L. H., Wells, S. Y., Thorp, S. R., Rauch, S. A. M., Cunningham, P. B., Tuerk, P. W., Grubbs, K. M., Golshan, S., Sohn, M. J., & Acierno, R. (2020). Home-based delivery of variable length prolonged exposure therapy: A comparison of clinical efficacy between service modalities. *Depression and Anxiety, 37*(4), 346–355. https://doi.org/10.1002/da.22979

Morland, L. A., Mackintosh, M.-A., Rosen, C. S., Willis, E., Resick, P., Chard, K., & Frueh, B. C. (2015). Telemedicine versus in-person delivery of cognitive processing therapy for women with posttraumatic stress disorder: A randomized noninferiority trial. *Depression and Anxiety, 32*(11), 811–820. https://doi.org/10.1002/da.22397

Nauphal, M., Swetlitz, C., Smith, L., & Rosellini, A. J. (2021). A preliminary examination of the acceptability, feasibility, and effectiveness of a telehealth cognitive-behavioral therapy group for social anxiety disorder. *Cognitive and Behavioral Practice, 28*(4), 730–742. https://doi.org/10.1016/j.cbpra.2021.04.011

Petersen, D., Salazar, B., & Kertz, S. J. (2020). Therapist and treatment-seeking students' perceptions of telemental health. *Journal of Technology in Behavioral Science, 5*(2), 113–120. https://doi.org/10.1007/s41347-019-00116-8

Peterson, A. L., Mintz, J., Moring, J. C., Straud, C. L., Young-McCaughan, S., McGeary, C. A., McGeary, D. D., Litz, B. T., Velligan, D. I., Macdonald, A., Mata-Galan, E., Holliday, S. L., Dillon, K. H., Roache, J. D., Bira, L. M., Nabity, P. S., Medellin, E. M., Hale, W. J., & Resick, P. A. (2022). In-office, in-home, and telehealth cognitive processing therapy for posttraumatic stress disorder in veterans: A randomized clinical trial. *BMC Psychiatry, 22*(1), 41. https://doi.org/10.1186/s12888-022-03699-4

Pineda, B. S., Mejia, R., Qin, Y., Martinez, J., Delgadillo, L. G., & Muñoz, R. F. (2023). Updated taxonomy of digital mental health interventions: A conceptual framework. *mHealth, 9*, 28. https://doi.org/10.21037/mhealth-23-6

Price, M., & Gros, D. F. (2014). Examination of prior experience with telehealth and comfort with telehealth technology as a moderator of treatment response for PTSD and depression in veterans. *The International Journal of Psychiatry in Medicine, 48*(1), 57–67. https://doi.org/10.2190/PM.48.1.e

Przeworski, A., & Newman, M. G. (2006). Efficacy and utility of computer-assisted cognitive behavioural therapy for anxiety disorders. *Clinical Psychologist, 10*(2), 43–53. https://doi.org/10.1080/13284200500378779

Rees, C. S., & Maclaine, E. (2015). A systematic review of videoconference-delivered psychological treatment for anxiety disorders. *Australian Psychologist, 50*(4), 259–264. https://doi.org/10.1111/ap.12122

Roddy, M. K., Rothman, K., Cicila, L. N., & Doss, B. D. (2019). Why do couples seek relationship help online? Description and comparison to in-person interventions. *Journal of Marital and Family Therapy, 45*(3), 369–379. https://doi.org/10.1111/jmft.12329

Scott, A. M., Bakhit, M., Greenwood, H., Cardona, M., Clark, J., Krzyzaniak, N., Peiris, R., & Glasziou, P. (2022). Real-time telehealth versus face-to-face management for patients with PTSD in primary care: A systematic review and meta-analysis. *The Journal of Clinical Psychiatry, 83*(4), 41146.

Shaker, A. A., Austin, S. F., Storebø, O. J., Schaug, J. P., Ayad, A., Sørensen, J. A., Tarp, K., Bechmann, H., & Simonsen, E. (2023). Psychiatric treatment conducted via telemedicine versus in-person modality in posttraumatic stress disorder, mood disorders, and anxiety disorders: Systematic review and meta-analysis. *JMIR Ment Health, 10*, e44790. https://doi.org/10.2196/44790

Simpson, S. G., & Reid, C. L. (2014). Therapeutic alliance in videoconferencing psychotherapy: A review. *Australian Journal of Rural Health, 22*(6), 280–299. https://doi.org/10.1111/ajr.12149

Song, L.-L., & Foster, C. (2022). Patients' and therapists' experiences of CBT videoconferencing in anxiety disorders. *The Cognitive Behaviour Therapist, 15*, e14. https://doi.org/10.1017/S1754470X22000083

Springer, P. R., Taylor, N. C., & Bischoff, R. J. (2025). Managing multiple therapeutic environments. In R. A. Cobb (Ed.), *The therapist's notebook for systemic teletherapy* (pp. 11–17). Routledge. https://doi.org/10.4324/9781003289920-3

Storch, E. A., Caporino, N. E., Morgan, J. R., Lewin, A. B., Rojas, A., Brauer, L., Larson, M. J., & Murphy, T. K. (2011). Preliminary investigation of web-camera delivered cognitive-behavioral therapy for youth with obsessive-compulsive disorder. *Psychiatry Research, 189*(3), 407–412. https://doi.org/10.1016/j.psychres.2011.05.047

Stubbings, D. R., Rees, C. S., Roberts, L. D., & Kane, R. T. (2013). Comparing in-person to videoconference-based cognitive behavioral therapy for mood and anxiety disorders: Randomized controlled trial. *Journal of Medical Internet Research, 15*(11), e258. https://doi.org/10.2196/jmir.2564

Sung, J., Bugatti, M., Vivian, D., & Schleider, J. (2023). Evaluating a telehealth single-session consultation service for clients on psychotherapy wait-lists. *PsyArXiv*. https://doi.org/10.31234/osf.io/k7u4r

Tarhan, G., Örsal, Ö., & Duru, P. (2023). The effect of telehealth interventions on anxiety management in the COVID-19 pandemic: A systematic review. *Journal of Psychiatric Nursing, 14*(1), 59–69. https://doi.org/10.14744/phd.2022.00378

Théberge-Lapointe, N., Marchand, A., Langlois, F., Gosselin, P., & Watts, S. (2015). Efficacy of a cognitive-behavioural therapy administered by videoconference for generalized anxiety disorder. *European Review of Applied Psychology, 65*(1), 9–17. https://doi.org/10.1016/j.erap.2014.10.001

Thomas, N., McDonald, C., de Boer, K., Brand, R. M., Nedeljkovic, M., & Seabrook, L. (2021). Review of the current empirical literature on using videoconferencing to deliver individual psychotherapies to adults with mental health problems. *Psychology and Psychotherapy: Theory, Research and Practice, 94*(3), 854–883. https://doi.org/10.1111/papt.12332

Tuerk, P. W., Yoder, M., Ruggiero, K. J., Gros, D. F., & Acierno, R. (2010). A pilot study of prolonged exposure therapy for posttraumatic stress disorder delivered via telehealth technology. *Journal of Traumatic Stress, 23*(1), 116–123. https://doi.org/10.1002/jts.20494

Turgoose, D., Ashwick, R., & Murphy, D. (2018). Systematic review of lessons learned from delivering tele-therapy to veterans with post-traumatic stress disorder. *Journal of Telemedicine and Telecare, 24*(9), 575–585. https://doi.org/10.1177/1357633x17730443

Valentine, L. M., Donofry, S. D., & Sexton, M. B. (2020). Demographic and psychiatric predictors of engagement in psychotherapy services conducted via clinical video telehealth. *Journal of Telemedicine and Telecare, 26*(1–2), 113–118. https://doi.org/10.1177/1357633x18801713

Vogel, P. A., Solem, S., Hagen, K., Moen, E. M., Launes, G., Håland, Å. T., Hansen, B., & Himle, J. A. (2014). A pilot randomized controlled trial of videoconference-assisted treatment for obsessive-compulsive disorder. *Behaviour Research and Therapy, 63*, 162–168. https://doi.org/10.1016/j.brat.2014.10.007

Wallin, E., Maathz, P., Parling, T., & Hursti, T. (2018). Self-stigma and the intention to seek psychological help online compared to face-to-face. *Journal of Clinical Psychology, 74*(7), 1207–1218. https://doi.org/10.1002/jclp.22583

Watts, S., Marchand, A., Bouchard, S., Gosselin, P., Langlois, F., Belleville, G., & Dugas, M. J. (2020). Telepsychotherapy for generalized anxiety disorder: Impact on the working alliance. *Journal of Psychotherapy Integration, 30*(2), 208–225. https://doi.org/10.1037/int0000223

Wrape, E. R., & McGinn, M. M. (2019). Clinical and ethical considerations for delivering couple and family therapy via telehealth. *Journal of Marital and Family Therapy, 45*(2), 296–308. https://doi.org/10.1111/jmft.12319

Yuen, E. K., Goetter, E. M., Herbert, J. D., & Forman, E. M. (2012). Challenges and opportunities in internet-mediated telemental health. *Professional Psychology: Research and Practice, 43*, 1–8. https://doi.org/10.1037/a0025524

Yuen, E. K., Goetter, E. M., Stasio, M. J., Ash, P., Mansour, B., McNally, E., Sanchez, M., Hobar, E., Forte, S., Zulaica, K., & Watkins, J. (2019). A pilot of acceptance and commitment therapy for public speaking anxiety delivered with group videoconferencing and virtual reality exposure. *Journal of Contextual Behavioral Science, 12*, 47–54. https://doi.org/10.1016/j.jcbs.2019.01.006

Yuen, E. K., Gros, D. F., Price, M., Zeigler, S., Tuerk, P. W., Foa, E. B., & Acierno, R. (2015). Randomized controlled trial of home-based telehealth versus in-person prolonged exposure for combat-related PTSD in veterans: Preliminary results. *Journal of Clinical Psychology, 71*(6), 500–512. https://doi.org/10.1002/jclp.22168

Yuen, E. K., Herbert, J. D., Forman, E. M., Goetter, E. M., Juarascio, A. S., Rabin, S. J., Goodwin, C., & Bouchard, S. (2013). Acceptance based behavior therapy for social anxiety disorder through videoconferencing. *Journal of Anxiety Disorders, 27*, 389–397. https://doi.org/10.1016/j.janxdis.2013.03.002

Chapter 8
Virtual Reality to Enhance Engagement in Exposure-Based Treatments

Andrew M. Sherrill, Natalie Hellman, and Barbara O. Rothbaum

Introduction

Exposure therapy is a component of cognitive behavioral therapy (CBT) for anxiety disorders that is based on the essential goal of helping the patient remove avoidant strategies that have been preventing the patient from learning they can tolerate distress evoked by certain internal and external stimuli (Foa & Kozak, 1986). This is an important goal, as the drive to avoid maintains psychopathology and can diminish treatment engagement. Virtual reality (VR), defined as an immersive and interactive simulated environment, has been used since the 1990s to optimize engagement in exposure therapy. Virtual reality exposure therapy (VRE) is defined as the use of VR hardware and software to deliver exposure therapy.

The VRE system is not a distinct therapy but rather a distinct tool. The hardware can include some or all of the following: head mounted display (HMD), stereo sound delivered via earphones, head and body position trackers, haptic vibrations, and scent machines. The clinician is also a part of the ecosystem, as they dynamically deploy specific elements and, when needed, insert their voice into virtual characters (e.g., a virtual audience member asking a difficult question within a fear of public speaking environment). This hardware, when used with immersive software, helps create simulations that engender a sense of presence, defined as the feeling of actually being in a virtual environment and/or with virtual objects (Schubert et al., 2001). Presence is a necessary condition for activating anxiety (Ling et al., 2014). Contemporary VRE systems allow therapists to create highly customizable environments tailored to the individual's specific fears or triggers. This flexibility enables a

A. M. Sherrill (✉) · N. Hellman · B. O. Rothbaum
Department of Psychiatry and Behavioral Sciences, Emory University School of Medicine, Atlanta, GA, USA
e-mail: andrew.m.sherrill@emory.edu

E. M. Goetter (ed.), *Optimizing Treatment Engagement Processes in CBT for Anxiety and Related Disorders*, CBT: Science Into Practice,
https://doi.org/10.1007/978-3-031-91439-3_8

gradual and controlled exposure process that the therapist can monitor in real-time. While comprehensive systems include many components, case conceptualization of the individual patient drives choice to deploy each component. The most important part of VRE is delivering good therapy to the patient. The therapist should never be distracted by the VR; rather, they should use it to enhance the patient's experience and engagement.

Background

While VRE is recently gaining attention due to widespread use of relatively affordable consumer-grade VR systems (e.g., Meta Quest 3), VRE has three decades of empirical support. Rothbaum et al. (1995) pioneered the field with a VRE system designed to treat fear of heights. VRE has since been examined in the treatment of several anxiety- and trauma-related disorders including other specific phobias (e.g., spiders and airline travel; Rothbaum et al., 2000), social anxiety disorder (SAD; Morina et al., 2023), posttraumatic stress disorder (PTSD; Difede et al., 2022), and panic disorder (Carl et al., 2019; Morina et al., 2015; Mishkind et al., 2017; Opriş et al., 2012). Outcomes of clinical trials indicate VRE protocols are largely comparable to conventional exposure therapies (e.g., Emmelkamp et al., 2002; Reger et al., 2019; Rothbaum et al., 2000). Further, VRE patients report high satisfaction and acceptability (Botella et al., 2015) and some data indicate VRE is more acceptable in initial exercises than conventional exposure (Garcia-Palacios et al., 2007). While the development and implementation of VRE has been promising for some anxiety-related psychopathology, empirical evidence should not be generalized to all related conditions. For example, further empirical investigation is needed on VRE for obsessive-compulsive disorder (OCD; Dehghan et al., 2022) and generalized anxiety disorder (GAD; Hungenberg et al., 2021).

The theoretical underpinnings of VRE start with conceptualizing trauma- and anxiety-related disorders the result of conditioning whereby neutral stimuli acquire the functions of aversive unconditioned stimuli (Myers & Davis, 2007; VanElzakker et al., 2014). For example, an innocuous song playing on the radio during a motor vehicle accident can later function as a signal for danger, thus activating a fear response. In VRE, like other exposure therapies, the patient systematically learns to inhibit fear-conditioned response through a series of exposures to the previously neutral stimuli presented in the context of no danger or threat. This is an experiential learning process called extinction training. Symptom severity improves as inhibitory responses to exposures become more robust than fear responses (Craske et al., 2014). Extinction training, the driving mechanism of VRE's effectiveness, is facilitated by the capacities of VR technology to a) present conditioned stimuli with precision and b) limit opportunities to avoid (Maples-Keller et al., 2023).

The choice to use VRE over conventional exposure is not based on evidence of higher efficacy or effectiveness but rather a clinical conceptualization of a specific patient that indicates VRE will enhance feasibility and patient engagement. For example, if a patient cannot afford conventional exposures (e.g., buying several plane trips to treatment fear of flying) or has previously demonstrated under-engagement (e.g., not engaging with vivid sensory details of a traumatic event during imaginal exposure to treat PTSD), a therapist can present VRE as a strategy to directly address those challenges. In practice, most VRE conceptualizations are largely based on addressing barriers identified from an *initial* CBT conceptualization that does not yet incorporate VR-facilitated learning experiences. Barriers to conventional exposure therapy are typically either (1) difficulty accessing external exposure stimuli (related to cost, availability, and practicality) or (2) difficulty retrieving internal exposure stimuli (related to willingness and abilities). Simply put, VRE should be used if there is reason to believe virtual simulations will make the individual's extinction training feasible.

While the prospect of home-based VRE is appealing given the rise of consumer-grade devices, more research is needed to understand the feasibility and effectiveness of home-based VRE systems that can be used as either self-help or between in-person therapy sessions (Lindner et al., 2017; Stevens & Sherrill, 2021). Home-based VRE may increase the frequency of exposure opportunities and potentially accelerate treatment gains; however, the risk of misuse is considerable and demands the development of research-based protocols. As VRE becomes more accessible, it is possible patients may attempt to use this modality for self-treatment outside of working with a therapist or may supplement their current therapy regimen without their therapist's knowledge. Without the guidance of therapist, a patient may use home-based VRE systems in a way that reinforces avoidance (e.g., subtle safety behaviors such as clenching teeth and deep breathing), thereby undermining their treatment efforts and gains. As described in this chapter, the therapist's behaviors and patient's engagement make VRE effective, not the tool.

Treatment Engagement

Engagement in exposure therapy requires the patient to willingly have experiences (e.g., emotion, thoughts, sensations, urges) that they typically avoid. The optimal level of engagement within exposures is defined functionally based on the question, "are they learning something adaptive through their experience?" The optimal range is not a predetermined intensity level. The control over stimuli afforded by VR allows the therapist to titrate the stimuli to create the "perfect" exposure. Very often, patients learn critically helpful information about themselves when they are experiencing and remaining in contact with a maximal level of distress. For example, although unusual, a patient who vomits during an imaginal exposure of a traumatic event can learn that vomiting, while unpleasant, is safe and tolerable.

When the patient's level of engagement is preventing new learning, the patient's experience can be characterized as either "over-engagement" or "under-engagement." In our experience in training exposure therapists, over-engagement is rare and can be addressed collaboratively without fragilizing the patient.

Over-engagement interferes with new learning by preventing the patient from being present and aware of their experience as safe and transient. Often, over-engagement presents as persistent dissociation throughout the exposure and the patient is not amenable to therapist prompts to bring the patient back to the present moment and location.

Compared to over-engagement during exposures, under-engagement is far more common and problematic. Under-engagement is suboptimal willingness or ability to confront external exposure stimuli and/or one's own internal experience that an exposure targets (i.e., memories, emotions, thoughts, and urges). For example, during imaginal exposure to a trauma memory, under-engagement can manifest as describing the event in superficial terms like a police report (e.g., "the cars collided, the other driver sustained an injury, and then I called for an ambulance") and not include vivid descriptions of the event and peritraumatic reactions (e.g., "I saw blood in the driver's mouth and hear guggling sounds as I try to talk to the dispatcher, but I'm so afraid that the words aren't coming out clearly"). Without confrontation of what the individual habitually avoids, nothing new can be learned. In contrast, under-engagement essentially reinforces avoidance strategies and unhelpful beliefs via the blocking or removal of unwanted experience. The primary focus of this chapter will be guidance on how VR can be used to create the optimal level of engagement, especially for under-engagers. The chapter concludes with two case examples that illustrate how clinicians can optimize engagement in exposure therapy using VR.

VRE Clinical Strategies to Promote Engagement

VR has been used for several decades to prevent and correct under-engagement in exposure therapy. In this chapter, we distinguish "VRE Technology Features" and "VRE Therapist Skills" as two distinct drivers of patient engagement. Given our emphasis on how the therapist can optimize exposure therapy, we more closely examine "VRE Therapist Skills." First, however, review Table 8.1 for an overview of the technology features that can make exposures more accessible and fruitful, thus facilitating engagement. These technology features are characterized elsewhere (Sherrill et al., 2020) and are typically viewed as intuitive and attractive by clinicians (Segal et al., 2011).

While VR has embedded technological features to enhance engagement, the art of enhancing engagement using VR is primarily the domain of clinical strategies. While VR may be a helpful tool, it is the therapist who wields the tool and understands how to use it effectively. Much like the mere possession of a chisel does not directly result in an artful sculpture, the mere possession of VRE equipment does not directly result in a therapeutic exposure. VRE involves a nuanced delivery that blends therapeutic expertise with a deep understanding of the technological and psychological aspects of VR, and always with a patient-centered approach.

Table 8.1 VR features to enhance engagement in exposure therapy

VRE technology feature	Example application for fear of public speaking
Feasibility	The therapist has difficulty recruiting and paying real people with whom the patient can practice public speaking. The VRE therapist introduces the possibility of using a virtual audience that is free to the patient and available every session
Customization	The patient needs to learn (1) she can talk to an audience who is bored and (2) she does not need humor to escape her own anxiety. The VRE therapist selects a virtual audience that is guaranteed to remain indifferent regardless of patient's humor attempts, thus not reinforcing safety behaviors
Clinician control	The patient reports that male audience members are especially activating and, therefore, would like to first engage in exposures using female audience members and then proceed to male audience members. The VRE therapist can switch from female to male audience members as soon as patient is ready, even during a single exposure session
Consistency	The patient reports a desire to gain mastery by delivering the same speech to the same audience several times and for the audience to respond as if they were hearing the speech for the first time. If using real people, the audience will not likely remain consistent across exposures. The VRE therapist can save a specific arrangement of stimuli from one exposure session and redeploy an exact copy of the arrangement for subsequent sessions
Privacy	The patient reports she needs to practice a speech that includes trade secrets that she cannot disclose to others outside her company. The VRE therapist assures patient that virtual audience members are not able to record patient's disclosures

Like all exposures, VRE sessions have four basic conditions that make the exposure *therapeutic* (Foa et al., 2019). First, the therapist must establish a therapeutic space that is safe and trustworthy. Second, the therapist must activate the specific experience that the patient and the therapist collaboratively agreed to activate—this typically includes the selection of appropriate activating stimuli according to the exposure hierarchy. Third, the patient must stay in the exposure long enough to experience information that is incompatible with expectations such as data that anxiety decreases over time, the feared outcome does not occur, the experience is generalizable, and the experience is worthwhile (i.e., values-consistent). Fourth, after the exposure, the patient must have an opportunity (post-exposure) to make sense of the experience with the goal of making explicit any new learning of incompatible information. When delivering exposure using VR, there are several therapist strategies that increase the likelihood of achieving these four conditions of a therapeutic experience. See Table 8.2 for a list of "VRE Therapist Skills" to enhance engagement.

Table 8.2 VRE therapist skills to enhance engagement in exposure therapy

VRE therapist skill	Example application for fear of public speaking
Sound rationale delivery	After several years of teleworking during the COVID-19 pandemic and developing safety behaviors during work meetings (e.g., bouncing legs and fidgeting hands off camera), a patient returns to the office and notices an acute increase in anxiety during meetings. The provider offers VRE as a way for the patient to address their specific concerns. The provider helps the patient see how "off camera" safety behaviors are maintaining anxiety and how VRE allows the provider to quickly notice and correct those behaviors during immersive virtual meetings
Fluid administration	The provider needs to seamlessly manipulate the virtual meeting (e.g., make avatars nod immediately after each good point articulated by patient) while also monitoring the patient's behavior and self-reported units of distress, and occasionally providing encouragement. If the clinician does not appropriately manipulate the environment (e.g., too long of delay on the audience nodding), it will distract the patient and not provide the desired reinforcement
Maintaining presence	The provider sets up a realistic context before the patient puts on the HMD, such as "you're about to walk into the conference room and give the work presentation you've been working on." during the exposure, when the patient self-soothes by saying, "the speech is not real," the provider does not start a discussion about "realness" but orients the patient back to the audience, perhaps by having one of the virtual characters interact with the patient (e.g., "tell me more about your last point")
Creative identification of content	The provider and patient want to incorporate the sound of a clicking pen (boss's signal of annoyance) but the VRE system does not have that sound. The provider finds an audio clip of a clicking pen on the internet, which is played during exposures
Generalization of new learning	After one particularly successful VR exposure, the patient reported that they were only able to succeed because they knew the audience was "fake." the provider helps patient see that the emotion they faced was real, as were their approach behaviors. They agreed the next step was to do an in-person exposure using the same "real" approach behaviors that were practiced during that session's exposure. Discussion following the in-person exposure included that the criticism the patient imagined from the audience was not real (i.e., accurate)
Correction of VR-specific barriers	The patient asked how to engage in VR exposure to audiences between sessions. Rather than attempting to set up home-based VR, the provider identified relevant in vivo exposures that did not require VR. Specifically, the provider and the patient proactively identified opportunities within group meetings at work in which the patient could present information to the full team

Rationale Delivery

Psychoeducation in VRE is no different from conventional exposure therapy. However, we recommend briefly introducing the equipment during the discussion which can help make the goals of treatment more tangible. Unlike therapies that are primarily verbal, when using VRE tools, the patient can see what they are getting into via looking at the equipment, seeing the scenarios that can be built by the software, etc. This step is very collaborative and patient-aligned, as presenting the tool and then involving the patient in goal-setting process fosters a sense of ownership and ensures that the exposures are personally meaningful. This process allows the patient and the provider to be aligned on treatment goals and exposure targets that lets VRE elements be customized to the patient and build a very personal hierarchy that is directly tailored to each patient. The equipment overview should aim to demystify the technology and make it approachable, which requires the clinician to present as technologically confident. Practicing prior to exposure exercises to show how the equipment works with non-targeted environments is often helpful (e.g., showing a simulated dog to a person with a fear of heights). Most systems have monitors that allow the therapist to see what the patient is seeing. When giving an overview of simulations that the patient may use, it is helpful to use learning checks while explaining the rationale to the patient. This allows you to explore their understanding and make any clarifications that are needed. A simple prompt to explore the patient's understanding is, "tell me how you can use this tool to overcome your anxiety?" Usually, patients find the clinical utility of VRE environment very intuitive. This simple question not only verifies their understanding, but also creates a collaborative environment. As mentioned above, creating a safe, trusting, and collaborative alliance sets the stage for therapeutic exposures.

When delivering the rationale for VRE, the clinician must address expectations and potential challenges. Patients should be clear that VR is just a tool, not a passive experience, and they are being asked to actively use the tool to learn new things about themselves. In effective VRE, the patient plays an active role in selecting simulations and choosing when to engage in each simulation, and when to advance each simulated experience to the next in their hierarchy. Just as in in vivo exposure, when selecting VRE for a patient, the therapist's rationale should not include what type of patient is the best match for this method, because research does not provide clear guidance. While some evidence suggests younger patients might respond better to VRE tools (Norr et al., 2018), which may reflect their familiarity with VR technology, more research is needed for clear exclusionary and inclusionary criteria beyond what is typically used for conventional exposure therapies. In a recent study with post-9/11 veterans and military service members with PTSD, VRE was more effective for those with comorbid major depression than standard prolonged imaginal exposure therapy (Difede et al., 2022).

Fluid Administration

While VR tools become more refined and more intuitive with each technological advancement, careful consideration for how to effectively integrate each VR component is necessary to have successful sessions. VRE providers should not only have competence in exposure therapy but also be comfortable with the VR technology. Just like any other tool used in cognitive behavior therapies (e.g., thought records, exposure hierarchies, biofeedback equipment), VRE therapists must navigate each session while administering this tool and maintaining a steady and calm presence. This requires multitasking capabilities, allowing them to be present with their patient while guiding the exposure using VR. Indeed, VRE sessions have many tasks (e.g., managing hardware, ensuring a dynamic virtual environment, monitoring patient engagement, and collecting their subjective units of distress) in addition to the regular elements of a traditional session that need thoughtful attendance. While the provider is multitasking, it is also critical to minimize their presence, so not to distract the patient from the exposure. Another way to minimize distraction is to not use VR elements that are not necessary—just because a virtual stimulus exists does not necessitate its use. A VRE provider does not aim to "show off" the technology. Fluid administration is often facilitated by the guideline that "less is more." Always the focus is on the patient and what they need and how they are responding.

The delivery of VRE sounds like a difficult task, but fear not! While using these VR tools can seem overwhelming and challenging to juggle during a session, there are many ways to build competency in this tool. In our experience, the best way to develop VRE multitasking skills is to practice using the VR equipment as much as possible prior to your patient's session, preferably with non-patients. We recommend inviting several colleagues to spend some breaks or after hours' time role-playing with the systems. In addition to building competency, we hope new learners also aim to have fun while gaining comfort with the system. The more a therapist can "play" with the equipment with non-patients, the more they can learn it is safe and user-friendly. Many are curious about VR and its constantly evolving capabilities, and spending time with peers to explore and practice VR is a great way to enhance not only an individual's learning, but also advance the field.

Maintaining Presence

Immersion in the environment is not solely determined by the level of "realism" of the simulation. Realistic visuals, sounds, and tactile feedback and opportunities to interact within the environment (e.g., manipulating virtual objects) may contribute to an authentic experience; however, willingness to engage with simulations and allow emotional responses is the product of the patient-clinician collaboration. Patients have experienced immersion since the 1990s, during early stages of VR technology with visuals that seem primitive by today's standards (Rothbaum et al., 1995). We have found that when exposing patients to fear cues in VR, the virtual environment does not have to be very realistic to evoke fear. We have found that it is not the level of realism (such as the level of realism in the video graphics or obtaining the exact smell) that makes VR an effective tool—instead, success when using VR is more attributed to the therapist's ability to play a substantial role in maintaining the patient's sense of presence. This is encouraging, as it means that one does not have to have the most realistic graphics to have successful VRE sessions. To help patients invest in the virtual environment as if it were a real environment, the therapist can contextualize the virtual experience in a way that matches real contexts. For example, when treating fear of storms, the VRE therapist asks the patient to describe the real settings they do not want to be in during a storm (e.g., their specific workplace at the end of the workday). One way of contextualizing the exposure is to actively describe why the task is important. For example, in a fear of heights case that is targeting the fear using elevators with large windows, the therapist and patient can build a narrative around the virtual elevator that is about visiting a real friend who lives on the 20th floor.

The therapist wants to eliminate any discussion that a VR environment is "just VR." The therapist, instead, needs to frame the simulation as if it is real. Of course, at no point will the patient forget it is a simulation. However, they can respond to the simulation as if it were real, and the fear stimuli *are* fear stimuli. For individuals with clinically significant anxiety and robust avoidance repertoires, it is typically easy to activate ecologically valid responses. For example, shortly after putting on the HMD for a patient with a fear of elevators, the therapist does not say, "see how immersive it is" but, rather, the VR provider might begin the exposure with the patient waiting for the elevator to arrive at the ground floor and say, "tell me about what you and your friend are going to do when you get to her place on the 20th floor." The patient might comment on the VR environment with statements such as, "wow, this elevator looks and sounds very real," or "these graphics are so old – my Xbox is much better." The therapist must redirect the patient to the context with a statement such as, "look out the window and estimate how high we are," or "what are you feeling in your body right now?" If the therapist treats the environment as real, the patient will as well. You do not want to diminish presence, which is important to activate anxiety (Ling et al., 2014). The more they perceive presence, the more likely they will tolerate the equipment (Weech et al., 2019).

Creative Identification of Content

VR tools continue to advance rapidly and many innovative adaptations are becoming more affordable with each expansion, thereby increasing the accessibility. As the field evolves, it is important to remember that no matter how far the field advances, VR capabilities will always be limited because there is no feasible way to predict all virtual stimuli that all patients will need. There will always be some detail that is inaccurate for a patient or some way that VR cannot be customized to be an exact replica of the feared experience. With this said, the core experience VR tools provide is an interactive and immersive multimedia environment that is relevant, not a replica, for each patient's targeted exposure experience.

A skillful VRE therapist is not limited by prepackaged environments or VR hardware. New elements can always be incorporated—either by digital files (e.g., an activating song by a virtual party host) or the VRE provider's voice (e.g., a specific question from a virtual party member). Indeed, this is nothing new for exposure therapists, who have a long history of finding stimuli in the real world to increase engagement within conventional exposure therapy. For example, during prolonged exposure for PTSD with a patient completing imaginal exposures to a trauma memory of a sexual assault, one method of increasing engagement during imaginal is to incorporate the smell of the perpetrators' cologne (a distressing reminder) into the session to further activate the trauma memory structure. Some VRE systems offer computer-controlled scent delivery with a large library of scents. However, in the absence of this VRE component, it is possible to simply hold a scent near the patient's nose during the exposure when the patient cues the therapist that the scent enters the narrative. When patients are using an HMD during the exposure, the equipment will block their vision and thereby block any preparatory self-soothing or bracing they may have done if they could watch the therapist gradually approach their nose while holding the scent. As with all VRE components, the patient should have full informed consent regarding when, why, and how each VR component will be used within the context of the exposure.

One method of using creativity in VRE is to repurpose existing content. Some VR environments happen to have elements that are useful for non-targeted clinical concerns. For example, the VRE provider may not have a VR scenario specifically for claustrophobia already available; however, the provider might have a fear of heights environment that uses an elevator to travel to top of a building—an elevator that is small enough to provide the perfect setting for a claustrophobia exposure.

One example of creative content identification was the treatment of a military veteran who experienced a traumatic event related to a military aircraft crash that included one fatality and several significant injuries. Virtual simulations of the combat aircraft with *Bravemind* (i.e., "Virtual Iraq and Virtual Afghanistan") were not available (Rizzo & Hartholt, 2005). However, a commercial aircraft was available on *Virtually Better: Fear of Flying* (Rothbaum & Hodges, 2008), which was used to facilitate imaginal exposure. Specifically, the sounds and tactile sensations of the aircraft taking off were used to activate the beginning of the memory and the sounds of turbulence to activate the end of the memory (i.e., the crash). The exposure was remarkably effective. The patient reported the deep and rumbling sounds of an aircraft engine and the constant vibrations under his feet made it easy to connect with the previously avoided memory.

Generalization of New Learning

VR tools can be incredibly helpful in increasing access to feared stimuli. As in all exposure therapy, it will be important to work with an exposure hierarchy and to assign in vivo exposure homework for the patient to conduct in between VR sessions. Evidence suggests VRE gains generalize to in vivo exposure (Morina et al., 2015), and incorporating exposures that can be conducted both in session (using VR) and in vivo for homework is essential in promoting the generalization of new learning.

Generalization of learning using VR tools is essential to patient progress, as treating the VR stimuli as the real world helps the patient build confidence for real-world events. When patients first engage in VR sessions, they may engage in some self-soothing thinking patterns such as "my doctor is here so I'm safe" or "this is a game and not reality." In addition to using the approach of treating the simulation as the real world (described earlier), the therapist should also be mindful that the patient may use our presence as a safety behavior, even though the HMD headset typically blocks the visual presence of the provider. To promote independent engagement with VRE, the provider may want to gradually phase out their prompts across sessions and direct the patient to initiate their interactions with stimuli (e.g., speak directly to virtual audience members, pet the virtual dog, and walk spontaneously on the virtual rooftop). This encourages the patients' independence and blocks the therapist's presence from being used as a safety signal.

To make generalization explicit, it is critical to have time after exposure to process the experience and explore new perspectives. In VRE, it is important to avoid talking about how "interesting" or "real" was the simulation. More important is examining the patient's experience (e.g., anxiety and its reduction) and the choices made during the exposure. During processing of VR exposures, it is natural for discussions to lead toward "real world" steps patients want to take between sessions. Indeed, gains in VR environments should not remain only in the virtual world. However, it is important to not communicate that gains do not "count" until they are somehow "verified" in real life. While the simulation may be artificial, their experience is fully valid and should be treated as such. They have encountered fearful stimuli and (hopefully) experienced decreased anxiety while continuing to encounter fearful stimuli. For example, when treating fear of public speaking, a VRE therapist reminds the patient that their initial fearful reactions to the virtual audience were identical to how they previously responded to real audience members (e.g., rushing the speech, breathing quickly, and focusing inwardly rather than toward the audience) and that adaptive behavior changes over course of treatment were "real" and are now available to use in "real" life contexts.

Correction of VR-Specific Barriers

There are some VRE-specific engagement pitfalls that need to be addressed early in treatment. First, "simulator sickness"—a sensation similar to motion sickness, is more common in people with a tendency to experience motion sickness. If the VRE provider keeps virtual environments simple and straightforward with no unnecessary movement, simulator sickness is uncommon. Simulator sickness is less common with newer HMDs with better resolution and refresh rates. Another caveat to navigating simulator sickness is to distinguish it from anxiety, as both can present similarly. Approaches to mitigate simulator sickness are to minimize quick movements, keep the room cool, keep time in the HMD to 40 min or under, and to remove less important or unnecessary stimuli (e.g., turning off scents). If a patient does report feeling queasy, introducing ginger, mint, or sweet carbonated sodas prior to and following exposures can be helpful.

Another VR-specific barrier is a mismatch between the available environment and the patient's needs. While VRE developers aim to make their environments useful and usable to as many end-users as possible, many desired simulations have yet to be developed and are therefore unavailable. The VRE therapist can help the patient anticipate these mismatches and, when appropriate, acknowledge and validate all reactions to design choices. For example, if we do not have the exact weapons fired for an exposure with a veteran with PTSD, acknowledging that this is all we have usually helps them accept the limitation without being distracted by it. Other mismatches might be related to multicultural factors such as the use of specific avatars, landscapes, and buildings that do not align with the patient's experience. VRE providers must be aware that VR is created and used in cultural contexts and should be prepared to discuss cultural concerns with patients that, if not addressed, might feel invalidating.

Related to diversity factors that could result in diminished access and acceptability, another VR-specific barrier is physiological limitations that prevent use of all VR components. For example, patients who are vision impaired or hard of hearing will not benefit from all VRE components. However, it is important to keep in mind the VRE is not solely determined by one form of simulation and that effective administration is often guided by the rule "less is more."

Case Examples

Fear of Flying

Ms. Earhart was a 40-year-old, white, female kindergarten teacher from the southeast United States who reported fear of flying throughout her adult life. She reported that she would take about one flight each year if she felt obligated (e.g., funerals, weddings, and invited vacations). She presented to the clinic with no psychiatric comorbidities or chronic health conditions. She reported significant anticipatory anxiety and panic-like symptoms during takeoff and with any signs of turbulence. To escape from anxiety, she consumed alcohol, fidgeted (hands and bouncing legs), distracted herself with headphones, and sought reassurance from travel partners and airline staff. She reported awareness that airline crashes are incredibly rare; however, this information did not function to reduce her anxiety. She was motivated for treatment because she was planning to get married in 6 months and her husband was planning a honeymoon in Maui.

From a CBT perspective, Ms. Earhart continued to experience fear of flying because avoidance was not allowing her to learn that she can handle the discomfort, that discomfort will eventually diminish, and that flying is safe and potentially comfortable and enjoyable. To treat this fear, exposure therapy indicated the patient should increase her frequency of flying and disengage from all avoidance behaviors during each flight. If a conventional exposure therapy approach were taken, the treatment plan for Ms. Earhart would include psychoeducation followed by training in anxiety management techniques such as cognitive restructuring, followed by in vivo exposure to the following elements: sitting in the terminal, walking down the Jetway, sitting in a parked airplane, taking off, flying without turbulence, flying with turbulence, and landing (see sample treatment session summary in Table 8.3). Due to the patient's avoidance repertoire, she would benefit from the presence of an exposure therapist to help identify and disengage from avoidance behaviors (e.g., leg bouncing, reassurance seeking) during initial exposures. The treatment plan would involve consuming significant cost and time resources (e.g., several plane tickets and trips to airport) and would not allow the patient to gain mastery of one component before automatically moving on to the next component (e.g., an airplane cannot stay parked until she reports a diminished fear response). This treatment plan would introduce significant barriers that would be challenging to navigate without the use of VRE tools.

When offered conventional exposure therapy for fear of flying, Ms. Earhart declined due to cost. She was referred to a VRE provider for the primary benefit of reduced cost. In the VRE treatment plan, her exposure hierarchy included the situations list above; however, using VR, each situation was individually targeted, allowing Ms. Earhart to remain in each situation a sufficient duration to learn information that was incompatible with anxiety-specific beliefs (e.g., the discomfort will diminish without using safety behaviors). All virtual flights were contextualized within the patient's honeymoon narrative. For example, during the exposure of waiting in the virtual terminal without avoidance behaviors, the therapist used their voice to simulate the following announcement: "Attention passengers of Flight 2857 to Maui, boarding has been delayed 30 min for a mechanical issue that is being addressed; however, please continue waiting near the gate as boarding may start sooner than expected." During the initial exposures inside the virtual airplane, Ms. Earhart bounced her legs and repeatedly scanned the fuselage, which the therapist observed and then helped the patient notice and stop. As predicted, the most significant discomfort was during the takeoff.

Table 8.3 VRE for fear of flying session overview

Session	Content
1	Information gathering, treatment rational, and treatment procedure review
2	Introduce and practice cognitive restructuring
3	Introduce and practice breathing retraining
4	Review prior content and conduct hyperventilation exposure (if history of panic)
5–8	Conduct virtual reality exposure

During the sixth session, Ms. Earhart committed to taking off five times during a single 50-min therapy appointment. Her anxiety peaked at the start of the exposure, during which she reported, “I’ll be okay – this is just VR.” To maintain a sense of presence, the therapist provided several orienting prompts such as, “tell me why you’re on this plane and why it’s important to fly where you’re flying” and “describe all the sounds you’re hearing in the airplane.” After the patient was able to maintain engagement with both the virtual environment and her emotion, she was about to experience gradual extinction and increases in self-reported confidence.

Ms. Earhart completed a full course of VRE of fear of flying without doing any exposures in actual airports or airplanes. She did take her flight to Maui and reported she was able to handle several sources of travel-related discomfort (e.g., airport construction, delays on tarmac, turbulence, and crying babies) without engaging in avoidant behavior. She was particularly proud of her ability to not drink alcohol while traveling. Critical to this case was shared decision-making each session, which allowed the patient to be more involved and take more ownership during the treatment course. Shared decision-making is a significant predictor of symptom and functioning outcomes (Glenn et al., 2013). Helpful prompts that encouraged collaboration with this patient were statements like, ‘tell me why this meaningful to you?” This process also included decisions within the environment. Incorporating interactive elements within simulations (e.g., handing a virtual plane ticket to the gate agent, walking through the Jetway) enhanced the patient’s sense of immersion and control, promoting active participation in exposure exercises.

Posttraumatic Stress Disorder

Mr. Blue was a 45-year-old, African American, male Army veteran of Operation Iraqi Freedom (OIF) who lived alone in a rural Midwestern town. He separated from the Army 10 years ago and received disability benefits from Veterans Affairs for a diagnosis of PTSD. His symptoms were anchored to an OIF event involving exposure to chemical agents while wearing a gas mask that interfered with combat operations required during the event. During this event, the patient believed he was going to die because the mask fell off while running to a shelter while carrying medical supplies needed for an injured soldier. Mr. Blue reported that ever since OIF, all alarms have given him a sense of doom. More recently, however, he reported that mandatory masking during the COVID-19 pandemic triggered distressing memories of his index trauma event. He also began to experience frequent nightmares related to the OIF event. To avoid having to wear a mask during the pandemic, Mr. Blue rarely left his home. Despite the removal of masking demands as COVID-19 rates reduced, Mr. Blue continued to isolate himself and experience trauma-related nightmares. When he experienced intrusive thoughts and memories related to OIF, he would distract himself with watching football and talking to his friends about football. In addition, he coped with trauma-related distress by chewing tobacco and working with his hands (e.g., building furniture and model airplanes). He presented with comorbid Persistent Depressive Disorder, obesity, diabetes, and high blood pressure. He was motivated for treatment because his adult children wanted him to visit them more often, which would require him to wear a mask.

From a CBT perspective, Mr. Blue continued to experience intrusive memories and nightmares because avoidance was not allowing him to learn OIF memories are safe and approachable and that he can handle discomfort related to thinking about OIF and its aftermath. The exposure therapy conceptual framework suggested he would benefit from revisiting the trauma memories without avoidance and for long enough to experience extinction learning. His original treatment plan included a conventional exposure therapy approach in which Mr. Blue would first receive psychoeducation, then in vivo exposure to surgical masks, and then imaginal exposure to the memory itself. However, during the first imaginal exposure, the patient reported that he could not revisit the memory because he struggled with visual imagination and he could only remember a handful of aspects of the memory, namely, his heavy breathing in the gas mask, the alarm, the complete darkness of that night, and being certain that he would die.

After rejecting the conventional approach to imaginal exposure, Mr. Blue was recommended for VRE for PTSD to help the patient activate and sustain as much of the trauma memory as possible and for a long enough duration to learn corrective information (see Table 8.4 for a session-by-session overview). The therapist did not have an environment specifically for the OIF event or for chemical warfare. However, the therapist was able to collaborate with the patient to find and combine stimuli that would help the patient revisit the memory. Specifically, Mr. Blue and the therapist decided to use all components of *Bravemind* (i.e., "Virtual Iraq"), except the visuals. The event occurred under complete darkness, so visuals were not needed. The selected components included scent (e.g., gun powder and burning trash), sound (e.g., explosions and alarms), and floor vibration (e.g., explosions). During the first VR-facilitated imaginal exposure, the patient said that not being able to breath activated the memory the most and, therefore, the memory was not

Table 8.4 VRE for PTSD session overview

Session	Content
1	Information gathering, treatment rational, treatment procedure review, introduce and practice breathing restraining
2	Review prior content, provide psychoeducation, introduce and assign in vivo exposure between sessions
3–4	Introduce and conduct imaginal exposure to trauma memory using VR, continue in vivo exposure between sessions
5	Truncate trauma narrative to "hot spots" and conduct VR imaginal exposure, continue in vivo exposure between sessions
5–9	Continue "hot spot" VR imaginal exposures, continue in vivo exposure between session
10	Conduct final VR imaginal exposure to full memory, review in vivo gains, and making plans to maintain gains

too distressing because he was reminding himself that he could now breathe just fine. Hearing this insight, the therapist and Mr. Blue collaboratively decided that Mr. Blue would wear a surgical mask during the imaginal exposure to simulate the sensations of wearing a gas mask. Of note, given that the specific chemical alarm that occurred during the OIF event was not a part of the existing VR system, Mr. Blue and the therapist found an audio clip of alarm online and incorporated it into the virtual environment. Imaginal exposure required the patient to describe everything that happened from beginning to end, including all thoughts and sensations experienced, and as soon as the patient described an element available within the VR system, the therapist would activate the simulation (e.g., when the patient said the alarm turned on, the therapist deployed the audio clip). The patient reported that stimuli helped activate more details regarding why he was running outdoors despite the alarm; namely, to provide life-saving medical equipment. After five sessions of revisiting the memories, the patient developed the perspective that he did the best he could to keep himself safe and that he did not hesitate to save the life of another soldier. He experienced extinction to the memory and the surgical mask. He reported that the alarm no longer activated a sense of doom but it continued to irritate him, which he decided was acceptable because he wanted all alarms to appropriately alert him to potential danger.

Mr. Blue completed a full course of VRE for PTSD, which included conventional in vivo exposure to trauma reminders (Sherrill et al., 2019). Although the patient experienced extinction learning while wearing the surgical mask, it was also important for him to not experience strong negative affect activated by wearing surgical masks in public settings (e.g., waiting rooms and grocery stores). He completed mask-related in vivo exposures between his in-person VR imaginal exposures. He did not complete VR-enabled exposures for homework assignments because conventional in vivo stimuli were feasible (e.g., walking outside during darkness, visiting loud public settings). At the end of treatment, Mr. Blue reported he was able to visit his children more frequently, talk with peers about his OIF experiences, and sleep without waking from nightmares.

Conclusion

For the past three decades, VR systems have been demonstrated to be useful and usable for the treatment of anxiety- and trauma-related symptoms. Importantly, within the context of VRE, virtual simulations are used simply as a tool to complement CBT, not a comprehensive treatment. The clinician is responsible to use the simulations as one way to help engage the patient in new, adaptive learning experiences. In this chapter, we highlighted several clinician skills that help optimize treatment engagement. The core of the work is to eliminate pathological avoidance and correct safety behaviors so that the patient can learn from their own new experiences that fear diminishes and/or they can handle strong emotion. The clinician is an active part of the clinical ecosystem and must prioritize case conceptualization prior to using any VR component. Demand for VRE will likely continue to increase due to general widespread use of relatively affordable consumer-grade VR systems. With continued training and consultation, clinicians are encouraged to build VR-related competencies (e.g., maintaining presence) upon of existing clinical skills in exposure therapy (see Table 8.2 for VRE Therapist Skills). Choosing VRE over conventional exposure should always been grounded in a clinical conceptualization of a specific patient.

Clinical Summary Points and Recommendations

- Virtual reality exposure therapy allows the therapist to address barriers to the accessibility of external exposure therapy stimuli (e.g., feared objects and settings) and internal exposure therapy stimuli (e.g., feared trauma memories).
- Virtual reality exposure therapy presents potent multi-model stimuli to facilitate engagement with experiences that patients typically avoid and escape.
- Many patients are willing to undergo virtual reality exposure therapy who might not consent to in vivo exposure therapy.
- There are several therapist skills specific to virtual reality exposure therapy (e.g., maintaining presence, creative identification of content, and correcting of modality-specific barriers) that increase the likelihood of achieving a therapeutic experience.

References

Botella, C., Serrano, B., Baños, R. M., & Garcia-Palacios, A. (2015). Virtual reality exposure-based therapy for the treatment of post-traumatic stress disorder: A review of its efficacy, the adequacy of the treatment protocol, and its acceptability. *Neuropsychiatric Disease and Treatment, 11*, 2533.

Carl, E., Stein, A. T., Levihn-Coon, A., Pogue, J. R., Rothbaum, B., Emmelkamp, P., et al. (2019). Virtual reality exposure therapy for anxiety and related disorders: A meta-analysis of randomized controlled trials. *Journal of Anxiety Disorders, 61*, 27–36.

Craske, M. G., Treanor, M., Conway, C. C., Zbozinek, T., & Vervliet, B. (2014). Maximizing exposure therapy: An inhibitory learning approach. *Behaviour Research and Therapy, 58*, 10–23.

Dehghan, B., Saeidimehr, S., Sayyah, M., & Rahim, F. (2022). The effect of virtual reality on emotional response and symptoms provocation in patients with OCD: A systematic review and meta-analysis. *Frontiers in Psychiatry, 12*, 733584.

Difede, J., Rothbaum, B. O., Rizzo, A. A., Wyka, K., Spielman, L., Reist, C., et al. (2022). Enhancing exposure therapy for posttraumatic stress disorder (PTSD): A randomized clinical trial of virtual reality and imaginal exposure with a cognitive enhancer. *Translational Psychiatry, 12*(1), 299.

Emmelkamp, P., Krijn, M., Hulsbosch, A., de Vries, S., Schuemie, M., & van der Mast, C. (2002). Virtual reality treatment versus exposure in vivo: A comparative evaluation in acrophobia. *Behaviour Research and Therapy, 40*(5), 509–516.

Foa, E. B., Hembree, E. A., Rothbaum, B. O., & Rauch, S. A. M. (2019). *Prolonged exposure therapy for PTSD: Therapist guide* (2nd ed.). Oxford University Press.

Foa, E. B., & Kozak, M. J. (1986). Emotional processing of fear: Exposure to corrective information. *Psychological Bulletin, 99*, 20–35.

Garcia-Palacios, A., Botella, C., Hoffman, H., & Fabregat, S. (2007). Comparing acceptance and refusal rates of virtual reality exposure therapy vs in vivo exposure by patients with specific phobias. *CyberPsychology and Behavior, 10*, 722–724.

Glenn, D., Golinelli, D., Rose, R. D., Roy-Byrne, P., Stein, M. B., Sullivan, G., et al. (2013). Who gets the most out of cognitive behavioral therapy for anxiety disorders? The role of treatment dose and patient engagement. *Journal of Consulting and Clinical Psychology, 81*(4), 639.

Hungenberg, M., Burke, S., Hansen-Guzman, A., Thompson, S., Lyon, C., & DeSanto, K. (2021). Virtual reality in the treatment of generalized anxiety disorder. *American Family Physician, 104*(6), 638–640.

Lindner, P., Miloff, A., Hamilton, W., Reuterskiöld, L., Andersson, G., Powers, M. B., & Carlbring, P. (2017). Creating state of the art, next-generation virtual reality exposure therapies for anxiety disorders using consumer hardware platforms: Design considerations and future directions. *Cognitive Behaviour Therapy, 46*, 404–420.

Ling, Y., Nefs, H. T., Morina, N., Heynderickx, I., & Brinkman, W.-P. (2014). A meta-analysis on the relationship between self-reported presence and anxiety in virtual reality exposure therapy for anxiety disorders. *PLoS One, 9*(5), e96144.

Maples-Keller, J. L., Sherrill, A. M., Reddi, P., Norrholm, S. D., & Rothbaum, B. O. (2023). Extinction-based exposure therapies using virtual reality. In M. Milad & S. D. Norrholm (Eds.), *Current topics in behavioral neurosciences: Fear extinction mechanisms*. Springer. Advanced Online Publication.

Mishkind, M. C., Norr, A. M., Katz, A. C., & Reger, G. M. (2017). Review of virtual reality treatment in psychiatry: evidence versus current diffusion and use. *Current Psychiatry Reports, 19*, 1–8.

Morina, N., Ijntema, H., Meyerbroker, K., & Emmelkamp, P. M. G. (2015). Can virtual reality exposure therapy gains be generalized to real-life? A meta-analysis of studies applying behavioral assessments. *Behaviour Research and Therapy, 74*, 18–24.

Morina, N., Kampmann, I., Emmelkamp, P., Barbui, C., & Hoppen, T. H. (2023). Meta-analysis of virtual reality exposure therapy for social anxiety disorder. *Psychological Medicine, 53*(5), 2176–2178.

Myers, K. M., & Davis, M. (2007). Mechanisms of fear extinction. *Molecular Psychiatry, 12*(2), 120–150.

Norr, A. M., Smolenski, D. J., Katz, A. C., Rizzo, A. A., Rothbaum, B. O., Difede, J., et al. (2018). Virtual reality exposure versus prolonged exposure for PTSD: Which treatment for whom? *Depression and Anxiety, 35*(6), 523–529.

Opriş, D., Pintea, S., García-Palacios, A., Botella, C., Szamosközi, Ş., & David, D. (2012). Virtual reality exposure therapy in anxiety disorders: A quantitative meta-analysis. *Depression and Anxiety, 29*(2), 85–93.

Reger, G. M., Smolenski, D., Norr, A., Katz, A., Buck, B., & Rothbaum, B. O. (2019). Does virtual reality increase emotional engagement during exposure for PTSD? Subjective distress during prolonged and virtual reality exposure therapy. *Journal of Anxiety Disorders, 61*, 75–81.

Rizzo, A., & Hartholt, R. (2005). *Bravemind: Virtual reality exposure therapy*. University of Southern California Institute for Creative Technologies.

Rothbaum, B. O., Hodges, L. F., Kooper, R., Opdyke, D., Williford, J., & North, M. (1995). Effectiveness of computer-generated (virtual reality) graded exposure in the treatment of acrophobia. *American Journal of Psychiatry, 152*, 626–628.

Rothbaum, B. O., & Hodges, L. (2008). *Virtual reality exposure therapy for fear of flying*. Virtually Better, Inc.

Rothbaum, B. O., Hodges, L., Smith, S., Lee, J. H., & Price, L. (2000). A controlled study of virtual reality exposure therapy for the fear of flying. *Journal of Consulting and Clinical Psychology, 68*(6), 1020.

Schubert, T., Friedmann, F., & Regenbrecht, H. (2001). The experience of presence: Factor analytic insights. *Presence: Teleoperators & Virtual Environments, 10*(3), 266–281.

Segal, R., Bhatia, M., & Drapeau, M. (2011). Therapists' perception of benefits and costs of using virtual reality treatments. *Cyberpsychology, Behavior, and Social Networking, 14*, 29–34.

Sherrill, A. M., Rothbaum, A. O., McSweeney, L. B., & Rothbaum, B. O. (2019). Virtual reality exposure therapy for posttraumatic stress disorder. *Psychiatric Annals, 49*, 343–347.

Sherrill, A. M., Goodnight, J. R., Burton, M. S., & Rothbaum, B. O. (2020). Use of virtual reality exposure therapy for trauma- and anxiety-related disorders. In G. M. Reger (Ed.), *Technology and mental health: A clinician's guide to improving outcomes*. Routledge.

Stevens, T. M., & Sherrill, A. M. (2021). A clinician's introduction to 360° video for exposure therapy. *Translational Issues in Psychological Science, 7*(3), 261–270.

VanElzakker, M. B., Dahlgren, M. K., Davis, F. C., Dubois, S., & Shin, L. M. (2014). From Pavlov to PTSD: The extinction of conditioned fear in rodents, humans, and anxiety disorders. *Neurobiology of Learning and Memory, 113*, 3–18.

Weech, S., Kenny, S., & Barnett-Cowan, M. (2019). Presence and cybersickness in virtual reality are negatively related: A review. *Frontiers in Psychology, 10*, 158.

Chapter 9
Culturally Responsive Approaches to Assessment and Case Conceptualization

Jessica LoPresti, Molly Sawdy, and Gerson Borrero

Introduction

When considering the prevalence of anxiety disorders within the United States (U.S.), it is beneficial to examine prevalence among specific populations instead of primarily utilizing aggregated general averages. This is based on findings that people who carry minoritized and marginalized identities may suffer from a higher prevalence of lifetime anxiety disorders in the U.S. than other groups (Alvarez et al., 2018; Ross et al., 2017; Szaflarski et al., 2017). For instance, the prevalence of anxiety disorder diagnoses is higher among people who identify as lesbian, gay, and bisexual than straight-identifying people (Ross et al., 2017). There is also a greater prevalence of anxiety disorder diagnoses among transgender and gender diverse people compared to those who identify as cisgender. Anxiety disorder prevalence also varies based on racial and ethnic identity (Alvarez et al., 2018) and nationality (Szaflarski et al., 2017). Moreover, contextual and cultural factors (e.g., discrimination, acculturation, and acculturative stress) affect the wellbeing and mental health help-seeking of people who carry racial and ethnic minoritized identities (LoPresti et al., 2023; Liu et al., 2022; Cariello et al., 2020; Thikeo et al., 2015).

J. LoPresti (✉) · M. Sawdy · G. Borrero
Department of Psychology, Suffolk University, Boston, MA, USA
e-mail: Jlopresti@suffolk.edu

E. M. Goetter (ed.), *Optimizing Treatment Engagement Processes in CBT for Anxiety and Related Disorders*, CBT: Science Into Practice,
https://doi.org/10.1007/978-3-031-91439-3_9

Stressors and Barriers to Quality and Effective Mental Healthcare

The Role of Power and Privilege and Social Determinants of Health

Prilleltensky and Gonick (1996) posit that oppression "entails a state of asymmetric power relations characterized by domination, subordination, and resistance, where the dominating persons or groups exercise their power by restricting access to material resources and by implanting in the subordinated persons or groups fear or self-deprecating views about themselves." Prilleltensky and Gonick (1996) emphasize how oppression arises and is perpetuated at a systemic level, thus creating and maintaining inequitable access to resources by groups that are minorities and marginalized by the dominant group (i.e., the group that holds more power or resources within a social context). Oppressive systems may be maintained by the dominant group through controlling which members of society have access to resources, such as education and wealth that may lead to a more equitable system. At an institutional level, examples of these oppressive systems include having less access to evidence-based interventions because the mental healthcare professionals at your community health center do not have access to training in these interventions. At an interpersonal level, racial macro- and micro-aggressions and other experiences of discrimination directed toward people who carry racial and ethnic minoritized identities are manifestations of oppression. An abundance of research demonstrates the frequency with which marginalized and minoritized people experience oppression, the pervasive nature of oppression, as well as the mental health consequences of cultural, systemic, institutional, and interpersonal oppression and their association with anxiety symptomology (Abdullah et al., 2021; LoPresti et al., 2023; Moagi et al., 2021; Nadal, 2011; Williams, 2020).

According to the Centers for Disease Control and Prevention (CDC), social determinants of health refer to life-enhancing resources (e.g., education, health care, and housing), which depending on the amount of distribution, determines a population's length and quality of life (Brennan Ramirez et al., 2008). *Power* is described as access to resources that enhance our ability to thrive and live safely as well as the ability to decide who has access to these resources, while *Privilege* gives unearned advantages and benefits to members of dominant groups in society. Access to the social determinants of health are inextricably tied to power and privilege, and thus the experience of anxiety. One such social determinant of health that pertains to the mental health field is health equity, or the idea that every individual should have the opportunity to attain their full health potential and that no individual should be disadvantaged from achieving this potential due to their social position (Brennan Ramirez et al., 2008). In other words, all individuals should have access to optimal psychological treatment for mental health conditions including anxiety disorders (which are particularly prevalent). Health disparities, on the other hand, refer to health inequities as a result of systematic, unequal distribution of resources (e.g., health care) (CDC, 2020).

Cultural Mistrust

A stressor that may contribute to anxiety for minoritized and marginalized populations navigating the mental healthcare system is highlighted by the phenomenon of cultural mistrust in mental healthcare providers. Cultural mistrust refers to the belief that White people cannot be trusted due to past and ongoing experiences of mistreatment perpetuated by White individuals against people of color (Terrell et al., 2009). There are over four centuries of biomedical research and healthcare infrastructure designed to exploit people of color, leading to modern day cultural mistrust of medical care setting (Washington, 2006). Specific examples of cultural mistrust in healthcare settings include mistrust of researchers and the healthcare system, fear related to research participation, inadequate information about research and opportunities to participate, inconvenience, questionable reputation of the research or research institution, and logistical concerns (Scharff et al., 2010). For instance, in the mid-1800s, a mental health disorder called Drapetomania described a Black American's uncontrollable urge to escape slavery, destroy property on the plantation, be disobedient, talk back, fight with their masters, and refuse to work (Poussaint & Alexander, 2000), which incorrectly pathologized valid human behavior and responses to racial trauma and oppression. Such injustices continue to be reflected in present-day health disparities amongst racial groupsand inequitable access to effective mental healthcare represents one of many factors that contribute to cultural mistrust in the mental health field by clients of color. Thus, when assessing experiences of anxiety, it is important to account for cultural mistrust when interpreting a client's endorsement of anxiety symptoms.

Factors that Heighten Experiences of Cultural Mistrust

Research has identified a number of factors that contribute to cultural mistrust. One factor is the limited availability of bilingual or linguistically trained mental health providers (American Psychiatry Association, 2017). For instance, it is estimated that less than 11% of psychologists are able to provide services in a language aside from in English, with only 5.5% of psychologists reporting they could do so in Spanish (Hamp et al., 2016). This limited availability for psychologists who may provide services aside from in English is a stark comparison to estimates from a US Census Bureau report of almost 1 in 5 people in the US speaking another language than English at home (Dietrich & Hernandez, 2022). Forcing clients to navigate clinical assessments not in their preferred language could potentially lead to miscommunication and misunderstanding of the client's psychological experiences, which could lead to an inaccurate diagnosis and inappropriate treatment recommendations.

Cultural Humility and Responsivity

Cultural competency, or "the ability to understand, appreciate and interact with people from cultures or belief systems different from one's own" (DeAngelis, 2015, p. 64) can help mitigate structural and interpersonal factors that contribute to health care disparities that impede treatment access and engagement. Cultural competency emphasizes a client-centered approach, such that it becomes the responsibility of the clinician to understand how their position(s) of power and privilege may play a role in the dynamic of their relationship with their client (Sue et al., 2008). For example, a White-identifying clinician instructing a client who identifies as an Asian woman with posttraumatic stress disorder (PTSD) to challenge safety-based cognitions, without acknowledging the increase of anti-Asian violence since the beginning of COVID-19 and the hate crime against Michelle Go in 2022, could invalidate the client's identity-based experiences and directly impede treatment engagement.

As the mental health field has evolved, there has been a shift from using the term cultural competency to an emphasis on cultural humility and cultural responsiveness. It is important to acknowledge the difference between cultural competency and cultural humility. Cultural competence implies a mastery of finite knowledge (Tervalon & Murray-Garcia, 1998) about clients' backgrounds. The expectation for a clinician to be culturally competent for shared and unshared identities for all clients they work with is an unrealistic expectation due to the vast number of sociocultural backgrounds that may be represented by clients. However, it is a realistic expectation for clinicians to strive toward cultural competency for all clients with whom they work (just as clinicians strive toward improvement in other areas of anxiety treatment, e.g. exposure implementation) because cultural competency exists on a spectrum not as a binary category (yes/no). A systematic review conducted by Kumaş-Tan et al. (2007) examined the ten most widely used quantitative measures of cultural competence, and highlighted six underlying, and problematic, assumptions that reinforce issues with providers' claims to cultural competency. *(1) Culture is typically equated to mean race and ethnicity.* This assumption does not account for a number of other sociocultural identities (e.g., gender identity, multilingualism, religion, immigration status, military status, adoption status, etc.) an individual brings to the therapy space. *(2) Culture is something only racial and ethnic minority groups have.* This fallacy fails to recognize that all racial and ethnic groups have culture regardless of their dominant or minoritized status. *(3) Cultural competency can be gained from sufficient awareness and knowledge gleaned from the client.* It is vital that clinicians do not solely rely on, or insist, that their clients educate them by having to share specialized knowledge about certain identities they may hold with which the clinician is less familiar. Doing so also places unfair pressure on the clients and fails to appreciate nuance within broad-based categorizations of identity. *(4) Cultural incompetence is an individual failure of the clinician.* Again, because cultural competency exists on a spectrum and not as a binary category, clinicians are no more able to claim they are culturally incompetent than they are able to claim they are culturally competent. It is the responsibility of the clinician to actively work to address areas of cultural incompetence to better serve their clients, foster treatment engagement, and work to bridge issues of cultural mistrust. The ability for clinicians to address their own biases and discomfort is a solid start to striving toward cultural humility and responsiveness. *(5) Cultural issues only arise when the client is from a racial or ethnic minority group.* Similar to number (2), a client's cultural background extends beyond their racial and ethnic identities. Thus, cultural issues within the dyad may occur based on any number of shared or unshared sociocultural identities between clinician and client (e.g., gender identity, multilingualism, religion, immigration status, Veteran status, adoption status, etc.). Moreover, even in instances where a clinician and client share identity factors, there may be very different lived experiences that require the clinician to maintain attention on cultural issues. *(6) Culturally competent providers are confident in themselves and comfortable with others.* The extent to which a clinician is confident in themselves and the extent to which a clinician is comfortable with others are not necessarily valid indicators of cultural competence. It is possible for a clinician to be highly confident in themselves and to feel highly comfortable with others, yet be perceived to have low cultural competency by the clients they work with. These six underlying assumptions that reinforce issues with clinicians' claims to cultural competency underscore the importance of shifting away from viewing cultural competence as a binary category and reframing cultural competence as a lifelong skill that exists on a spectrum that clinicians should strive toward throughout their career. Tervalon and Murray-Garcia (1998) use the term cultural humility to describe a lifelong commitment to self-evaluation and self-critique to understand the power imbalance in the provider-client dyad and to strive toward mutually beneficial partnerships with communities through individuals. Moreover, Jones-Smith (2018, p. xxviii) posited the term cultural responsiveness as a provider's ability to recognize cultural influences between a client and their presenting problems and also between the therapeutic dyad. Continuing to shift the emphasis from cultural competency to cultural humility and cultural responsiveness is evidenced by the American Psychological Association's (APA), 2017 Multicultural Guidelines, which oblige clinicians to improve the experiences of clients engaging in mental healthcare services. For instance, Guideline 5 states, "Psychologists aspire to recognize and understand historical and contemporary experiences with power, privilege and oppression. As such, they seek to address institutional barriers and related inequities, disproportionalities, and disparities of law enforcement, administration of criminal justice, educational, mental health, and other systems as they seek to promote justice, human rights, and access to quality and equitable mental and behavioral health services" (APA, 2017, p. 45). Because the identities of power and privilege that exist within the therapeutic dyad are social identities, the ways in which these identities interact and intertwine shift and adapt based on the current sociopolitical landscape. Thus, a clinician's skillset related to cultural humility and cultural responsiveness need to be just as dynamic and enduring to optimally serve their clients and foster their engagement in treatment.

Psychological Assessment Considerations for the Culturally Responsive Clinician

As posited in Guideline 9 of APA's Multicultural Guidelines (APA, 2017, p. 83), it is crucial for the field of psychology to train current and future generations of mental health providers not only as culturally responsive and humble therapists, but to also support the creation of, modification of, and training in culturally responsive clinical assessments and associated assessment practices marked by cultural humility. As put forth by Hays (2016), foundational parts of psychological assessment include: (1) ongoing involvement in one's own cultural self-assessment, (2) learning about minority and dominant groups' views/language/terminology, (3) understanding a client's unique identity and context, (4) accounting for the interaction between the identities within the therapeutic dyad, and (5) establishing positive alliance between clinician and client.

Part of administering assessment as a culturally responsive and humble therapist is recognizing when an assessment has not been validated in a population to which your client belongs or identifies with. As an example, consider a clinician working with an older client (i.e., 65 years or older) aiming to assess the client's anxiety symptoms. A unique experience to the older adult population includes specific fear situations such as fear of being a burden to their families (Kogan & Edelstein, 1997), which may not necessarily be as prevalent or even included in anxiety assessment tools for adult clients between the ages of 18–64. Thus, the clinician accounting for the client's age and having familiarity and comfort with administering a psychometrically validated assessment tool for older adults like the Geriatric Anxiety Inventory (GAI; Pachana et al., 2007) is one of many instances they may demonstrate cultural responsiveness and humility. Moreover, cultural responsiveness and humility will inherently strengthen interactions between clinicians and their clients, educators and the training communities, and researchers and their participants, regardless of their shared and non-shared identities. To strive toward growing as a culturally responsive and humble clinical assessor is to understand the power of assessment and to understand how clinical assessment is a continual part of understanding a client's experience to optimally provide mental healthcare services. Even if formally established culturally responsive assessments are unavailable to the clinician, or perhaps not yet validated for the client sitting across from them based on the identities they hold, it is still possible for clinicians to demonstrate their cultural responsiveness and humility through thoughtfully navigating the measure or questionnaire and recognizing potential power imbalances as reflected within the dyad and within society at large. Most importantly, because of the multiple and ongoing identity-based experiences clients have, and their impact on psychological functioning, it is critical for clinical assessment to occur throughout the treatment process. Furthermore, it is critical for clinical assessment to not pathologize valid, human responses that may occur among minoritized individuals navigating an oppressive system. To strive toward administering culturally responsive and humble clinical assessment is to infuse the development of critical consciousness from the individual level (e.g., clinical assessor) to the systemic level (e.g., dismantling barriers to accessing effective mental health experienced by minoritized and marginalized populations).

The Role of Identity Exploration

A central tenant of culturally responsive assessment is identity exploration. Identity is defined as a sense of who you are based on group membership and lived experience (Hays, 2008). Identity exploration is a foundational aspect of assessment for every client and it is important that clinicians include discussion of identity with all clients, regardless of the intersecting identities they hold. Intersectionality theory (Crenshaw, 1991) is framework that posits that our experiences are directly influenced by our multiple, cultural identities (e.g., race, gender, and social class) and that these experiences cannot be effectively or adequately understood by considering these cultural identities independently (Bauer et al., 2021). Whether one is aware of it or not, the identities one holds shape how we see ourselves, and the world. For instance, someone who celebrates Christian holidays (e.g., Christmas) might not know what it feels like to have their religious holidays go unacknowledged in education, employment, and community settings. Understanding this context might help a clinician integrate the experience of invisibility and anxiety for a client who identifies as Jewish or Muslim. A person who identifies as cisgender (i.e., gender aligns with sex they were assigned at birth) might not understand the anxiety that arises for transgender and gender nonconforming people when a primary care physician refer to them as "it" during a medical visit and the feelings of dehumanization associated with that experience. The historical assumption that identity only matters to those with minoritized or marginalized identities serves to uphold systems of power and oppression by not forcing those with privileged identities to acknowledge and gain awareness of oppression and inequities. In discussing identities with all clients, therapists facilitate treatment engagement by working to repair preexisting cultural mistrust and demonstrating an act of allyship and advocacy.

The importance of identity exploration holds true for therapists and clients in several ways. First, therapists must begin by gaining awareness of their intersecting cultural identities, the power, privilege, and oppression they hold in the context of these identities, and how these identities affect their viewpoints and perspectives. This level of awareness should be ongoing and provides a foundation for therapists to support clients in similar work.

Cultural Identity Assessment

The ADDRESSING and RESPECTFUL Frameworks

Hays (2008) presents an acronym, the ADDRESSING framework that helps therapists begin to attend to their own identities and the diverse backgrounds and lived experiences of clients. Specifically, this framework focuses on nine cultural identity factors that merit attention in the context of assessment and diagnosis (the parenthetical additions are our own expansions): Age and generational influences, Development disabilities, acquired Disabilities, Religion and spiritual orientation, Ethnicity (and race), Socioeconomic status, which includes education, Sexual orientation, Indigenous heritage, National origin (citizenship and immigrant status), and Gender. In addition, D'Andrea and Daniels (2001) present the RESPECTFUL model of interviewing. This model presents 10 dimensions of identity including Religion/spirituality, Economic/social class background, Sexual identity, Personal style and education, Ethic/racial identity, Chronic/lifespan status and challenges, Trauma/crisis, Family background and history, Unique physical characteristics, and Location of residence/language differences. We recommend therapists use one of these frameworks for gathering information about clients' cultural identities and how those identities juxtapose with their own cultural identities. As therapists gather information related to cultural identities of clients, it is clinically important to assess for the link between identity-related experiences and the development and maintenance of clients' anxiety. Specifically, there is an abundance of literature demonstrating that identity-based oppression contributes to the development and maintenance of anxiety (MacIntyre et al., 2023; Sosoo et al., 2020; Williams et al., 2023) and assessing for these experiences necessitates first understanding the intersecting cultural identities of our clients.

The Cultural Formulation Interview

The Cultural Formulation Interview, which can be found in the DSM5 (American Psychiatric Association, 2013), is a semi-structured 16-item assessment that presents an additional model for culturally responsive identity-based assessment. Clinicians can use the questions within the cultural formulation to guide the process of understanding the ways in which clients' cultural identities and related experiences are associated with the development and maintenance of their anxiety symptoms. Incorporating such models adeptly will serve to not only built therapeutic rapport, but will also enhance culturally responsive clinical assessment and case conceptualization to promote engagement in treatment.

The Process of Cultural Identity Assessment

To begin engaging with these identity models, clinicians are recommended to place themselves in the context of the identity categories presented and spend time reflecting on their lived experiences in society based on their intersecting identities. Therapists can ask themselves several questions:

- How do you identify within each category?
- How has this identity affected your life experiences?
- How much time do you spend thinking about this identity?
- Have you experienced oppression, barriers, or stigma targeting your identity (ies)?

Engaging in this self-reflective work provides a foundation for therapists to see the contrast between their own identity-related experiences and those of their clients. For instance, a therapist who has not experienced racial oppression and is unaware of the ways in which racial oppression is embedded in society can unintentionally cause harm to clients of color by ignoring the link between their identity-related experiences and anxiety making clients feel unseen, unheard, and dehumanized in the assessment process. Awareness guards against blind-spots associated with privilege and helps clinicians avoid making assumptions about clients or their experiences based on their own identity-related experiences.

Consider the example of Marta (a Black cisgender woman) who came to therapy experiencing social anxiety during her hospital rotations as a medical resident. Specifically, she reported having trouble finding her words when speaking to supervisors and fellow residents. Marta's therapist engaged in some social skills training with Marta and set up exposure scenarios where Marta would plan to have lunch with her fellow residents, speak up in small team chart review sessions, and make small talk with her Chief Resident. Marta engaged in these exposure scenarios for 6 weeks and saw no change in her symptoms or experience. Upon further exploration, Marta's therapist was able to understand that Marta's experience of social anxiety was tied to her perception that her White male superiors did not believe that she was intelligent enough to be a doctor. For Marta's case conceptualization and treatment plan, it was important for her therapist to understand her experiences related to her intersecting minoritized identities as a Black woman and about her historical experiences of having her intelligence questioned by White male supervisors frequently. Once the therapist understood these experiences through further assessment, she was able to tailor Marta's fear hierarchy, exposure experiences, and overall treatment plan more effectively.

Clinicians must also attend to contextual issues of power, privilege, and marginalization in clients' lives. The impact of these constructs on the lived experiences of clients who hold intersecting minoritized and marginalized identities as well as the impact of these constructs within the therapy space, is foundational to culturally responsive assessment. When introducing and discussing experiences of oppression with clients it is important for clinicians to understand and acknowledge that people with minoritized or marginalized identities often get the message that discussing oppression across difference (e.g., with White, heterosexual, cisgender, able-bodied, etc., identities) can be threatening and lead to negative consequences (e.g., loss of employment, lack of opportunities, and social isolation). This fear contributes to clients with marginalized identities introducing or discussing their experiences of oppression with therapist who do not hold similar identities. This context threatens the effectiveness of assessment and therapeutic outcomes in many ways. First, clients' valid assumptions of threat in discussing these experiences across difference undermines the development of a strong therapeutic alliance which contributes to positive mental health outcomes. Additionally, identity-related experiences can be linked to clients' experiences of anxiety and without exploration of these experiences, therapists are missing important aspects of case conceptualization which can undermine proper diagnosis, effective intervention choices, and ultimately positive therapeutic outcomes. Finally, clients feeling that they cannot authentically discuss their experiences in therapy can lead to lack of engagement in the therapy process as well as premature termination. Therefore, clinicians should introduce the topic of oppression early in assessment and check in with clients about their fears of discussing oppression in therapy with a clinician who does not hold their identities.

As an example, consider a therapist, who identifies as White, European American, and heterosexual, working with a client who identifies as Chinese-American and queer. Notably, the therapist holds multiple privileged identities, while the client is sitting at the intersection of multiple minoritized and marginalized identities (i.e., being of a nondominant racial and ethnic and sexual orientation group). In this instance, the culturally responsive clinician would want to inquire about the client's experiences within those identities. The therapist might ask the client about the identities that are important to them, inquire about the strengths within their identity-based communities, as well as their experiences of oppression in the context of their intersecting, marginalized identities (i.e., being Chinese-American and queer includes unique experiences of oppression compared to those who are Chinese-American and heterosexual and those who are part of the LGBTQIA+ community and of another non-minoritized, racial identity). Moreover, the clinician would want to present these questions in a way that (1) acknowledges the client's intersecting identities, (2) acknowledges how the therapist's own dominant group identities may impact how the client chooses to respond sequentially, and (3) acknowledges how the therapist's own dominant group identities may play a role in their automatic interpretation of the client's responses. Below we provide an example of what this conversation might look like.

Therapist: Many people who identify as a person of color and queer experience racism, heterosexism, and other forms of oppression that can amplify anxiety or just be distressing in their own right. Have you had these types of experiences?

Client: Yes, definitely. I can think of many instances across my life where people have made assumptions about because I'm Chinese-American.

Therapist: How have these experiences affected you?

Client: In so many ways. Maybe more than I can even think of.

Therapist: What would it be like to talk about these experiences with me given that I am a White heterosexual woman?

Client: I'm not really sure. I feel uneasy talking about these things in general.

Therapist: Thanks for sharing that. I know that it can feel uncomfortable, or even unsafe, to talk about these things for a number of reasons. I also know that it can be hard to talk about them with people who hold different identities and that you may have gotten the message, or had the experience, that talking about oppression with White people is not a validating or emotionally safe experience. (Pause)

Therapist: Would it be okay if we discussed these experiences a bit more as we unpack the anxiety you've been experiencing?

Client: Yes, I think so…

Clinicians can begin by introducing the topic of oppression through the intake process and allow the clients to drive the conversation. Specifically, we recommend that therapists include valid and reliable assessments of oppression-related stress in their intake packets and inquire about their responses in the first session. These assessments include The Race-Based Traumatic Stress Symptom Scale (RBTSSS; Carter et al., 2013), The Schedule of Racist Events (SRE; Landrine & Klonoff, 1996), The General Ethnic Discrimination Scale (GEDS; Landrine et al., 2006), The Racial and Ethnic Microaggressions Scale (REMS; Nadal, 2011), The Racial Microaggressions Scale (RMAS; Torres-Harding et al., 2012). Clinicians can also reference the DSM 5 Cultural Formulation Interview (APA, 2013) as a guide for culturally responsive assessment. This introduction accomplishes several things that can promote treatment engagement. First, the clinician is validating the client's experiences and humanity by acknowledging that oppression is something that clients with minoritized and marginalized identities experience with frequency. Additionally, by starting this conversation, clinicians send a message to clients that therapy provides an opportunity to discuss these experiences and that you, as the clinician have some understanding of the severe negative mental health consequences of oppression.

Strengths-Based Approaches to Identity Exploration

One important aspect of identity exploration is approaching this process with a strengths-based perspective. Client's often have diverse identity-related experiences inclusive of the values, traditions, and strength associated with their identities. Specifically, there is literature to suggest positive racial and ethnic identity can buffer the negative impacts of oppression on anxiety (Willis et al., 2021; Woo et al., 2019). Additionally, evidence suggests that finding strength in community, resistance against oppression, and shared values and traditions is in direct contrast to the negative messages marginalized clients often receive about their identities and can contribute to wellness (Silverman et al., 2023). Clinicians are socialized to approach identity exploration from a deficit perspective, which assumes that minoritized and marginalized clients have solely challenging identity-related experiences (e.g., oppression). This approach can contribute to the internalization of the overwhelming messages minoritized clients receive about their worth and value. While it is crucial to assess for oppressive experiences, it is equally important to engage with clients in the importance, values, and strength they associate with their identities, the empowerment they experience based on the shared values within their communities, and the ways they resist oppression. These aspects of clients' identities often unearth organic coping resources that can be integrated into the case conceptualization and intervention strategies, which in turn fosters treatment engagement.

The Role of Critical Consciousness

When assessing the role of clients' intersecting identities, a central focus must be on the importance of these identities to clients as well as the role of critical consciousness. Critical consciousness is described as an in-depth knowledge about social, political, and economic systems that contribute to societal inequities (Freire, 1970). This in-depth knowledge can facilitate advocacy, self-agency, and esteem in the face of societal inequities and oppression (Freire, 1970). In addition to awareness of clients' identities and identity-related experiences, level of critical consciousness helps clinicians meet clients where they are in terms of readiness to approach identity-related challenges (e.g., racism-related stress and internalized oppression). An example of the integration of critical consciousness and assessment practices are demonstrated in the case of Rebecca, an 18-year-old Black young woman. Rebecca came to therapy struggling with a history of generalized anxiety disorder with current anxiety associated with her performance in her new job as a first-year associate at a law firm. She reported significant worry and stress related to the quality of her work product, lack of sleep due to perseveration on mistakes she anticipated, and inability to engage with her (mostly White) colleagues in meetings. As her therapist worked from the ADDRESSING Framework (Hays, 2008) several things became clear: (1) The client racially identified as Black and ethnically as African American; (2) the client did not identify any clear connection between the anxiety she was feeling and her identity-related experiences; and (3) at the time of her intake, the client was not ready to make the aforementioned connection. Below we provide an example of introducing identity to the therapy context while allowing the client to think about the connection between her identity-related experiences and the anxiety she is experiencing.

Therapist: As we've talked about several aspects of your identity, it seems like your identity as a Black woman is important to you.

Rebecca: Well, yes. I would say that I'm proud to be a Black woman.

Therapist: Can you tell me a bit more about that pride?

Rebecca: I'm just proud. I'm not sure what else to say about it.

Therapist: How has being a Black woman affected your experiences as an associate at your firm?

Rebecca: Well, I'm one of a few people of color. It's pretty typical in law firms. But, I'm not sure that has anything to do with my experiences of stress. The job is hard, I'm new, and I keep making mistakes.

Therapist: It makes sense that you are experiencing anxiety given how stressful the job is. As we continue therapy I hope we can continue to explore factors in your work environment that might be contributing to the anxiety you're experiencing.

Here, the therapist skillfully introduced and integrated a discussion of identity as they began to delve deeper into the client's experiences of stress at work. However, it was evident that the client did not initially connect her intersecting minoritized identities (i.e., being a woman, being Black, African American) to her experiences of stress at work. Specifically, it is possible that there is no connection. So as not to undermine treatment engagement, the culturally responsive clinician sensitively follows the clients' lead in these types of situations while considering alternative hypotheses, such as no connection exists, a connection does exist and the client is not ready to discuss it with the therapist, or the client is unaware of the connection entirely.

The Role of Self-Report Assessments

An additional way to begin the conversation about oppression with clients is through the use of self-report measures. There are many validated and reliable self-report measures that assess the experience of racial discrimination. The Schedule of Racist Events (SRE; Landrine & Klonoff, 1996) is an 18-item self-report measure that assesses the frequency and stress associated with racist experiences. Items include, "How many times have you been treated unfairly by your co-workers, fellow students, or colleagues because you are Black?". The Race-Based Traumatic Stress Symptom Scale (RBTSSS; Carter et al., 2013) is a 52-item self-report measure that assesses stress reactions to racism. Items include, "As a consequence of the memorable encounter I had with racism, I try not to think about, talk about, or have feelings about the event." The General Ethnic Discrimination Scale (GEDS; Landrineet al., 2006) is an 18-item measure that assesses lifetime and past-year frequency and stress associated with ethnic discrimination. Items include, "How often have you been treated unfairly by your co-workers, fellow students and colleagues because of your race/ethnic group?". The Racial and Ethnic Microaggressions Scale (REMS-45; Nadal, 2011) is a checklist that assesses the frequency of microaggressions over the past 6 months. Items included, "An employer or coworker was unfriendly or unwelcoming toward me because of my race." The Racial Microaggressions Scale (RMAS; Torres-Harding et al., 2012) is a 32-item measure that assesses the frequency and distress appraisal associated with racial microaggressions. Items include, "People act like they are scared of me because of my race" or "People suggest that I am 'exotic' in a sexual way because of my race." Clinicians should encourage their clinics, community health centers, and practices to include validated and reliable self-report measures of oppression in their intake questionnaire packets. This is an organic and evidence-based way to introduce and integrate discussions of oppression. After clients complete an intake packet that includes an assessment of oppression, clinicians might say, "I see that you endorsed experiencing racism/heterosexism/homophobia/transphobia and very reasonable stress associated with those experiences. Would it be okay if I asked you a bit about those experiences and how they are affecting your anxiety?". If the client agrees, you might begin with asking questions like, "How has racism affected your ability to engage at school, work, or in your community?", "How has heterosexism affected your ability to focus on the things in your life that are meaningful to you" (e.g., spending time with loved ones and thriving in your career), " How has transphobia affected your belief that you are safe?". Each of these assessment questions begins to target underlying psychological mechanisms that lead to anxiety from evidence-based cognitive behavioral models.

Integration of Assessment with Evidence-Based Cognitive Behavioral (CBT) Models

Culturally responsive assessment and conceptualization involves the integration of evidence-based cognitive behavioral therapy models. Specifically, it is important for clinicians to understand the ways in which oppressive experiences affect a client's perceptions of themselves and their contexts, emotional experiences, as well as their behaviors. In fact, this is consistent with a CBT conceptualization of anxiety: Clients experience events, perceive those events, emote in response to those perceptions, and behave based on those emotions.

Consider a college student who presents with public speaking anxiety. She discloses to the therapist that she has been experiencing anxiety because she gave a class presentation where she stuttered and lost her train of thought several times (**EVENT**), then perceived that everyone in the class viewed her as unintelligent (**APPRAISAL**), and experienced sadness and shame about the situation (**EMOTION**). She desires to avoid public speaking and anticipates dropping courses that include a public speaking component (**BEHAVIORAL AVOIDANCE**). While her avoidance of public speaking and related courses assuages her anxiety in the short-term, this behavioral avoidance exacerbates her long-term experiences of anxiety because of her goals to graduate and pursue a career in marketing. From a traditional CBT framework, the clinician has several avenues for conceptualization and subsequent intervention of the public speaking anxiety including the irrational nature of the client's perception, the lack of emotion regulation skills, or the avoidance behavior. Now, let's add some context to this client's experience. The college student identifies as a Muslim woman who has been ostracized in the past for her quiet and "introverted nature" and has also experienced significant Islamophobia on her college campus including racial and ethnic slurs and her headscarf being pulled off at the dining hall. In terms of assessment of her public speaking anxiety, the clinician should avoid prematurely conceptualizing her perceptions as irrational and instead seek to understand more about the ways the client's anxiety might reflect or be amplified by the internalization of the oppression she has experienced. Failing to assess for discrimination and oppression-related experiences would render the case conceptualization incomplete and could lead to serious consequences for treatment engagement. After establishing that the client has experienced racism through the intake process, the clinician might ask questions like, "what do these experiences mean about you?" or "How have these experiences changed the way you think about yourself" or "How have these experiences affected your self-confidence or the ways that you value yourself." A culturally responsive conceptualization of this client's experience of public speaking anxiety is more complete in consideration of the client's social and cultural context. See Fig. 9.1.

Assessing for the internalization of oppression (e.g., "I don't belong," "I'm not valuable," and "I don't deserve compassion") provides an important target for intervention. Clinicians must avoid assessment tactics that question the validity or veracity of clients' experience of oppression. For example, therapists should avoid asking questions like, "*Are you sure what you experienced was racism?*", "*What evidence do you have that your boss is racist*?", "*Did your professor intend to say something that hurt you?*". This type of assessment serves to compound the client's experiences of oppression in the therapy room and can undermine engagement or cause a client to discontinue treatment completely. Instead, clinicians should focus on asking clients how these experiences affect self-esteem, self-worth, feelings of being valued, and perceptions of their own worth. This line of questioning sets the stage for work on supporting clients in building their self-esteem, sense of worth and value, while maintaining and validating that racism is real and can contribute to the development and maintenance of anxiety. By understanding the ways in which clients internalize oppression, therapists can develop a treatment plan that includes engagement in restructuring the negative self-focused thoughts that arise as a consequence of racism. Context matters and it is important for clinicians to attend to the context during assessment and continue to attend to context throughout treatment.

The integration of cultural responsivity and evidence-based practice is not only applicable in traditional CBT conceptualizations. Consider the lens of acceptance-based behavioral therapy (ABBT) models. From an ABBT perspective, anxiety is developed and maintained through a narrow focus on future oriented threat, fusion

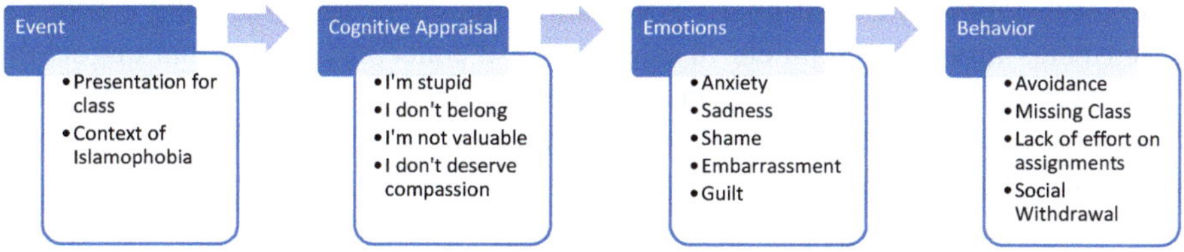

Fig. 9.1 Integration of culturally specific example and traditional CBT model

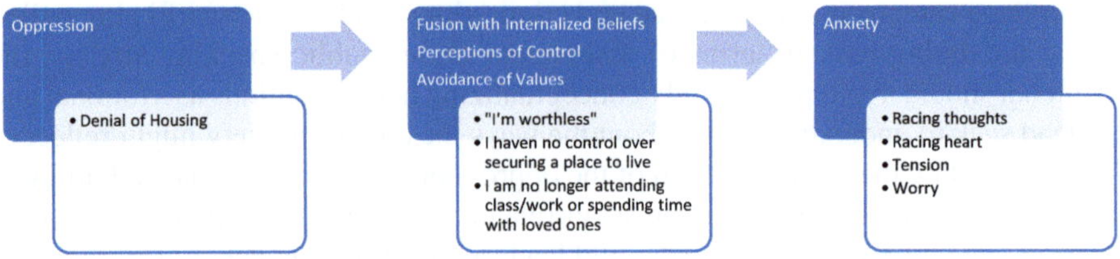

Fig. 9.2 Mechanisms linking oppression and anxiety

with negative thoughts, responding negatively to internal experiences (e.g., thoughts, physiology, and emotions), and behaviorally avoiding the most meaningful activities in one's life (Roemer & Orsillo, 2009).

Consider the case of Alex, a Latinx, transgender man who comes to therapy due to pervasive worry associated with housing and healthcare. Alex's fifth apartment rental application in 2 weeks was denied. He is currently sleeping on a friend's couch. He reports constant stress and worry about where he will sleep and if he will ever be able to find permanent housing. He reports feeling "worthless" and experiences daily panic attack symptoms (e.g., heart palpitations, sweaty palms, and light headed) that have led him to stop going to work and attending classes at his university. Additionally, he has begun isolating from friends and family. In this case, Alex's clinician should assess for the client's perception of oppression in the context of these life stressors. In many cases, barriers to accessing resources related to the social determinants of health are connected to systemic inequities. It is important for clinicians to be able to make these types of connections while assessing for the underlying mental health consequences of oppression. These assessment considerations would inform an adapted version of the above ABBT model to include Alex's experience of internalized oppression (e.g., fusion with thoughts of worthlessness), feeling a lack of control over his safety and ability to thrive (e.g., housing), as well as the avoidance of the things that are most meaningful to him (e.g., classes, work, and time with friends and family). See Fig. 9.2.

Using Alex's example, a therapist might tailor their assessment questions to target the internalized beliefs that arise in the face of racism. For example, a therapist might ask, "How does racism make you feel about your value or worth?". Targeting perceptions of control a therapist might ask, "do you feel that you have control over your safety or access to the things you need to thrive?". Finally, targeting values-based living a therapist might ask, "How does racism get in the way of you doing the things that are most meaningful to you?". Asking these types of assessment questions achieves several goals: (1) Ensures the client feels seen and heard; (2) contributes to the development of effective case conceptualization that targets the underlying psychological mechanisms maintaining anxiety (e.g., perceptions of control and avoidance of valued living); and (3) enables the therapist to choose effective interventions that include coping with identity-related experiences (e.g., racism).

Conclusion

Culturally responsive assessment has been highlighted by the governing bodies of our field as foundational to ethical clinical practice. The practice of culturally responsive assessment sets the stage for treatment engagement, retention, and effective outcomes for people who hold marginalized and minoritized identities. Engagement in culturally responsive assessment, and clinical practice more broadly, requires ongoing self-reflection, attention to issues of power, privilege, and oppression, as well as commitment to integrating identity and evidence-based practice throughout the assessment process.

Clinical Summary Points and Recommendations

- Therapists must explore their own identities and develop an awareness of the power and privilege they hold in reference to these identities, as well as the oppression they experience in the context of these identities.
- Therapists should endeavor to gain knowledge about their clients' identities throughout the assessment process.
- Culturally responsive and humble assessment approaches are the foundation of ethical clinical practice. Several models and assessment methods can be integrated into evidence-based clinical assessment and case conceptualization. Therapists should work to integrate identity-related factors into evidence-based CBT models for anxiety.

References

Abdou, C. M., Fingerhut, A. W., Jackson, J. S., & Wheaton, F. (2016). Healthcare stereotype threat in older adults in the health and retirement study. *American Journal of Preventive Medicine, 50*(2), 191–198. https://doi.org/10.1016/j.amepre.2015.07.034

Abdullah, T., Graham-LoPresti, J. R., Tahirkheli, N. N., Hughley, S. M., & Watson, L. (2021). Microaggressions and posttraumatic stress disorder symptom scores among black Americans: Exploring the link. *Traumatology, 27*(3), 244–253. https://doi.org/10.1037/trm0000259

Alvarez, K., Fillbrunn, M., Green, J., Jackson, J. S., Kessler, R. C., McLaughlin, K. A., Sadikova, E., Sampson, N. A., & Alegría, M. (2018). Race/ethnicity, nativity, and lifetime risk of mental disorders in US adults. *Social Psychiatry and Psychiatric Epidemiology, 54*(5), 553–565. https://doi.org/10.1007/s00127-018-1644-5

American Psychiatric Association. (2013). *Diagnostic and statistical manual of mental disorders* (5th ed.). American Psychiatric Association.

American Psychiatry Association. (2017). *Mental health facts.* [Fact Sheet]. https://www.psychiatry.org/psychiatrists/diversity/education/mental-health-facts#section_0

American Psychological Association (APA). (2017). *Multicultural guidelines: An ecological approach to context, identity, and intersectionality,* 2017. https://www.apa.org/about/policy/multicultural-guidelines.pdf

Bauer, G. R., Churchill, S. M., Mahendran, M., Walwyn, C., Lizotte, D., & Villa-Rueda, A. A. (2021). Intersectionality in quantitative research: A systematic review of its emergence

and applications of theory and methods. *SSM - Population Health, 14*, 100798. https://doi.org/10.1016/j.ssmph.2021.100798
Brennan Ramirez, L. K., Baker, E. A., & Metzler, M. (2008). *Promoting health equity: A resource to help communities address social determinants of health.* https://www.cdc.gov/nccdphp/dch/programs/healthycommunitiesprogram/tools/pdf/SDOH-workbook.pdf; https://doi.org/10.1016/j.ssmph.2021.100798
Cariello, A. N., Perrin, P. B., Williams, C. D., Espinoza, G., Paredes, A. M., Moreno, O., & Trujillo, M. A. (2020). Moderating influence of enculturation on the relations between minority stressors and physical health via anxiety in Latinx immigrants. *Cultural Diversity & Ethnic Minority Psychology, 26*(3), 356–366. https://doi.org/10.1037/cdp0000308
Carter, R. T., Mazzula, S., Victoria, R., Vazquez, R., Hall, S., Smith, S., Sant-Barket, S., Forsyth, J., Bazelais, K., & Williams, B. (2013). *Race-based traumatic stress symptom scale (RBTSSS).* [database record]. APA PsycTests. https://doi.org/10.1037/t19426-000
Centers for Disease Control and Prevention. (2020). *Health disparities among youth.* [Fact Sheet]. https://www.cdc.gov/healthyyouth/disparities/index.htm
Crenshaw, K. (1991). Mapping the margins: Intersectionality, identity politics, and violence against women of color. *Stanford Law Review, 43*, 61.
D'Andrea, M., & Daniels, J. (2001). RESPECTFUL Counseling: An Integrative Model for Counselors. In D. Pope-Davis, & H. Coleman (Eds.), *The Interface of Class, Culture and Gender in Counseling* (pp. 417–466). Thousand Oaks, CA: Sage.
DeAngelis, T. (2015). In search of cultural competence. *Monitor on Psychology, 46*(3) http://www.apa.org/monitor/2015/03/cultural-competence
Dietrich, S. & Hernandez, E. (2022). *Language use in the United States: 2019*. American Community Survey Reports. https://www.census.gov/content/dam/Census/library/publications/2022/acs/acs-50.pdf
Freire, P. (1970). *Pedagogy of the oppressed*. Seabury Press.
Hamp, A., Stamm, K., Lin, L., & Christidis, P. (2016). *2015 APA survey of psychology health service providers*. American Psychological Association. https://www.apa.org/workforce/publications/15-health-service-providers
Hays, P. A. (2008). *Addressing cultural complexities in practice: Assessment, diagnosis, and therapy* (2nd ed.). American Psychological Association. https://doi.org/10.1037/11650-000
Hays, P. A. (2016). Conducting a culturally responsive assessment. In I. P. A. Hays (Ed.), *Addressing cultural complexities in practice: Assessment, diagnosis, and therapy* (3rd ed., pp. 127–160). American Psychological Association. https://doi.org/10.1037/14801-007
Jones-Smith, E. (2018). *Culturally diverse counseling: Theory and practice*. SAGE Publications.
Kogan, J. N., & Edelstein, B. (1997, November). Fears in middle-aged and older adults: Relations to daily functioning and satisfaction with life. In *Poster presented at the 31st annual convention of the Association for Advancement of behavior therapy*.
Kumaş-Tan, Z., Beagan, B., Loppie, C., MacLeod, A., & Frank, B. (2007). Measures of cultural competence: Examining hidden assumptions. *Academic Medicine, 82*(6), 548–557. https://doi.org/10.1097/ACM.0b013e3180555a2d
Landrine, H., & Klonoff, E. (1996). The schedule of racist events: A measure of racial discrimination and a study of its negative physical and mental health consequences. *Journal of Black Psychology, 22*(2), 144–168. https://doi.org/10.1177/009579849602220022
Landrine, H., Klonoff, E. A., Corral, I., Fernandez, S., & Roesch, S. (2006). Conceptualizing and measuring ethnic discrimination in health research. *Journal of Behavioral Medicine, 29*, 79–94.
Liu, S., He, L., Wei, M., Du, Y., & Cheng, D. (2022). Depression and anxiety from acculturative stress: Maladaptive perfectionism as a mediator and mindfulness as a moderator. *Asian American Journal of Psychology, 13*(2), 207–216. https://doi.org/10.1037/aap0000242
LoPresti, J., Abdullah-Swain, T., Borrero, G., & Scott, D. (2023). Racial microaggressions and trauma symptoms in a black sample: The moderating role of self-compassion. *Journal of Contextual Behavioral Science, 29*, 209–218. https://doi.org/10.1016/j.jcbs.2023.06.010

MacIntyre, M. M., Zare, M., & Williams, M. T. (2023). Anxiety-related disorders in the context of racism. *Current Psychiatry Reports, 25*(2), 31–43. https://doi.org/10.1007/s11920-022-01408-2
Moagi, M. M., van Der Wath, A. E., Jiyane, P. M., & Rikhotso, R. S. (2021). Mental health challenges of lesbian, gay, bisexual and transgender people: An integrated literature review. *Health SA Gesondheid, 26*(1), 1487. https://doi.org/10.4102/hsag.v26i0.1487
Nadal, K. L. (2011). The racial and ethnic microaggressions scale: Construction, reliability, and validity. *Journal of Counseling Psychology, 58*, 470–480. https://doi.org/10.1037/a0025193
Pachana, N. A., Byrne, G. J., Siddle, H., Koloski, N., Harley, E., & Arnold, E. (2007). Development and validation of the geriatric anxiety inventory. *International Psychogeriatrics, 19*(1), 103–114. https://doi.org/10.1017/S1041610206003504
Poussaint, A. F., & Alexander, A. (2000). *Lay my burden down: Unraveling suicide and the mental health crisis among African-Americans*. Beacon Press.
Prilleltensky, I., & Gonick, L. (1996). Polities change, oppression remains: On the psychology and politics of oppression. *Political Psychology, 127-148*, 127. https://doi.org/10.2307/3791946
Roemer, L., & Orsillo, S. (2009). *Mindfulness and acceptance-based behavioral therapies in practice*. The Guiford Press.
Ross, L. E., Salway, T., Tarasoff, L. A., MacKay, J., Hawkins, B., & Fehr, C. (2017). Prevalence of depression and anxiety among bisexual people compared to gay, lesbian, and heterosexual individuals: A systematic review and meta-analysis. *Journal of Sex Research, 55*(4–5), 435–456. https://doi.org/10.1080/00224499.2017.1387755
Silverman, D. M., Rosario, R. J., Hernandez, I. A., & Destin, M. (2023). The ongoing development of strength-based approaches to people who hold systemically marginalized identities. *Personality and Social Psychology Review, 27*(3), 255–271.
Scharff, D. P., Mathews, K. J., Jackson, P., Hoffsuemmer, J., Martin, E., & Edwards, D. (2010). More than Tuskegee: Understanding mistrust about research participation. *Journal of Health Care for the Poor and Underserved, 21*(3), 879. https://doi.org/10.1353/hpu.0.0323
Sosoo, E. E., Bernard, D. L., & Neblett, E. W., Jr. (2020). The influence of internalized racism on the relationship between discrimination and anxiety. *Cultural Diversity and Ethnic Minority Psychology, 26*(4), 570. https://doi.org/10.1037/cdp0000320
Steele, C. M., & Aronson, J. (1995). Stereotype threat and the intellectual test performance of African Americans. *Journal of Personality and Social Psychology, 69*(5), 797. https://doi.org/10.1037/0022-3514.69.5.797
Sue, D. W., Nadal, K. L., Capodilupo, C. M., Lin, A. I., Torino, G. C., & Rivera, D. P. (2008). Racial microaggressions against black Americans: Implications for counseling. *Journal of Counseling & Development, 86*(3), 330–338. https://doi.org/10.1037/0735-7028.39.3.329
Szaflarski, M., Cubbins, L. A., & Meganathan, K. (2017). Anxiety disorders among US immigrants: The role of immigrant background and social-psychological factors. *Issues in Mental Health Nursing, 38*(4), 317–326. https://doi.org/10.1080/01612840.2017.1287790
Terrell, F., Taylor, J., Menzise, J., & Barrett, R. K. (2009). Cultural mistrust: A core component of African American consciousness. In H. A. Neville, B. M. Tynes, & S. O. Utsey (Eds.), *Handbook of African American psychology* (pp. 299–309). Sage Publications, Inc.
Tervalon, M., & Murray-Garcia, J. (1998). Cultural humility versus cultural competence: A critical distinction in defining physician training outcomes in multicultural education. *Journal of Health Care for the Poor and Underserved, 9*(2), 117–125. https://doi.org/10.1353/hpu.2010.0233
Thikeo, M., Florin, P., & Ng, C. H. (2015). Help seeking attitudes among Cambodian and Laotian refugees: Implications for public mental health approaches. *Journal of Immigrant and Minority Health, 17*(6), 1679–1686. https://doi.org/10.1007/s10903-015-0171-7
Torres-Harding, S. R., Andrade, A. L., & Romero-Diaz, C. E. (2012). The racial microaggressions scale (RMAS): A new scale to measure experiences of racial micoaggressions in people of color. *Cultural Diversity and Ethnic Minority Psychology, 18*, 153–164. https://doi.org/10.1037/a0027658
Washington, H. A. (2006). *Medical apartheid: The dark history of medical experimentation on black Americans from colonial times to the present*. Random House, Inc.

Williams, M. T. (2020). Microaggressions: Clarification, evidence, and impact. *Perspectives on Psychological Science, 15*(1), 3–26. https://doi.org/10.1177/1745691619827499

Williams, M., Osman, M., & Hyon, C. (2023). Understanding the psychological impact of oppression using the trauma symptoms of discrimination scale. *Chronic Stress, 7*, 24705470221149511. https://doi.org/10.1177/24705470221149511

Willis, H. A., Sosoo, E. E., Bernard, D. L., Neal, A., & Neblett, E. W. (2021). The associations between internalized racism, racial identity, and psychological distress. *Emerging Adulthood, 9*(4), 384–400. https://doi.org/10.1177/21676968211005598

Woo, B., Fan, W., Tran, T. V., & Takeuchi, D. T. (2019). The role of racial/ethnic identity in the association between racial discrimination and psychiatric disorders: A buffer or exacerbator? *SSM - Population Health, 7*, 100378. https://doi.org/10.1016/j.ssmph.2019.100378

Chapter 10
Building a Positive Racial and Ethnic Identity to Support Treatment Engagement

Monnica T. Williams, Ruo Ying Feng, Sonya C. Faber, and Rehman Y. Abdulrehman

Introduction

Ethnic identity is about how people develop and experience a sense of belonging to their culture and roots. It sometimes, but not always, correlates to national origin. Traditions, customs, national history, and feelings about a person's heritage are all important aspects of ethnic identity. From a young age, people progress through different stages as they learn to identify with their culture, whereby they come to understand their group's customs and values so that they can feel they are a part of their ethnic group. Research has found that a stronger ethnic identity is correlated with better psychological well-being, whereas lower levels of ethnic identity are correlated to depression and anxiety in some ethnic groups (Williams et al., 2012a, 2012b). Ethnic identity seems to have an important buffering effect against the negative consequences of racial discrimination by combating negative cognitions about individuals' racial or ethnic group, increasing self-esteem, and increasing positive coping strategies (Williams et al., 2018a, 2018b).

M. T. Williams (✉) · R. Y. Feng
School of Psychology, University of Ottawa, Ottawa, ON, Canada
e-mail: Monnica.Williams@uOttawa.ca

S. C. Faber
School of Psychology, University of Ottawa, Ottawa, ON, Canada

School of Epidemiology and Public Health, University of Ottawa, Ottawa, ON, Canada

R. Y. Abdulrehman
Department of Clinical Health Psychology, University of Manitoba, Winnipeg, MB, Canada

E. M. Goetter (ed.), *Optimizing Treatment Engagement Processes in CBT for Anxiety and Related Disorders*, CBT: Science Into Practice,
https://doi.org/10.1007/978-3-031-91439-3_10

Ethnic Identity and its Importance to Treatment Engagement

Ethnic identity is important to treatment engagement because it contributes to self-efficacy, or an individual's belief in their ability to control their own behavior and attain specific goals (Booth et al., 2017). In the context of psychotherapy, self-efficacy is a key component to treatment outcomes, both for clients and for therapists (e.g., Gori et al., 2022). Self-efficacy is also crucial for the treatment engagement processes, providing motivation for treatment (Longo et al., 1992), increasing adherence (Roncoroni et al., 2019), and preventing dropout (Keshen et al., 2017). For cognitive behavioral therapy (CBT), self-efficacy may play even larger roles as change mechanisms often involve clients re-appraising their own thoughts or changing specific behavior/thought patterns. A growing amount of research illustrates the role of self-efficacy (see Chap. 2) in CBT engagement and treatment outcomes for several disorders including panic disorder (Fentz et al., 2014), social anxiety disorder (Goldin et al., 2012), anxiety symptoms (Brown et al., 2014), obsessive-compulsive disorder (Leeuwerik et al., 2023; Merling et al., 2022), and posttraumatic stress disorder (Brown et al., 2016; Titcombe-Parekh et al., 2018).

Lastly, for therapists, an understanding of ethnic identity is crucial as it relates to the ability to work well with an increasingly diverse client population with various ethnic and racial identities, leading to a strong therapeutic alliance. The associations between therapeutic alliance, treatment outcomes, and engagement have been well established (see Chap. 1). A stronger therapeutic alliance is associated with higher treatment engagement, lower dropout, as well as global reductions in symptoms (Bourke et al., 2021; Sharf et al., 2010). In the context of exposure therapy for anxiety disorders, research shows a strong link between the therapeutic alliance and treatment engagement, with particular emphasis on goal and task agreement (Buchholz & Abramowitz, 2020). Treatment adherence was a key factor explaining this relationship, highlighting the importance of the therapeutic alliance in promoting adherence in exposure therapy, ultimately facilitating positive therapeutic outcomes. An understanding of ethnic identity is also key for therapist's cultural humility, an ongoing process of self-reflection, openness to learning, and challenge of ongoing biases, which also plays a key role in therapeutic alliance and repairing cultural ruptures (Mosher et al., 2017).

Race Versus Ethnicity

It is important to understand what ethnic identity refers to and how it differs from racial identity. Many people have been socialized to avoid, dismiss, or ignore these constructs, often conflating race and ethnicity, and this lack of understanding tends to hinder open and frank discussions, even for therapists. Recognizing and understanding the distinctions between race and ethnicity are necessary for clinicians to offer culturally competent and inclusive care. This, in turn, can improve treatment engagement by more cogently addressing barriers to care, fostering trust, improving rapport, and tailoring interventions to meet the unique needs of diverse populations.

While there can be intersections and overlaps between ethnicity and race, they are distinct concepts. Ethnic identity emphasizes cultural connections and social belonging, whereas race often focuses on *perceived* physical characteristics and social categorizations that have been used to create and perpetuate systemic inequalities. Where race is a label applied to us by perceptions of others, ethnicity is a label we apply ourselves arising from a nuanced understanding of our intersecting identities, based on both our actual and identified heritage.

Embracing ethnic diversity can contribute to cultural richness, mutual understanding, and appreciation of different traditions, but race has been used to create and perpetuate systems of power, privilege, and discrimination. The historical and ongoing implications of race have led to social inequalities, marginalization, and injustices against racialized groups. It is also important to appreciate that the concept of race does not always apply internationally, where identity is more often determined by ethnicity, as bloodlines or perceived race becomes more complex. Ethnic identity is inclusive in a way that race is not; for example, the following are ethnic identities: Palestinian Christian, Ethiopian-Mizrahi Jewish, Arab-Dutch, Somali-Muslim, and French-Canadian-Hawaiian, while "racial categories" are White, Black, Asian, and Indigenous/Native American.

Race is a social construct with no biological basis and is derived from White supremacy, an ideology that assumes the superiority of White people and White culture over people of color and the cultures of people of color (Haeny et al., 2021). Race is mutually exclusive and externally defined, often by governments for purposes of population control. Critically, these definitions affect people's perception of race and of themselves. For example, consider that "Hispanic" used to be considered a race, but then the US Census Bureau changed it to an ethnic group, although many Hispanic people do not identify with any race other than "Hispanic or Latino." Brown Hispanic people are left with no suitable options beyond "Other."

Ethnicity, in contrast with race, can have overlapping and simultaneous categories and can be self-defined in a way that race cannot. It is more reflective of how identity is determined outside a colonialist perspective. Finally, the ability to self-identify and have overlapping ethnic identities critically provides individuals with *agency* in defining and expressing their own sense of belonging and cultural heritage. It can more accurately reflect one's own history and lineage and be more reflective of the intersectional identity that most of us actually carry (Table 10.1).

Whereas being racialized is something done to people based on a limited set of categories, ethnically identifying is something people can describe based on a greater depth of understanding of themselves. When clients and therapists have a common language to discuss the important parts of a person's identity, it promotes understanding and treatment engagement. A client explaining their own identity is more empowering than a therapist defining their identity for them.

Table 10.1 Differences between race and ethnicity

Race	Ethnicity	Why does it matter for treatment engagement?
Arbitrary categorization: Individuals are classified into mutually exclusive categories based on skin shade and visual features.	**Self-identification**: Reflects how individuals personally identify, can encompass genetic, ancestral, cultural, historical, fluid, and overlapping factors.	Speaks to importance of cultural assessment and understanding personal salience of identity factors; opens client's eyes to nuance.
Social construction for control: A tool for establishing hierarchy and dividing populations. Invented and instrumentalized in colonialism, slavery, and discrimination. Immutable.	**Self-construct for culture:** Often encompasses shared cultural practices, traditions, and languages and can evolve over time due to migration, assimilation, or other societal changes.	Social oppression factors prevent trust in systems and subsequent care-seeking in these settings and show clients the origins of identity-based oppression that may amplify mental health and anxiety disorder symptoms.
External imposition: Individuals are subjected to "racialization," where identity is imposed from outside based on appearance and presumed ancestry.	**Agency in definition**: Allows individuals to define themselves and their identity based on culture. Offers a more respectful approach, acknowledging more freedom to self-define.	Allows for a better understanding of clients in the context of intersecting cultural values and worldview; allows clients to have agency over identity; promotes autonomy in treatment; minimizes unhelpful power dynamics that perpetuate oppression and work against alliance building and collaborative treatment engagement.
Non-overlapping categories: Defined by governing bodies and based on public perceptions, these categories can change based on the needs of those in power.	**Diverse expression**: Studies reveal approximately 650 self-defined ethnic groups across 190 countries, demonstrating a rich diversity of human identity. Categories often overlap.	Speaks to importance of making cultural modifications to treatments to promote engagement; gives client permission to embrace and resolve multiple identities.
Genetic fallacies: Susceptible to attributing inaccurate traits based on perceived race.	**Genetics:** May make up one or zero components of ethnicity.	Has contributed to oppressive practices in psychology that have perpetuated stereotypes, contributed to clinician bias, and eroded trust in systems that work against treatment engagement; fits genes into identity in a healthy way that does not undermine self-agency.

The Mental Health Impact of Racism

Racism is a public health problem that leads to death and disability (Mendez et al., 2021; Williams et al., 2022b), and many anxiety-related conditions are caused or exacerbated by racism (MacIntyre et al., 2023). Racism and anxiety are intricately interconnected, as individuals who face racial discrimination may constantly live in fear of prejudice or violence, leading to chronic stress and heightened anxiety. For example, consider a young Black student who regularly faces racial slurs at school. Each day, he feels a growing sense of dread and develops symptoms like constant worry, difficulty concentrating, and insomnia, indicative of anxiety. Further, if he is assaulted, he may wonder if law enforcement will come to his aid or blame him for the altercation, due to false stereotypes about the dangerousness of dark-skinned men. His experience illustrates how repeated exposure to racism can directly lead to the development of anxiety symptoms, which may in turn require clinical attention. Notably, connections have been found between racism and generalized anxiety disorder (GAD; e.g., Soto et al., 2011), posttraumatic stress disorder (PTSD; e.g., Flores et al., 2010), social anxiety disorder (Kline et al., 2021), and OCD (Williams et al., 2017).

Being a product of Western socialization, clinicians are not immune from the influence of racism, and when not conscious of their own biases, may reenact racist patterns with clients in ways that perpetuate problems (Williams, 2020). When clients experience even small acts of bias from their therapists, they are less likely to attend sessions regularly, complete homework, or be open about their difficulties (Williams & Halstead, 2019). As such, clinicians must do their own learning to become anti-racist and engage in practices that help mitigate the damage caused by racism in their work with clients (Williams et al., 2022a). One important first step is understanding clients' sense of identity around their race and ethnicity.

Ethnic and Racial Identity Development

Ethnic identity has been researched across cultures, primarily in youth. Because ethnic identity is thought to develop in childhood through young adulthood, relatively less is known about the ethnic identity development processes in older adults, although ethnic identity can continue to develop well after adolescence (Maehler, 2022). The strength and salience of one's ethnic identity can also vary according to demographic factors. For example, among African Americans, ethnic identity is stronger in the southern United States compared to other regions, due to the larger African American population and longstanding traditional ethnic institutions, such as Black churches and Historically Black Colleges and Universities (HBCUs; Williams et al., 2018a, 2018b).

The Identity Exploration Process

To achieve a positive sense of ethnic identity, individuals must navigate a meaningful process of exploration of their ethnic groups (Abdulrehman, 2024; Phinney, 1989). Phinney (1989) described three stages of the exploration process: unexamined stage, searching stage, and achieved or integrated stage. Abdulrehman (2024) approached the concept of ethnic and cultural identity development as fluid, and that where a person of color is in this process varies over time and depends upon experiences of personal racism and systemic racism that devalue the identities of people of color in a White-dominant world.

People who have not explored or examined their culture remain in the unexamined stage (Phinney, 1989). This stage may also include negative feelings toward having a minoritized ethnicity due to the lack of direct connection to it. The searching stage is when people become more interested in what it means to be a part of their ethnic group and begin to develop their own ethnic identity. This is characterized by efforts to express their commitment to their identity. But these stages of development are not fixed, and a person of color having awareness is not guaranteed to sustain that awareness and identity development, because ongoing forces of racism invalidate the worldviews of people of color, thus oppressing identity development. In an achieved or integrated stage, a person has developed an awareness of the existence of others' identities, recognizes their worldview as valuable, appreciates that they have an ethnic heritage to share, and has developed a sense of resiliency (Abdulrehman, 2024).

Identity Development in People of Color

Several models have been developed to determine how identity development differs across groups. Cross (1978) developed an early and highly influential five-stage model called Nigrescence to explain the process of identity development in African Americans. In the revised model, the original five stages were reduced to three stages of group racial identity attitudes: pre-encounter, immersion-emersion, and internalization. The pre-encounter stage includes opposition or low acceptance to Black racial identity and culture; at this stage a person may experience self-hatred and be driven to assimilate into the dominant White society. In the immersion-emersion process, individuals recognize the value of their Black roots and their desire to exhibit their heritage increases as they reject other cultures. The final stage, internalization, reflects an acceptance of self and other cultures and positive reconciliation within a multicultural society.

The Cross model was later expanded by other scholars to include all people of color (Sue et al., 2019). These models typically include stages referred to as conformity, dissonance, resistance, introspection, and integrative awareness, as shown in Table 10.2, along with an example of how this might impact treatment engagement (also see Williams, 2018).

Table 10.2 Minority identity development model and impact on treatment engagement

Stage	Description	Therapist example	Client example
Conformity	Accepts values of white culture; values white role models, white standards of beauty and success, and believes it preferable to be white; negative emotions toward self.	South Asian therapist uses anglicized name on professional website, and changes her photo to look as light-skinned as possible.	Rejects a same-race therapist and views white therapists as more desirable and competent in treating anxiety disorders.
Dissonance	Begins to acknowledge racism when a triggering event causes re-examination of own assumptions and beliefs; becomes more aware of racism; confusion and conflict toward the dominant cultural system arise.	Asian American therapist is called a "banana" by an Asian client. Feels upset and stops taking clients of color.	Therapist makes stereotypical assumptions about black client, saying "maybe you just need to work harder" in response to workplace harassment; asks client to practice social anxiety exposure in situation that is objectively harassing; client quits therapy.
Resistance	Actively rejects dominant culture and immerses self in own culture; may feel hostility and reject white people in this stage.	Makes pointed comments toward white clients about having unconscious hatred of black people.	Client of color will not consider working with a white therapist to address their PTSD, even when no therapists of color are available.
Introspection	Starts to question the values of own ethnic group and dominant group; more open to connecting with white people to better learn and understand differences.	Starts working with interracial couples to help better understand how they navigate their differences.	Client of color starts working with a white therapist to address PTSD and probes therapist with questions about their own "experience of whiteness" while processing a racially related traumatic experience.
Integrative awareness	Develops cultural identity based on both minoritized and dominant cultural values; feels comfortable with self and identity as a person of color in a multicultural society.	Appreciates client's differing cultural beliefs and can use them to advance therapeutic goals, even when those beliefs are not shared by therapist.	Will benefit from therapist of any race if they take a culturally informed approach, and values different cultural perspectives on addressing anxiety-related difficulties.

White Identity Development

White people in dominant White culture also traverse a process of ethnoracial identity development, although this may be less salient to those who remain in the earlier stages of growth. Helms and Carter (1990) defined the structure and stages of development, which depict six intertwining ego statuses, as shown in Table 10.3.

Table 10.3 White identity development

Stage	Description	Therapist example	Client example
Contact	Denies racism, cultural differences, and dominant group membership; may be colorblind or insensitive to racial differences.	Therapist says, "let's hope that wasn't due to racism," when client of color describes being called a racial slur. The client does not return to therapy.	White client says "I just treat everyone the same" when racial topics arise in session.
Disintegration	Experiences conflict over moral dilemmas between choosing own group versus greater humanity goals.	White therapist realizes he has unfairly waived no-show fees and extended sessions times with white clients only	White client is upset about racial conversation at work and seeks validation from therapist for being a silent bystander.
Reintegration	Finds some resolution of dilemma by becoming intolerant of other groups and taking a racial superiority bias.	Tells a black client that they only were admitted to their prestigious university through affirmative action.	Tells therapist that as white people he is glad they both understand what it means to appreciate American values.
Pseudo-independence	Begins limited acceptance of racism and efforts to connect with people of color that share similarities.	Invites a colleague of color to speak about PTSD symptoms in children in Africa.	Decides to start working with a therapist of color to help better understand diversity issues but selects a white-passing Latin American therapist.
Immersion/emersion	Develops increased understanding and acceptance of white privilege but may still act based on guilt.	Doesn't push a client of color as assertively as white clients to complete anxiety self-monitoring homework for fear of making their life harder	Asks the therapist if they have clients of color and if they are worse off due to racism.
Autonomy	Gained acceptance of own whiteness; understands personal role in perpetuating racism; values diversity; feels less fearful and guilty about the reality of racism.	Organizes educational seminar on cultural competency for psychology trainees completing anxiety rotation on internship and ends up defending the premise of the course against hostile white senior psychologists.	Sees white joggers calling 911 on black teenagers minding their own business in a park and stays to tell the cops it was all a mistake. Proud to share this with therapist.

Redefining Whiteness and White Allyship

To extinguish notions of superiority White people can learn to redefine what it means to be White. Aspects that they consider negative parts of their identity (e.g., racist history and unearned privileges) can become positives when thoughtfully used in the service of racial justice (Liu, 2020). Although White allyship can sometimes be difficult, having a White identity gives a therapist special power to bring attention, intervention, and justice to situations in which a peer of color would not be able to take action (Williams et al., 2022a, 2022b).

A White ally is someone who, while benefiting from White privilege, actively seeks to challenge and eradicate racism. This role involves continuous learning about systemic racism and White supremacy, listening and respecting the perspectives of people of color, confronting racism, and using their platform to amplify marginalized voices. For instance, a White therapist working in an anxiety-specialty clinic may advocate within their organization to enhance inclusive practices (e.g., recruiting staff of color, ensuring representation of people of color in clinic materials, and inviting speakers on issues of culturally responsive CBT practices for implementing exposure therapy) that may improve the clinical experience for clients of color. When being "White" is not the sole identifying factor for identity, and culture is more openly integrated into a person's identity, we see a healthier balance toward connection with others and a removal of privilege. White therapists must become racial justice allies themselves before they can help their clients grow in this way and be most effective in working with clients of color (Williams et al., 2022a).

Building a Strong Ethnoracial Identity in People of Color: Clinical Strategies to Enhance Treatment Engagement

Acknowledge and Attend to the Importance of a Strong Ethnoracial Identity

Negative social messages about people of color are pervasive. A strong ethnoracial identity can help POC develop more resilient cognitions or beliefs about themselves, preventing the development of internalized racism. This can in turn support a more positive self-concept and greater self-efficacy, which can mitigate symptoms of anxiety and traumatic stress and promote treatment engagement (Roncoroni et al., 2019; Titcombe-Parekh et al., 2018). Further, understanding one's experiences through the lens of ethnoracial identity can provide a cognitive framework that aids in interpreting and navigating personal experiences of oppression and ultimately greater cognitive flexibility to combat against constricting stereotypes. Consider how this could potentially improve treatment engagement in the context of a person of color with GAD who comes to therapy to address discriminatory stress at work with a White boss, which is amplifying generalized worries about financial security. Consider too, how the empowering nature of social action could be part of the healing process from conditions like racial trauma, as it can return a lost sense of self-determination that occurs as a result of racism (e.g., Carlson et al., 2018).

As such, perspectives that acknowledge the positives about a person's ethnoracial group are needed to provide a critical counterpoint to pathological stereotypic narratives about people of color. Often parents are the ones helping children do this, but this does not happen in all families—in such cases, leaving adolescents to feel like they do not fit in as they develop into adults. For therapists who wish to support positive development of ethnoracial identity in clients of color with anxiety and related disorders, it is important to promote (Williams & Faber, 2024): (1) an appreciation of their group through cultural knowledge and practicing cultural traditions, (2) acquisition of knowledge about their culture; celebration of cultural strengths, (3) critical thinking about racial differences (e.g., healthy suspicion of stereotypes and systems that reinforce White supremacy), (4) understanding of the nature of racism, and (5) determining what their ethnic group and race mean to them personally.

Provide Psychoeducation

Cultural Strengths and Practicing Cultural Traditions

CBT interventions for anxiety and related disorders may incorporate the aforementioned by discussing the positive aspects of clients' ethnic groups, exploring their history and the accomplishments of others from their background, and encouraging participation in traditional cultural activities to foster a stronger sense of ethnoracial pride (Williams, 2020). Another approach is to utilize cultural bridging techniques that capitalize on traditional practices by incorporating cultural strengths and healing practices into CBT (Hwang et al., 2006). For instance, mindfulness principles from Buddhism may be integrated within CBT protocols for GAD to strengthen treatment adherence and effectiveness if culturally relevant.

Consider each client of color individually, taking into account their unique cultural background and experiences, and reflect on the information they have shared about their culture to identify sources of cultural strength that resonate with them. If clients have not disclosed much about their cultural background, therapists should exhibit curiosity and actively inquire about their heritage, family dynamics, and community involvement during sessions. Clients should be encouraged to express what aspects of their ethnic group give them pride. The Cultural Formulation Interview (CFI; American Psychiatric Association, 2013) provides a helpful framework, including questions that assess significant aspects of cultural identity. When therapists are unfamiliar with a client's ethnic group, they should take the initiative to educate themselves. This ensures that clients are not burdened with the sole responsibility of educating their therapists about their culture.

Consider the example of Lenora, a biracial client with OCD and BDD, whose mother was Black and father was White. Even though she was racially ambiguous, she identified as Black and would feel a great deal of distress when people asked, "What are you?" This led to obsessive ruminations about whether or not she was "Black enough" and if her physical features were properly commensurate with her identity. She wore her hair in a large afro to enhance the perception of being Black.

She would take pictures of her face from many different angles to try to determine if her nose looked like "an African American nose." She told her therapist she wanted rhinoplasty to make her nose look "more ethnic." The White therapist, in a stage of pseudo-independence, was initially uncertain how to respond to the client's plan of action, although he felt sure surgery would not be a good solution. The client in this case was demonstrating a weak sense of ethnoracial identity, and it was important for her to understand that the look she wanted was based on Black stereotypes, which are inherently racist and fail to appreciate the nuances of ethnicity. The therapist working solely to discourage OCD and BDD behaviors would risk undermining the client's treatment engagement by failing to consider the important aspect of her ethnoracial identity development. A more culturally responsive approach in this case would be to help the client understand the many different international physical representations of Black people.

Racial Differences and the Myth of Biological Racism

A vital step in the education process is understanding that racial categories are simply social conventions. Many are taught that races of humans represent real biologically based group differences, which is unscientific. Part of the confusion around genes and race stems from the conflation of the understanding that genes define heritable traits such as height, blood type, and skin color, and then adding assumptions about how related individuals may be based on skin tone. But belief in genetic relatedness based on skin color is no more sensible than assuming individuals must be related because they are the same height.

Clients of color who have adopted these false beliefs are likely to suffer from internalized racism. Internalized racism can be described as a negative view of the self-based on the perceived inferiority of one's own ethnic or racial group, which can cause shame and self-blame. People with internalized racism will tend to embrace White standards of beauty and role models and believe that it is better to be White. Internalized racism has been linked to anxiety symptoms and can cause problems like social anxiety disorder due to negative perceptions about one's physical appearance and worries about rejection from others (Graham et al., 2016; Kline et al., 2021).

To combat internalized racism, psychoeducation using helpful reading materials can include *National Geographic*'s special issue, *There's No Such Thing as Race—It's a Made Up Category* (Kolbert, 2018). It is important to explain how the concept of "race" is at odds with population genetics and that humans cannot be categorized neatly into biologically distinct subcategories based on appearance. Some may have a hard time understanding this is a myth, as it is so firmly embedded across identities and educational levels. However, common sense can also be helpful as it may be easier to explain that all people with brown hair do not share personality traits or genetic predispositions compared to people with black hair or blonde hair—and the same goes for skin color.

How Racism Works

Helping clients understand how racism works can strengthen ethnoracial identity and facilitate treatment. For example, pathological stereotypes about racial groups can lead to internalized racism. These are false generalizations about people in specific groups that do not change when presented with accurate information. Pathological stereotypes about people are a means of explaining and justifying differences between groups and using these differences to oppress the out-group (Williams et al., 2012b). As an example, a particular group may have higher unemployment rates caused by discrimination, leading to pathological stereotypes that the marginalized group is intellectually deficient and lazy to explain the higher unemployment rate, which in turn justifies the denial of educational and employment opportunities, perpetuating the problem. People of color who are aware of these stereotypes may believe them and think something is wrong with their people group and by extension themselves. They may develop anxiety and negative self-talk around educational pursuits or even drop out of higher education, believing themselves to be less intelligent. Consider how internalized racism may amplify negative self-referential beliefs for a person with social anxiety disorder or PTSD. Therapists can help clients understand the role of racism in this false belief and bolster confidence and self-efficacy through cognitive restructuring, leading to reduced internalized racism and better treatment outcomes in anxiety and related disorders. Similarly, therapists should ensure they do not ask clients of color with anxiety disorders to participate in objectively unsafe exposure exercises that may reinforce harmful, racist interactions.

Encourage Self-Reflection

Developing a strong sense of ethnoracial identity often involves an introspective journey. There are many good CBT protocols for addressing anxiety disorders, but few start with taking time to understand a client's culture first, which can help promote engagement in treatment. This can start with an examination of a person's family's history, traditions, languages, and experiences, and reflecting on what this means to the client on a personal level. They should consider the values, customs, attitudes, and beliefs acquired from their culture and think about how being a part of their ethnic group has shaped their worldview and influenced daily life (see Chap. 8).

Most people will at some point reflect on their experiences of exclusion related to their race or ethnicity. This might involve reflecting on experiences that have occurred in their community, school, workplace, or broader society. Experiences of bias or discrimination may have impacted a client's sense of self (Cénat et al., 2022). Likewise, negative stereotypes may cause some people to want to distance themselves from their group (Cokley, 2002). Clients should also consider the role models from their group who inspire them and how this may factor into their sense of pride.

Finally, clients should also reflect on intersectionality, as race and ethnicity interact with other aspects of identity like gender, class, religion, and sexual orientation. Often a person may feel more connected to an intersectional identity that includes one's ethnoracial group than an ethnoracial group alone (e.g., identifying as a Latina queer woman).

Recognize Challenges to Ethnoracial Identity Formation in People of Color

Therapists working with diverse adolescents and college students will certainly see many young people who struggle with their ethnoracial identities, particularly children of immigrants and biracial/multiethnic youth.

Immigrant parents may not realize the identity conflict experienced by their children as the children become socialized into a system that may be at complete odds with the values of their country of origin. Similarly, White parents raising children of color (e.g., through adoption or interracial marriage) may struggle to provide the racial socialization necessary to help their children thrive due to lack of awareness. This can cause confusion and anxiety in young people when faced with common racial stressors, such as microaggressions in school.

The struggles of biracial people are often ignored, despite the fact that they are just as impacted by racism as their monoracial peers (e.g., Williams et al., 2018b). Biracial young people have been found to have lower levels of ethnoracial identity, which puts them at risk for more serious emotional issues and makes it more difficult for them to feel good about themselves. They may feel less of a sense of belonging even within their own families and experience rejection from ethnic or racial groups that they think should be accepting because they do not fit appearance-wise into neat racial categories. Because of these identity issues, they may have more mental health problems, such as increased depression, suicidality, and illicit substance use (Choi et al., 2006; Jahn et al., 2021). Perceptions of being a "misfit" or "not belonging" can lead to social anxiety and isolation. Among biracial individuals, social pressure to identify as monoracial has been found to predict social anxiety and fear of negative evaluation (Coleman & Carter, 2007).

Therapists should learn more about what clients' many identities mean to them and not assume clients have resolved these challenges or can even completely articulate their struggles. It can be demoralizing when therapists tell such clients, "You are the expert on you," because often confusion surrounding their identity is the very thing that brings the person into therapy, so they do not feel like much of an expert at all. Feelings of shame around conflicting identities can cause a loss of engagement in treatment if the client feels they are expected to "know it all" surrounding these issues. Therapists should acknowledge this process is a struggle that can be difficult. Therapists can help by providing context to the challenges based on what clients did and did not learn growing up, encouraging more connection to their various ethnic communities, and providing affirmation by highlighting the benefits of greater intercultural competence.

Incorporate Microaffirmations and Racial Uplifts for Cognitive Restructuring and Empowerment

Literature on ethnic and racial identity has not focused on the lives of racialized people in terms of what commonplace experiences lead to improved mental health or resilience. Ong and colleagues (2022) have advanced the importance of "racial uplifts," observable behaviors that are culturally positive and improve the well-being of people of color based on research on daily events (e.g., having conversations about overcoming racial obstacles and seeing members of one's racial group depicted in a positive light).

It is common for therapists to be so concerned about offending clients that they say nothing about the client's race, ethnicity, or culture—even when clients bring it up (Michaels et al., 2018). However, this silence only reinforces the notion that there is something shameful about the client's identity, so shameful, in fact, that it cannot be discussed; this can lead to a loss of engagement in treatment as clients start to feel they cannot discuss these issues, which may in fact be central to their presenting problem.

Therapists can encourage open conversation and growth by directly supporting a client's ethnoracial identity by engaging in deliberate supportive statements with clients, sometimes referred to as microaffirmations. Racial microaffirmations, specifically, are small acts that help people of color feel supported. Such practices may include active listening, especially in terms of matters related to race or culture. It includes recognizing and validating experiences shared, such as expressing sorrow toward experiences of racism or showing interest and enthusiasm about cultural activities.

Therapists should also help clients by focusing on actions that will heal, empower, or bring about useful learning. Consider activities clients can do to reduce injustice in their environment (Riley et al., 2021). Carlson et al. (2018) describe social advocacy as a step that naturally evolved in groups for treating racial trauma in veterans. Over the course of treatment and with the encouragement of therapists, the veterans began engaging in values-based behaviors they would have previously avoided. They began assertively addressing racism, leading to enhanced self-esteem and an improved sense of control. One veteran garnered support from his neighbors and engaged in legal action against his hometown over environmental racism involving funneling polluted rainwater to the historically Black side of the neighborhood. Another led an effort to hold a veterans' organization accountable for using a confederate flag in a local parade. He ultimately rescinded his own group's participation in the parade, which led to a major sponsor also withdrawing their plans to provide food at the parade, and the city boycotted it as well.

Carefully Support Clients Teaching Others about the Nature of Racism

In certain circumstances, clients may wish to teach others about the nature of racism. This can be an empowering action that fosters ethnoracial identity development, yet it can be emotionally challenging as it is often a result of a microaggression committed by another. It is common to feel anxiety and uncertainty about how to proceed when one experiences these acts, and ongoing experiences of racism are stressful and can lead to a host of mental health problems, including PTSD (Williams et al., 2022b). There is some important nuance in choosing how to respond to everyday racism. The type of response should vary based on the relationship between the client and the one who requires educating, as that dictates the level of vulnerability appropriate for the situation (Williams et al., 2023). Friends, family members, and coworkers are more appropriate people to teach about racism, as there is an existing relationship to help reinforce the importance of the lesson.

When the person to be educated is a close friend or caring family member, the client can appeal to the quality of the relationship to help bring about mutual understanding and positive change. They can share how acts of racism make them feel, differentiate between intent and impact, and appeal to the other person's values and principles to stress the importance of the matter. When the person to educate is a co-worker or acquaintance, the client can attempt to gently educate the person about stereotypes and racism in a more straightforward manner that requires less vulnerability. Although others may not show appreciation for being educated in the moment, over time they may come to understand how they can commit racist acts, allowing them to become more informed and less hurtful. But more importantly, these actions empower the client to take action against racism in a way that is positive and maintains personal integrity. These confrontations can be conceptualized as exposures that will become easier with practice (Williams et al., 2023) and thus can be easily integrated into a CBT protocol for anxiety. Role-play with the therapist is a good way to build skills in this area.

Example of Behavioral Intervention to Address Act of Racism

Due to problems like colonization and the trans-Atlantic slave trade, challenges with developing a positive ethnoracial identity are a global issue, and the associated barriers to the development of positive ethnoracial identity are often pervasive and insidious. One author shares an experience that happened to her biracial/bicultural adolescent daughter at school, related to her curly hair due to her African American heritage, where other students would grab, touch, or pull it out of curiosity.

Unwanted hair touching is a form of racism, yet many of those in power tend to dismiss it as harmless (i.e., teachers and school administrators). The implicit message is that White people are allowed to violate Black people, and it demonstrates public ownership of something that should belong to the individual alone. It also teaches children that if they are touched by someone else, no one will do anything to help, which could incur risk for later interpersonal trauma. Fighting back against this kind of assault can be difficult for victims because the associated compliment, "I love your hair," makes the violation more insidious.

As is typically presented as psychoeducation to individuals with PTSD, assault is not defined by intent. As such, ignoring this violation is compounded by legitimizing it. It sends a message that some students are less valuable, can be assaulted in public, and nothing will be done about it. This is important also because experiencing racism in schools can lead to social anxiety, low self-esteem, and academic disengagement (Steketee et al., 2021). Like bullying, even small acts of racism can be problematic if they are ongoing, leading to traumatization. As such, teachers need to be educated, and in this case, the author had a meeting with the school to explain the problem. It is important to teach clients how to respond in the moment when these events occur, as this will make them feel more confident and competent when they experience or witness microaggressions and other forms of racism.

Conclusion

In a racist society, developing a strong, positive ethnoracial identity is essential for the mental health and well-being of people of color. It is also an important foundation for building self-identity because it provides a sense of identification with group cultural values, kinship, and beliefs. Clients who did not receive positive messages about their ethnoracial group growing up may need to be supported in learning to appreciate their identities. Culturally attuned therapists must be attentive to ethnoracial identity in their conceptualization and in their efforts to foster engagement in treatment, particularly given the ways in which it may intersect with anxiety and related conditions like PTSD. To facilitate treatment engagement, when clients have marginalized identities, it is therapeutically important to problematize, pathologize, and address dysfunctional systems and racist narratives, rather than focusing only on the resultant anxiety and the internal coping resources of the client (Bartlett et al., 2022). As such, each client should be encouraged and empowered in their ethnoracial identity development and learn to understand the mechanisms of covert racial oppression to become increasingly skilled at warding off negative messages that would conspire to make people of color feel inferior, devalued, and dejected (Pierce, 1970).

Clinical Summary Points and Recommendations

- Understanding ethnic and racial identity enables therapists to work more effectively with diverse clients. This is associated with a strong therapeutic alliance and improved engagement in treatment.
- Client ethnoracial identity development can impact the engagement based on therapist ethnoracial identity.
- The impact of racism in the development of anxiety disorders is discussed with examples.
- Therapists can support the formation of a healthy, positive ethnoracial identity to foster engagement.

References

Abdulrehman, R. (2024). *Developing anti-racist cultural competence*. Hogrefe.

American Psychiatric Association. (2013). *Diagnostic and statistical manual of mental disorders* (5th ed.). American Psychiatric Publishing.

Atkinson, D., Morten, G., & Sue, D. (1998). *Counseling American minorities*. McGraw Hill.

Bartlett, A., Faber, S., Williams, M., & Saxberg, K. (2022). Getting to the root of the problem: Supporting clients with lived-experiences of systemic discrimination. *Chronic Stress, 6*, 1–10. https://doi.org/10.1177/24705470221139205

Booth, M. Z., Abercrombie, S., & Frey, C. J. (2017). Contradictions of adolescent self-construal: Examining the interaction of ethnic identity, self-efficacy and academic achievement. *Mid-Western Educational Researcher, 29*(1), 3–19.

Bourke, E., Barker, C., & Fornells-Ambrojo, M. (2021). Systematic review and meta-analysis of therapeutic alliance, engagement, and outcome in psychological therapies for psychosis. *Psychology and Psychotherapy: Theory, Research and Practice, 94*(3), 822–853. https://doi.org/10.1111/papt.12330

Brown, A. D., Kouri, N. A., Rahman, N., Joscelyne, A., Bryant, R. A., & Marmar, C. R. (2016). Enhancing self-efficacy improves episodic future thinking and social-decision making in combat veterans with posttraumatic stress disorder. *Psychiatry Research, 242*, 19–25. https://doi.org/10.1016/j.psychres.2016.05.026

Brown, L. A., Wiley, J. F., Wolitzky-Taylor, K., Roy-Byrne, P., Sherbourne, C., Stein, M. B., et al. (2014). Changes in self-efficacy and outcome expectancy as predictors of anxiety outcomes from the CALM study. *Depression and Anxiety, 31*(8), 678–689. https://doi.org/10.1002/da.22256

Buchholz, J. L., & Abramowitz, J. S. (2020). The therapeutic alliance in exposure therapy for anxiety-related disorders: A critical review. *Journal of Anxiety Disorders, 70*, 102194. https://doi.org/10.1016/j.janxdis.2020.102194

Carlson, M. D., Endsley, M., Motley, D., Shawahin, L. N., & Williams, M. T. (2018). Addressing the impact of racism on veterans of color: A race-based stress and trauma intervention. *Psychology of Violence, 8*(6), 748–762. https://doi.org/10.1037/vio0000221

Cénat, J. M., Darius, W. P., Dalexis, R. D., Kogan, C. S., Guerrier, M., & Ndengeyingoma, A. (2022). Perceived racial discrimination, internalized racism, social support, and self-esteem among black individuals in Canada: A moderated mediation model. *Cultural Diversity and Ethnic Minority Psychology*. Advance online publication, *30*, 118. https://doi.org/10.1037/cdp0000542

Choi, Y., Harachi, T. W., Gillmore, M. R., & Catalano, R. F. (2006). Are multiracial adolescents at greater risk? Comparisons of rates, patterns, and correlates of substance use and violence between monoracial and multiracial adolescents. *American Journal of Orthopsychiatry, 76*(1), 86–97.

Cokley, K. O. (2002). Testing Cross's revised racial identity model: An examination of the relationship between racial identity and internalized racialism. *Journal of Counseling Psychology, 49*(4), 476–483. https://doi.org/10.1037/0022-0167.49.4.476

Coleman, V. H., & Carter, M. M. (2007). Biracial self-identification: Impact on trait anxiety, social anxiety, and depression. *Identity: An International Journal of Theory and Research, 7*(2), 103–114.

Cross, W. E. (1978). The Thomas and Cross models of psychological Nigrescence. *A review: The Journal of Black Psychology, 5*, 13–31.

Fentz, H. N., Arendt, M., O'Toole, M. S., Hoffart, A., & Hougaard, E. (2014). The mediational role of panic self-efficacy in cognitive behavioral therapy for panic disorder: A systematic review and meta-analysis. *Behaviour Research and Therapy, 60*, 23–33. https://doi.org/10.1016/j.brat.2014.06.003

Flores, E., Tschann, J. M., Dimas, J. M., Pasch, L. A., & de Groat, C. L. (2010). Perceived racial/ethnic discrimination, posttraumatic stress symptoms, and health risk behaviors among Mexican American adolescents. *Journal of Counseling Psychology, 57*(3), 264–273.

Goldin, P. R., Ziv, M., Jazaieri, H., Werner, K., Kraemer, H., Heimberg, R. G., & Gross, J. J. (2012). Cognitive reappraisal self-efficacy mediates the effects of individual cognitive-behavioral therapy for social anxiety disorder. *Journal of Consulting and Clinical Psychology, 80*(6), 1034–1040. https://doi.org/10.1037/a0028555

Gori, A., Topino, E., Brugnera, A., & Compare, A. (2022). Assessment of professional self-efficacy in psychological interventions and psychotherapy sessions: Development of the therapist self-efficacy scale (T-SES) and its application for eTherapy. *Journal of Clinical Psychology, 78*(11), 2122–2144. https://doi.org/10.1002/jclp.23391

Graham, J. R., West, L. M., Martinez, J., & Roemer, L. (2016). The mediating role of internalized racism in the relationship between racist experiences and anxiety symptoms in a black American sample. *Cultural Diversity and Ethnic Minority Psychology, 22*(3), 369–376. https://doi.org/10.1037/cdp0000073

Haeny, A., Holmes, S., & Williams, M. T. (2021). The need for shared nomenclature on racism and related terminology. *Perspectives on Psychological Science, 16*(5), 886–892. https://doi.org/10.1177/17456916211000760

Helms, J. E., & Carter, R. T. (1990). Toward a model of the white racial identity development. In J. E. Helms (Ed.), *Black and white racial identity: Theory, research, and practice* (pp. 49–66). Greenwood Press.

Hwang, W. C., Wood, J. J., Lin, K. M., & Cheung, F. (2006). Cognitive-behavioral therapy with Chinese Americans: Research, theory, and clinical practice. *Cognitive and Behavioral Practice, 13*(4), 293–303. https://doi.org/10.1016/j.cbpra.2006.04.010

Jahn, Z. W., Lopez, J., de la Salle, S., Faber, S., & Williams, M. T. (2021). Racial/ethnic differences in prevalence for hallucinogen use by age cohort: Findings from the 2018 National Survey on drug use and health. *Journal of Psychedelic Studies, 5*(2), 69–82. https://doi.org/10.1556/2054.2021.00166

Keshen, A., Helson, T., Town, J., & Warren, K. (2017). Self-efficacy as a predictor of treatment outcome in an outpatient eating disorder program. *Eating Disorders, 25*(5), 406–419. https://doi.org/10.1080/10640266.2017.1324073

Kline, E. A., Warner, C. M., Grapin, S. L., Reyes-Portillo, J. A., Bixter, M. T., Cunningham, D. J., et al. (2021). The relationship between social anxiety and internalized racism in black young adults. *Journal of Cognitive Psychotherapy, 35*, 53. https://doi.org/10.1891/JCPSY-D-20-00030

Kolbert, E. (2018). Skin deep: What is race, exactly? Science tells us there is no genetic or scientific basis for it. Instead it's largely a made-up label, used to define and separate us.

National Geographic, 233(4), 28–41. https://www.nationalgeographic.com/magazine/article/race-genetics-science-africa

Leeuwerik, T., Caradonna, G., Cavanagh, K., Forrester, E., Jones, A. M., Lea, L., et al. (2023). A thematic analysis of barriers and facilitators to participant engagement in group exposure and response prevention therapy for obsessive–compulsive disorder. *Psychology and Psychotherapy: Theory, Research and Practice, 96*(1), 129–147. https://doi.org/10.1111/papt.12430

Liu, H. (2020). White Allyship. In *Redeeming leadership: An anti-racist feminist intervention* (1st ed., pp. 141–156). Bristol University Press.

Longo, D. A., Lent, R. W., & Brown, S. D. (1992). Social cognitive variables in the prediction of client motivation and attrition. *Journal of Counseling Psychology, 39*(4), 447–452. https://doi.org/10.1037/0022-0167.39.4.447

MacIntyre, M. M., Zare, M., & Williams, M. T. (2023). Anxiety-related disorders in the context of racism. *Current Psychiatry Reports, 25*(2), 31–43. https://doi.org/10.1007/s11920-022-01408-2

Maehler, D. B. (2022). Determinants of ethnic identity development in adulthood: A longitudinal study. *British Journal of Developmental Psychology, 40*(1), 46–72. https://doi.org/10.1111/bjdp.12384

Mendez, D. D., Scott, J., Adodoadji, L., Toval, C., McNeil, M., & Sindhu, M. (2021). Racism as public health crisis: Assessment and review of municipal declarations and resolutions across the United States. *Frontiers in Public Health, 9*, 686807.

Merling, L. F., Siev, J., Delucia, C., & Davidtz, J. (2022). I think I can: The role of self-efficacy in exposure to contamination. *Journal of Social and Clinical Psychology, 41*(5), 423–443. https://doi.org/10.1521/jscp.2022.41.5.423

Michaels, T. I., Gallagher, N., Crawford, M., Kanter, J. W., & Williams, M. T. (2018). Racial differences in the appraisal of microaggressions through cultural consensus modeling. *The Behavior Therapist, 41*(7), 314–321.

Mosher, D. K., Hook, J. N., Captari, L. E., Davis, D. E., DeBlaere, C., & Owen, J. (2017). Cultural humility: A therapeutic framework for engaging diverse clients. *Practice Innovations, 2*(4), 221–233. https://doi.org/10.1037/pri0000055

Phinney, J. (1989). Stages of ethnic identity development in minority group adolescents. *Journal of Early Adolescence, 9*, 34–49.

Pierce, C. (1970). Offensive mechanisms. In F. Barbour (Ed.), *In the black seventies* (pp. 265–282). Porter Sargent.

Riley, T. N., DeLaney, E., Brown, D., Lozada, F. T., Williams, C. D., The Spit for Science Working Group, & Dick, D. M. (2021). The associations between African American emerging adults' racial discrimination and civic engagement via emotion regulation. *Cultural Diversity and Ethnic Minority Psychology, 27*(2), 169–175. https://doi.org/10.1037/cdp0000335

Roncoroni, J., Tucker, C. M., Wall, W., Wippold, G., & Ratchford, J. (2019). Associations of health self-efficacy with engagement in health-promoting behaviors and treatment adherence in rural patients. *Family & Community Health, 42*(2), 109–116. https://doi.org/10.1097/FCH.0000000000000219

Sharf, J., Primavera, L. H., & Diener, M. J. (2010). Dropout and therapeutic alliance: A meta-analysis of adult individual psychotherapy. *Psychotherapy: Theory, Research, Practice, Training, 47*(4), 637–645. https://doi.org/10.1037/a0021175

Soto, J. A., Dawson-Andoh, N. A., & BeLue, R. (2011). The relationship between perceived discrimination and generalized anxiety disorder among African Americans, afro Caribbeans, and non-Hispanic whites. *Journal of Anxiety Disorders, 25*(2), 258–265.

Steketee, A., Williams, M., Valencia, B., Printz, D., & Hooper, L. M. (2021). Racial and language microaggressions in the school ecology. *Perspectives on Psychological Science, 16*(5), 1075–1098. https://doi.org/10.1177/1745691621995740

Sue, D. W., Sue, D., Neville, H. A., & Smith, L. (2022). *Counseling the culturally diverse: Theory and practice* (9th ed.). John Wiley & Sons.

Sue, D. W., & Sue, D. (2016). Racial/cultural identity development in people of color: Therapeutic implications, chapter 11. In D. W. Sue & D. Sue (Eds.), *Counseling the culturally diverse: Theory and practice* (7th ed.). Wiley.

Sue, D. W., Sue, D., Neville, H. A., & Smith, L. (2019). Racial, ethnic, cultural (REC) identity attitudes in people of color: Counseling implications, chapter 11. In *Counseling the culturally diverse: Theory and practice* (8th ed., p. 233). Wiley.

Titcombe-Parekh, R. F., Chen, J., Rahman, N., Kouri, N., Qian, M., Li, M., et al. (2018). Neural circuitry changes associated with increasing self-efficacy in posttraumatic stress disorder. *Journal of Psychiatric Research, 104*, 58–64. https://doi.org/10.1016/j.jpsychires.2018.06.009

Williams, M. (2018, March). Ethnic and Racial Identity and the Therapeutic Alliance. *Culturally Speaking*. Psychology Today. https://www.psychologytoday.com/us/blog/culturally-speaking/201803/ethnic-and-racial-identity-and-the-therapeutic-alliance

Williams, M. T. (2020). *Managing microaggressions: Addressing everyday racism in therapeutic spaces*. Oxford University Press.

Williams, M. T., Chapman, L. K., Wong, J., & Turkheimer, E. (2012a). The role of ethnic identity in symptoms of anxiety and depression in African Americans. *Psychiatry Research, 199*(1), 31–36. https://doi.org/10.1016/j.psychres.2012.03.049

Williams, M. T., Duque, G., Chapman, L. K., Wetterneck, C. T., & DeLapp, R. C. T. (2018a). Ethnic identity and regional differences in mental health in a national sample of African American young adults. *Journal of Racial and Ethnic Health Disparities, 5*(2), 312–321. https://doi.org/10.1007/s40615-017-0372-y

Williams, M., & Faber, S. (2024). Building a positive racial and ethnic identity. In G. P. Koocher, A. M. La Greca, N. L. Reilly, & O. Moorehead-Slaughter (Eds.), *The parents' guide to psychological first aid: Helping children and adolescents cope with predictable life crises*. Oxford University Press.

Williams, M., Faber, S. C., & Duniya, C. (2022a). Being an anti-racist clinician. *The Cognitive Behaviour Therapist, 15*(e19), 1–22. https://doi.org/10.1017/S1754470X22000162

Williams, M. T., Gooden, A. M., & Davis, D. (2012b). African Americans, European Americans, and pathological stereotypes: An African-centered perspective. In G. R. Hayes & M. H. Bryant (Eds.), *Psychology of culture* (pp. 25–46). Nova Science Publishers.

Williams, M., & Halstead, M. (2019). Racial microaggressions as barriers to treatment in clinical care. *Directions in Psychiatry, 39*(4), 265–280.

Williams, M. T., Holmes, S., Zare, M., Haeny, A. H., & Faber, S. C. (2023). An evidence-based approach for treating stress and trauma due to racism. *Cognitive and Behavioral Practice, 30*(4), 565–588. https://doi.org/10.1016/j.cbpra.2022.07.001

Williams, M. T., Khanna Roy, A., MacIntyre, M. P., & Faber, S. (2022b). The traumatizing impact of racism in Canadians of colour. *Current Trauma Reports, 8*(2), 17–34.

Williams, M. T., Printz, D., & DeLapp, R. C. T. (2018b). Assessing racial trauma with the trauma symptoms of discrimination scale. *Psychology of Violence, 8*(6), 735–747. https://doi.org/10.1037/vio0000212

Williams, M. T., Taylor, R. J., Mouzon, D. M., Oshin, L. A., Himle, J. A., & Chatters, L. M. (2017). Discrimination and symptoms of obsessive–compulsive disorder among African Americans. *American Journal of Orthopsychiatry, 87*(6), 636–645.

Part II
Engagement with Specific Populations

Chapter 11
Social Anxiety Disorder

Katharina Meyerbröker and Paul M. G. Emmelkamp

Background

Cross-Cultural Classification and Prevalence

Social anxiety disorder (SAD) is a highly disabling condition that is marked by persistent fear of being humiliated or scrutinized by others in social situations (APA, 2022; WHO, 2022). The situations vary from walking into a room where others are, eating or drinking in front of others, talking to others, interacting with strangers, attending parties or social gatherings, going to work or school, making eye contact or to perform in front of others. The fear usually concerns saying or doing something that will be negatively evaluated by others. Children with SAD fear not only negative evaluation of other children and adults, but they often are afraid that others will notice their sweating, trembling, or blushing, which eventually may result in avoidance of all social situations. The estimated age of onset of SAD is about 10.6 years with a confidence interval from 6 to 14 years. Adults may misinterpret clinging and crying as oppositional behavior rather than as symptoms of social anxiety, which may lead to missed opportunities for intervention (Morris & D'Souza, 2023).

Cultural differences in symptom expression may also lead to missed opportunities and lead to an underestimation of SAD in some countries, as DSM-5 diagnostic criteria for SAD do not capture all culturally specific aspects. *Taijin kyofusho*, or

K. Meyerbröker (✉)
Department of Clinical Psychology, Utrecht University, Utrecht, The Netherlands

Altrecht Academic Anxiety Centre, Altrecht, Utrecht, Netherlands
e-mail: K.Meyerbroker@uu.nl

P. M. G. Emmelkamp
University of Amsterdam, Amsterdam, Netherlands

E. M. Goetter (ed.), *Optimizing Treatment Engagement Processes in CBT for Anxiety and Related Disorders*, CBT: Science Into Practice,
https://doi.org/10.1007/978-3-031-91439-3_11

Hikikomori, or a fear of being offensive to others, is one example of a culturally specific clinical expression of SAD that primarily presents in Japan (e.g., APA, 2022; Hofmann et al., 2010). In recent epidemiological studies, prevalence rates vary between 3% and 6% for lifetime and 1% and 4% for the past 12 months (McGrath et al., 2023; Stein et al., 2017).

Comorbidity

Approximately 50–80% of patients with SAD have at least one other mental disorder, typically an additional anxiety disorder, mood disorder, or substance abuse disorder (Piccirillo & Rodebaugh, 2022). Major depressive disorder is often especially highly comorbid with SAD (Koyuncu et al., 2019; Stein et al., 2017). SAD is characterized by fear of social scrutiny, leading to avoidance behaviors that reinforce negative self-perception and contribute to depressive symptoms (e.g., guilt and negative self-referential cognitions), which complicate treatment engagement as symptoms overlap and influence each other, with decreased activity and anhedonia further heightening social inadequacy and worthlessness. Addressing these intertwined symptoms through targeted interventions could improve treatment outcomes by focusing on enhancing self-evaluation and reducing negative beliefs.

Not surprisingly, SAD is also highly comorbid with avoidant personality disorder (Emmelkamp & Meyerbröker, 2019). Avoidant personality disorder is characterized by social avoidance, together with hypersensitivity to negative evaluation, fears of rejection, and feelings of inferiority, which are also primary characteristics of SAD. Studies comparing SAD and avoidant personality disorder have led to the conclusion that both disorders are not qualitatively different but only differ in severity of dysfunction (Emmelkamp & Meyerbröker, 2019). There is some evidence, however, that SAD and avoidant personality disorder are correlated but separable constructs, with differences in both the genetic and environmental risk factors for the two disorders (see Welander-Vatn et al., 2018). For treatment engagement, it may help to include schema therapy sessions for patients with both SAD and avoidant personality disorder (Baljé et al., 2024).

Theoretical Models Underpinning CBT for SAD

Cognitive behavioral therapy (CBT) for SAD combines cognitive and behavioral techniques to modify maladaptive cognitions and avoidance behaviors. CBT has shown good outcomes for SAD, with stable long-term results (Carpenter et al., 2018; van Dis et al., 2020) that generalize to clinical settings (e.g., Morina et al., 2023b).

There are three predominant theoretical models of social anxiety disorder (SAD) that underpin CBT for SAD, which are necessary to understand to adequately explain the treatment rationale to patients and increase their engagement: the cognitive model by Clark and Wells (1995), the cognitive-behavioral model by Rapee and Heimberg (1997), and Hofmann's cognitive model (Hofmann, 2007).

The Clark and Wells model (1995) emphasizes self-focused attention, negative self-beliefs, and safety behaviors. Individuals with SAD focus excessively on themselves in social situations, leading to heightened self-awareness and scrutiny. This self-focus amplifies perceived social threats and fosters negative self-beliefs, such as fear of negative evaluation. Safety behaviors, like avoiding eye contact, reinforce the belief that they cannot cope without these behaviors, potentially leading to avoidance of social situations altogether (Piccirillo et al., 2016).

The cognitive-behavioral model by Rapee and Heimberg (1997) complements Clark and Wells model by incorporating attentional biases and anticipatory processing of social threats. While both models highlight self-focused attention and fear of negative evaluation, Rapee and Heimberg emphasize the role of external environmental cues. They propose a positive feedback loop where biased detection of negative evaluations (e.g., frowning) increases focus on negative self-representations (Rapee et al., 2017; Schultz & Heimberg, 2008; Wong & Rapee, 2016).

In Hofmann's model (2007), the focus is on maladaptive social beliefs and negative self-imagery. Individuals with SAD hold unrealistically high standards for social performance and fear negative evaluation. They engage in safety behaviors like avoidance and excessive self-monitoring, which prevent them from noticing others' responses. This inward focus on anxiety symptoms reinforces negative beliefs about themselves (Mörtberg et al., 2015), similar to the other models.

All three models emphasize the role of cognitions as self-focused attention, safety behaviors, and cognitive biases in maintaining social anxiety, highlighting different aspects of internal and external influences on SAD. To optimize treatment engagement processes, when working with patients with SAD, it is important that the therapist carefully investigates which model fits the best for the patient to explain the treatment rationale.

Problems with Engagement in Treatment

Barriers to Treatment and Premature Dropout

Several studies have indicated barriers to successful treatment engagement among individuals with SAD. A self-guided internet intervention study found high unmet need among individuals with social anxiety symptoms in the community (Powell et al., 2020). Even after treatment is accessed, dropout is a concern. For instance, a meta-analysis of effectiveness studies revealed that dropout from CBT for SAD is approximately 15% (Hans & Hiller, 2013). Higher dropout risks from CBT in general are associated with comorbid depression, outpatient settings (vs. clinical trials), and e-therapy (Fernandez et al., 2015), though specific data on SAD is limited.

Avoidance and Safety Behaviors

Avoidance and safety behaviors (actions perceived necessary to prevent feared outcomes) are considered key factors in maintaining SAD. Recent studies investigated the relationship between fear, avoidance, and safety behaviors in SAD. During challenging situations, safety behaviors can hinder performance in social interactions, and reductions of safety behaviors generally lead to better CBT outcomes (Gray et al., 2019; Rodebaugh et al., 2024). However, initial use of safety behaviors can also make treatment more acceptable, with gradual fading proving as efficacious as immediate elimination (Levy & Radomsky, 2016).

The very nature of social anxiety revolves around fear and avoidance of social situations, interactions, or performance scenarios where one is subject to potential scrutiny or evaluation, which inherently makes it challenging to approach therapy, which in itself can represent a high-stakes social exposure. Additionally, social anxiety often involves essential aspects of daily life (e.g., making eye contact with others), making exposure to social situations even more threatening. Avoidance behavior is a common coping strategy and undermines successfully engaging in therapy, particularly given the exposure component central to evidence-based treatment for SAD. As such, the therapist needs to optimize engagement early on in treatment and consider engagement carefully when explaining the rationale for treatment, as this may be aversive to individuals with high levels of social avoidance. The rationale of how anxious complaints influence behavior and how this behavior (i.e., avoidance) in the long run maintains and worsens complaints (McManus et al., 2008) needs to be presented with a lot of compassion to encourage the patient to engage in the first steps of exposure. Therefore, a patient's strong understanding of the rationale will be facilitative of engagement and speaks further to how important it is, that the therapist comprehend the different, aforementioned theoretical models and how exposure relates to negative cognitions and self-awareness. Generally, it is important that first exposure steps are successful and will not be experienced as a failure by the patient (Meyerbröker & Emmelkamp, 2025). Therefore, the therapist needs to listen closely to what would be achievable for a patient to do.

As social anxiety is characterized by heightened self-focused attention, negative self-perception, and distorted cognitions about social situations (Clark & Wells, 1995), the therapist can expect that these cognitive aspects will intensify the anxiety response during exposure and often trigger avoidance or safety behaviors. Individuals with social anxiety commonly engage in anticipatory anxiety and employ safety behaviors, such as avoiding eye contact or rehearsing sentences before a social interaction (Heimberg et al., 2014). These safety behaviors may serve as coping mechanisms, hindering the effectiveness of exposure by maintaining avoidance and preventing the confrontation of feared stimuli. The therapist also needs to be aware of subtle avoidance behaviors specifically for SAD, which could include avoiding eye contact. Given that these safety behaviors and subtle avoidance behaviors can perniciously undermine treatment engagement, the therapist is encouraged to be especially thorough in their assessment, monitoring, and interruption of such behaviors.

Shame and Stigma

In addition to the clinical symptoms of avoidance, others refer to the social aspects that can manifest as barriers, such as stigma (Goetter et al., 2018), or psychological aspects, such as shame (Goetter et al., 2018; Swee et al., 2021). Several theorists have proposed a strong association between shame and core features of social anxiety, including self-critical cognitions (Cox et al., 2004), social avoidance, interaction anxiety, and distress (e.g., Moscovitch, 2009; Swee et al., 2021). The cognitions associated with shame and social anxiety are remarkably similar, as both involve viewing oneself as lacking or defective (Gilbert & Procter, 2006). Behaviorally, both shame and social anxiety are associated with withdrawal, avoidance, and submissive behaviors (e.g., Gilbert & Procter, 2006; Piccirillo et al., 2016).

Given this substantial conceptual overlap, it seems highly unlikely that one would experience significant social anxiety or SAD without experiencing some level of shame. The perceived negative evaluation central to SAD closely aligns with the self-conscious nature of shame, suggesting an intrinsic link between these experiences, which relates to the Rapee–Heimberg model of SAD (1997).

The updated Rapee–Heimberg model of SAD proposes that individuals with SAD form a mental representation of how they believe others perceive them in social situations. This representation closely aligns with spontaneous images of how they view themselves in social situations (Heimberg et al., 2014). Empirical studies support this model, showing that individuals with SAD are more prone to experiencing negative, distorted observer-perspective imagery. This means they tend to visualize themselves from an external viewpoint, often seeing themselves as displaying anxiety symptoms that they believe will be judged negatively by others (Swee et al., 2021).

Practical and Logistical Barriers

Practical barriers can also impact treatment engagement for individuals with SAD. Both logistical issues and financial constraints can form an obstacle, and a lack of knowledge about where to seek treatment can also be a hindrance (Goetter et al., 2018). In a prior study of barriers to treatment that included individuals with SAD, the number of perceived barriers increased with symptom severity, speaking to the importance of considering barriers for those with more severe presentations.

Cultural Misattunement

In the same study, the number of perceived barriers was higher among those with minoritized racial and ethnic identities, even when controlling for symptom severity (Goetter et al., 2018). The findings suggest a need for increased education about treatment options and culturally sensitive outreach initiatives to reduce barriers to engaging in treatment.

Most culturally adapted psychological interventions are based on cognitive behavioral therapies adapted for use with minorities (Emmelkamp, 2023). While CBT developed in Western countries provides a conceptual framework that uses reasoning approaches, this can be inconsistent with other cultural understandings of symptom distress and, at worst, potentially invalidating if delivered without consideration of an individual's diverse identities and cultural and social context.

Treatment Non-response

Although CBT is the most effective treatment for SAD, many patients with SAD do not show clinically significant improvements as a result of CBT (Loerinc et al., 2015), and—when including drop-out rates—more than 40% of patients show no or hardly any improvement (Auyeung et al., 2020). SAD shows the lowest recovery rates among anxiety disorders (Steinert et al., 2013), and even among those who initiate treatment, not all individuals respond equally to treatment for SAD, thus signaling potential barriers to treatment engagement as discussed above. In contrast with large effect sizes after CBT for other anxiety disorders, only small to moderate effect sizes are reported after CBT for SAD (Carpenter et al., 2018). In contrast to moderators of treatment of other anxiety disorders, researchers have not been able to identify moderators of SAD treatment outcome (Erceg-Hurn et al., 2023). Few studies with patients with SAD provide information with respect to factors associated with drop-out of CBT and inadequate success of CBT of patients treated for SAD. However, interesting data were provided by a very large study conducted by Altmann et al. (2020). Patients with SAD with the lowest remission rate were mostly unmarried or living without a partner. Thus, the lack of quality in partner relationships, or the quality of social support more broadly, is a relevant factor. Interestingly, initial depressive symptom severity and interpersonal problems did not discriminate the groups of high responders and patients with no remission. Another interesting finding in this study was that higher initial attachment anxiety predicted non-remission, which suggests that therapists should adapt the treatment strategy according to the emotion regulation strategies associated with an insecure and anxious attachment (see Brenk-Franz et al., 2015).

Reasons for nonresponse vary. For example, the severity of SAD and comorbid disorders (e.g., depression, generalized anxiety, and addictive disorder) may affect the success of treatment for social anxiety. Depressed patients may be unable to do homework exercises for SAD given their low motivation and beliefs that these exercises will not help to overcome social anxiety (Rozen & Aderka, 2022). Other factors that may affect treatment outcome of SAD may include intolerance of uncertainty (Carleton, 2016; Erceg-Hurn et al., 2023) and fear of negative evaluation (e.g., Wong & Rapee, 2016).

Unfortunately, the results of studies that have investigated moderators of treatment outcomes for SAD are inconclusive. For example, a meta-analysis by Rozen and Ardeka (2022) found hardly any evidence that comorbidity of depression was associated with worse outcomes of treatment for SAD. In a study by Erceg-Hun et al. (2023), only 2 out of 15 potential moderators of treatment outcome for SAD were found to predict outcome: (1) baseline severity of SAD and (2) fear of negative evaluation. However, the effect sizes for moderating the outcome of treatment for SAD of fear of negative evaluation were rather small. Intolerance of uncertainty, self-esteem, comorbid generalized anxiety, and number of comorbid diagnoses did not moderate treatment outcome. Interestingly, individuals with a comorbid diagnosis of depression improved as much as individuals who were not depressed. Thus, results of the studies of Rozen and Ardeka (2022) and of Erceg-Hurn et al. (2023) suggest that there is no reason to exclude patients with SAD and comorbid depression or generalized anxiety for treatment of SAD in routine clinical practice or to think that their outcomes will necessarily be limited.

Clinical Considerations to Maximize Engagement in Evidence-Based Treatment

Functional Problem Analysis

Individual case conceptualizations are crucial in maximizing SAD treatment engagement, as patients with this condition are not homogeneous (see case below). Ideally, therapists should develop hypotheses to explain problem behaviors and devise treatments to test these hypotheses. Two levels of functional analysis are important: (1) macro-analysis: establishes relationships between co-occurring syndromes to determine treatment priorities (e.g., SAD vs. depression) and (2) micro-analysis: provides a detailed analysis of symptoms and their relationship to behaviors like avoidance. For example, in cases of comorbid SAD and depression, a macro-analysis can help determine which condition to treat first. Similarly, when substance use disorder co-occurs with SAD, it is generally recommended to address substance use first (Emmelkamp & Vedel, 2006) as it is considered avoidance or safety behavior.

A micro-analysis or functional analysis creates a hypothetical working model of the problem behavior, informing specific treatment interventions. This approach allows therapists to target avoidance behavior with exposure exercises and identify necessary social skills training. Collaborating with patients to develop a functional analysis and providing a theoretical rationale for interventions do enhance treatment engagement (Bluett et al., 2016). This individualized approach is essential for effective treatment of SAD, considering the diverse factors that may contribute to and maintain the disorder in different patients. It may help to have the patient complete a self-monitoring diary or daily record to elucidate the conditions under which the behavior (e.g., social anxiety, avoidance, and thoughts) occurs.

Motivational Interviewing

Motivational interviewing (MI; see Chap. 4) and between-session assignments (see homework assignments) are promising components to engage an individual more strongly in the therapy process. MI is a technique widely used in patients with addiction (Emmelkamp & Vedel, 2006), but it may also have added value in the treatment of individuals with anxiety disorders (Marker & Norton, 2018), but effects of motivational interviewing on CBT are smaller for individuals with SAD (Westra & Dozois, 2006) as compared to other disorders. In a more recent study (Peters et al., 2019), motivational interviewing was used as a three-session preparation for CBT in a large sample of individuals with SAD. However, no significant differences were found in the outcome in comparison with the control group, who received supportive counseling. It was found that the group who received motivational interviewing first was better at completing homework assignments, but this did not lead to better outcomes. A potential explanation could be that especially patients with SAD profit more from behavioral interventions leading to changes in cognitions than vice versa (Lervik et al., 2022).

Exposure Therapy

In a study evaluating mechanisms of change in CBT, the main research questions sought to determine whether changing cognitions leads to behavior change or if changing behavior leads to changes in cognitions (Lervik et al., 2022). In a sample of patients with SAD who received CBT, it was found that avoidance behavior predicted cognitions at later timepoints but not the other way around (Lervik et al., 2022). Therefore, exposure therapy is specifically important in individuals with SAD. Indeed, a recent meta-analysis suggested that the exposure component of CBT in particular enhances treatment outcomes (Parker et al., 2018).

Exposure therapy, particularly in vivo exposure, is considered the gold standard for treating anxiety disorders, including SAD (Abramowitz et al., 2019; Böhnlein et al., 2020). It involves gradually exposing patients to anxiety-provoking situations until habituation occurs (Emmelkamp, 2013). However, creating a hierarchy of social situations for exposure in SAD is challenging due to the unpredictability of social interactions. Clinical trials often combine exposure with other components, such as social skills training, which may have benefits in reducing social distress and improving social behavior (Beidel et al., 2014).

Recent trends have shifted toward virtual reality exposure therapy (VRET) due to the challenges of in vivo exposure in uncontrollable social situations (Emmelkamp et al., 2020). While VRET has shown efficacy across anxiety disorders (Emmelkamp & Meyerbröker, 2021), its results for SAD are mixed (Horigome et al., 2020; Morina et al., 2023a). Nonetheless, advancements in technology have made VRET a promising alternative, allowing real-time interaction with avatars (Emmelkamp et al., 2020). Especially in SAD, the use of VRET overcomes challenges inherent to the unpredictability and uncontrollability of social situations. With the use of VRET in SAD, therapists can improve the efficiency of exposure to maximize engagement (i.e., if patients experience earlier successes and gains, they may be more likely to persist in treatment). By developing more positive exposure experiences, the confidence of being able to manage a future exposure situation will help to stay engaged in treatment (Meyerbröker & Emmelkamp, 2025).

When considering engagement in exposure therapy, clinicians must keep in mind that negative exposure experiences can lead to a decrease in patients' self-efficacy in managing social situations. This can lead to increased avoidance behaviors and reduced confidence in their ability to cope with anxiety-provoking situations (Racz et al., 2024). Reduced confidence in one's ability to cope with a social situation in combination with avoidance behavior has a tremendous effect on engagement with exposure therapy. Engaging in safety behaviors (e.g., avoiding eye contact and rehearsing speech) and avoidance behavior can prevent individuals from fully engaging in exposure tasks, which are critical for the success of exposure (Butler et al., 2021). These behaviors can also reinforce the belief that they cannot cope with social situations without these crutches. Clinicians should work to ensure success experiences, particularly early on (see Chap. 5).

Cognitive Therapy

Cognitive therapy based on Clark and Wells model targets beliefs and self-focused attention as primary maintaining factors. It uses experiential exercises to highlight the negative effects of self-focused attention and safety behaviors (Schreiber et al., 2015). Techniques include external-focused attention training and video feedback to correct distorted self-images (Warnock-Parkes et al., 2017). Behavioral experiments during therapy test negative predictions while dropping safety behaviors. Decatastrophizing and discrimination training (i.e., helping individuals with social difficulties to recognize and differentiate between various social cues, such as facial expressions, tone of voice, and body language) are used as well to enhance engagement in CBT. More recently, imagery rescripting may be added to address early social trauma (Morina et al., 2017; Landkroon et al., 2022; Strohm et al., 2021). Overall, cognitive therapy offers a structured approach to SAD, focusing on modifying cognitive processes and behaviors that maintain anxiety and has been found efficacious compared with other active treatments (e.g., Aune et al., 2021; Clark et al., 2023; Thew et al., 2020; Warnock-Parkes et al., 2022).

Individuals with SAD often hold unrealistic social standards and high self-expectations, such as the belief that they must always appear calm and composed. These beliefs can lead to anxiety about meeting these standards and hinder engagement in therapy, as individuals may fear failure or judgment during therapeutic exercises. Other cognitions that hinder engagement in treatment are associated with negative self-perception. People with SAD frequently view themselves rather negatively. This self-focused attention and negative self-view can result in a reluctance to participate in exposure exercises and therapy more broadly. Additionally, individuals with SAD tend to overestimate the negative consequences of their behavior. They often overestimate the likelihood and impact of negative social outcomes. This cognitive distortion can in turn lead to more avoidance behaviors, which directly conflict with the exposure-based components of CBT, thereby reducing engagement. Therapists may consider prioritizing these distorted beliefs to mitigate the potential risk of disengagement in treatment.

Homework Assignments in CBT

Homework is considered crucial in CBT for allowing patients to practice and reinforce skills learned in therapy sessions in real-life contexts (Kazantzis et al., 2018). This is particularly relevant for SAD, where exposure to social situations is a key component of treatment (Kazantzis et al., 2016; Ryum et al., 2024). However, engagement in homework can be challenging. Early engagement, positive experiences, and a strong therapeutic alliance appear to be key factors in promoting homework compliance and effectiveness.

In a recent systematic review (Ryum et al., 2023), it was found that higher early homework engagement was associated with higher subsequent homework engagement throughout group CBT for SAD. This suggests that establishing good homework habits early in treatment is important. The same study found that experiencing positive consequences from homework (e.g., mastery and progress) was reciprocally related to a stronger working alliance throughout therapy. Simply stated, successful homework engagement was associated with a stronger therapeutic relationship. Non-engagement with homework assignments may signal that the client is fundamentally opposing the treatment with possible negative consequences of further avoidance behavior, which could be a warning sign of eventually dropping out of therapy. In a recent study with patients with SAD receiving group CBT (McEvoy et al., 2024), it was found that early homework engagement was associated with higher engagement throughout therapy. Generally, it has been suggested that homework non-adherence rates range from approximately 20–50% in adult clients receiving CBT, highlighting that homework compliance remains a significant challenge in clinical practice (Kazantzis et al., 2016). In patients treated with CBT for SAD, there is a positive association between the amount of homework completed and anxiety reduction after CBT (e.g., Hawley et al., 2016). Thus, one way to increase homework compliance may be to increase expectations for change; that is, expectations about a positive outcome may motivate individuals to engage in difficult homework tasks.

Social Skills

There is some evidence that social skills deficits are associated with SAD, but whether this is due to a real skills deficit or to the fact that socially anxious individuals may exhibit negative cognitive biases in evaluating their own social skills is still a matter of discussion. In one study (Habibi Asgarabad et al., 2023), reduced social skills predicted the development of social anxiety in middle childhood, suggesting that teaching adequate social skills may be important in a substantial number of children with SAD (James et al., 2020). Generally, a larger reduction in social anxiety is found when social skills training is included in CBT for SAD in children and adolescents (e.g., del Mar et al., 2023).

Relatively few studies have investigated the effects of social skills training in adults with SAD. Beidel et al. (2014) investigated the additive impact of social skills training on imaginal and in vivo exposure therapy. The combination of social skills training and exposure therapy was slightly more effective than exposure therapy alone on measures of social skills and general clinical status. Teaching social skills may enhance engagement by increasing mastery and confidence and potentially increase positive expectancies for treatment, but more research is needed to definitively draw such conclusions.

Case Example

We present an adult case of an individual with SAD. In the case, we will link symptoms to treatment indications, treatment engagement strategies, and implications.

Case Description and Conceptualization

Emily is a 32-year-old graphic designer who has been experiencing challenges with social anxiety since she was 11 years old. Despite her creative talents and professional success, Emily finds herself increasingly overwhelmed by her fear of social interactions, hindering her personal and career growth. For the past 8 months, her mood has been consistently low, and she has begun to have feelings of purposelessness and hopelessness.

In her professional life, Emily's social anxiety is impactful such that she avoids or endures with great distress networking events, client presentations, and team meetings. Her fear of making any mistakes and receiving criticism paralyzes her, leading to either avoidance by calling in sick or safety behaviors, which include bringing her notebook and pretending to take extensive notes to divert attention away from herself and minimize the pressure of being the center of attention. In personal conversations, she rehearses and scripts potential conversations in her mind before social interactions, hoping that this preparation will prevent awkward moments or perceived failures. Emily's relationships have been strained due to her reluctance to engage in social interactions.

When faced with a social situation, Emily experiences a range of physical symptoms, such as muscle tension, rapid heartbeat, and a sense of breathlessness. Additionally, she often endures persistent feelings of self-consciousness, embarrassment, and fear of being scrutinized by others. Despite her expertise and talent as a graphic designer, Emily's social anxiety has limited her career progression. Opportunities for promotions, collaborations, and new projects are often passed over due to her fear of interpersonal interactions.

The therapist, an experienced cognitive behavioral therapist, initiated treatment with a comprehensive assessment to support Emily's engagement. This process involved a thorough evaluation of Emily's social anxiety and comorbid depressive symptoms. Given the severity of her symptoms and the seriousness of her avoidance behavior, they agreed together that treatment would address avoidance behavior with exposure therapy and social skills training, including role-playing. The therapist discussed the specific anxiety-triggering social situations and Emily's coping mechanisms and safety behaviors. Based on this assessment, the therapist developed a nuanced case conceptualization based on the SAD model of Rapee and Heimberg (1997). This conceptualization highlighted the chronic nature of Emily's SAD, its significant impact on her functioning, and would ensure focus on such potential obstacles as low motivation and avoidance tendencies.

Treatment Approach and Engagement Strategies

The therapist clearly articulated the CBT treatment rationale to Emily, explaining the interconnection between thoughts, emotions, and behaviors in maintaining social anxiety. This approach aimed to foster Emily's engagement from the beginning by providing a clear understanding of the therapeutic process. Here the therapist worked collaboratively with Emily, asking her for a recent situation in which she experienced high social anxiety. When analyzing the situation, the therapist worked out the CBT model and discussed with her a good starting point. Although Emily responded that she thinks challenging her thoughts would be a good starting point, the therapists asked her whether she would be open to working with her behavior, as this seems to be a more impactful route (Parker et al., 2018), and although it might be more anxiety provoking, it would probably lead to faster change. Emily was hesitant but said that she was willing to give it a try.

To support Emily's engagement and mitigate the risk of dropout or nonresponse, the therapist worked to implement several evidence-based strategies. To start, he worked collaboratively with Emily to identify her goals. Together, they worked to make Emily's goals measurable and achievable to enhance her sense of agency and commitment to treatment (Kazantzis et al., 2016).

Emily's treatment began with exposure to social situations that trigger anxiety, starting with less intimidating scenarios and progressing to more challenging ones. Especially when addressing the feared social situations, the therapist realized it was important to tailor these individually to Emily's ability and to make it a successful exposure experience. Experiencing a successful exposure was intended to build up Emily's confidence in her own ability and strengthen treatment engagement. Additionally, in therapy sessions, she practiced shifting her attention from internal perceptions to external objects or social interaction partners. The therapist used role-play to model social skills and provide Emily with opportunities for practice.

At the same time, to enhance Emily's social skills, the focus during therapy expanded to include effective communication and self-expression. Role-playing and real-life practice contributed to increased confidence in various social settings. Exposure exercises were incorporated not only in Emily's private life to increase engagement in social interactions but also in her professional context. The exposure exercises were conducted alongside behavioral activation techniques to address depressive symptoms. By this, the therapists aimed to combat low motivation and potential barriers to homework completion and session attendance and thus also mitigate disengagement from treatment. In between sessions, Emily practiced, and her therapist emphasized the importance of these assignments in relation to the collaboratively formulated goals.

The therapist regularly checked in with Emily using the Social Phobia Inventory (SPIN; Connor et al., 2000) to track Emily's symptoms and progress. This feedback guided treatment adjustments and was used to relate to the goals previously formulated.

The therapist remained vigilant to potential red flags for low treatment engagement, such as Emily's reported low mood suggesting comorbid depression, which, if not addressed, may have made it hard for her to behaviorally engage in treatment and also eroded her confidence in the treatment's effectiveness.

At the end of Emily's therapy, she demonstrated significant progress in managing her SAD. Her ability to perform daily work tasks with reduced distress marked a notable improvement. This positive change led to increased job satisfaction as Emily's growing confidence in her professional abilities became evident. The enhanced self-assurance had a ripple effect, motivating Emily to engage more actively in exposure exercises. This created a positive feedback loop, where successful exposures further bolstered her confidence, encouraging her to tackle increasingly challenging social situations. Quantitative assessment of Emily's progress showed substantial improvement. Her score on the SPIN decreased dramatically from her initial assessment.

During the final sessions, Emily reflected on the elements of therapy that were most beneficial to her. She highlighted the effectiveness of the role-playing exercises conducted with her therapist. Although Emily recognized that the exposure exercises were quite challenging for her at times, she found them invaluable in building up her confidence. The successful navigation of doing the exposure exercises and practicing role-plays with her therapist provided Emily with concrete evidence of her capabilities, even in the face of anxiety. The skills and confidence gained through role-playing allowed her to approach actual social interactions with greater ease and less apprehension. She reported feeling more relaxed in various social contexts, attributing this improvement to the practical experience gained during therapy. The therapist's attention to theory-driven case conceptualization, collaborative goal-setting, regular symptom monitoring, and the development of successful, mastery-building exposures and role-play exercises worked to enhance Emily's engagement in treatment and ultimately optimize treatment outcome.

Conclusion

SAD is one of the most common psychiatric diagnoses and the most common anxiety disorder. It is also one of the earliest manifesting anxiety disorders with far-reaching consequences that can impact attainment of developmental milestones (van Est-Bitincka et al., 2023) and further limit in personal and professional life achievements. As social interactions are complex and reflective of subjective experience, the therapeutic approach, grounded in evidence-based CBT approaches, must be nuanced to optimize outcomes and engagement. The problem of engagement in treatment for individuals with SAD is multifaceted. Studies indicate high unmet need in the community, with notable barriers to engagement including stigma and shame, the latter of which closely aligns with core SAD features. Practical aspects, including the knowledge about how to seek therapy, hinder treatment engagement as well (Goetter et al., 2018). The nature of SAD (i.e., fear of scrutiny and negative evaluation) makes approaching therapy challenging. Even after initiating treatment, the therapist must be attentive to behaviors that can undermine effective engagement in treatment. Heightened self-focus and distorted cognitions intensify anxiety during exposure. Safety behaviors undermine the effectiveness of exposure exercises, which is considered the most effective part of CBT in anxiety disorders (Parker et al., 2018). Addressing these barriers requires therapists to carefully explain the treatment rationale, monitor subtle avoidance behavior, and provide culturally sensitive and individually tailored care to optimize engagement and prevent dropout. SAD has lower recovery rates compared to other anxiety disorders. Studies of potential moderators of treatment outcome and engagement are limited and largely inconclusive. These findings underscore the complexity of treating SAD and the need for further research to improve treatment engagement and outcomes.

To enhance treatment engagement, it is important to use an elaborated individual case conceptualization and conduct thorough macro- and micro-level functional analyses to identify treatment priorities and inform specific interventions, which is of utmost importance. Taking a collaborative approach, therapists can enhance engagement and target avoidance behaviors effectively while working toward mutually agreed-upon treatment goals. Clinicians must also guide patients through successful first exposure experiences. Using VRET, monitoring avoidance and safety behaviors, and combining social skills training may be especially important considerations. When considering how to modify cognitive processes that maintain SAD, several techniques such as external-focused attention training and video feedback to correct distorted self-images can be added as therapeutic instruments. It is essential to address unrealistic social standards and negative self-perceptions that may hinder engagement in therapy. Homework can be challenging, but early engagement in and positive experiences with homework can strengthen the therapeutic alliance and improve compliance (Kazantzis et al., 2016). In summary, the treatment of SAD presents unique challenges that require a multifaceted and idiosyncratic approach to maximize engagement and outcome.

Clinical Summary Points and Recommendations

- Prevalence rates of SAD vary between 3% and 6% for lifetime and 1% and 4% for the past 12 months. SAD has the youngest age of onset with a mean of 10.5 years. CBT is considered the most effective treatment, but engagement is hindered by barriers to treatment (e.g., shame and stigma), premature drop-out, and nonresponse.
- Close collaboration in treatment goal-setting between therapist and patient is considered an important aspect in fostering a strong therapeutic alliance and supporting treatment engagement.
- Behavioral interventions, including exposure exercises, are considered crucial for long-term change in SAD. Working from a theoretically consistent rationale, fostering positive treatment expectancies, designing successful early exposures, incorporating social skills training, and implementing virtual reality exposure can enhance engagement in exposure exercises and build mastery. Behavioral exercises in SAD predict later changes in cognitions, and homework assignments are considered crucial for real-life changes.
- Avoidance and safety behaviors require close monitoring and individually tailored therapist-guided interventions to keep patients engaged in treatment.

References

Abramowitz, J. S., Deacon, B. J., & Whiteside, S. P. H. (2019). *Exposure therapy for anxiety: Principles and practice* (2nd ed.). The Guilford Press.

Altmann, U., Gawlytta, R., Hoyer, J., Leichsenring, F., Leibing, E., Beutel, M., Willutzki, U., Herpertz, S., & Strauss, B. (2020). Typical symptom change patterns and their predictors in patients with social anxiety disorder: A latent class analysis. *Journal of Anxiety Disorders, 71*, 102200. https://doi.org/10.1016/j.janxdis.2020.102200

Association, A. P. (2022). Diagnostic and statistical manual of mental disorders: DSM-5-TR. In *America Psychiatric Association, 6(11), 951–952* (5th ed.). American Psychiatric Association.

Aune, T., Juul, E. M. L., Beidel, D. C., Nordahl, H. M., & Dvorak, R. D. (2021). Mitigating adolescent social anxiety symptoms: The effects of social support and social self-efficacy in findings from the Young-HUNT 3 study. *European Child & Adolescent Psychiatry, 30*(3), 441–449. https://doi.org/10.1007/s00787-020-01529-0

Auyeung, K., Hawley, L. L., Grimm, K., McCabe, R., & Rowa, K. (2020). Fear of negative evaluation and rapid response to treatment during cognitive behaviour therapy for social anxiety disorder. *Cognitive Therapy and Research, 44*, 526–537.

Baljé, A. E., Greeven, A., Deen, M., van Giezen, A. E., Arntz, A., & Spinhoven, P. (2024). Group schema therapy versus group cognitive behavioral therapy for patients with social anxiety disorder and comorbid avoidant personality disorder: A randomized controlled trial. *Journal of Anxiety Disorders, 104*. https://doi.org/10.1016/j.janxdis.2024.102860

Beidel, D. C., Alfano, C. A., Kofler, M. J., Rao, P. A., Scharfstein, L., & Wong Sarver, N. (2014). The impact of social skills training for social anxiety disorder: A randomized controlled trial. *Journal of Anxiety Disorders, 28*(8), 908–918. https://doi.org/10.1016/j.janxdis.2014.09.016

Bluett, E. J., Landy, L. L., Twohig, M. P., & Arch, J. J. (2016). Does the theoretical perspective of exposure framing matter? Acceptance, fear reduction/cognitive reappraisal, and values-framing of exposure for social anxiety. *Journal of Cognitive Psychotherapy, 30*(2), 77–93. https://doi.org/10.1891/0889-8391.30.2.77

Böhnlein, J., Altegoer, L., Muck, N. K., Roesmann, K., Redlich, R., Dannlowski, U., & Leehr, E. J. (2020). Factors influencing the success of exposure therapy for specific phobia: A systematic review. *Neuroscience & Biobehavioral Reviews, 108*, 796–820. https://doi.org/10.1016/j.neubiorev.2019.12.009

Brenk-Franz, K., Strauss, B., Tiesler, F., Fleischhauer, C., Ciechanowski, P., Schneider, N., & Gensichen, J. (2015). The influence of adult attachment on patient self-management in primary care-the need for a personalized approach and patient-centred care. *PLoS One, 10*(9), e0136723.

Butler, R. M., O'Day, E. B., Swee, M. B., Horenstein, A., & Heimberg, R. G. (2021). Cognitive behavioral therapy for social anxiety disorder: Predictors of treatment outcome in a quasi-naturalistic setting. *Behavior Therapy, 52*(2), 465–477. https://doi.org/10.1016/j.beth.2020.06.002

Carleton, R. N., Duranceau, S., Shulman, E. P., Zerff, M., Gonzales, J., & Mishra, S. (2016). Self-reported intolerance of uncertainty and behavioural decisions. *Journal of Behavior Therapy and Experimental Psychiatry, 51*, 58–65. https://doi.org/10.1016/j.jbtep.2015.12.004

Carpenter, J. K., Andrews, L. A., Witcraft, S. M., Powers, M. B., Smits, J. A. J., & Hofmann, S. G. (2018). Cognitive behavioral therapy for anxiety and related disorders: A meta-analysis of randomized placebo-controlled trials. *Depression and Anxiety, 35*(6), 502–514. https://doi.org/10.1002/da.22728

Clark, D., & Wells, A. (1995). A cognitive model of social phobia. In *Social phobia: Diagnosis, assessment, and treatment* (pp. 69–93).

Clark, D. M., Wild, J., Warnock-Parkes, E., Stott, R., Grey, N., Thew, G., & Ehlers, A. (2023). More than doubling the clinical benefit of each hour of therapist time: A randomised controlled trial of internet cognitive therapy for social anxiety disorder. *Psychological Medicine, 53*(11), 5022–5032. https://doi.org/10.1017/S0033291722002008

Connor, K. M., Davidson, J. R. T., Churchill, L. E., Sherwood, A., Weisler, R. H., & Foa, E. (2000). Psychometric properties of the Social Phobia Inventory (SPIN): New self-rating scale. *British Journal of Psychiatry, 176*(4), 379–386. https://doi.org/10.1192/bjp.176.4.379

Cox, B. J., Fleet, C., & Stein, M. B. (2004). Self-criticism and social phobia in the US national comorbidity survey. *Journal of Affective Disorders, 82*(2), 227–234. https://doi.org/10.1016/j.jad.2003.12.012

del Mar Díaz-Castela, M., Martínez, J. A. M., López, L. J. G., & Fernández, L. E. (2023). The state of psychological treatments for social anxiety disorder in children and adolescents: An umbrella review. *Revista de Psicología Clínica Con Niños y Adolescentes, 10*(1), 3.

Emmelkamp. (2013). Behavior therapy with adults. In M. J. Lambert (Ed.), *Bergin and Garfield's handbook of psychotherapy and behavior change*. John Wiley & Sons.

Emmelkamp, P. M. G., & Meyerbröker, K. (2021). Virtual reality therapy in mental health. *Annual Review of Clinical Psychology, 17*. https://doi.org/10.1146/annurev-clinpsy-081219-115923

Emmelkamp, P. M. G. (2023). Mental health of adult refugees. In *Mental health of refugees: Etiology and treatment* (pp. 1–49). Springer.

Emmelkamp, P. M. G., & Meyerbröker, K. (2019). Personality disorders. *Personality Disorders*. https://doi.org/10.4324/9781351055901

Emmelkamp, P. M. G., Meyerbröker, K., & Morina, N. (2020). Virtual reality therapy in social anxiety disorder. *Current Psychiatry Reports, 22*(7), 32. https://doi.org/10.1007/s11920-020-01156-1

Emmelkamp, P. M. G., & Vedel, E. (2006). *Evidence-based treatment for alcohol and drug abuse: A practitioner's guide to theory, methods, and practice*. Routledge/Taylor & Francis Group.

Erceg-Hurn, D. M., Campbell, B. N. C., & McEvoy, P. M. (2023). What explains the failure to identify replicable moderators of symptom change in social anxiety disorder? *Journal of Anxiety Disorders, 94*, 102676.

Fernandez, E., Salem, D., Swift, J. K., & Ramtahal, N. (2015). Meta-analysis of dropout from cognitive behavioral therapy: Magnitude, timing, and moderators. *Journal of Consulting and Clinical Psychology, 83*(6), 1108–1122. https://doi.org/10.1037/ccp0000044

Gilbert, P., & Procter, S. (2006). Compassionate mind training for people with high shame and self-criticism: Overview and pilot study of a group therapy approach. *Clinical Psychology & Psychotherapy, 13*(6), 353–379. https://doi.org/10.1002/cpp.507

Goetter, E. M., Frumkin, M. R., Palitz, S. A., Swee, M. B., Baker, A. W., Bui, E., & Simon, N. M. (2018). Barriers to mental health treatment among individuals with social anxiety disorder and generalized anxiety disorder. *Psychological Services, 17*(1), 5–12. https://doi.org/10.1037/ser0000254

Gray, E., Beierl, E. T., & Clark, D. M. (2019). Sub-types of safety behaviours and their effects on social anxiety disorder. *PLoS One, 14*(10). https://doi.org/10.1371/journal.pone.0223165

Habibi Asgarabad, M., Steinsbekk, S., & Wichstrøm, L. (2023). Social skills and symptoms of anxiety disorders from preschool to adolescence: A prospective cohort study. *Journal of Child Psychology and Psychiatry, 64*(7), 1045–1055. https://doi.org/10.1111/jcpp.13787

Hans, E., & Hiller, W. (2013). A meta-analysis of nonrandomized effectiveness studies on outpatient cognitive behavioral therapy for adult anxiety disorders. *Clinical Psychology Review, 33*(8), 954–964. https://doi.org/10.1016/j.cpr.2013.07.003

Hawley, L. L., Rector, N. A., & Laposa, J. M. (2016). Examining the dynamic relationships between exposure tasks and cognitive restructuring in CBT for SAD: Outcomes and moderating influences. *Journal of Anxiety Disorders, 39*, 10–20. https://doi.org/10.1016/j.janxdis.2016.01.010

Heimberg, R. G., Brozovich, F. A., & Rapee, R. M. (2014). *Chapter 24 – A cognitive-behavioral model of social anxiety disorder* (pp. 705–728). Academic Press. https://doi.org/10.1016/B978-0-12-394427-6.00024-8

Hofmann, S. G. (2007). Cognitive factors that maintain social anxiety disorder: A comprehensive model and its treatment implications. *Cognitive Behaviour Therapy, 36*(4), 193–209. https://doi.org/10.1080/16506070701421313

Hofmann, S. G., Anu Asnaani, M. A., & Hinton, D. E. (2010). Cultural aspects in social anxiety and social anxiety disorder. *Depression and Anxiety, 27*(12), 1117–1127. https://doi.org/10.1002/da.20759

Horigome, T., Kurokawa, S., Sawada, K., Kudo, S., Shiga, K., Mimura, M., & Kishimoto, T. (2020). Virtual reality exposure therapy for social anxiety disorder: A systematic review and meta-Analysis. *Psychological Medicine, 50*(15), 2487–2497. https://doi.org/10.1017/S0033291720003785

James, A. C., Reardon, T., Soler, A., James, G., & Creswell, C. (2020). Cognitive behavioural therapy for anxiety disorders in children and adolescents. *Cochrane Database of Systematic Reviews, 11*. https://doi.org/10.1002/14651858.CD013162.pub2

Kazantzis, N., Luong, H. K., Usatoff, A. S., Impala, T., Yew, R. Y., & Hofmann, S. G. (2018). The processes of cognitive behavioral therapy: A review of meta-analyses. *Cognitive Therapy and Research, 42*(4), 349–357. https://doi.org/10.1007/s10608-018-9920-y

Kazantzis, N., Whittington, C., Zelencich, L., Kyrios, M., Norton, P. J., & Hofmann, S. G. (2016). Quantity and quality of homework compliance: A meta-analysis of relations with outcome in cognitive behavior therapy. *Behavior Therapy, 47*(5), 755–772. https://doi.org/10.1016/j.beth.2016.05.002

Koyuncu, A., İnce, E., Ertekin, E., & Tükel, R. (2019). Comorbidity in social anxiety disorder: Diagnostic and therapeutic challenges. *Drugs in Context, 8*, 212573. https://doi.org/10.7573/dic.212573

Landkroon, E., Meyerbröker, K., Salemink, E., & Engelhard, I. M. (2022). Future-oriented imagery rescripting facilitates conducting behavioral experiments in social anxiety. *Behaviour Research and Therapy*, 104130. https://doi.org/10.1016/j.brat.2022.104130

Lervik, L. V., Hoffart, A., Knapstad, M., & Smith, O. R. F. (2022). Exploring the temporal associations between avoidance behavior and cognitions during the course of cognitive behavioral therapy for clients with symptoms of social anxiety disorder. *Psychotherapy Research, 32*(2), 195–208. https://doi.org/10.1080/10503307.2021.1930243

Levy, H. C., & Radomsky, A. S. (2016). Are all safety behaviours created equal? A comparison of novel and routinely used safety behaviours in obsessive-compulsive disorder. *Cognitive Behaviour Therapy, 45*(5), 367–379. https://doi.org/10.1080/16506073.2016.1184712

Loerinc, A. G., Meuret, A. E., Twohig, M. P., Rosenfield, D., Bluett, E. J., & Craske, M. G. (2015). Response rates for CBT for anxiety disorders: Need for standardized criteria. *Clinical Psychology Review, 42*, 72–82. https://doi.org/10.1016/j.cpr.2015.08.004

Marker, I., & Norton, P. J. (2018). The efficacy of incorporating motivational interviewing to cognitive behavior therapy for anxiety disorders: A review and meta-analysis. *Clinical Psychology Review, 62*, 1–10. https://doi.org/10.1016/j.cpr.2018.04.004

McEvoy, P. M., Johnson, A. R., Kazantzis, N., & Egan, S. J. (2024). Predictors of homework engagement in group CBT for social anxiety: Client beliefs about homework, its consequences, group cohesion, and working alliance. *Psychotherapy Research, 34*(1), 68–80. https://doi.org/10.1080/10503307.2023.2286993

McGrath, J. J., Al-Hamzawi, A., Alonso, J., Altwaijri, Y., Andrade, L. H., Bromet, E. J., Bruffaerts, R., de Almeida, J. M. C., Chardoul, S., Chiu, W. T., Degenhardt, L., Demler, O. V., Ferry, F., Gureje, O., Haro, J. M., Karam, E. G., Karam, G., Khaled, S. M., Kovess-Masfety, V., et al. (2023). Age of onset and cumulative risk of mental disorders: A cross-national analysis of population surveys from 29 countries. *The Lancet Psychiatry, 10*(9), 668–681. https://doi.org/10.1016/S2215-0366(23)00193-1

McManus, F., Sacadura, C., & Clark, D. M. (2008). Why social anxiety persists: An experimental investigation of the role of safety behaviours as a maintaining factor. *Journal of Behavior Therapy and Experimental Psychiatry, 39*(2), 147–161. https://doi.org/10.1016/j.jbtep.2006.12.002

Meyerbröker, K., & Emmelkamp, P. (2025). Take a Look at Me Now: The Use of Virtual Reality in the Treatment of Social Anxiety Disorder. *Journal of Clinical Psychology*, n/a(n/a). https://doi.org/10.1002/jclp.23782

Morina, N., Lancee, J., & Arntz, A. (2017). Imagery rescripting as a clinical intervention for aversive memories: A meta-analysis. *Journal of Behavior Therapy and Experimental Psychiatry, 55*, 6–15. https://doi.org/10.1016/j.jbtep.2016.11.003

Morina, N., Kampmann, I., Emmelkamp, P., Barbui, C., & Hoppen, T. H. (2023a). Meta-analysis of virtual reality exposure therapy for social anxiety disorder. *Psychological Medicine, 53*(5), 2176–2178. https://doi.org/10.1017/S0033291721001690

Morina, N., Seidemann, J., Andor, T., Sondern, L., Bürkner, P.-C., Drenckhan, I., & Buhlmann, U. (2023b). The effectiveness of cognitive behavioural therapy for social anxiety disorder in routine clinical practice. *Clinical Psychology & Psychotherapy, 30*(2), 335–343. https://doi.org/10.1002/cpp.2799

Morris, T. L., & D'Souza, J. (2023). Treatment of social anxiety in children and adolescents BT - Handbook of child and adolescent anxiety disorders. In D. McKay & E. A. Storch (Eds.), (pp. 299–313). Springer International Publishing. https://doi.org/10.1007/978-3-031-14080-8_20

Mörtberg, E., Hoffart, A., Boecking, B., & Clark, D. M. (2015). Shifting the focus of one's attention mediates improvement in cognitive therapy for social anxiety disorder. *BEHAVIOURAL AND COGNITIVE PSYCHOTHERAPY, 43*(1), 63–73. https://doi.org/10.1017/S1352465813000738

Moscovitch, D. A. (2009). What is the core fear in social phobia? A new model to facilitate individualized case conceptualization and treatment. *Cognitive and Behavioral Practice, 16*(2), 123–134.

Parker, Z. J., Waller, G., Duhne, G. S., & P., & Dawson, J. (2018). The role of exposure in treatment of anxiety disorders: A meta-analysis. *International Journal of Psychology and Psychological Therapy, 18*(1).

Peters, L., Romano, M., Byrow, Y., Gregory, B., McLellan, L. F., Brockveld, K., Baillie, A., Gaston, J., & Rapee, R. M. (2019). Motivational interviewing prior to cognitive behavioural treatment for social anxiety disorder: A randomised controlled trial. *Journal of Affective Disorders, 256*, 70–78. https://doi.org/10.1016/j.jad.2019.05.042

Piccirillo, M. L., & Rodebaugh, T. L. (2022). Personalized networks of social anxiety disorder and depression and implications for treatment. *Journal of Affective Disorders, 298*, 262–276. https://doi.org/10.1016/j.jad.2021.10.034

Piccirillo, M. L., Taylor Dryman, M., & Heimberg, R. G. (2016). Safety behaviors in adults with social anxiety: Review and future directions. *Behavior Therapy, 47*(5), 675–687. https://doi.org/10.1016/j.beth.2015.11.005

Powell, J., Williams, V., Atherton, H., Bennett, K., Yang, Y., Davoudianfar, M., Hellsing, A., Martin, A., Mollison, J., Shanyinde, M., Yu, L.-M., & Griffiths, K. M. (2020). Effectiveness and cost-effectiveness of a self-guided internet intervention for social anxiety symptoms in a general population sample: Randomized controlled trial. *Journal of Medical Internet Researc, 22*(1), e16804. https://doi.org/10.2196/16804

Racz, J. I., Bialocerkowski, A., Calteaux, I., & Farrell, L. J. (2024). Determinants of exposure therapy implementation in clinical practice for the treatment of anxiety, OCD, and PTSD: A systematic review. *Clinical Child and Family Psychology Review, 27*(2), 317–341. https://doi.org/10.1007/s10567-024-00478-3

Rapee, R. M., & Heimberg, R. G. (1997). A cognitive-behavioral model of anxiety in social phobia. *Behaviour Research and Therapy, 35*(8), 741–756. https://doi.org/10.1016/S0005-7967(97)00022-3

Rapee, R. M., Lyneham, H. J., Wuthrich, V., Chatterton, M. L., Hudson, J. L., Kangas, M., & Mihalopoulos, C. (2017). Comparison of stepped care delivery against a single, empirically validated cognitive-behavioral therapy program for youth with anxiety: A randomized clinical trial. *Journal of the American Academy of Child & Adolescent Psychiatry, 56*(10), 841–848. https://doi.org/10.1016/j.jaac.2017.08.001

Rodebaugh, T. L., Grossman, J. T., Tonge, N. A., Shin, J., Frumkin, M. R., Rodriguez, C. R., Ortiz, E. G., & Piccirillo, M. L. (2024). Avoidance and fear day by day in social anxiety disorder. *PSYCHOTHERAPY RESEARCH*. https://doi.org/10.1080/10503307.2023.2297994

Rozen, N., & Aderka, I. M. (2022). The effect of depression on treatment outcome in social anxiety disorder: An individual-level meta-analysis. *Cognitive Behaviour Therapy, 51*(3), 185–216. https://doi.org/10.1080/16506073.2021.1966089

Ryum, T., Bennion, M., & Kazantzis, N. (2023). Integrating between-session homework in psychotherapy: A systematic review of immediate in-session and intermediate outcomes. *Psychotherapy, 60*(3), 306–319. https://doi.org/10.1037/pst0000488

Ryum, T., Bennion, M., & Kazantzis, N. (2024). Homework as a driver of change in psychotherapy. *Journal of Clinical Psychology, 80*(4), 733–743. https://doi.org/10.1002/jclp.23627

Schreiber, F., Heimlich, C., Schweitzer, C., & Stangier, U. (2015). Cognitive therapy for social anxiety disorder: The impact of the "self-focused attention and safety behaviours experiment" on the course of treatment. *BEHAVIOURAL AND COGNITIVE PSYCHOTHERAPY, 43*(2), 158–166. https://doi.org/10.1017/S1352465813000672

Schultz, L. T., & Heimberg, R. G. (2008). Attentional focus in social anxiety disorder: Potential for interactive processes. *Clinical Psychology Review, 28*(7), 1206–1221. https://doi.org/10.1016/j.cpr.2008.04.003

Stein, D. J., Lim, C. C. W., Roest, A. M., de Jonge, P., Aguilar-Gaxiola, S., Al-Hamzawi, A., Alonso, J., Benjet, C., Bromet, E. J., Bruffaerts, R., de Girolamo, G., Florescu, S., Gureje, O., Haro, J. M., Harris, M. G., He, Y., Hinkov, H., Horiguchi, I., Hu, C., et al. (2017). The cross-national epidemiology of social anxiety disorder: Data from the World Mental Health Survey Initiative. *BMC Medicine, 15*(1), 143. https://doi.org/10.1186/s12916-017-0889-2

Steinert, C., Hofmann, M., Leichsenring, F., & Kruse, J. (2013). What do we know today about the prospective long-term course of social anxiety disorder? A systematic literature review. *Journal of Anxiety Disorders, 27*(7), 692–702. https://doi.org/10.1016/j.janxdis.2013.08.002

Strohm, M., Siegesleitner, M., Kunze, A. E., Ehring, T., & Wittekind, C. E. (2021). Imagery rescripting versus cognitive restructuring for social anxiety: Treatment effects and working mechanisms. *Clinical Psychology in Europe, 3*(3). https://doi.org/10.32872/cpe.5303

Swee, M. B., Hudson, C. C., & Heimberg, R. G. (2021). Examining the relationship between shame and social anxiety disorder: A systematic review. *Clinical Psychology Review, 90*. https://doi.org/10.1016/j.cpr.2021.102088

Thew, G. R., Ehlers, A., Grey, N., Wild, J., Warnock-Parkes, E., Dawson, R. L., & Clark, D. M. (2020). Change processes in cognitive therapy for social anxiety disorder delivered in routine clinical practice. *Clinical Psychology in Europe, 2*(2).

van Dis, E. A. M., van Veen, S. C., Hagenaars, M. A., Batelaan, N. M., Bockting, C. L. H., van den Heuvel, R. M., Cuijpers, P., & Engelhard, I. M. (2020). Long-term outcomes of cognitive behavioral therapy for anxiety-related disorders: A systematic review and meta-analysis. *JAMA Psychiatry, 77*(3), 265–273. https://doi.org/10.1001/jamapsychiatry.2019.3986

van Est-Bitincka, L. A. C., Schuiringa, H. D., van der Heijden, P. T., van Aken, M. A. G., & Laceulle, O. M. (2023). Youth's social environments: Associations with mental problems and achievement of developmental milestones in times of crises. *Adolescents, 3*(2), 366–381. https://doi.org/10.3390/adolescents3020025

Warnock-Parkes, E., Wild, J., Stott, R., Grey, N., Ehlers, A., & Clark, D. M. (2017). Seeing is believing: Using video feedback in cognitive therapy for social anxiety disorder. *Cognitive and Behavioral Practice, 24*(2), 245–255. https://doi.org/10.1016/j.cbpra.2016.03.007

Warnock-Parkes, E., Wild, J., Thew, G., Kerr, A., Grey, N., & Clark, D. M. (2022). "I'm unlikeable, boring, weird, foolish, inferior, inadequate": How to address the persistent negative self-evaluations that are central to social anxiety disorder with cognitive therapy. *Cognitive Behavior Therapist, 15*. https://doi.org/10.1017/S1754470X22000496

Welander-Vatn, A., Torvik, F. A., Czajkowski, N., Kendler, K. S., Reichborn-Kjennerud, T., Knudsen, G. P., & Ystrom, E. (2018). Relationships among avoidant personality disorder, social anxiety disorder, and normative personality traits: A twin study. *Journal of Personality Disorders, 33*(3), 289–309. https://doi.org/10.1521/pedi_2018_32_341

Westra, H. A., & Dozois, D. J. A. (2006). Preparing clients for cognitive behavioral therapy: A randomized pilot study of motivational interviewing for anxiety. *Cognitive Therapy and Research, 30*(4), 481–498. https://doi.org/10.1007/s10608-006-9016-y

Wong, Q. J. J., & Rapee, R. M. (2016). The aetiology and maintenance of social anxiety disorder: A synthesis of complementary theoretical models and formulation of a new integrated model. *Journal of Affective Disorders, 203*, 84–100. https://doi.org/10.1016/j.jad.2016.05.069

World Health Organisation. (2022). *The ICD-11 Classification of Mental and Behavioural Disorders: Clinical descriptions and diagnostic guidelines, tenth revision.* World Health Organization. https://www.who.int/publications/i/item/9241544228%0Ahttps://books.google.com/books?hl=en&lr=&id=DFM0DgAAQBAJ&oi=fnd&pg=PR1&dq=World+Health+Organization.+ICD-10+Classification+of+Mental+and+Behavioral+Disorders+1992+Geneva,+Switzerland+World+Health+Organi

Chapter 12
Generalized Anxiety Disorder

Lizabeth Roemer, Elizabeth H. Eustis, and Ana M. González-Garzón

Background

Generalized anxiety disorder (GAD) is centrally defined by excessive worry (i.e., thinking about things that might go wrong) that is difficult to control (APA, 2013). Associated features include muscle tension, feeling on edge, trouble sleeping, fatigue, irritability, and trouble concentrating. To meet diagnostic criteria, worry has to occur more days than not for at least 6 months. Lifetime prevalence of GAD is 3.7% globally, and GAD is highly comorbid, with major depression the most common comorbid diagnosis (Ruscio et al., 2017). Although GAD is sometimes misunderstood as a disorder of the "worried well," it is, in fact, associated with significant role impairment and disruption (Ruscio et al., 2017).

A recent review (Newman et al., 2022) concluded that cognitive behavioral therapy packages (which typically include psychoeducation, cognitive restructuring, and behavioral strategies such as self-monitoring and relaxation strategies) are efficacious for both GAD and comorbid presentations, although typically only 50% of clients demonstrate substantial improvements. As a result, several researchers have drawn on ongoing research on the nature of worry and GAD to enhance these interventions; each enhancement has shown promise (e.g., acceptance-based behavioral therapy (ABBT), emotion regulation therapy, and cognitive behavior therapy targeting intolerance of uncertainty; see Newman et al., 2022 for a review). Our clinical suggestions are grounded in our work developing and delivering ABBT (Roemer & Orsillo, 2020; Roemer et al., 2021), which is grounded in a model of GAD that

L. Roemer (✉) · A. M. González-Garzón
University of Massachusetts Boston, Boston, MA, USA
e-mail: Lizabeth.Roemer@umb.edu

E. H. Eustis
Boston University, Boston, MA, USA

E. M. Goetter (ed.), *Optimizing Treatment Engagement Processes in CBT for Anxiety and Related Disorders*, CBT: Science Into Practice,
https://doi.org/10.1007/978-3-031-91439-3_12

stems from both behavioral and acceptance-based interventions (e.g., Hayes et al., 2012; Linehan, 2014; Segal et al., 2018), and focuses on reducing experiential avoidance and increasing values-based actions.

ABBT for GAD is grounded in an evidence-based transdiagnostic model that identifies three interrelated aspects of GAD and its associated disorders (adapted from acceptance and commitment therapy's (ACT) hexaflex; Hayes et al., 2012). Individuals develop a narrow, critical, fused relation with their internal experiences (thoughts, emotions, sensations). This naturally leads to rigid efforts to avoid these experiences (i.e., experiential avoidance), which exacerbates the problematic relation to them. Both processes naturally interfere with intentional, present engagement in actions that matter to the individuals, which deepens distress, furthering the cycle. Therefore, ABBT helps clients to develop a compassionate, decentered (seeing thoughts as thoughts rather than centrally defining; Safran & Segal, 1990) relation with their internal experiences, respond more flexibly to those experiences with willingness to experience whatever arises, clarify what matters to them, and take actions consistent with those values.

In our studies, we have found that ABBT significantly improved GAD, worry, depressive symptoms, comorbid disorders, and quality of life in a waitlist RCT (Roemer et al., 2008) and yielded comparable effects to applied relaxation, an empirically supported treatment for GAD, on clinician-rated and self-reported GAD symptoms, clinician-rated comorbid diagnoses, and self-reported depressive symptoms and quality of life (Hayes-Skelton et al., 2013). In both studies, a high proportion of individuals treated with ABBT fell into the nonclinical range on measures following treatment. Efficacy has also been demonstrated outside the continental United States. ABBT yielded significantly more GAD symptom reduction than medication alone in a small RCT in Iran (Zargar et al., 2012), more rapid change in GAD and anxiety symptoms for a group-based ABBT treatment compared to a nondirective supportive group therapy in Brazil (de Almeida Sampaio et al., 2020), and comparable effects to CBT on reports of worry among primary care patients in Puerto Rico (Vera et al., 2021). Additional studies have found support for decentering, experiential avoidance, and mindfulness as mechanisms of ABBT (Hayes-Skelton et al., 2015; Eustis et al., 2016; Millstein et al., 2015).

Barriers to Engagement in Treatment for People with GAD

Many people who meet criteria for GAD do not pursue treatment or do not persist in treatment. In a large-scale global epidemiological study, slightly less than half the participants who met criteria for current GAD had pursued treatment, with higher rates of treatment seeking for those with comorbid disorders (55.8%) or severe role impairment (59.4%; Ruscio et al., 2017). A meta-analysis of RCT studies of GAD revealed a 16.99% rate of dropout in these studies, with no significant predictors of dropout (Gersh et al., 2017); our own trials (Roemer et al., 2008; Hayes-Skelton et al., 2013) yield similar dropout rates. This rate may be partially elevated due to the typically less flexible nature of research studies; nonetheless, we need to consider factors that will increase initiation and persistence in therapy.

Only one quantitative study has examined barriers to treatment specifically among people diagnosed with GAD. Goetter et al. (2020) examined self-reported barriers to treatment among individuals diagnosed with GAD. The most commonly endorsed reasons were wanting to handle problems themselves, feeling embarrassed about needing help, not knowing where to go for treatment, not having time for treatment, and being worried about the cost of treatment. Symptom severity, low income, and racial and ethnic minority status all predicted more self-reported barriers to treatment. These findings suggest that we need to consider how to address stigma and shame around symptoms, as well as cost and logistics, to make treatment better fit into people's lives. More research is needed to determine why barriers are higher for those with minoritized racial and ethnic identities; however, this finding suggests that therapy should address contextual and cultural factors to increase engagement. In a systematic review of barriers to attending first sessions for any mental health problems (with many studies including people with anxiety), Sweetman et al. (2021) similarly highlighted beliefs about symptoms and treatment (e.g., stigma and confidence that therapy can help), practical considerations, and social and cultural factors as barriers that need to be addressed. In a review of cultural considerations in treating GAD, Xie (2020) also noted that language barriers, experiences of discrimination, and concerns about not being understood by a racially/ethnically different therapist can all prevent individuals from seeking help.

Toledo-Chávarri et al. (2020) conducted a qualitative evidence synthesis to better understand implementation of care and treatment preferences for patients with GAD in primary care settings specifically. Individuals with GAD frequently present in primary care rather than mental health settings (Roy-Byrne & Wagner, 2004), so this is an important context for considering their engagement. Toledo-Chávarri and colleagues identified that individuals with GAD often have a long course of the disorder, with relapse common, which can be discouraging. Studies revealed that individuals desire more information about GAD, its course, and its treatment. While individuals indicated a wide range of treatment preferences, many identified honesty, trust, and empathy as important therapist characteristics, while pessimism, judgment, and directive styles were barriers to engagement. The authors noted a lack of racial, ethnic, and national diversity in the samples of the studies they reviewed, a limitation given the common finding of social determinants of engagement in therapy. In a qualitative study with White older adults and healthcare professionals, Lawrence et al. (2019) also observed a desire for empathic listening from therapists among older adults with GAD. Healthcare professionals who were interviewed identified that physical and cognitive problems can interfere with the success of therapy, highlighting the importance of considering and attending to contextual factors when promoting engagement in therapy. Taken together, these findings highlight the importance of providing information about GAD, its course, and treatment, empathic listening, cultivation of trust, as well as attention to contextual factors.

GAD-Specific Barriers and Challenges

Specific aspects of GAD may be barriers to beginning and persisting in treatment. As noted above, Toledo-Chávarri et al. (2020) found that the long course and common relapse of GAD were often identified as discouraging, creating a potential barrier to treatment. Also, Lawrence et al. (2019), who focused specifically on the feasibility and acceptability of ACT for older adults, reported that individuals with GAD identified worry as useful, while also recognizing it may not always be helpful. Consistent with these reports of older adults with GAD, many studies have demonstrated that people with GAD are ambivalent about the worry they habitually engage in—they have both positive beliefs about the worry (e.g., that it helps them plan, prepare for, or superstitiously avoid negative outcomes) and negative beliefs about it (e.g., that it's uncontrollable; e.g., Penney et al., 2013). These positive beliefs about worry may discourage people from seeking treatment. This led Westra and Duzois (2006) to explore the usefulness of motivational interviewing sessions added to CBT for GAD to enhance engagement, which led to modest improvements, as well as reduced resistance and increased agency for clients (see Newman et al., 2022, for a review). Lawrence et al. (2019) reported that participants with GAD identified habits of avoidance as hard to address and held beliefs that sometimes avoidance is helpful. This avoidance characteristic of GAD could also interfere with engaging in therapy. Finally, as Goetter et al. (2020) note, GAD is characterized by anxiety about (or intolerance of) uncertainty, which may make initiating and persisting in therapy more challenging.

Cultural, Systemic, and Contextual Barriers to Engagement for GAD

Although many psychological models for GAD and other psychological disorders focus primarily on internal processes, recognition of the importance of acknowledging contextual, systemic, and cultural factors to promote engagement and psychological health is growing (e.g., Graham-LoPresti et al., 2020). For instance, we need to recognize and address racism-related stress and other forms of discrimination. A cross-sectional study of Black Americans found that racial stress was significantly associated with reports of worry, with intolerance of uncertainty fully mediating the association (Rucker et al., 2010), indicating that racism-related stress may generate chronic worry, as well as intolerance of uncertainty. In another correlational study, racial discrimination was associated with reports of mental health stigma among people of color (Krill Williston et al., 2019), indicating one potential mechanism for the increased barriers to engagement among people of color (Goetter et al., 2020). A study of Australian adolescents found that those for whom English is not a first language had higher levels of personal GAD-related stigma (Calear et al., 2017). Thus, experiences of marginalization may contribute to both stigma and worry, and addressing marginalization-related stressors may address stigma and therefore improve engagement.

In their discussion of culturally responsive assessment and treatment of GAD, Graham-LoPresti et al. (2020) note that experiences of discrimination naturally lead to an experience of a lack of control over safety, livelihood, and environments, and that this absence of control and experience of uncertainty can contribute to stress and anxiety, including GAD. In this context, worry is an understandable response, but it can interfere with functioning. Relatedly, they note that discriminatory experiences (interpersonal and systemic) can lead to avoidance, which may in turn interfere with values-based living. Failure to acknowledge the reality of these contexts can be a barrier to engagement in treatment. Boot-Haury (2023) similarly noted that discrimination within and outside the medical system can naturally heighten anxiety among transgender clients and that failure to intentionally provide affirming care can be a barrier to treatment engagement for these clients.

In a small qualitative study following a trial of ABBT for GAD, participants with marginalized identities shared that they appreciated the focus on acceptance and values-based living in the treatment and flexibility in between-session practices (Fuchs et al., 2016). One challenge they noted was that they wanted time to focus on specific stressors in their lives, which was not a focus during psychoeducation and skills training. This again highlights the importance of acknowledging and validating the realities of clients' stressors while also trying to help them develop new ways of responding to these stressors. Some clients also reported that some mindfulness exercises, specifically those involving imagery like putting their thoughts on leaves floating on a stream, did not resonate with them and did not apply to their current stressors. In a small pilot study of a Taoist Cognitive Therapy for GAD with Chinese American immigrants (Chang et al., 2020), clients reflected positively on the flexibility of the intervention, providing multiple options for coping and empowering clients to collaborate in the treatment. These clients also emphasized feeling validated and accepted by their therapists.

Cultural Barriers to Consider in Delivering ABBT

A review of potential cultural barriers to engagement and responsiveness to ABBTs is beyond the scope of the chapter; we encourage readers to review extensive writing in this area (e.g., Hall et al., 2011; Harrell, 2018; Martinez et al., 2022; Proulx et al., 2018; Sobczak & West, 2013; Watson-Singleton et al., 2019). One consistent theme these authors raise, which echoes the GAD-specific considerations raised above, is the importance of acknowledging systemic, structural, and interpersonal racism, including the colonial history of mindfulness in therapy (Martinez et al., 2022). Further, clients may have reactions to mindfulness-based approaches due to concerns they do not resonate with their religious background (e.g., Watson-Singleton et al., 2019; although Fuchs et al., 2016 found participants saw ABBT as congruent with their non-Buddhist religious backgrounds). Further, like CBTs,

ABBTs have been developed and studied in largely White-dominated spaces (Proulx et al., 2018). Similarly, these approaches are often grounded in independent construals of self, which may not resonate with clients from collectivist backgrounds who have more interdependent self-construals (Hall et al., 2011; Watson-Singleton et al., 2019). Further, metaphors and practices may be culture bound and should be adapted, collaboratively with clients, to be more culturally congruent (e.g., Fuchs et al., 2016). Finally, when working with clients to increase values-based actions, ignoring real structural and contextual barriers, as well as culturally based values, will interfere with engagement (Martinez et al., 2022; Sobczak & West, 2013).

Additional Observations from Trials of ABBT

We gave clients in Hayes-Skelton et al. (2013) several opportunities to share their reflections on treatment during the follow-up period. Clients regularly referred to specific aspects of the treatments (validation, flexibility, focus on values clarification and values-based action, learning to relate to internal experiences differently) as strengths. Some clients felt there was sufficient time for specific life concerns, while others felt the focus on psychoeducation and skills did not allow sufficient time for support and reflection. This highlights a challenge of treating GAD—on the one hand, validation and support are, of course, important. On the other hand, clients are often caught in cycles of worry so that time spent listening and processing these worries may strengthen habits of worry, rather than disrupt these patterns and cultivate new, alternative ways of responding. Finding (and clearly communicating about) an adaptive balance will promote engagement and effectiveness. This balance will differ depending on the context of treatment—with more time for support and validation in long-term therapy than in short-term contexts.

Some clients also expressed a desire for structures to help them continue practicing mindfulness, acceptance, and values-based actions. Some clients also noted that they faced more challenges applying their new skills in specific contexts (e.g., parenting and health concerns). Particularly when providing shorter-term treatments, engagement and treatment response may be facilitated by providing some supplemental supports (e.g., digital mental health interventions [DMHIs] that provide reminders or opportunities for practice, other online supports, materials to revisit, context-specific psychoeducation) so that clients can maintain and deepen their therapeutic gains.

Barriers in Digital Mental Health Approaches

DMHIs include a wide range of services that are delivered using technology and can be implemented in multiple ways (e.g., as stand-alone treatments with or without human support, while client is on a waitlist, as an adjunct during treatment, for relapse prevention after treatment). DMHIs based in CBT have generally been found to be effective for anxiety disorders, and also GAD, specifically (e.g., Andrews et al., 2018; Eilert et al., 2021). While DMHIs have the potential to significantly increase access to care and can address some of the barriers to accessing traditional in-person treatment, current data suggests that the same disparities are seen with access to DMHIs, with middle-aged White cisgender women being the most common users of these interventions (Schueller et al., 2019). Important work is being done to co-develop and tailor DMHIs for specific populations, including people who have been racially minoritized (e.g., Salamanca-Sanabria et al., 2020; Watson-Singleton et al., 2023), but there has been a lack of attention to cultural responsiveness in the field in general (Ramos et al., 2021; Eustis et al., 2023). Identified variables important to engagement with DMHIs in general include perceived fit (i.e., whether the intervention feels relevant for the individual, their culture, and values), mental health literacy (i.e., knowledge about mental health symptoms and treatments), digital literacy (i.e., possessing skills needed to use a specific technology), and digital health literacy (i.e., the ability to use technology to identify and engage with health resources; Borghouts et al., 2021).

Summary of Barriers That Clinicians Can Target

Based on the available literature, clinicians can be aware of and target a number of barriers to treatment for GAD. In general, clinicians should be mindful that many people feel shame and stigma around their experience with GAD. People may not have access to quality information about GAD and treatment options and may be unsure of what type of treatment to seek out. In addition, people often have concerns about the logistics of engaging in treatment, including cost and the required time investment. Clients may also have positive beliefs about worry that reduce their motivation for treatment. There are also barriers related to contextual, systemic, and cultural factors, including racism-related stress and other forms of discrimination, and a lack of culturally responsive care. In terms of therapist characteristics, research suggests that individuals with GAD may be less likely to engage with treatment if they perceive their clinician as pessimistic, judgmental, or not empathic. If clinicians use a DMHI with a client, potential barriers to consider include a lack of perceived fit with the intervention (e.g., the intervention does not feel relevant to the individual) and low digital health literacy.

Clinical Recommendations for Increasing Engagement in ABBT

A comprehensive description of ABBT is beyond the scope of this chapter (see Roemer et al., 2021 for a chapter-length description and Roemer & Orsillo, 2020 for a book length one). Briefly, ABBT is grounded in the model presented earlier and helps clients to (1) change the nature of their relationship with their internal experiences so it is broader, more compassionate, and less fused; (2) accept internal experiences as they arise, rather than trying to get rid of them; and (3) intentionally engage in personally meaningful actions. Therapists develop an empathic, collaborative therapeutic relationship with clients, beginning by developing and sharing an acceptance-based behavioral model of their presenting concerns that incorporates contextual factors and explanations. Therapy includes validation and exploration within the therapeutic relationship, psychoeducation, skills development and application, and values clarification and values-based actions. The therapeutic relationship and psychoeducation both help clients to begin to relate to their internal experiences with more compassion and less criticism and judgment, as well as decentering, or treating thoughts and feelings as phenomena that naturally rise and fall, rather than as permanent and self-defining. Mindfulness and other acceptance-based practices help develop new habits of responding to internal distress that minimize entanglement with those responses, while values clarification and action help to redirect control efforts from internal experiences to one's own actions. Therapy helps clients to begin to see the ongoing process of this growth and change, so they are prepared for future lapses in response to stressful contexts, and can re-engage their skills and practices as needed.

Collaborative Case Formulation

As with all CBT approaches, an important initial step in ABBT is a thorough assessment that leads to a collaborative case formulation that is linked to the treatment approach, with the therapist addressing any questions the client has and ensuring that the approach meets the client's expectations and desires for treatment. In addition to traditional domains of assessment, we include exploration of the ways that clients respond to their internal experiences, including both experiential and behavioral avoidance, as well as the ways their symptoms have been getting in the way of fully engaging with their lives (Roemer & Orsillo, 2020). The therapist then connects what they've heard from the client to share the ways that their presenting challenges make sense through an ABBT perspective (e.g., they have learned to react negatively and judgmentally to distressing thoughts, feelings, and sensations [including feelings of uncertainty], developed ways of responding that diminish distress in the short term but maintain it in the long run, and these understandable habits have diminished their satisfaction in their lives in certain specific ways).

External realities, such as experiences of discrimination, health concerns, or trauma histories, are included in this formulation, highlighting the way that the client's responses are learned and their avoidance has served a function. The therapist seeks feedback on the model and addresses and incorporates any elements that are missing. Next, the therapist explains how these patterns can be addressed through treatment, answering any additional questions raised in response to this explanation.

The case conceptualization can be tailored to explicitly address issues of engagement. For instance, a thorough, culturally responsive case formulation can address some of the barriers Goetter et al. (2020) identified in their review. A detailed explanation for why the challenges of worry and avoidance make sense can counter the guilt and shame that often interfere with treatment engagement, as well as offer a model for why it is reasonable to seek help instead of addressing problems on one's own. The explanations for discomfort associated with uncertainty can help clients begin to see that their reluctance or fear about therapy is tied to their presenting problems, so continuing with treatment can address them. In addition, the formulation provides information about GAD, its course, and treatment, addressing themes in Toledo-Chávarri et al.' (2020) qualitative synthesis. This formulation highlights that worry is a habit that can be altered and weakened with practice, although worries will still arise at times, and that therapy can provide support in making meaningful behavioral changes so that worry no longer reduces meaningful engagement in life. A clear, responsive rationale that is tied to treatment can bolster confidence that treatment can help (Sweetman et al., 2021). Recognition of contextual stressors (e.g., how experiences of discrimination have led to worries about workplace conflict and harm) and their integration in the formulation can help marginalized clients see how the proposed treatment is specifically responsive to their experiences, potentially minimizing the barriers tied to marginalization. This case formulation also incorporates the ways that worry can seem to be helpful (e.g., it seems to avoid low base rate negative events and creates a sense of feeling prepared), giving the therapist an opportunity to name and validate ambivalence about reducing worry because it may seem that it is tied to a client's success. Therapists can acknowledge how understandable that fear is while also reassuring clients that they will work with them to make changes that enhance, rather than impair, their lives.

Therapists continually return to the shared formulation throughout treatment, explaining the reasoning behind each intervention. When the form of particular practices doesn't fit well for a client, the therapist can return to the case formulation and the function of a given intervention to adapt it to enhance engagement. Consider a client who has a negative reaction to writing in self-monitoring forms. These are used to help clients begin to notice each sign of anxiety (physical, cognitive, emotional, and behavioral) as it arises so that new, noncritical responses can replace well-worn but problematic habits. Instead, the therapist can consider alternative ways of interrupting habits and promoting awareness, such as leaving voice notes or taking simple tallies of specific experiences and then reflecting on them later in a voice note to enhance awareness and clarity and set the stage for new learning.

Therapists also return to this case formulation when any barriers to engagement arise. For example, clients may mistakenly assume that mindfulness practices are meant to calm them, or clear their minds, and then may experience frustration or feelings of failure when their minds are busy or their anxiety persists while practicing mindfulness. The therapist can revisit the case formulation to clarify that the practices are intended to develop new habits of awareness and compassion so that when busy minds and anxiety arise, they can notice these phenomena and, rather than getting entangled in trying to get rid of them, remain aware of the present moment so that they can make meaningful choices in the actions they take. Given this, busy minds and anxiety during practice help make the practice more relevant to their treatment goals to live fuller, more meaningful lives.

Culturally and Relationally Responsive Engagement Sessions

In a RCT comparing ABBT to applied relaxation for GAD, with independent assessors (Hayes-Skelton et al., 2013), participants received an engagement session with the therapist prior to the beginning of the protocol for both treatments. These sessions were included to begin to establish a therapeutic relationship. Session components included the following: asking clients to share their experiences and understandings of their worry; understanding what had helped them in the past; asking about barriers to treatment; discussing identity-based differences between client and therapist; and asking about associated values held by the client. Therapists adopted a stance of validation, empathy, openness, curiosity, and deference to the client's self-expertise. For example, to open a conversation about identity-related differences between therapist and client, the therapist said, "Sometimes people come into therapy with an idea about the kind of therapist that they want to see in terms of gender, race, background, etc. Did you have any of these thoughts before you came in?" This allowed clients to discuss apparent differences in visible identities or to describe invisible identities that were important to them. When clients said they had no concerns, therapists invited them to share any concerns that arose at any point in therapy and conveyed their commitment to working toward their treatment goals in ways that incorporated the client's full self.

This session created an expectation that therapists were open to talking about any barriers that arose over the course of the protocol therapy. These sessions helped clients and therapists to form positive working relationships overall, and we recommend considering incorporating aspects of this session in therapy.

Values Clarification and Values-Based Action as a Mechanism of Treatment Engagement

Values clarification (e.g., identifying that being open and honest with family members is a value) and values-based action (e.g., communicating honestly with one's child) represent another potential mechanism of treatment engagement that clinicians can use when providing ABBT (see Orsillo & Roemer, 2016; Roemer & Orsillo, 2020 for more in-depth discussions of this). Discussing values can help to address clients' early concerns that treatment won't help, ambivalence about giving up their worry, or unrealistic expectations, like hoping to be worry-free by the end of treatment, and to set realistic expectations in several ways. Therapists can highlight how clarifying values and taking values-based actions can help clients feel more engaged in their lives and what matters to them. Talking about values also gives clients more information about one of the new concrete strategies they will learn that can help them move toward their treatment goals (i.e., that they aren't just losing worry, they're gaining ways to enhance their lives). This discussion can also help to set realistic expectations that while clients likely won't be worry-free at the end of treatment, they will be able to still do things that are important to them in the face of worry. In addition, there may be some overlap between values clarification and motivational interviewing, a client-centered and directive approach to help clients cultivate intrinsic motivation for change that has been incorporated into CBT for GAD with modest improvements in engagement and treatment response (Westra & Duzois, 2006). In both approaches, therapists strive to provide validation and empathy, to help clients to identify what is important to them, and to identify ways in which they may not be living in line with their values and to then increase values-based actions. Therefore, these approaches may increase intrinsic motivation and ensure that values are coming from the specific client versus from the therapist or someone else, ultimately increasing treatment engagement.

Addressing Situational and Contextual Stressors in Treatment

As we noted above, psychological models, including CBT and ABBT, often emphasize internal processes over external realities in explaining psychological distress. This is inherently invalidating, particularly for individuals who are faced with interpersonal and structural forms of discrimination, which can naturally contribute to experiences of anxiety linked to potential threats in the environment and lack of control or agency (e.g., Graham-LoPresti et al., 2020). For instance, a Black woman client who worries about being seen as incompetent at work might be told that her worries are unrealistic and she should develop more accurate beliefs when, in fact, she receives societal and interpersonal messages that she is seen as less competent than her White coworkers. An essential element of engaging, responsive, effective therapy involves explicit recognition of these factors, opportunities for clients to explore their experiences of stress and discrimination, and therapists clearly affirming marginalized identities. Clinicians should also consider ways to make their practice explicitly inclusive, anti-racist, and affirming so that treatment itself does not present additional stressors through marginalizing or exclusionary language or messages. Guidelines of trans and gender diverse affirming strategies provide one example of considerations for clinicians in promoting engagement and minimizing harm (Puckett et al., 2023a).

While ABBT for GAD focuses on helping clients identify changes they can make (in how they relate to internal experiences and in taking actions), validating the reality of their context is also essential. While worry in GAD is defined as "excessive," it is not necessarily unrealistic; clients often present with worry about real threats, including structural and global factors (for instance, the climate crisis). Therapists help clients to identify effective responses to these real stressors, which might include problem-solving rather than worrying, identifying meaningful ways to address structural or other external barriers they experience, or finding support in the midst of challenges that aren't easily addressed. Validating the understandable nature of an anxious response to contextual stressors serves the therapeutic purpose of reducing the intensification of anxiety and worry that can result from invalidation of natural responses, modeling self-compassion, and helping clients to feel that therapy is responsive to their full context.

Recognition of the validity of interpersonal and structural forms of discrimination is particularly essential to facilitate engagement and a therapeutic alliance with clients from marginalized backgrounds (Graham et al., 2013; Puckett et al., 2023b). Given the common erasure and denial of experiences of discrimination, therapists need to take extra care to convey their recognition of harmful, minimizing experiences that clients face and the injustice of these experiences, such as acknowledging that worries about being seen as incompetent can be related to racist stereotypes. Studies have found that therapists often question the veracity of clients' reports or suggest they should try to see situations differently, rather than recognize and name the oppression they face (e.g., Puckett et al., 2023b). Instead of trying to change perceptions of these experiences, therapists can help clients to accurately attribute those experiences to external sources, rather than internalizing them and taking them as information about their worth. Therapists should also acknowledge and name sociopolitical realities, such as anti-trans laws, that may be affecting clients, indicating they are able to see the client's full lived experience (Puckett et al., 2023b).

One challenge for therapists to address, transparently, with clients is the need to reserve time for exploring new learning so that clients can make the changes they're seeking while also making time to hear about weekly stressors. Clients with strong habits of worry can easily spend time telling therapists all the things they are afraid will happen in ways that strengthen their habits of worry, rather than helping them to interrupt this process and develop new habits that expand their lives. Once clients have been taught about the cycle of worry and the importance of interrupting well-worn habits so new habits can be strengthened, therapists can directly ask clients whether it might make sense to move on to new material or a discussion of values-based action, rather than rehearsing the stressors. Therapists can apply the skills building or values clarification work of the session to some of the stressors introduced as a way of continuing to validate and recognize these realities while still continuing with the development of new skills and ways of responding. The work in establishing a strong alliance, validating the realities of clients' stressors, and encouraging open communication sets the stage for finding this balance collaboratively so the therapeutic alliance is maintained and treatment engagement is optimized.

The recognition of external, structural barriers also shapes the content of treatment. Clients may identify some contexts in which avoidance is, in fact, a chosen values-based action because of micro- or macro-aggressive experiences in a given context that make the cost of engagement higher than the possible reward. In addition, clients may identify values-based actions that address systemic barriers directly and promote collective well-being (Harrell, 2018), adding efforts to create a world they want to live in to the overarching goal of being the person they want to be in the world (Martinez et al., 2022).

Cultural Adaptations

In addition to acknowledging and addressing the reality of external, structural, and systemic stressors, therapists can address barriers to engagement experienced by clients from cultural backgrounds that have been historically excluded and marginalized in the discipline of psychology through culturally responsive adaptations throughout treatment. In-depth discussion of these considerations is beyond the scope of this chapter (see Hays, 2022; Hook et al., 2017; Iwamasa & Hays, 2018; Sue et al., 2019); one consistent theme is the importance of adaptations that capitalize on existing resources and knowledge of the targeted population. We highlight a few specific considerations for ABBT for GAD.

Harrell (2018) notes that culture is an inherent part of human experience, yet contemplative practice often fails to describe culture, and, as noted above, the psychological interventions that incorporate mindfulness and contemplative practice often emerge from White-centric perspectives (Proulx et al., 2018). Harrell (2018) has developed Soulfulness, an integrative, culturally attuned approach grounded in themes from the African diaspora that emphasizes connectedness, wholeness, and liberation from oppression. Within her rich, integrative approach, she blends traditional mindfulness practices like focusing on the breath or observing thoughts with culturally resonant music, art, and poetry. Clinicians can similarly adapt methods and practices so they are culturally congruent. For instance, participants in Woods-Giscombe and Gaylord's (2014) qualitative study with African American adults recommended using activities like knitting or shelling peas as mindfulness practices to promote present-moment focus and counter anxiety and stress. We have also worked with clients who incorporate mindful awareness into prayer. When a client does not feel connected to a specific practice (e.g., imagining putting thoughts on leaves as they go down a stream; Hayes et al., 2012), the therapist can consider the function of the practice and develop a new practice that is more meaningful. We use this practice as a way of decentering from worries that arise and grabbing clients' attention. We could instead imagine putting worries on cars as they drive by a window, or writing worry thoughts on billboards, or putting them on a conveyor belt.

Although values-based work allows flexibility that can use cultural values to benefit and engage clients (Castellanos & Flory, 2022), therapists should still bring cultural awareness to the process of clarifying values and identifying values-based actions. Values clarification can promote engagement in that it centers the values of the client rather than those of the therapist, the field of psychology, or dominant society. While values are often described as "personally meaningful," clients may have interdependent self-construals that lead their values to reflect those of their community or family (Hall et al., 2011). Therapists should not impose an independent self-construal on clients and should respect the way that clients' values and chosen actions may reflect a collectivist orientation, including values like harmony or *familismo* (dedication, commitment, and loyalty to family). Therapists should also be attuned to both internal (e.g., emotions and thoughts) and external (e.g., racism, discrimination, cost, and time) barriers to taking values-based action and explicitly name these external barriers when exploring chosen actions with clients. The framework of values allows clients to consider anxiety-provoking situations and make an intentional decision about what available option feels the most values aligned to them in that moment (e.g., avoiding someone who has microaggressed against them in the past, volunteering in their community, choosing a nourishing or soothing activity when a context has been activating). While challenging, it can also be empowering to recognize and name contextual barriers and the pain that comes from them, while also intentionally deciding how to respond, which may include directly addressing systemic barriers (Martinez et al., 2022).

The Role of Flexibility in Treatment Engagement

Clients have identified flexibility in the delivery of treatment as a strength of ABBT, so clinicians should consider how they can incorporate flexibility into their work. One way we do this is by teaching numerous types of mindfulness practices and adapting them to clients' lives. Clients are asked to try out many practices and then encouraged to develop consistent practice of a few. We include some longer practices but also brief practices, as well as informal mindfulness practice (i.e., bringing compassionate awareness to daily tasks and gradually more challenging tasks), which does not add any additional time to one's day. Relatedly, we work with clients flexibly around between-session exercises. First, we make sure that we provide a clear rationale for between-session practice (i.e., interrupting strong habits requires repeated practice of new habits, so time outside of session is needed for this). Next, we make sure to check on between-session exercises and address any barriers that arise. One barrier to engagement can come when clients feel they are "failing" at therapy because they don't do between-session work. We validate the difficulty of fitting things in and remembering them and help clients find ways to do the practices in some form, reinforcing any attempts at practice and countering any self-criticism or shame with validation and compassion. We might suggest waking up 10 min early to do a mindfulness practice or spending 15 min less on social media in order to fit practice in. We have also found that sometimes very busy clients (for instance, parents of infants and toddlers) cannot fit in formal practices (i.e., setting aside time to practice mindfulness), but they can do tasks mindfully (informal practice, such as folding laundry or feeding their baby). Informal practice was associated with maintenance of treatment gains after therapy ended, while formal practice was not (Morgan et al., 2014), suggesting that this adjustment may not negatively impact treatment progress.

The Role of Digital Mental Health in Treatment Engagement

Resources are available to help clinicians learn more about how they can use DMHIs to support their work with clients with GAD (e.g., Newby et al., 2021). We recommend clinicians consider whether their clients have regular access to the Internet and devices needed to access specific interventions. We recommend clinicians try to find programs that are culturally responsive and that they talk with clients about their experience of using a program and whether it feels culturally relevant to them. Awareness of potential barriers with DMHIs allows clinicians to discuss them and troubleshoot collaboratively. In general, some form of human support has been found to increase engagement with DMHIs through increased accountability and other factors, and this type of communication can also validate clients' lived experiences and barriers, which are all likely to increase engagement.

Case Examples

Case Formulation and Values Clarification Addressing Stigma

Miguel is a 24-year-old Latin American cisgender man, a Spanish native speaker, with a physical disability that affects his gait. He moved to the United States from Venezuela a year prior to pursue a master's degree in physical therapy. He currently lives alone in Boston and communicates daily with family back home. Miguel came to therapy endorsing symptoms consistent with GAD. He described worrying about different things linked to his transition to a new country, including not being good at making friends or holding conversations with strangers, failing in school, getting sick while living alone in Boston without family support, thinking that his family was not doing well back home without him, and thinking that his anxiety might be an indicator that he was not good enough to thrive in the United States. Among these, Miguel noted feeling most distressed by how anxious and paralyzed he got when interacting with strangers and peers from the graduate program, as he reported this had negatively impacted his ability to connect socially with others and adjust to the city. Miguel's disability and stigma seemed linked to his anxiety as he feared that people would judge his gait or think he was "weak" for being nervous all the time. He also reported an overall dissatisfaction with his quality of life.

Miguel remembered being somewhat anxious all his life, most particularly around peers and experiencing other kids making fun of his gait when younger. However, he noted that his transition to a new country made his anxiety more intense and that he found himself more isolated at home over the weekends and between classes to avoid feared social interactions. Miguel was ambivalent about coming to therapy and had not shared with his family what he was going through, as he felt embarrassed to be struggling with something "so stupid" and he feared that his family would think he was not strong enough to make it in the United States. During the initial session, Miguel asked the therapist to help him develop skills to cope with his anxiety, worry less, and look "more normal" so he could make friends and have others like him more.

The first three sessions were focused on developing a case formulation, introducing and practicing mindfulness skills, and introducing the concept of values. During Session 2, the therapist shared the case formulation with Miguel, which included validating the humanness of his responses and connecting them to the external context (e.g., how it made sense for Miguel to feel anxious given the challenges involved in adapting to a new country and being isolated from family who were his central source of social support, acknowledging the ways his fear of being judged by others and avoiding situations to protect himself from that made sense given the unjust experiences of discrimination he had in high school, etc.), and describing the ways some of his understandable behavioral responses (e.g., isolating at home) could be contributing in the long term to his sense of loneliness, low mood, and making the adjustment to Boston harder. Given that Miguel was initially emphatic about wanting the therapist to help him develop skills to cope with his anxiety to look "more normal" and have others like him more, the therapist also discussed the ways that ableism could be linked to Miguel's desires to change for the sake of making other people like him and used this to reframe treatment goals so that rather than trying to help Miguel feel different and "be more likable," they could work together to help him live his life in ways that felt meaningful to him.

During session 4, the therapist helped Miguel clarify his values in the interpersonal dimension and used them to frame and motivate flexibility to change the ways he responds to feared social situations. Before this session, the therapist introduced values as things in life that matter to Miguel and ways of being in his life that are personally meaningful or important, and Miguel had done a between-session writing assignment reflecting on how he would like to be in social situations if he didn't experience worry. Through the valued writing assignment and reflections in the session, Miguel identified that he valued being open and warm in relationships, developing intimate relationships where he could express and receive care from others, practicing self-care, and being curious about seeking new experiences.

Miguel came to this session sharing an anxiety-provoking situation with his classmates that happened the night before that he had been feeling disappointed and distressed by.

Miguel: …last night after we finished classes, a group of my classmates and I were waiting for the T and they were talking about going to dinner but for some reason, even while I was standing there, I wasn't directly invited and I felt kind of ignored and very anxious honestly. I don't think they wanted me to come and I thought about joining regardless but I just couldn't stop worrying about them staring or laughing at me about my gait or even my accent or thinking that I am weird…or that I would just be silently awkward making them feel more uncomfortable. Anyway…I just froze and ended up going home as I always do…I suck at this. And now I am worried they'll think that I don't like them.
Therapist: I think as human beings we all wish to be liked by others, and it is very reasonable to not want to be judged by others. It is a hard thing to experience, and it must be harder to expose yourself to social interactions in a new country and with people that are new to you. Going home made sense for you at the time because you wanted to protect yourself from being judged, as it has unfairly happened to you before.
Client: Then why do I feel so bad about it?
Therapist: Well, avoiding the dinner probably made you feel relieved in the moment and certainly prevented you from being vulnerable and facing the risk of having other people judge you. However, in the long run it also prevented you from opening yourself to the possibility of making friends and seeking new experiences, which you mentioned is important to you.
Client: Well, that makes sense.
Therapist: Let's think through something together: if you had not been worrying or feeling anxious at all about what they would think about you, would you have done anything differently?
Client: mhh well, it would have actually been nice to go to this new restaurant as I have been wanting to check it out for a while now. It is very popular and has great reviews.
Therapist: anything else?
Client: mhh one of my classmates seems nice and I just realized that she was somewhat sad yesterday because her mom is very sick…it would have been nice to cheer her up. I do tend to feel deeply when I see people struggling. I wish I could have helped her...
Therapist: So it seems that worrying about how your classmates were perceiving you got in the way of things you wanted to do and were meaningful for you at that moment…
Client: yeah, I guess that is true…at that moment I didn't even realize this.
Therapist: Of course—it's hard to notice these habits when we have such strong, understandable reactions in the moment.

After the therapist and Miguel discussed future opportunities to practice valued-based actions (e.g., inviting a classmate for coffee and having a meaningful and mindful conversation with them), Miguel brought a concern to the therapist linked to stigma around his disability and anxiety. The therapist used this as an opportunity to acknowledge these, validate their impact, and help Miguel find ways to live consistently with his values even in the midst of barriers that are real and unfair.

Client: I think I could try to invite this classmate for coffee this week but… what if she actually doesn't like me or makes fun of my gait or my shaky anxious voice? I feel this is making me wonder if this is really worth it…

Therapist: It makes a lot of sense to fear this scenario and feel reluctant about exposing ourselves to the risk of being rejected. No one likes to be rejected, and it is something that could happen... Let's go there for a moment and say you meet this classmate for a coffee, what would your fear be?

Client: That I find out that she tells others that I am weird and makes fun of my gait or how I speak very anxiously.

Therapist: What would that say about her?

Client: That she is not nice...

Therapist: What would that say about you, knowing that you were intentional about opening up and connecting with her?

Client: Well...that I did what I could.

Therapist: And how would that make you feel?

Client: Well…good about myself because I was nice and showed up how I wanted to.

Therapist: Exactly. It is true that we can't control how others behave, but choosing to act aligned with our values can be inherently fulfilling independent of the response of others.

Client: It would still be painful, though. I am not sure I would want to go through that again.

Therapist: Of course, it would be painful. We live in a society where unfortunately this could happen. Ableism is a real problem in society where some people are erroneously socialized to believe that having a physical disability or experiencing anxiety are indicators of weakness and it is an unfair, unjust and problematic situation that you should not have to deal with. It not only makes a lot of sense for you to want to avoid people that discriminate against others based on who they are, but it is also important to protect oneself.

Therapist: Considering that you expressed valuing opening up in relationships while also practicing self-care, would you consider hanging out again with this classmate if you learned she is like this?

Client: I don't think so.

Therapist: In what other ways could you hold your value of opening up to and connecting with new people while taking care of and protecting yourself?

Client: I guess finding other classmates that are not like this and getting closer to them.

The therapist continued to explore with Miguel ways to identify and lean into social opportunities where he could thrive and engage in values-based actions, while intentionally avoiding those he chose to because others were not treating him well. Throughout the therapy process and across similar situations that the client brought up in sessions, the therapist validated Miguel's feelings and fears of being rejected given previous experiences and ableist contexts and used his values (e.g., desire for connections and practice self-care) to guide his chosen actions in the midst of his fear.

Incorporating DMHI into Therapy

Naomi is a 40-year-old Asian cisgender woman who identifies as Japanese American and lives with her wife and 1-year-old daughter. At the start of treatment, she reported frequent uncontrollable worry about work, her relationships, and climate change. She reported that she spent a significant amount of time over-preparing for work tasks and always double-checked all of this work. This led to working long hours, leaving less time to spend with her wife and daughter. This led to arguments with her wife, exacerbating worries about their relationship. She reported that her worries were strongest at night and that she would often lie in bed wide awake for hours before she could fall asleep, and once asleep, she would typically wake up multiple times during the night and find it challenging to fall back to sleep.

As treatment progressed, it became clear that Naomi's sleep problems were an important part of the clinical picture. While she reported that using ABBT-based skills was helping to reduce her anxiety and helping her to engage more fully in her life and with her family, she shared that falling and staying asleep were still significant concerns. Naomi's therapist did not have training in CBT for insomnia (CBT-i), an evidence-based treatment for insomnia. The therapist and Naomi discussed the possibility of including an evidence-based CBT-i app in their treatment plan. Naomi expressed interest in this idea as she had used other health-related apps before, and she felt it would provide her with another resource to learn more about sleep problems specifically and strategies to address them. This would allow the therapist and Naomi to continue to focus more of their time in session on her anxiety and ABBT skills. The therapist knew of a CBT-i app that had been found to significantly reduce insomnia symptoms in a peer-reviewed research study. The therapist downloaded and reviewed the app, including the privacy policy and the content, to make sure the content was consistent with their treatment plan, identify any contradictions, and identify additional content to discuss and orient the client to. The therapist determined that some content was consistent with ABBT (e.g., mindfulness practices with similar framing) and that the app also provided unique content and features related to sleep. They noticed that the illustrations and examples seemed to focus on White women. They looked for more culturally responsive apps that included a range of identities in examples. The therapist also reached out to several colleagues for recommendations. One colleague recommended the same app the therapist had found based on its effectiveness. Unfortunately, the therapist did not find another CBT-i app that seemed to be more culturally responsive. During the next session, the therapist shared what they found with Naomi:

Therapist: Since we last met, I looked into different apps that use CBT-i, which is an evidence-based treatment for insomnia. I've found one that is available in the app store. I downloaded it and overall I think it could be a helpful addition to our work together. Some of the content is similar to what we're working on, like mindfulness exercises, while some of it is different and focuses on sleep.

Naomi: Thank you for looking into that. It sounds like that's a good option.

Therapist: You're welcome. There is one part of the app I'd like to talk about with you. I noticed when I was reviewing it that the examples and pictures were all about White women. After noticing this, I went back to my search to try to find another option that is more culturally responsive. Unfortunately, I was not able to find one. I recognize that there may be other parts of the app that are not *culturally responsive* or that don't include a range of experiences, and that I may not have noticed those as a White person. I wanted to share this observation with you and to see how you'd like to proceed.

Naomi: Thank you for sharing that. It is often frustrating to feel like you don't see yourself reflected in the content of a lot of apps. I am still interested in giving it a try. If it could help with my sleep it could still be worth it to me.

Therapist: I am sorry that I don't have an option that is more culturally responsive and has examples with a wider range of identities to offer you. I'd like to check in with you next session to see what your initial experience of the app is like. If it raises any concerns for you, or doesn't feel relevant, those would be important things for us to discuss. If there are parts that do not feel relevant, I would be happy to discuss them together and see if we can make the content feel more relevant and helpful for you and your goals. What do you think about that?

Naomi: That sounds like a good plan to me. It will be helpful to talk more about it once I give the app a try.

During this session, the therapist offered that Naomi could download and set up the app during the session if she would like to. While the therapist hypothesized that Naomi had a high level of digital health literacy, as she previously referred to using other health apps, the therapist still wanted to offer this to ensure Naomi had support getting started if it would be helpful. Naomi said she felt comfortable doing this on her own given her familiarity with health apps. In the next session, the therapist made time to ask Naomi about whether she had downloaded and started using the app. They specifically asked what her experience was like, if the app felt relevant to her, and if she ran into any challenges or barriers or had any concerns about it. Naomi reported that despite the lack of cultural responsiveness, she had found the app content helpful that week and wanted to continue using it. During the next session, the therapist checked in about the app, and Naomi reported that she had intended to use it but had forgotten multiple times. Since they were discussing values, the therapist and Naomi connected using the app to her value of taking care of herself. Naomi then made a plan to use the app over the next week as an example of a values-based action. She also decided that she wanted to turn on the notification feature in the app to provide reminders at specific times that would work for her schedule. The therapist checked in about this during the following session, and Naomi reported that conceptualizing using the app as a values-based action and also having the notification feature helped her engage with it.

Naomi used the app for the remainder of the treatment period. She noted that some of the exercises were similar to session content, and some of the features were unique and helped with her sleep (e.g., sleep diaries). The therapist continued to check in with Naomi about what content she was engaging with in the app and if any of it felt inconsistent with their work together to be able to address any discrepancies. At the end of treatment, the therapist and Naomi discussed ways for her to maintain the gains she had made. Naomi stated that she would like to continue to use the app to monitor her sleep and mindfulness practices. The app also had a journal feature, which she decided to use to track values-based actions she took. She felt that the app could help her to continue practicing the new habits she had built in treatment and to provide some structure and accountability after therapy. She continued to use the notification feature on the app for reminders to check in with herself during this period and to ensure she was continuing to apply what she learned during treatment in her daily life. Naomi also liked knowing that, in addition to reaching back out to her therapist in the future, she could use the app more frequently if her symptoms worsened again or if she wanted a refresher.

Conclusion

While there are evidence-based CBTs for GAD, many people with GAD do not pursue, or do not persist in, treatment. Although some barriers to engagement are systemic and need to be addressed outside of therapy, this chapter offers specific recommendations for therapists to increase engagement in treatment for people with GAD. Clinicians can use collaborative case formulation, culturally responsive engagement sessions, values clarification, addressing situational and contextual stressors in treatment, cultural adaptations, and flexibility in treatment elements to address stigma, avoidance, unrealistic expectations for therapy, fear of uncertainty, and sociocultural barriers to engagement. Clinicians may also consider utilizing DMHIs to increase engagement, though should be mindful of potential barriers to these approaches. Most importantly, a strong therapeutic alliance that allows for open communication can help therapists address any barriers that arise before they lead to disengagement.

Clinical Summary Points and Recommendations

- A collaborative case formulation that presents realistic expectations for therapy, addresses the role of uncertainty and positive beliefs about worry in the client's current challenges and how they relate to treatment, and connects symptoms and treatment to enhancing meaning and purpose in the client's life (i.e., values clarification and values-based actions) will enhance engagement and persistence in clients with GAD.
- Clinicians should assess, consider, and explore contextual and situational stressors throughout treatment, making sure to validate the reality of systemic stressors, apply skills to the reactions to those stressors, and help clients identify and enact meaningful, values-based actions in response to stressors (e.g., Martinez et al., 2022).
- A rich case conceptualization and consideration of the function of specific interventions can help clinicians to flexibly adjust interventions so they are culturally and contextually responsive, further enhancing engagement and persistence.

References

American Psychiatric Association. (2013). *Diagnostic and statistical manual of mental disorders* (5th ed.). American Psychiatric Association.

Andrews, G., Basu, A., Cuijpers, P., Craske, M. G., McEvoy, P., English, C. L., & Newby, J. M. (2018). Computer therapy for the anxiety and depression disorders is effective, acceptable and practical health care: an updated meta-analysis. *Journal of Anxiety Disorders, 55*, 70–78. https://doi.org/10.1016/j.janxdis.2018.01.001

Boot-Haury, J. W. (2023). Cultural competence for clinicians working with rural transgender clients with generalized anxiety disorder. *Journal of LGBTQ Issues in Counseling, 17*(2), 164–183. https://doi.org/10.1080/26924951.2023.2128970

Borghouts, J., Eikey, E., Mark, G., De Leon, C., Schueller, S. M., Schneider, M., et al. (2021). Barriers to and facilitators of user engagement with digital mental health interventions: Systematic review. *Journal of Medical Internet Research, 23*(3), e24387. https://doi.org/10.2196/24387

Castellanos, R., & Flory, K. (2022). Mindfulness, culture, and clinical practice: Clinician experiences utilizing mindfulness and acceptance with Hispanics/Latinx population. In C. M. Fleming, V. Y. Womack, & J. Proulx (Eds.), *Beyond white mindfulness: Critical perspectives on racism, well-being and liberation* (pp. 40–63). Routledge. https://doi.org/10.4324/9781003090922-4

Calear, A. L., Batterham, P. J., Griffiths, K. M., & Christensen, H. (2017). Generalized anxiety disorder stigma in adolescents: Personal and perceived stigma levels and predictors. *Stigma and Health, 2*(3), 208–215. https://doi.org/10.1037/sah0000046

Chang, D. F., Ng, N., Chen, T., Hung, T., Miao, I. Y., Cao, Y., & Zhang, Y. (2020). Let nature take its course: Cultural adaptation and pilot test of taoist cognitive therapy for Chinese American immigrants with generalized anxiety disorder. *Frontiers in Psychology, 11*, 547852. https://doi.org/10.3389/fpsyg.2020.547852

de Almeida Sampaio, T. P., Jorge, R. C., Martins, D. S., Gandarela, L. M., Hayes-Skelton, S., Bernik, M. A., & Lotufo-Neto, F. (2020). Efficacy of an acceptance-based group behavioral therapy for generalized anxiety disorder. *Depression and Anxiety, 37*(12), 1179–1193. https://doi.org/10.1002/da.23021

Eilert, N., Enrique, A., Wogan, R., Mooney, O., Timulak, L., & Richards, D. (2021). The effectiveness of Internet-delivered treatment for generalized anxiety disorder: An updated systematic review and meta-analysis. *Depression and Anxiety, 38*(2), 196–219. https://doi.org/10.1002/da.23115

Eustis, E. H., Hayes-Skelton, S. A., Roemer, L., & Orsillo, S. M. (2016). Reductions in experiential avoidance as a mediator of change in symptom outcome and quality of life in acceptance-based behavior therapy and applied relaxation for generalized anxiety disorder. *Behaviour Research and Therapy, 87*, 188–195. https://doi.org/10.1016/j.brat.2016.09.012

Eustis, E. H., LoPresti, J., Aguilera, A., & Schueller, S. M. (2023). Cultural responsivity in technology-enabled services: Integrating culture into technology and service components. *Journal of Medical Internet Research, 25*, e45409. https://doi.org/10.2196/45409

Fuchs, C. H., West, L. M., Graham, J. R., Kalill, K. S., Morgan, L. P., Hayes-Skelton, S. A., et al. (2016). Reactions to an acceptance-based behavior therapy for GAD: Giving voice to the experiences of clients from marginalized backgrounds. *Cognitive and Behavioral Practice, 23*(4), 473–484. https://doi.org/10.1016/j.cbpra.2015.09.004

Gersh, E., Hallford, D. J., Rice, S. M., Kazantzis, N., Gersh, H., Gersh, B., & McCarty, C. A. (2017). Systematic review and meta-analysis of dropout rates in individual psychotherapy for generalized anxiety disorder. *Journal of Anxiety Disorders, 52*, 25–33. https://doi.org/10.1016/j.janxdis.2017.10.001

Goetter, E. M., Frumkin, M. R., Palitz, S. A., Swee, M. B., Baker, A. W., Bui, E., & Simon, N. M. (2020). Barriers to mental health treatment among individuals with social anxiety disorder and generalized anxiety disorder. *Psychological Services, 17*(1), 5–12. https://doi.org/10.1037/ser0000254

Graham, J. R., Sorenson, S., & Hayes-Skelton, S. A. (2013). Enhancing the cultural sensitivity of cognitive behavioral interventions for anxiety in diverse populations. *The Behavior Therapist, 36*(5), 101–108.

Graham-LoPresti, J. R., Abdullah, T., & Calloway, A. (2020). Culturally responsive assessment and treatment of generalized anxiety disorder. *Handbook of cultural factors in behavioral health: A guide for the helping professional*, 231–245. https://doi.org/10.1007/978-3-030-32229-8_17

Hall, G. C. N., Hong, J. J., Zane, N. W. S., & Meyer, O. L. (2011). Culturally competent treatments for Asian Americans: The relevance of mindfulness and acceptance-based psychotherapies. *Clinical Psychology: Science and Practice, 18*(3), 215–231. https://doi.org/10.1111/j.1468-2850.2011.01253.x

Harrell, S. P. (2018). Soulfulness as an orientation to contemplative practice: Culture, liberation, and mindful awareness. *The Journal of Contemplative Inquiry, 5*(1), 9–40. https://digscholarship.unco.edu/joci/vol5/iss1/6

Hayes, S. C., Strosahl, K. D., & Wilson, K. G. (2012). *Acceptance and commitment therapy: The process and practice of mindful change* (2nd ed.). Guilford Press.

Hayes-Skelton, S. A., Calloway, A., Roemer, L., & Orsillo, S. M. (2015). Decentering as a potential common mechanism across two therapies for generalized anxiety disorder. *Journal of Consulting and Clinical Psychology, 83*, 395–404. https://doi.org/10.1037/a0038305

Hayes-Skelton, S. A., Roemer, L., & Orsillo, S. M. (2013). A randomized clinical trial comparing an acceptance-based behavior therapy to applied relaxation for generalized anxiety disorder. *Journal of Consulting and Clinical Psychology, 81*(5), 761–773. https://doi.org/10.1037/a0032871

Hays, P. A. (2022). *Addressing cultural complexities in counseling and clinical practice: An intersectional approach.* American Psychological Association.

Hook, J. N., Davis, D., Owen, J., & DeBlaere, C. (2017). *Cultural humility: Engaging diverse identities in therapy. American Psychological Association.* https://doi.org/10.1037/0000037-000

Iwamasa, G. Y., & Hays, P. A. (Eds.). (2018). *Culturally responsive cognitive behavior therapy: Practice and supervision* (2nd ed.). American Psychological Association. https://doi.org/10.1037/0000119-000

Krill Williston, S., Martinez, J. H., & Abdullah, T. (2019). Mental health stigma among people of color: An examination of the impact of racial discrimination. *International Journal of Social Psychiatry, 65*(6), 458–467. https://doi.org/10.1177/0020764019858651

Linehan, M. M. (2014). *DBT skills training manual*. Guilford Press.

Lawrence, V., Kimona, K., Howard, R. J., Serfaty, M. A., Wetherell, J. L., Livingston, G., et al. (2019). Optimising the acceptability and feasibility of acceptance and commitment therapy for treatment-resistant generalised anxiety disorder in older adults. *Age and Ageing, 48*(5), 741–750. https://doi.org/10.1093/ageing/afz082

Martinez, J. H., Suyemoto, K. L., Abdullah, T., Burnett-Ziegler, I., & Roemer, L. (2022). Mindfulness and valued living in the face of racism-related stress. *Mindfulness, 13*(5), 1112–1125. https://doi.org/10.1007/s12671-022-01826-6

Millstein, D. J., Orsillo, S. M., Hayes-Skelton, S. A., & Roemer, L. (2015). Interpersonal problems, mindfulness, and therapy outcome in an acceptance-based behavior therapy for generalized anxiety disorder. *Cognitive Behaviour Therapy, 44*(6), 491–450. https://doi.org/10.1080/16506073.2015.1060255

Morgan, L. P., Graham, J. R., Hayes-Skelton, S. A., Orsillo, S. M., & Roemer, L. (2014). Relationships between amount of post-intervention mindfulness practice and follow-up outcome variables in an acceptance-based behavior therapy for Generalized Anxiety Disorder: The importance of informal practice. *Journal of Contextual Behavioral Science, 3*(3), 173–117. https://doi.org/10.1016/j.jcbs.2014.05.001

Newby, J., Mason, E., Kladnistki, N., Murphy, M., Millard, M., Haskelberg, H., et al. (2021). Integrating internet CBT into clinical practice: A practical guide for clinicians. *Clinical Psychologist, 25*(2), 164–178. https://doi.org/10.1080/13284207.2020.1843968

Newman, M. G., Basterfield, C., Erickson, T. M., Caulley, E., Przeworski, A., & Llera, S. J. (2022). Psychotherapeutic treatments for generalized anxiety disorder: Cognitive and behavioral therapies, enhancement strategies, and emerging efforts. *Expert Review of Neurotherapeutics, 22*(9), 751–770.

Orsillo, S. M., & Roemer, L. (2016). *Worry less, live more: The mindful way through anxiety workbook*. Guilford Press. https://doi.org/10.1080/14737175.2022.2125800

Penney, A. M., Mazmanian, D., & Rudanycz, C. (2013). Comparing positive and negative beliefs about worry in predicting generalized anxiety disorder symptoms. *Canadian Journal of Behavioural Science, 45*(1), 34–41. https://doi.org/10.1037/a0027623

Puckett, J. A., Wiklund, L. O., Louis, C., Gallik, C., Brown-Wren, L., Chu, H., et al. (2023a). Clinical practice with transgender and gender diverse clients: Setting up an inclusive practice and training considerations. *Practice Innovations*. https://doi.org/10.1037/pri0000209

Puckett, J. A., Kimball, D., Glozier, W. K., Wertz, M., Dunn, T., Lash, B. R., et al. (2023b). Transgender and gender diverse clients' experiences in therapy: Responses to sociopolitical events and helpful and unhelpful experiences. *Professional Psychology: Research and Practice, 54*(4), 265–274. https://doi.org/10.1037/pro0000513

Proulx, J., Croff, R., Oken, B., Aldwin, C. M., Fleming, C., Bergen-Cico, D., et al. (2018). Considerations for research and development of culturally relevant mindfulness interventions in American minority communities. *Mindfulness, 9*, 361–370. https://doi.org/10.1007/s12671-017-0785-z

Ramos, G., Ponting, C., Labao, J. P., & Sobowale, K. (2021). Considerations of diversity, equity, and inclusion in mental health apps: A scoping review of evaluation frameworks. *Behaviour Research and Therapy, 147*, 1–15. https://doi.org/10.1016/j.brat.2021.103990

Roemer, L., & Orsillo, S. M. (2020). *Acceptance-based behavioral therapy: Treating anxiety and related challenges*. Guilford Press.

Roemer, L., Eustis, E. H., & Orsillo, S. M. (2021). An acceptance-based behavioral therapy for generalized anxiety disorder. In D. H. Barlow (Ed.), *Clinical handbook of psychological disorders: A step-by-step treatment manual* (6th ed., pp. 184–216). Guilford Press.

Roemer, L., Orsillo, S. M., & Salters-Pedneault, K. (2008). Efficacy of an acceptance-based behavior therapy for generalized anxiety disorder: Evaluation in a randomized controlled trial. *Journal of Consulting and Clinical Psychology, 76*(6), 1083–1089. https://doi.org/10.1037/a0012720

Roy-Byrne, P. P., & Wagner, A. (2004). Primary care perspectives on generalized anxiety disorder. *Journal of Clinical Psychiatry, 65*, 20–26. https://pubmed.ncbi.nlm.nih.gov/15384933/

Rucker, L. S., West, L. M., & Roemer, L. (2010). Relationships among perceived racial stress, intolerance of uncertainty, and worry in a black sample. *Behavior Therapy, 41*(2), 245–253. https://doi.org/10.1016/j.beth.2009.04.001

Ruscio, A. M., Hallion, L. S., Lim, C. C., Aguilar-Gaxiola, S., Al-Hamzawi, A., Alonso, J., et al. (2017). Cross-sectional comparison of the epidemiology of DSM-5 generalized anxiety disorder across the globe. *JAMA Psychiatry, 74*(5), 465–475. https://doi.org/10.1001/jamapsychiatry.2017.0056

Safran, J., & Segal, Z. V. (1990). *Interpersonal process in cognitive therapy*. Jason Aronson.

Salamanca-Sanabria, A., Richards, D., Timulak, L., Connell, S., Mojica Perilla, M., Parra-Villa, Y., & Castro-Camacho, L. (2020). A culturally adapted cognitive behavioral internet-delivered intervention for depressive symptoms: Randomized controlled trial. *JMIR Mental Health, 7*(1), e13392. https://doi.org/10.2196/13392

Schueller, S. M., Hunter, J. F., Figueroa, C., & Aguilera, A. (2019). Use of digital mental health for marginalized and underserved populations. *Current Treatment Options in Psychiatry, 6*, 243–255.

Segal, Z., Williams, M., & Teasdale, J. (2018). *Mindfulness-based cognitive therapy for depression*. Guilford Publications.

Sobczak, L. R., & West, L. M. (2013). Clinical considerations in using mindfulness- and acceptance-based approaches with diverse populations: Addressing challenges in service delivery in diverse community settings. *Cognitive and Behavioral Practice, 20*(1), 13–22. https://doi.org/10.1016/j.cbpra.2011.08.005

Sue, D. W., Sue, D., Neville, H. A., & Smith, L. (2019). *Counseling the culturally diverse: Theory and practice* (8th ed.). Wiley.

Sweetman, J., Knapp, P., Varley, D., Woodhouse, R., McMillan, D., & Coventry, P. (2021). Barriers to attending initial psychological therapy service appointments for common mental health problems: A mixed-methods systematic review. *Journal of Affective Disorders, 284*, 44–63. https://doi.org/10.1016/j.jad.2021.01.089

Toledo-Chávarri, A., Ramos-García, V., Torres-Castaño, A., Trujillo-Martín, M. M., Peñate Castro, W., Del Cura-Castro, I., et al. (2020). Framing the process in the implementation of care for people with generalized anxiety disorder in primary care: A qualitative evidence synthesis. *BMC Family Practice, 21*, 1–12. https://doi.org/10.1186/s12875-020-01307-6

Vera, M., Obén, A., Juarbe, D., Hernández, N., & Pérez-Pedrogo, C. (2021). Randomized pilot trial of cognitive-behavioral therapy and acceptance-based behavioral therapy in the treatment of Spanish-speaking Latino primary care patients with generalized anxiety disorder. *Journal of Behavioral and Cognitive Therapy, 31*(2), 91–103. https://doi.org/10.1016/j.jbct.2020.11.007

Watson-Singleton, N. N., Black, A. R., & Spivey, B. N. (2019). Recommendations for a culturally-responsive mindfulness-based intervention for African Americans. *Complementary Therapies in Clinical Practice, 34*, 132–138. https://doi.org/10.1016/j.ctcp.2018.11.013

Watson-Singleton, N. N., Pennefather, J., & Trusty, T. (2023). Can a culturally-responsive mobile health (mHealth) application reduce African Americans' stress?: A pilot feasibility study. *Current Psychology, 42*(2), 1434–1443. https://doi.org/10.1007/s12144-021-01534-9

Westra, H. A., & Dozois, D. J. (2006). Preparing clients for cognitive behavioral therapy: A randomized pilot study of motivational interviewing for anxiety. *Cognitive Therapy and Research, 30*, 481–498. https://doi.org/10.1007/s10608-006-9016-y

Woods-Giscombé, C. L., & Gaylord, S. A. (2014). The cultural relevance of mindfulness meditation as a health intervention for African Americans: Implications for reducing stress-related health disparities. *Journal of Holistic Nursing: Official Journal of the American Holistic Nurses' Association, 32*(3), 147–160. https://doi.org/10.1177/0898010113519010

Xie, D. (2020). Cultural perspectives in understanding, treating, and studying: Worry and generalized anxiety disorder (GAD). In *Generalized anxiety disorder and worrying: A comprehensive handbook for clinicians and researchers* (pp. 173–201). https://doi.org/10.1002/9781119189909.ch9

Zargar, F., Asgharnejad Farid, A. A., Atef-Vahid, M. K., Afshar, H., Maroofi, M., & Omranifard, V. (2012). Effect of acceptance-based behavior therapy on severity of symptoms, worry and quality of life in women with generalized anxiety disorder. *Iranian Journal of Psychiatry and Behavioral Sciences, 6*(2), 23–32. https://www.ncbi.nlm.nih.gov/pmc/articles/pmid/24644479/

Chapter 13
Panic Disorder

Emily H. Mintz, Dhea Kothari, Claire M. Hotchkin, Annie-Lori Joseph, and Amanda W. Baker

Background

Panic disorder (PD) is characterized by recurrent and unexpected panic attacks (abrupt surges of intense fear or discomfort, involving several physical symptoms), followed by worry about future attacks, significant maladaptive changes in behavior, or avoidance of associated places or activities, with symptoms persisting for at least 1 month (American Psychiatric Association, 2013; Cackovic et al., 2023). Panic attacks can be present in individuals diagnosed with other anxiety, mood, psychotic, and substance use disorders. Though panic attacks typically occur without warning, some individuals with PD may exhibit concurrent agoraphobia, which is a fear of situations in which receiving help or finding an escape is challenging. Differentiating panic attacks from PD is crucial for accurate diagnosis and

Emily H. Mintz and Dhea Kothari contributed equally with all other contributors.

E. H. Mintz · D. Kothari · C. M. Hotchkin
Department of Psychiatry, Massachusetts General Hospital, Boston, MA, USA
e-mail: emintz1@mgh.harvard.edu; dkothari2@mgh.harvard.edu; claire.h@uci.edu

A.-L. Joseph
Department of Psychiatry, Massachusetts General Hospital, Boston, MA, USA

Department of Psychology, Suffolk University, Boston, MA, USA
e-mail: ajoseph24@mgh.harvard.edu

A. W. Baker (✉)
Department of Psychiatry, Massachusetts General Hospital, Boston, MA, USA

Department of Psychiatry, Harvard Medical School, Boston, MA, USA
e-mail: awbaker@mgh.harvard.edu

E. M. Goetter (ed.), *Optimizing Treatment Engagement Processes in CBT for Anxiety and Related Disorders*, CBT: Science Into Practice,
https://doi.org/10.1007/978-3-031-91439-3_13

treatment engagement. Individuals with PD experience recurrent worry and behavior changes associated with the attacks and typically misinterpret physical symptoms as having dangerous catastrophic outcomes, triggering anxiety and avoidance behaviors as they anticipate another panic attack, perpetuating a cycle of fear and avoidance (American Psychiatric Association, 2013). Misinterpretation of and difficulty expressing symptoms, avoidance behaviors, and limited awareness of or access to treatment options make treatment seeking and engaging in treatment challenging for individuals with PD.

Cognitive Behavioral Therapy (CBT) for Panic Disorder and Its Effectiveness

PD involves catastrophic misinterpretations of physiological sensations. Thus, the cognitive-behavioral approach to PD treatment entails individuals learning new responses to previously feared cues to produce a sense of safety and security (Otto & Deveney, 2005). Cognitive behavioral therapy (CBT) for PD includes psychoeducation, a collaborative process in which an overview of CBT treatment for PD is provided and the clinician and patient work together to discuss treatment goals. The cognitive component of PD treatment involves discussing the relationship between thoughts and physiological symptoms of anxiety, as well as how to challenge these thoughts (e.g., by countering probability overestimation). Exposure exercises are a primary component and include exposure to catastrophic thoughts related to panic and interoceptive exposures, which focus on the patients' feared bodily sensations (e.g., hyperventilation and heart palpitations). During these exercises, which are initially therapist-assisted and then practiced independently, patients work to create a new relationship with sensations of anxiety and distress and reexamine the belief that catastrophic outcomes will occur. In vivo exposures are also utilized in treatment, which are centralized around the external circumstances in which feared psychological experiences develop or are amplified (e.g., crowded spaces and riding public transportation), with the goal being able to reduce agoraphobic-related avoidance and to reduce the use of safety behaviors that may temporarily alleviate panic symptoms (Otto & Deveney, 2005). Over time and with repeated practice, the goal of these exposure interventions is that individuals will no longer associate their physiological sensations with danger, they will no longer avoid the environmental situations previously associated with feared sensations or outcomes, and their anxiety will decrease (Rayburn & Otto, 2003; Baker & Levine, 2023).

Among the various therapeutic approaches available (see Rabasco et al., 2022 for a review), CBT has emerged as a leading evidence-based treatment for PD. Numerous randomized controlled trials have consistently demonstrated the effectiveness of CBT in reducing panic symptoms, decreasing the frequency and severity of panic attacks, and improving overall functioning and quality of life, with maintenance of treatment gains over time (Otto & Deveny, 2005; McHugh et al., 2007). Moreover, a systematic review and network meta-analysis found CBT for PD (face-to-face group, face-to-face individual, and guided self-help) to be more efficacious than treatment as usual (e.g., assessment or psychoeducation, with little clinician contact and no routine pharmacological treatment) (Papola et al., 2023). CBT has demonstrated an advantage in preventing relapse after treatment discontinuation and can benefit those who are resistant to pharmacotherapy (Heldt et al., 2006). While efficacious, CBT for PD may be difficult for patients to engage with initially, given the inherent difficulty in facing feared sensations and situations associated with subjectively grave consequences.

As such, there is still room for improvement in CBT treatment for PD in terms of accessibility, treatment engagement, and outcomes. For example, online platforms and smartphone applications for internet-based cognitive behavioral therapy (iCBT) and virtual reality interventions can provide additional resources and allow for greater flexibility and convenience for patients, potentially increasing access and patient engagement in treatment. Investigating novel treatment techniques, understanding the underlying mechanisms of change during treatment, and identifying specific subgroups that may benefit from tailored interventions can contribute to improving the efficacy of CBT and patient engagement. Additionally, it is important to consider how to address treatment for comorbidities, as over 80% of individuals with panic disorder experience at least one lifetime comorbid mental health condition (Gorman & Coplan, 1996; Kessler et al., 2006; American Psychiatric Association, 2013; Lai et al., 2015). Addressing these comorbidities concurrently within the CBT framework can improve overall treatment outcomes by streamlining the treatment process and targeting the interconnected nature of these conditions, which may increase engagement with treatment through individually tailored treatments rather than one-size-fits-all protocols that fail to appreciate individual differences.

Scope of the Problem of Engagement in Treatment

A study found that on average, patients with PD are symptomatic for 4.5 years before seeking treatment (Benatti et al., 2016). The fact that people delay treatment (often due to avoidance or stigma) contributes to unmet need. In fact, a study of 231 participants investigating the perceived unmet need of PD treatment in primary care settings revealed that 38% of people endorsed an unmet need in treatment, which was operationalized as barriers to accessing or partaking in mental health care (Craske et al., 2005). Given these realities, it is important to optimize engagement early on once individuals present for CBT. Tzavela et al. (2018) conducted a qualitative study that focused on the importance of patient experience and engagement early in treatment and categorized the early experience in four categories: approaching the problem, easing in and opening up, building trust and bonding, and making sense of panic. It is important to attend to these processes early in treatment and be attentive to signs of patient engagement and disengagement. For instance, encouraging signs of engagement may look like attentively immersing in treatment (versus mind racing off), being inspired by and trusting the method (versus passive expectancies of relief), and believing in one's capabilities or relying on therapist (versus the inability to do the same) (Tzavela et al., 2018).

Disengagement is a common experience for which therapists must be prepared. Disengagement may be a reason why individuals are symptomatic post-treatment (Arch & Craske, 2009) and at its most extreme manifests as dropout from treatment. Dropout in CBT for PD has been documented in some studies to be close to 20% (White et al., 2010). Disengagement, though, can take other milder forms, including cognitive and emotional avoidance, conflicting feelings toward symptom improvement, or a lack of belief in CBT's efficacy or the therapist's expertise. While CBT has demonstrated effectiveness for treating panic disorder, therapists must be attentive to the processes that exist prior to and early on in treatment, which may undermine engagement. Barriers to treatment seeking and engagement are present among a sizable percentage of individuals with PD and exist at the individual, contextual, and systematic levels, discussed in further detail below.

Barriers and Facilitators to Treatment Seeking, Engagement, and Retention

Individual Barriers

Individual barriers to seeking CBT for PD can be complex and multifaceted. Foremost, PD is defined by avoidance behaviors, as people with panic disorder may have a fear of experiencing panic attacks or the situations that trigger them. This fear and avoidance can make it challenging to engage in therapy sessions that involve exposure to feared situations or sensations. Additionally, a specific consideration in the treatment of PD is that individuals may be resistant to initiating psychological treatment due to difficulty expressing or understanding the symptoms that they are experiencing. For individuals with panic disorder, medical or biological causes are often assumed, and seeking treatment from a cognitive-behavioral therapist may not be initially considered.

Additionally, engaging in therapy requires motivation and a readiness to make changes. Some individuals with panic disorder may initially struggle with low motivation or feel hesitant about confronting their fears, and there is evidence to suggest that low patient motivation (as rated by therapists) can impede outcomes in CBT for PD (Huppert et al., 2006). For some, it may take time to build the necessary motivation and readiness to actively participate in CBT. Once treatment is underway, a lack of homework adherence, often related to issues of motivation, may also make it difficult for CBT skills and concepts to be reinforced or inhibit a successful progression through the treatment modules. A lack of homework compliance has been cited as one of the top reasons that CBT is unsuccessful for a given patient (Tang &

Kreindler, 2017), likely due to the importance of practicing skills between sessions (Conklin et al., 2021).

However, in addition to the patient's internal and motivational processes, there may be practical challenges to consider, such as conflicting or inflexible work schedules. This may limit one's ability to attend therapy sessions during normal business hours. Many individuals may be unable to take off from work to accommodate therapy appointments during clinician hours because they may lose pay. Stigma associated with various psychological conditions may also prevent an individual from seeking treatment (Craske et al., 2005) and may prevent individuals from formally requesting time off for appointments. Moreover, distance to a therapist's office may be a barrier to receiving care, particularly for those with agoraphobic fears. Additionally, people may not know where to go for help, what treatment options are available, and what treatment may be most appropriate for their presenting concerns, or whether or not treatment could help alleviate symptoms.

Lastly, although less definitive, there are also certain individual demographic factors that may be predictive of CBT treatment dropout for PD. Level of education and motivation to engage in treatment, when examined concurrently, has been associated with dropout in CBT for PD (Keefe et al., 2021). Further, patients who were unemployed, on disability, or had higher self-reported functional impairment were more likely to drop out from treatment (Keefe et al., 2021).

Individual Facilitators

Given the nature of PD, psychoeducation early on is key for helping patients understand the role of avoidance and the nature of the physical sensations they are experiencing. In theory, this should help the patient understand the need for a CBT intervention, as opposed to a medical intervention for instance. Therapists can work to increase engagement by utilizing motivational interviewing as a pre-treatment preparation, which could span multiple sessions prior to beginning cognitive restructuring and/or exposure (Westra et al., 2009, 2016). Motivational interviewing (see Chap. 4) is a therapeutic strategy intended to increase patient engagement in change behavior (e.g., therapy engagement). In the case of PD, no studies have singularly assessed the role of MI in CBT for PD, but a therapist might explore the patient's goals for treatment, reasons for change, hesitations about change, and attitudes toward treatment (Rollnick & Miller, 1995). Yet, such interventions can naturally coincide with the psychoeducation phase of CBT for PD. The therapist may also use this as an opportunity to discuss the benefits of treatment and prepare the patient for what is to be expected during treatment (Rollnick & Miller, 1995).

To overcome some of the logistical and stigma-related individual barriers, there is promise in utilizing digital treatment options for PD. Digital mental health interventions (DMHIs) are a burgeoning focus of research that address several engagement issues and could also potentially increase access to evidence-based mental health resources. DMHI can range from self-help programs (iCBT, mobile applications) to videoconference-mediated therapies. Technology enhances convenience for patients who live far away or need more flexibility with fitting in their appointments with work schedules. Additionally, patients may be more inclined to start or engage in treatment for PD if it is delivered via telehealth or if it is self-guided (e.g., iCBT) when privacy is a concern or if agoraphobic fears prevent them from presenting to treatment in person. A meta-analysis of 21 studies investigating treatment outcomes in remotely delivered CBT (including telehealth and iCBT) for PD in adults found that remote CBT is effective, as demonstrated by the large within-group effects (g = 1.18; 95% CI: 0.99–1.36) and between-group differences (i.e., CBT *versus* inactive controls) in PD symptoms (g = 0.82; 05% CI: 0.44–1.20) (Efron & Wootton, 2021).

In addition to telehealth and iCBT, there are currently three main use cases for mobile applications. The first is a self-help app, which is a stand-alone intervention that is not connected to any form of therapy with a clinician. The second type is a therapy adjunct, which provides additional skills when providers do not have adequate training (e.g., using an app to deliver CBT for insomnia when a patient with PD has co-occurring sleep issues, but the therapist is not trained in CBT-I). The third and final type is therapy extenders, which support CBT through lessons and homework (e.g., Rootd, which can be used for panic attacks or anxiety symptoms). Preliminary research suggests that engagement is highest when a digital intervention is paired with support from a mental health provider (Borghouts et al., 2021). These apps also provide validation, psychoeducation, and rationale for treatment. They can also be used to keep digital records of various worksheets that are filled out over the course of CBT, which may be helpful for patients to refer back to and for clinicians to review.

Regardless of the therapy format, homework or *between-session* practice plays a large role in CBT for anxiety, depression, and PD, and homework adherence, which is often a proxy for patient engagement, is facilitative of outcome (Rees et al., 2005; Cammin-Nowak et al., 2013). In an effort to improve homework adherence throughout treatment, clinicians should spend sufficient time in the beginning of treatment to explain the purpose of completing homework as well as take time throughout the course of treatment to check in about homework and address any concerns. Each session should begin with a discussion of homework to reinforce its importance and allow time to assess and troubleshoot lack of homework adherence if necessary. This might involve identifying barriers to homework completion (e.g., panic-related avoidance and scheduling), engaging in motivational interviewing, or providing psychoeducation on the importance of repeated practice. Smartphones may have the potential to overcome homework adherence issues due to how ubiquitous they are. There are several potential benefits of using smartphone applications as a way of recording CBT homework. Clinicians can view homework completion in real time, provide feedback, or communicate any issues that may come up between sessions. However, it is important to acknowledge the potential concerns of utilizing smartphone-delivered homework, which include therapist–patient boundaries outside of session confidentiality and ensuring that these homework assignments are created collaboratively and in a culturally responsive manner (Tang & Kreindler,

2017). While additional research is needed to understand how and for whom smartphone-delivered homework assignments may work best, it may be an acceptable and feasible solution to thwarting homework adherence issues. Further research in the area of DMHI needs to be done to identify who benefits the most from technology-based interventions (e.g., stand-alone self-help apps, therapy adjuncts, or therapy extenders) and when they should be utilized. Future work should also be done to tailor these interventions specifically for CBT for panic disorder and to improve user experience and design.

Self-efficacy (see Chap. 3) and anxiety sensitivity are potential key mechanisms of change in CBT for PD. Targeting these processes may support engagement via the optimization of CBT for PD. Emotional self-efficacy refers to an individual's confidence in their emotional functioning capabilities, including their ability to understand and manage their emotions (Kirk et al., 2008). Self-efficacy, in the context of panic, refers to an individual's belief in their ability to effectively use strategies to manage their PD symptoms (Casey et al., 2004). Emotional self-efficacy and panic-related self-efficacy have been seen to improve in the latter half of CBT (Gallagher et al., 2013; Kothari et al., 2024), whereas anxiety sensitivity symptoms (catastrophic negative thoughts) appear to improve most notably in the first part of treatment (Gallagher et al., 2013). Panic self-efficacy and anxiety sensitivity could potentially be independent mediators of change, but further research with rigorous design is needed to draw firm conclusions (Fentz et al., 2014). Therapists can still work to develop and target anxiety sensitivity and self-efficacy early in treatment to promote gains, which could potentially mitigate risk for treatment drop-out as patients experience improvements.

Contextual Barriers

Contextual barriers to treatment of PD include psychosocial and cultural factors external to and within treatment that may hinder success. First, family dynamics play an important role in having a patient engage fully with CBT treatment. For instance, well-meaning family members might accommodate the patient by adjusting their own behaviors to make their loved one feel better, often inadvertently reinforcing panic-related avoidance and dependence on the family member. For example, a family member might run important errands (e.g., going to the grocery store) for a loved one because they fear having a panic attack if they leave the house. Family accommodation can be treatment interfering and is related to the severity of symptoms and functional impact across anxiety disorders and obsessive-compulsive disorder (Lebowitz et al., 2016). In addition, there are within-treatment, contextual factors that may contribute to ending treatment early. These factors may include dissatisfaction with the treatment, the treatment procedures, the therapeutic relationship, or limited improvement (Keijers et al., 2001). Lack of cultural attunement by the therapist may also contribute to early termination due to variation in how PD symptoms present across cultures. For example, symptoms of PD can be experienced differently, and specific symptoms of panic may be endorsed at higher or lower rates across racial and ethnic groups (Barrera et al., 2010). As such, clients whose cultural context differs from a therapist's may not feel understood by the therapist. Further, if the therapist lacks familiarity with such variations in presentation, the consequence on alliance building, case conceptualization, and subsequent treatment planning could be significant. Further, lifetime prevalence of comorbid conditions such as anxiety disorders (93.6%), major depressive episodes (38.5%), and substance use disorders (37.3%) is extremely common among those with PD with agoraphobia (Kessler et al., 2006). It is important to consider these factors when developing a thoughtful treatment plan, which could potentially lead to higher treatment retention rates and better treatment outcomes.

Contextual Facilitators

It is crucial, therefore, for a clinician to extend psychoeducation of CBT treatment not only to the patient but also to their support system. As part of the psychoeducation process, the support system is given additional information about the treatment and learns how to avoid accommodation of avoidance behaviors. Therapists may provide psychoeducation related to the avoidance cycle and facilitate a conversation between the patient and their supports about not providing accommodation, even when it is requested by their loved one. Further, ensuring a shared, culturally responsive case conceptualization will help build rapport and enhance both the client's and therapist's understanding of treatment targets and goals. Importantly, factors related to the client's context should also be considered. For instance, exposures should be challenging, though objectively safe for that individual, tailored to the client's current context, and respect their values and culture. Therapists are encouraged to use shared decision-making—initially and throughout treatment—to personalize a treatment plan for PD that the client agrees with and does not pose a threat to their well-being given their current context, identities, and values.

Systemic Barriers

Systemic barriers are perhaps the most complicated to consider and overcome but must be recognized in the ways in which they impact the ability to receive CBT for PD. These barriers include the cost of mental health care, obtaining insurance coverage, getting an appointment with a mental health professional when demand is high and availability is limited, and getting through to the provider's office on the phone (Craske et al., 2005). Since the COVID-19 pandemic, these systemic barriers have become even more apparent. The 2022 COVID-19 Practitioner Impact Survey, conducted by the American Psychological Association (APA), surveyed 2295 clinicians and observed that psychologists noted increases in anxiety disorders among their patients but also highlighted that 60% of psychologists indicated that they had no openings for new patients (American Psychological Association, 2022).

Systemic Facilitators

Facilitating treatment on a system level requires a multifaceted and coordinated response that is beyond the scope of this chapter. Nonetheless, some areas are worth noting, as systems consider how to facilitate treatment for individuals with PD. Improving access to mental health resources and streamlining the intake process when initiating treatment are some factors that may assist in overcoming barriers to CBT treatment for PD (Craske et al., 2005). Psychotherapy provided over telehealth may also eliminate systemic barriers (as well as individual barriers) to receiving care. Compared to other anxiety disorders, internet-based CBT (iCBT) has been well researched among individuals with PD and has the potential to provide evidence-based care with less demand on therapist time. For instance, iCBT with minimal therapist support over email led to outcomes that were comparable to traditional in-person CBT for PD (Carlbring et al., 2005; Kiropoulos et al., 2008). Additionally, brief CBT for PD can potentially reduce the cost of psychiatric care and expand access to evidence-based care while still providing improvement in PD symptoms (Otto et al., 2012). Single-session interventions for PD may also be effective and show promise in reducing barriers to treatment access or engagement, although additional research in this area is needed with larger sample sizes (Mitsopoulou et al., 2020; Bertuzzi et al., 2021).

Clinical Strategies and Techniques for Promoting Treatment Engagement

To promote treatment engagement, therapists are encouraged to consider the use of the following treatment engagement strategies, which are further illustrated through case examples.

Encourage Persistence in Treatment

For various reasons, including stigma related to mental health treatment, cultural beliefs about mental illness, or level of familiarity with therapy, patients may be hesitant to begin or persist in treatment. Clinicians are encouraged to explore treatment-seeking beliefs, anticipate and problem solve potential barriers, and, if necessary, use motivational interviewing to support and encourage change efforts.

Disrupt Family Accommodation of Patient Symptoms

Family members or social supports may inadvertently engage in over-accommodating patients' avoidance behaviors, thus helping maintain panic symptoms. Clinicians are encouraged to provide psychoeducation to the patient and their loved ones to ensure supports are not changing their behaviors to make the patient feel better while in turn maintaining anxiety. It is important to disrupt these accommodations, but such interventions must be done compassionately, expressing an understanding as to why such behavioral patterns have become established in the first place.

Support Treatment Flexibility with Technology

Consistency is an important element of treatment engagement. Depending on their circumstances, clients may need flexibility from the therapist to support consistent engagement. Telehealth allows for greater flexibility and treatment consistency when treating panic disorder. Flexibility with using telehealth is especially helpful for groups that may find it difficult to attend in-person appointments, for example, those living in rural areas, students with busy schedules, or working parents. Previous research suggests CBT for panic via videoconferencing is noninferior to in-person therapy for panic and does not impact the ability to build a strong working alliance or complete key aspects of treatment (e.g., interoceptive exposures; Bouchard et al., 2020). Flexibility with telehealth at the onset of treatment may be particularly helpful for individuals struggling with panic-related agoraphobia. Therapists are also encouraged to consider how integrating technology solutions (e.g., mobile apps) may foster homework adherence to support engagement.

Implement a Culturally Responsive Case Conceptualization

Assessing how cultural factors and context might play a role in presenting problems is of great importance in case conceptualization and treatment planning. At a minimum, the therapist should assess idiosyncratic experiences of the physical sensations of panic, relevant interpretations as they relate to physical, somatic, and psychological symptoms, cultural and family beliefs about seeking treatment, and the client's important and potentially minoritized identities. This assessment will support alliance building and enable the therapist and client to collaboratively determine what aspects of their background may be key in the functional analysis of thoughts and behaviors. Together, this will be essential to forming a culturally responsive case conceptualization and treatment plan that supports the client's treatment engagement (see Chap. 9).

Attend to Concurrent Medication and Substance Use

Medication and substance use can interfere with treatment engagement. For instance, though benzodiazepines are prescribed to relieve PD symptoms, they only provide short-term relief and can lead to dependence and increased reliance on medications to feel panic relief. As such, it is crucial for clinicians to discuss benzodiazepine usage with patients and work collaboratively with medical professionals throughout CBT treatment. Similarly, alcohol use can reinforce avoidant behaviors, lead to a substance use disorder, and increase the severity of panic symptoms over time due to alcohol's influence on the body's chemical and physiological processes. Clinicians should provide psychoeducation related to alcohol use and offer information about how alcohol can impair learning in treatment, disrupt sleep patterns, and lead to increased feelings of anxiety and panic. A referral may also be made for treatment specifically for substance use. Depending on the extent to which alcohol use might interfere with the efficacy of CBT for PD, treatment may occur concurrently or prior to starting treatment for PD.

Case Example

Celine identified as a Black cisgender woman who studied art history and photography in New York City. She often visited museums for class assignments or during her free time with some of her friends in the art department at her college. When Celine visited one of her favorite museums to see a new photography exhibit a few months ago, she experienced her first panic attack. Celine described feeling extremely dizzy, her "heart beating outside of her chest," and "detached from herself." While everyone at the exhibit seemed to feel fine, Celine began to sweat and had trouble breathing. She wondered why this was happening to her and if she was going to die. Since that first panic attack, Celine has not gone back to that museum or any other museums in the city. This has interfered with her schoolwork—she missed several assignments that required reviewing art in various museums. Celine's mom was extremely concerned about her daughter and wanted to help in any way that she could, but she wasn't sure how, as no one in their family had ever sought mental health treatment before. Celine also avoided socializing with many of her friends in the art department, as she feared they would ask her to go to a crowded museum, and she might have another panic attack. As a result, she was feeling lonely and badly about doing poorly in school.

CBT Engagement Issue: Hesitancy for Treatment

For the first couple of sessions, Celine and her therapist worked through clinical assessments to get a better sense of symptom presence and intensity and to rule out any other medical conditions. Once the therapist gave Celine a diagnosis of panic disorder, they discussed treatment, including what CBT for panic disorder entails and the estimated duration of treatment. Her therapist provided psychoeducation, which Celine reported as helpful for better understanding why she was panicking. In addition, her therapist provided Celine's mother with handouts describing the CBT for panic treatment so that Celine's loved ones could learn about how to best support her during treatment.

Nevertheless, Celine was somewhat hesitant to engage in CBT, as she was unsure how therapy could make her feel better. She also had a very busy schedule and limited resources as a college student, which impacted her ability to fully engage in treatment. The following discussions between Celine and her therapist highlight how to build willingness and buy-in at various stages of treatment for PD, including psychoeducation and exposure.

Excerpts from Psychoeducation

Many patients have not engaged in therapy before they start panic treatment. The following excerpt illustrates how to provide psychoeducation around panic and CBT in general for someone who is new to treatment and unsure of its efficacy.

Therapist: Let's talk a bit about what's happening in your body when you experience those intense feelings of panic. Have you heard of the "fight or flight" response before?

Celine: I think I've heard the term, but I'm not entirely sure what it means.

Therapist: The fight or flight response is a natural and automatic reaction that our bodies have when we perceive a threat. It's a survival mechanism that's hardwired into our biology. When your brain senses danger, it sends signals to your body to prepare to either face the threat (fight) or run away from it (flight).

Celine: So, my body thinks there's a threat even though I'm just in a museum?

Therapist: Exactly. In places like museums where there might not be a physical threat, your body's alarm system can sometimes get triggered by something else, like crowded spaces or even just the idea of being in that environment. Your brain reacts as if there's a danger present, and that's why you might feel your heart racing, your breathing getting faster, and an overwhelming sense of fear.

Celine: That makes sense, but why does it feel so intense?

Therapist: Great question. When the fight or flight response is activated, your body releases hormones like adrenaline. These hormones help to prepare your body for action, like increasing your heart rate to pump more blood to your muscles so you can either fight or run. In situations where there isn't a real threat, like a museum, this response can feel overwhelming because your body is getting ready for something that isn't actually happening.

Celine: That's helpful to understand. But—I'm not quite sure how just talking about this will help me stop panicking when I'm in museums.

Therapist: That's a common concern! In CBT, we'll work together on changing the way you're thinking about your panic attacks, which is the cognitive portion of treatment—or the "C" in CBT. We'll also do many exercises to help you get used to the feelings of panic, like your heart race increasing, and practice approaching situations that might make you start to feel panicky. This is the behavioral portion of treatment—or the "B." By doing this, you'll get used to these panicky feelings and will be able to get back to going to museums without worrying about whether you'll panic. I'm confident that by the end of treatment, even if you do start to feel panicky for whatever reason, you'll be able to handle it.

Celine: Okay, that's helpful to understand what treatment will look like. It feels like less of a mystery now and makes more sense to me than what was described online.

Teaching point Many clients are hesitant to engage in exposure-based treatments for a variety of reasons, including lack of familiarity with CBT or therapy, beliefs about therapy, and time/resources. As such, meeting clients where they are and providing psychoeducation to emphasize the rationale for treatment is an important first step. Breaking down each aspect of CBT can help demystify the treatment and therapy in general. Therapists are encouraged to use the client's own words and examples when providing psychoeducation.

Excerpts from Exposures

Patients are often hesitant to get started with exposure exercises because they involve approaching the exact activity or feeling they have been trying so hard to avoid. The following excerpts from interoceptive and in vivo exposures demonstrate how to overcome this challenge in panic treatment.

Imaginal Exposure

Therapist: Today, we're going to work on a technique called imaginal exposure. This technique is designed to help you confront and reevaluate the anxious thoughts that contribute to your panic attacks. Are you open to giving it a try?

Celine: I'm willing to try anything that might help.

Therapist: Great, let's start by identifying a specific anxious thought related to your panic attacks. What's a thought that tends to go through your mind when you're feeling anxious or having a panic attack?

Celine: Well, lately I've just been having moments of terror where my heart races, I start shaking, and I feel like I can't breathe. I worry that I am going to pass out.

Therapist: Close your eyes and take a few slow, deep breaths. I'm going to guide you through a scenario. I want you to imagine that you're experiencing a panic attack right now. You might start feeling dizzy and lightheaded, and the fear of passing out might be intensifying.

Celine: Okay, but if I start feeling that way, I worry I'll actually have a panic attack and pass out. I'm not sure I want to do that.

Therapist: A scary thought! Let's examine it further. What do you think the likelihood of that happening is? Have you ever had a panic attack and passed out?

Celine: No.

Therapist: Okay—and what if you did pass out? What is the worst that might happen?

Celine: I guess it would be really scary and I'd feel out of control.

Therapist: That makes sense, panic attacks can feel scary. Why might you still do the exposure, even if there is a very low likelihood of passing out? How might doing the exposure fit with your goals in our treatment together?

Celine: Well…approaching the sensations would mean I'm not avoiding them. Which, like you've said, wouldn't feel so great in the short term, but will help me in the long run.

Therapist: Exactly. How are you feeling about trying one together, just to see what happens?

Celine: Okay, I'll give it a try since we're here together.

Therapist: That's great—I know this isn't easy. Okay, we'll start by picturing yourself in this scenario, let yourself experience the sensations and the fear. Notice any images, thoughts, or feelings that come up.

Celine: It's really uncomfortable. I can feel my heart racing.

Therapist: That's expected. Stay with the discomfort for a few more moments.

Celine: I'm trying to stay with this imagined scenario, but the fear is pretty strong. I really might need to stop.

Therapist: You're doing great, stick with that image. I'll check in with you in a few minutes. How are you doing?

Celine: I think it's starting to feel a bit less overwhelming.

Therapist: Stay with that image for a few more moments. Now, let's slowly bring the exercise to a close. Open your eyes and take a few deep breaths. How are you feeling now?

Celine: I'm a bit relieved that I made it through, even though it was just in my imagination. I was definitely uncomfortable though, and I still feel a little panicky.

Therapist: That's a significant step. Imaginal exposure is challenging, but it's an important tool for helping you confront your fears in a controlled way and you did it! You stuck with it and have shown great courage.

Celine: It's a process, but I can see how it might help.

Therapist: Absolutely, it's a gradual process that can lead to meaningful change. You said you still feel a little panicky—can you tell me more about that?

Celine: I guess since this is my first time doing this sort of exercise, it's still so new to me and a bit scary to work through some of the symptoms I'm experiencing.

Therapist: That makes a ton of sense! Of course it can feel scary to do something new, like face anxiety you've been avoiding for a long time. What did you learn about yourself today?

Celine: I guess that I can do it. That I did do it, even though it was hard. I guess, I can see how over time, this exercise is going to be very helpful in confronting, processing, and coping some of the physiological experiences I've been trying so hard to avoid.

Teaching point Clients with low self-efficacy related to handling their emotions may benefit from additional validation and acknowledgement of the successes they have had thus far. When a client is concerned or unsure about proceeding with an exposure, therapists are advised to reinforce the rationale for exposure. Asking patients to provide their own rationale and to link exposure back to their goals can be particularly helpful. Additionally, the therapist can help foster the formation of positive self-efficacy-related beliefs when processing the exposure.

Interoceptive Exposure

Therapist: I'd like to introduce a technique called "interoceptive exposures." It's a way to help you gradually become more comfortable with the physical sensations you experience during panic attacks. The idea is that as you confront these sensations in a controlled way, your body and mind can learn that they aren't as dangerous as they might feel.

Celine: So, you want me to intentionally make myself feel like I'm having a panic attack? I don't know if I can get on board with that—how would making myself feel worse help me get better?

Therapist: It's completely natural to feel a bit apprehensive, and you're right—it sounds paradoxical to induce the sensations that you've tried so hard to avoid. Remember, the goal is to help you build confidence in managing these sensations, so when you feel these sensations in real life, like if you're out with your friends at a museum, you feel prepared and ready to handle them.

Celine: I do want to be able to hang out with my friends without worrying about this…I really miss them. There are also a few new exhibits I'd like to see to help me prepare for my next term paper.

Therapist: Exactly—interoceptive exposures, though challenging at first, will gradually allow you to learn how to tolerate these very uncomfortable, scary feelings in service of doing these activities you enjoy.

Celine: Okay, I'm willing to at least give it a try. What do I need to do?

Celine: Great! We'll take it step by step at a pace that feels comfortable for you. To start, we'll practice experiencing a number of different physical sensations to determine which are most relevant for your experience of panic. Based on some of the symptoms you shared with me when we first met, this might include practice experiencing a rapid heart rate, shortness of breath, dizziness, or even tingling sensations. Right now, which of those options feels like something you'd be willing to try out first?

Teaching point Interoceptive exposures can be particularly daunting. Therapists are encouraged to meet clients where they are by starting with an exposure they are willing to try rather than arbitrarily starting with any particular number on their

SUDs scale. In other fear-based disorders, like OCD, research suggests that willingness to do an exposure is related to greater symptom reduction (Reid et al., 2017). As such, allowing the patient to start with exposures that they feel they can complete will likely build self-efficacy and ultimately increase the likelihood that they will continue with "harder" exposures.

In Vivo Exposure

Therapist: Now that we've gotten some practice with interoceptive exposure, let's talk about in vivo exposures, which involve facing your fears directly in real-life situations. The idea is to gradually and systematically expose yourself to the situations that trigger your panic attacks. By doing this, you give yourself the chance to learn that these situations aren't as dangerous as your mind might be telling you. I know you mentioned how important it is for you to visit art museums, but you haven't been able to go to some of these places. Can you tell me more about this?

Celine: Sure…I haven't been going for a couple of reasons, I guess. The big museum I was referring to I try to avoid because I worry I'll have a panic attack there. But I've also avoided some other smaller museums around the city, too. One time when I was at a smaller museum, I was walking around the gift shop for a while trying to pick out a gift for my mom. I was taking my time, and I noticed I was being followed by the museum security. Looking around at the time, I was the only person of color, and I really felt I was being followed for that reason. Because of that, I've been worried about going back to smaller museums out of fear they might accuse me of stealing or something else.

Therapist: I'm very sorry to hear that happened to you. It must have been unsettling and maybe even scary to have been targeted because of your racial identity. As we work together to build an exposure plan, we want to make sure you're practicing exposure in situations that are objectively safe. I would never ask you to go into a situation where you are a target of racial discrimination. However, we may want to consider how to practice getting to the big museum, because it sounds like in that situation you specifically fear having a panic attack. With any exposure, we'll assess together the reason why you avoid those places, and only choose those you avoid for the purpose of avoiding panic. Do you have any questions about that?

Celine: No, that makes sense.

Therapist: For the situations we decide are safe to practice confronting, we'll do it in a careful and gradual way. It's about taking small steps that build your confidence over time. Remember, the goal isn't to overwhelm you, but rather to help you learn that you can handle these situations without experiencing a panic attack.

Celine: Okay. I am thinking it will take a lot for me to work both going to museums and coming here for therapy into my schedule, especially since it's coming up on midterms week. Plus, even with my student discount, it can be expensive for me to go to a museum without a reason for a class or for a specific exhibit.

Therapist: Completely understandable—you have a lot going on! We'll work together to create an exposure plan that is feasible and fits with your schedule the best we can. This plan will start with situations that are a bit challenging but manageable for you. Something that can be helpful for busy students is doing some sessions virtually, so we can be a little more flexible around your schedule. You would still need to find a private space, which I know can be difficult on campus—but how would that sound?

Celine: That would be a huge help actually. I can probably make it work if that's the case. I'll be honest, though—virtual or in-person, I'm just very nervous to go at all. Maybe you can give me an example of what an exposure might look like?

Therapist: Of course. Let's say right now going to a museum feels like a 10 on your anxiety scale, with 10 being the most anxiety-provoking. We'll begin with a situation that's maybe a 3 or 4 on that scale. It could be spending a short amount of time near a museum or looking at pictures of artworks from museums.

Celine: That doesn't sound too bad. When I go to the museum—could I bring someone with me? I'd be worried about going alone.

Therapist: We want to find a starting point that doesn't overwhelm you—I know your mom mentioned she wants to help—so you might start by taking her with you. Once you feel comfortable with that step, we'll gradually move up the ladder, facing more challenging situations—like going by yourself on a crowded weekend day. The goal is for you to build confidence and prove to yourself that you can handle these situations without a panic attack.

Celine: That sounds good about bringing my mom. I'll feel a little safer knowing she is there—she can help me get out of the museum if I start panicking or can calm me down. She's really good at that.

Therapist: Ah—so I understand why you would want your mom there to start with exposures—however, I'll ask you and your mom to make an agreement about what her supportive role might look like. We want to make sure that your mom serves as a support if you need help staying in the exposure, not an escape from the exposure. Does that make sense?

Celine: Oh, okay. So, having my mom calm me down might be a way to avoid feeling panicky?

Therapist: Exactly! We want to make sure you learn that you can handle these uncomfortable feelings on your own without escaping them. If it's helpful and okay with you, we can discuss this with your mom before you do your first exposure together so we are all have a good sense of the plan.

Celine: That would be great, I know she really wants to help. So, if these initial exposures go okay, how will I know when to move to the next step?

Therapist: That's a great question, and it's great to hear you're already thinking about next steps. We'll work collaboratively on this. If you feel that a particular step is becoming easier for you and isn't causing intense anxiety, that's a sign that you're ready to move up the ladder. If you ever feel overwhelmed, we can take a step back and adjust the plan. Let's work on creating that ladder now, which we call the fear hierarchy.

Teaching Point Functional assessment related to avoidance is especially important. For instance, Celine's experience of racial profiling and subsequent avoidance of that museum is neither maladaptive nor a consequence of panic disorder, and thus exposure should not challenge adaptive avoidance given that her safety may be at risk in that space. Additionally, flexibility is key. When possible, allowing telehealth appointments may increase a client's ability to consistently attend appointments. Further, therapists can work on building readiness to engage in treatment through motivational interviewing, identifying the patient's values, and connecting back to a patient's treatment goals. If a patient is hesitant to get started with between-session exposures, it may be helpful to build willingness by designing an exposure hierarchy that involves a trusted person, like a family member or close friend. We suggest providing psychoeducation to this person to avoid overaccommodation during the exposure, which can act as a form of avoidance.

Conclusion

Cognitive behavioral therapy is an effective treatment for panic disorder, but some patients do not access treatment, under-engage or drop out early from treatment, or remain symptomatic after treatment. While much of the CBT for panic disorder literature focuses on efficacy, additional empirical attention is needed on issues of engagement, adherence, and retention to foster optimal outcomes. Notable advances that have been made include the use of telehealth or self-guided, internet-based CBT for PD, brief or single-session interventions for PD, technology-based enhancements of treatment such as smartphone applications to record homework and thus promote between-session engagement, and more targeted treatments that focus on specific mechanisms of change such as self-efficacy or anxiety sensitivity. Practically, it is important for clinicians to create a personalized and accessible course of treatment and to be attentive to engagement in treatment at all stages of CBT to maximize its effectiveness. Clinicians can support engagement by implementing a thorough evaluation session, reviewing relevant barriers to treatment, considering culture and context, discussing treatment options in a manner that emphasizes shared decision-making, fostering flexibility, supporting self-efficacy, enhancing motivation, and remaining aware of PD-specific avoidance behaviors that may undermine engagement. This process will occur throughout treatment, as the clinician will continue to monitor potential barriers to treatment engagement to maximize outcomes.

Clinical Summary Points and Recommendations

- Engagement is a significant issue in CBT for PD, with dropout rates as high as 20% (White et al., 2010; Keijers et al., 2001).
- Techniques such as motivational interviewing and cognitive restructuring can help increase willingness to engage in panic-related interoceptive and in vivo exposures. In turn, patients will build self-efficacy and feel more prepared for real-life encounters with panic-related sensations and situations.
- Continual assessment of individual (e.g., benzodiazepine use) and contextual (e.g., family accommodation) treatment-interfering factors will enhance treatment engagement and symptom improvements. Providers are encouraged to provide consistent psychoeducation to patients and their family members related to these factors.
- Incorporating technology into treatment (e.g., tracking via apps) may help facilitate greater engagement in homework and therefore better overall treatment outcomes.

References

American Psychiatric Association (Ed.). (2013). *Diagnostic and statistical manual of mental disorders: DSM-5* (5th ed., p. 947). American Psychiatric Association.

American Psychological Association. (2022). *2022 covid-19 practitioner impact survey*. American Psychological Association. https://www.apa.org/pubs/reports/practitioner/2022-covid-psychologist-workload

Arch, J. J., & Craske, M. G. (2009). First-line treatment: A critical appraisal of cognitive behavioral therapy developments and alternatives. *Psychiatric Clinics, 32*(3), 525–547

Baker, A. W., & Levine, D. S. (2023). Cognitive-behavioral therapy for panic disorder. In *The Massachusetts General Hospital handbook of cognitive behavioral therapy* (pp. 81–93). Springer International.

Benatti, B., Camuri, G., Dell'Osso, B., Cremaschi, L., Sembira, E., Palazzo, C., Oldani, L., Dobrea, C., Arici, C., Primavera, D., Carpiniello, B., Castellano, F., Carrà, G., Clerici, M., Baldwin, D. S., & Altamura, A. C. (2016). Which factors influence onset and latency to treatment in generalized anxiety disorder, panic disorder, and obsessive-compulsive disorder? *International Clinical Psychopharmacology, 31*(6), 347–352. https://doi.org/10.1097/YIC.0000000000000137

Bertuzzi, V., Fratini, G., Tarquinio, C., Cannistrà, F., Granese, V., Giusti, E. M., et al. (2021). Single-session therapy by appointment for the treatment of anxiety disorders in youth and adults: A systematic review of the literature. *Frontiers in Psychology, 12*, 721382.

Barrera, T. L., Wilson, K. P., & Norton, P. J. (2010). The experience of panic symptoms across racial groups in a student sample. *Journal of Anxiety Disorders, 24*(8), 873–878. https://doi.org/10.1016/j.janxdis.2010.06.010

Bouchard, S., Allard, M., Robillard, G., Dumoulin, S., Guitard, T., Loranger, C., Green-Demers, I., Marchand, A., Renaud, P., Cournoyer, L. G., & Corno, G. (2020). Videoconferencing psychotherapy for panic disorder and agoraphobia: Outcome and treatment processes from a non-randomized non-inferiority trial. *Frontiers in Psychology, 11*, 2164. https://doi.org/10.3389/fpsyg.2020.02164

Borghouts, J., Eikey, E., Mark, G., De Leon, C., Schueller, S., Schneider, M., Stadnick, N., Zheng, K., Mukamel, D., & Sorkin, D. (2021). Barriers to and facilitators of user engagement with digital mental health interventions. *Journal of Medical Internet Research, 23*(3), e24387. https://doi.org/10.2196/24387

Cackovic, C., Nazir, S., & Marwaha, R. (2023, January). Panic disorder. [Updated 2023 Aug 6]. In *StatPearls* [Internet]. StatPearls Publishing. https://www.ncbi.nlm.nih.gov/books/NBK430973/

Cammin-Nowak, S., Helbig-Lang, S., Lang, T., Gloster, A. T., Fehm, L., Gerlach, A. L., et al. (2013). Specificity of homework compliance effects on treatment outcome in CBT: Evidence from a controlled trial on panic disorder and agoraphobia. *Journal of Clinical Psychology, 69*(6), 616–629.

Carlbring, P., Nilsson-Ihrfelt, E., Waara, J., Kollenstam, C., Buhrman, M., Kaldo, V., et al. (2005). Treatment of panic disorder: Live therapy vs. self-help via the Internet. *Behaviour Research and Therapy, 43*(10), 1321–1333.

Casey, L. M., Oei, T. P., & Newcombe, P. A. (2004). An integrated cognitive model of panic disorder: The role of positive and negative cognitions. *Clinical Psychology Review, 24*(5), 529–555.

Craske, M. G., Edlund, M. J., Sullivan, G., Roy-Byrne, P., Sherbourne, C., Bystritsky, A., & Stein, M. B. (2005). Perceived unmet need for mental health treatment and barriers to care among patients with panic disorder. *Psychiatric Services, 56*(8), 988–994.

Conklin, L. R., Curreri, A. J., Farchione, T. J., & Barlow, D. H. (2021). Homework compliance and quality in cognitive behavioral therapies for anxiety disorders and obsessive-compulsive disorder. *Behavior Therapy, 52*(4), 1008–1018. https://doi.org/10.1016/j.beth.2021.01.001

Efron, G., & Wootton, B. M. (2021). Remote cognitive behavioral therapy for panic disorder: A meta-analysis. *Journal of Anxiety Disorders, 79*, 102385. https://doi.org/10.1016/j.janxdis.2021.102385

Fentz, H. N., Arendt, M., O'Toole, M. S., Hoffart, A., & Hougaard, E. (2014). The mediational role of panic self-efficacy in cognitive behavioral therapy for panic disorder: A systematic review and meta-analysis. *Behaviour Research and Therapy, 60*, 23–33.

Gallagher, M. W., Payne, L. A., White, K. S., Shear, K. M., Woods, S. W., Gorman, J. M., & Barlow, D. H. (2013). Mechanisms of change in cognitive behavioral therapy for panic disorder: The unique effects of self-efficacy and anxiety sensitivity. *Behaviour Research and Therapy, 51*(11), 767–777.

Gorman, J. M., & Coplan, J. D. (1996). Comorbidity of depression and panic disorder. *The Journal of Clinical Psychiatry, 57*, 34–41.

Heldt, E., Manfro, G. G., Kipper, L., Blaya, C., Isolan, L., & Otto, M. W. (2006). One-year follow-up of pharmacotherapy-resistant patients with panic disorder treated with cognitive-behavior therapy: Outcome and predictors of remission. *Behaviour Research and Therapy, 44*(5), 657–665.

Huppert, J. D., Barlow, D. H., Gorman, J. M., Shear, M. K., & Woods, S. W. (2006). The interaction of motivation and therapist adherence predicts outcome in cognitive behavioral therapy for panic disorder: Preliminary findings. *Cognitive and Behavioral Practice, 13*(3), 198–204.

Keefe, J. R., Chambless, D. L., Barber, J. P., & Milrod, B. L. (2021). Predictors and moderators of treatment dropout in cognitive-behavioral and psychodynamic therapies for panic disorder. *Psychotherapy Research: Journal of the Society for Psychotherapy Research, 31*(4), 432–442. https://doi.org/10.1080/10503307.2020.1784487

Keijsers, G. P., Kampman, M., & Hoogduin, C. A. (2001). Dropout prediction in cognitive behavior therapy for panic disorder. *Behavior Therapy, 32*(4), 739–749.

Kessler, R. C., Chiu, W. T., Jin, R., Ruscio, A. M., Shear, K., & Walters, E. E. (2006). The epidemiology of panic attacks, panic disorder, and agoraphobia in the National Comorbidity Survey Replication. *Archives of General Psychiatry, 63*(4), 415–424. https://doi.org/10.1001/archpsyc.63.4.415

Kiropoulos, L. A., Klein, B., Austin, D. W., Gilson, K., Pier, C., Mitchell, J., & Ciechomski, L. (2008). Is internet-based CBT for panic disorder and agoraphobia as effective as face-to-face CBT? *Journal of Anxiety Disorders, 22*(8), 1273–1284.

Kirk, B. A., Schutte, N. S., & Hine, D. H. (2008). Development and preliminary validation of an emotional self-efficacy scale. *Personality and Individual Differences, 45*(5), 432–436. https://doi.org/10.1016/j.paid.2008.06.010

Kothari, D., Robinaugh, D. J., Kabel, K. E., Coppersmith, D. L., & Baker, A. W. (2024). *Cognitive behavioral therapy for panic disorder increases emotional self-efficacy* [Poster Abstract]. Association for Behavioral and Cognitive Therapies (ABCT) 57th Annual Convention, Seattle, WA.

Lai, H. M. X., Cleary, M., Sitharthan, T., & Hunt, G. E. (2015). Prevalence of comorbid substance use, anxiety and mood disorders in epidemiological surveys, 1990–2014: A systematic review and meta-analysis. *Drug and Alcohol Dependence, 154*, 1–13.

Lebowitz, E. R., Panza, K. E., & Bloch, M. H. (2016). Family accommodation in obsessive-compulsive and anxiety disorders: A five-year update. *Expert Review of Neurotherapeutics, 16*(1), 45–53.

McHugh, R. K., Otto, M. W., Barlow, D. H., Gorman, J. M., Shear, M. K., & Woods, S. W. (2007). Cost-efficacy of individual and combined treatments for panic disorder. *Journal of Clinical Psychiatry, 68*(7), 1038.

Mitsopoulou, T., Kasvikis, Y., Koumantanou, L., Giaglis, G., Skapinakis, P., & Mavreas, V. (2020). Manualized single-session behavior treatment with self-help manual for panic disorder with or without agoraphobia. *Psychotherapy Research, 30*(6), 776–787.

Otto, M. W., & Deveney, C. (2005). Cognitive-behavioral therapy and the treatment of panic disorder: Efficacy and strategies. *Journal of Clinical Psychiatry, 66*(Suppl 4), 28–32.

Otto, M. W., Tolin, D. F., Nations, K. R., Utschig, A. C., Rothbaum, B. O., Hofmann, S. G., & Smits, J. A. (2012). Five sessions and counting: Considering ultra-brief treatment for panic disorder. *Depression and Anxiety, 29*(6), 465–470.

Papola, D., Ostuzzi, G., Tedeschi, F., Gastaldon, C., Purgato, M., Del Giovane, C., et al. (2023). CBT treatment delivery formats for panic disorder: A systematic review and network meta-analysis of randomised controlled trials. *Psychological Medicine, 53*(3), 614–624.

Rabasco, A., McKay, D., Smits, J. A., Powers, M. B., Meuret, A. E., & McGrath, P. B. (2022). Psychosocial treatment for panic disorder: An umbrella review of systematic reviews and meta-analyses. *Journal of Anxiety Disorders, 86*, 102528.

Rees, C. S., McEvoy, P., & Nathan, P. R. (2005). Relationship between homework completion and outcome in cognitive behaviour therapy. *Cognitive Behaviour Therapy, 34*(4), 242–247.

Reid, A. M., Garner, L. E., Van Kirk, N., Gironda, C., Krompinger, J. W., Brennan, B. P., Mathes, B. M., Monaghan, S. C., Tifft, E. D., André, M. C., Cattie, J., Crosby, J. M., & Elias, J. A. (2017). How willing are you? Willingness as a predictor of change during treatment of adults with obsessive-compulsive disorder. *Depression and Anxiety, 34*(11), 1057–1064. https://doi.org/10.1002/da.22672

Rollnick, S., & Miller, W. R. (1995). What is motivational interviewing? *Behavioural and Cognitive Psychotherapy, 23*(4), 325–334.

Rayburn, N. R., & Otto, M. W. (2003). Cognitive-behavioral therapy for panic disorder: A review of treatment elements, strategies, and outcomes. *CNS Dpectrums, 8*(5), 356–362.

Tang, W., & Kreindler, D. (2017). Supporting homework compliance in cognitive behavioural therapy: Essential features of mobile apps. *JMIR Mental Health, 4*(2), e5283.

Tzavela, E. C., Mitskidou, P., Mertika, A., Stalikas, A., & Kasvikis, Y. (2018). Treatment engagement in the early phase of cognitive-behavior therapy for panic disorder: A grounded theory analysis of patient experience. *Psychotherapy Research, 28*(6), 842–860.

Westra, H. A., Arkowitz, H., & Dozois, D. J. (2009). Adding a motivational interviewing pretreatment to cognitive behavioral therapy for generalized anxiety disorder: A preliminary randomized controlled trial. *Journal of Anxiety Disorders, 23*(8), 1106–1117.

Westra, H. A., Constantino, M. J., & Antony, M. M. (2016). Integrating motivational interviewing with cognitive-behavioral therapy for severe generalized anxiety disorder: An allegiance-controlled randomized clinical trial. *Journal of Consulting and Clinical Psychology, 84*(9), 768.

White, K. S., Allen, L. B., Barlow, D. H., Gorman, J. M., Shear, M. K., & Woods, S. W. (2010). Attrition in a multicenter clinical trial for panic disorder. *The Journal of Nervous and Mental Disease, 198*(9), 665–671.

Chapter 14
Obsessive-Compulsive Disorder

Michael G. Wheaton

Background

Obsessive-compulsive disorder (OCD) is a neuropsychiatric disorder that is estimated to have a worldwide prevalence rate of 1.3% (Fawcett et al., 2020). OCD is characterized by impairing and/or distressing obsessions (intrusive thoughts and bothersome thoughts, images, or urges to complete actions) that provoke distress, which are typically coupled with compulsions, defined as mental or behavioral acts that function to relieve distress or prevent feared consequences (APA, 2013). Empirical and theoretical work (e.g., Mataix-Cols et al., 2005; McKay et al., 2004) has identified four "symptom dimensions": (1) contamination-related obsessions and compulsive washing/cleaning, (2) fears of being responsible for harm or making mistakes coupled with checking compulsions, (3) unacceptable/taboo thoughts relating to violence, sexual, and/or religious themes, and (4) concerns relating to the need for symmetry, order, and completion. OCD symptoms typically begin during childhood and adolescence, with OCD having a median onset age around 19 years old (Anholt et al., 2014). These symptoms tend to follow a chronic course when not adequately treated (APA, 2013). Importantly, OCD symptoms are impairing not only for sufferers but also cause societal burden in terms of economic impact (i.e., work impairment) and health care costs (Murray & Lopez, 1996).

Effective treatments have been developed for OCD, including medication and psychotherapy. Serotonin reuptake inhibitors (SRIs) are the first-line medications prescribed to treat OCD (Koran & Simpson, 2013) but typically lead to only a partial reduction in symptoms (Skapinakis et al., 2016). The most extensively tested and empirically supported psychotherapy for OCD is a form of cognitive-behavioral

M. G. Wheaton (✉)
Department of Psychology, Barnard College, New York, NY, USA
e-mail: mwheaton@barnard.edu

E. M. Goetter (ed.), *Optimizing Treatment Engagement Processes in CBT for Anxiety and Related Disorders*, CBT: Science Into Practice,
https://doi.org/10.1007/978-3-031-91439-3_14

therapy (CBT) consisting of exposure and response/ritual prevention (ERP). Meta-analyses consistently report that ERP effectively reduces OCD symptoms in both adult (Öst et al., 2015) and child/adolescent samples (McGuire et al., 2015) with large effect sizes. In fact, ERP is often considered the "gold standard" OCD treatment and is recommended as a first-line treatment in practice guidelines, including the American Psychiatric Association's practice guidelines (Koran & Simpson, 2013) as well as the United Kingdom's National Institute for Health and Care Excellence (NICE) evidence-based recommendations (NICE, 2013). However, ERP is not universally effective. Although approximately 75–80% of recipients typically experience a treatment response with a standard course of ERP, only about half experience remission (Simpson et al., 2006; Whittal & McLean, 1999). New data suggest that adding additional ERP sessions can improve remission rates (e.g., up to ~70%; Simpson et al., 2021). However, a substantial subgroup of individuals are not fully helped by ERP. Moreover, others end treatment prematurely, with premature discontinuation rates of ~20% typically reported (Ong et al., 2016; Stanley & Turner, 1995).

Although various factors have been investigated as potential contributors to poor outcomes with ERP, one prominent factor has to do with patient engagement in treatment. Across multiple different patient groups and approaches to psychotherapy, engagement with the psychotherapy process appears to be a critically important component of successful treatment outcomes (Holdsworth et al., 2014). This chapter will focus specifically the issue of engagement in treatment with ERP for OCD.

Barriers to Successful Treatment Engagement

Practical Barriers

One category of variables that may affect ERP treatment engagement concerns a set of practical barriers that affect the ability of participants to seek, have access to, and utilize ERP.

In order to engage in ERP treatment, patients must have the ability to find community providers who are available and affordable to them. Problems of lack of access to ERP providers have been noted (Bekker et al., 2017) as not all community clinicians are trained in this specialized form of psychotherapy. Moreover, cost and affordability have been noted as barriers to ERP (Senter et al., 2021), as lack of access to health care and financial resources to afford ERP may be barriers for some OCD patients. To remedy these issues, new directions have been explored to increase the accessibility and cost-effectiveness of ERP.

One approach has been to disseminate ERP by training community clinicians to be able to administer this specialized form of CBT. Recent work has attempted to establish competency standards to inform, advance, and offer a model for clinical practice and training for OCD (Sookman et al., 2021). The International OCD

Foundation (IOCDF) runs the Behavior Therapy Training Institute (BTTI), a therapist training program designed to train therapists to deliver ERP for OCD, which has been found to increase utilization of ERP among clinicians (Reese et al., 2016). Recent work has also explored online training programs to disseminate ERP to community clinicians in practice, with promising results as completers of the online training had increased self-reported comfort in assessing and treating OCD and greater use of ERP (Jacoby et al. 2019).

Another promising approach to increase access and reduce costs has been the development of Internet-based approaches to delivering ERP for OCD (e.g., Andersson et al., 2012; Patel et al., 2018), which typically involve therapist support via either online messages or phone calls. These approaches have the practical advantage of being accessible nearly anywhere, making ERP available even in geographically remote locations where therapists might not be physically present. Although these forms of treatment are new, emerging data suggest they are cost-effective compared with face-to-face ERP (Lundström et al., 2022). Adoption of Internet-based CBT for OCD has been highly variable. Although this treatment has not yet proliferated widely in the United States, in other countries adoption has been much more widespread. For example, in Sweden, Internet-administered CBT is recommended in national guidelines for provision within Swedish primary care (Brantnell et al., 2020).

Another innovation to overcome practical barriers to ERP engagement has been the development of concentrated forms of treatment. Concentrating treatment may make treatment more affordable by reducing the number of sessions and the duration of treatment. Moreover, the shorter period of treatment means participants may have less disruption in seeking treatment (as compared to the typical 2–3 months of outpatient treatment), which may make treatment easier to engage with. For example, in the Bergen 4-day Treatment (B4DT), ERP is delivered over only four consecutive days. This approach has demonstrated positive results as up to 80–90% of patients show a treatment response (Kvale et al., 2018; Launes et al., 2019), and despite the brief treatment duration, positive treatment outcomes are generally maintained both at 1-year and even at 4-year follow-up (Hansen et al., 2018).

Intra-individual Barriers

Individual attitudes, beliefs, and behaviors also pose potential barriers to treatment. For patients with access to ERP providers, a prerequisite for engagement in ERP is willingness to receive it. In this regard, patient treatment preferences are key to willingness to engage with treatment. Research on treatment preferences among individuals with OCD shows that a majority of patients prefer ERP, though a sizable minority of patients report that they would prefer medications (Patel & Simpson, 2010). Importantly, preference for medication as an alternative to ERP may not actually diminish the effectiveness of ERP if patients are willing to try it: in a randomized controlled trial comparing risperidone to ERP (Simpson et al., 2013), prior to group assignment, patients were asked whether they preferred to be randomized to the medication or ERP. A subsequent analysis (Wheaton et al. 2016a, b) found that ERP was actually equally effective for those who stated that they would have preferred to receive risperidone, as they had equivalent OCD symptom reduction as compared to those who preferred ERP. These results suggest that ERP can be effective even for patients who do not list it as their first treatment preference.

Once ERP has begun, therapy tasks take significant effort on the part of the patient. ERP is an active, present-focused form of therapy in which patients are instructed to confront the situations that provoke obsessional distress via exposures. These practices frequently take up to 90 min and involve purposefully experiencing distress. Moreover, both during exposure trials and in between exposures, patients practice response/ritual prevention in which they are instructed to refrain from engaging in compulsive behaviors. Therefore, the intensive and potentially stressful nature of ERP requires substantial commitment from patients. In particular, unwillingness to endure the distress associated with ERP is a potential intra-individual barrier to successful engagement with ERP therapy tasks. Several contributing factors linked to OCD may serve as potential barriers to engagement in ERP, as measured prior to treatment. For example, some research linked OCD to distress tolerance, finding that individuals with OCD have greater difficulty tolerating distress than healthy controls (Cougle et al., 2011). Similarly, cross-sectional research has linked OCD to the construct of experiential avoidance (EA), which has been defined as an unwillingness to experience or remain in contact with unpleasant emotions, thoughts, and sensations coupled with deliberate attempts to escape from and avoid these experiences (Hayes et al., 1996). Specifically, OCD symptoms have been associated with heightened EA as reported in a recent meta-analysis (Angelakis & Pseftogianni, 2021).

Treatment Engagement and Its Relation to Treatment Outcomes in ERP

Assessing engagement in ERP is challenging given the multicomponent nature of the treatment. In one seminal study, Abramowitz et al. (2002) collected ratings on engagement with ERP tasks from the clinicians who treated 28 adults with OCD with ERP at a fee for service clinic. The ratings separated out four different components of ERP treatment: (1) patient understanding the treatment rationale; (2) compliance with in-session exposure instructions; (3) compliance with between-session homework exposure instructions; and (4) completion of self-monitoring forms. For each of these ERP components, therapists rated patients using a Likert-type scales ranging from 0 (poor) to 6 (outstanding). Patients who demonstrated a clinically significant treatment response had significantly higher ratings on the extent to which they understood the treatment rationale and were more compliant with both within-session exposures and exposure homework. Compliance ratings for completion of self-monitoring forms were not associated with ERP outcomes.

Engagement with within-session procedures has been assessed in some studies (Leeuwerik et al., 2019), but the majority of research on engagement in ERP has focused on compliance with between-session therapy tasks (i.e., "homework assignments"), which is understandable given that within-session compliance occurs under the supervision of the therapist (Leeuwerik et al., 2019). As recently reviewed (Wheaton & Chen, 2021), numerous studies find a significant association between engagement with ERP homework tasks and ERP outcomes. For example, in a secondary analysis of an ERP trial, De Araujo (1996) reported on the association between early homework compliance (during the first week of treatment) and posttreatment outcomes. Results showed that successful completion of homework tasks (quantified as percentage completed) predicted change in scores on the YBOCS (Goodman et al., 1989a, b; assessing obsession and compulsion severity separately), as well as greater improvement on the CGI (Guy, 1976) at posttreatment. In addition, early compliance predicted improvement assessed at 32-week follow-up.

In order to track patient engagement with ERP tasks, Simpson et al. (2010b) developed the Patient ERP Adherence Scale (PEAS). This scale consists of three items, which are completed by the clinician at each session. The first two items track the percent of homework exposures completed and their quality, respectively. The third item involves rating success with ritual prevention (by calculating the percent of compulsions that the patient was able to successfully resist engaging in). Among a sample of 30 adults with OCD receiving ERP, Simpson et al. (2011) reported that completion of ERP homework as assessed by the PEAS predicted posttreatment OCD severity (outcomes) as well as likelihood of remission (defined as minimal OCD symptoms at posttreatment). Moreover, a subsequent study in this sample showed that adherence to between-session homework also predicted long-term ERP outcome, as PEAS scores measured during ERP treatment predicted OCD severity at 6-month follow-up (Simpson et al., 2012). A subsequent study in an independent sample of 37 adults who received ERP as part of a clinical trial replicated the finding that adherence to ERP homework predicts ERP outcomes (Wheaton et al. 2016a, b). In addition, the authors analyzed the three PEAS items separately and found that PEAS item C, which assesses success with between-session response prevention practice, was particularly strongly related to treatment outcomes, above and beyond compliance with homework exposures. In particular, engagement with response prevention accurately forecast which patients would achieve remission later in treatment (Wheaton et al. 2016a, b). In summary, there is strong support between the degree of engagement and treatment outcome with ERP for OCD.

Predictors of Treatment Engagement in ERP

Given the importance of engagement in ERP therapy tasks, it is important to identify variables that predict poor engagement, given that individuals demonstrating these vulnerabilities are presumably at risk for poorer outcomes. One early study identified low motivation as a factor in problems with engagement: Foa et al. (1983) surveyed clinical observations on why nearly 100 OCD patients refused or dropped out of ERP treatment and found that a "lack of motivation" was a key factor, though this finding should be caveated by the potential for biased responses among clinicians.

Several investigations have explored factors associated with homework completion in the context of ERP, using the PEAS as an indicator of ERP homework adherence. In a subsequent analysis of data derived from the initial PEAS sample, Maher et al. (2012) investigated baseline variables that significantly correlated with subsequent PEAS scores. Six baseline variables demonstrated a positive association with enhanced homework completion: higher patient assessments of quality of the therapeutic alliance, greater expectations for treatment success, increased readiness for change, reduced levels of work impairment, fewer hoarding symptoms, and heightened treatment readiness (based on the readiness ruler). In a final regression model with these six potential predictors, only the strength of the working alliance, readiness for treatment, and fewer hoarding symptoms emerged as significant independent predictors of homework engagement. Notably, these factors also predicted outcomes of ERP, with a significant indirect effect through adherence to ERP homework. These findings suggest that patients exhibiting fewer hoarding symptoms, higher readiness for change, and a robust working alliance with their therapist are more likely to engage in treatment (i.e., adhere to homework tasks), resulting in OCD symptom improvement.

In a subsequent investigation that utilized an independent sample, Wheaton et al. (2016a, b) attempted to replicate the earlier finding that the strength of the therapeutic alliance serves as a predictor for improved outcomes in ERP via engagement (i.e., enhanced patient adherence to homework). However, results showed that the overall strength of the alliance as rated by patients on the Working Alliance Inventory-Short Form (WAI; Hatcher & Gillapsy, 2006) did not significantly predict outcomes in ERP in a group of patients ($n = 37$) undergoing this treatment. Notably, a subsequent analysis focusing on WAI subscales revealed a significant predictive association between the Task subscale (i.e., agreement on therapy tasks) and ERP outcomes (adjusted for baseline severity on the YBOCS). Additionally, the strength of the working alliance as pertains to therapy-related tasks emerged as a predictor of homework adherence (i.e., PEAS scores), with a meditational analysis suggesting that increased completion of homework mediated the connection between task-alliance and enhanced treatment outcomes (Wheaton et al. 2016a, b). In sum, these findings suggest that a high level of agreement between the therapist and patient regarding therapy tasks (assessed prior to beginning exposure homework) is associated with enhanced engagement with subsequent ERP homework, which in turn is associated with a reduction in OCD symptoms.

Dowling et al. (2016) utilized a modified version of the PEAS to quantify engagement with ERP tasks during intensive residential treatment for OCD, a modality that relies on extensive ERP tasks. Results showed that improved adherence to ERP tasks, as measured by PEAS scores, was associated with higher levels of treatment readiness, enhanced insight, and reduced avoidance. Similarly, in a recent investigation involving outpatients undergoing twice-weekly ERP, Wheaton et al. (2018) observed that individuals exhibiting significant behavioral avoidance at baseline (defined as moderate or severe avoidance on the YBOCS avoidance item) demonstrated lower PEAS levels throughout treatment, indicating poorer engagement with homework. Furthermore, the diminished adherence to between-session ERP tasks served as a significant mediating factor in the relationship between baseline avoidance and unfavorable treatment outcomes (Wheaton et al., 2018). Lastly, in a study involving 49 youth with OCD, Lewin et al. (2011) noted a significant correlation between homework compliance and pretreatment treatment expectations as reported by both parents and treating clinicians. Specifically, when parents and clinicians held more optimistic expectations regarding the treatment's effectiveness, there was a higher level of homework completion and, subsequently, a greater improvement in OCD symptoms.

Taken together, these findings underscore how important engagement with between-session homework is to successful outcomes in ERP. Additionally, these findings highlight the importance of fostering a strong working alliance (particularly agreement on therapeutic tasks), ensuring readiness, targeting avoidance, and promoting positive treatment expectations, which appear to promote outcomes indirectly via homework compliance.

Clinical Considerations That Pertain to ERP Engagement

Before describing strategies to maximize ERP engagement, it is important to consider patients for whom engaging with ERP may *not* be appropriate. In particular, the data reviewed above suggest that patients with hoarding symptoms seem to have lower ERP engagement. The majority of these studies considered hoarding as a symptom of OCD and predate the publication of DSM-5 (American Psychiatric Association, 2013), which established hoarding disorder as an independent condition. Therefore, rather than ERP, individuals with hoarding symptoms should be recommended to engage in hoarding-specific treatment (Tolin et al., 2015).

In addition, depression (particularly when severe) might be a clinical consideration that precludes initiation of ERP. The research literature is mixed in terms of whether comorbid depression predicts worse ERP outcomes. Some studies find no association, while others suggest that depression may interfere with ERP when the depression is severe. For example, Anholt et al. (2011) found no association between depression and ERP outcome when analyzed continuously or categorically (present/absent comorbid depression). However, Abramowitz et al. (2000) analyzed depression with thresholded categories for severity and found that participants with severe comorbid depression had worse ERP outcomes. Severe depression, which includes amotivation and lack of energy, might make engagement with ERP more challenging for some. In addition, patients who are expressing active suicidal thoughts or behaviors would require additional clinical attention and would not be appropriate for ERP. These patients might begin treatment for depression prior to treatment for their OCD. However, patients who are not suicidal and are able to engage with ERP often find that depressive symptoms improve along with OCD (Wheaton & Gallina, 2019), and indeed a meta-analysis of the literature failed to find a consistent link between depression and OCD treatment outcomes with CBT (Knopp et al., 2013). Therefore, thorough risk assessments, collaborative discussions with patients, and clinical judgment are required when deciding whether to begin ERP with patients experiencing OCD with comorbid depression. Moreover, this is something that may require ongoing assessment throughout treatment.

Clinical Strategies for Engaging Patients with OCD in ERP

The research literature reviewed above has direct clinical implications for the successful treatment of OCD using ERP. Specifically, the data are clear that engagement with treatment is a critical factor in ERP treatment outcomes. To benefit from treatment, recipients of ERP need to be able to access the treatment, but merely attending therapy sessions is not sufficient to expect positive outcomes. Rather, it seems that effort and engagement with therapy tasks robustly account for success. Engagement with multiple treatment elements has been found to relate to the degree of subsequent improvement. From these data, it is possible to draw clinical recommendations for treating OCD with ERP.

Provide Clear Psychoeducation About the Rationale for ERP

It is essential to provide an adequate rationale for the procedures involved in ERP in order for patients to be willing to engage in them. It is important to frame the rationale in a way that is understandable in plain terms and uses examples from the patients' own experiences. Typically, this involves describing anxiety as the body's alarm system, which like any alarm system, can have false alarms. The process of exposures is to recalibrate the alarm to see that the situations and stimuli that provoke obsessional distress are less dangerous than they seem. At the same time, ritual prevention is framed as a way to reduce reliance on compulsive behaviors as a way to relieve anxiety and prevent feared consequences. Newer approaches to conducting exposures, as exemplified in inhibitory learning approaches (Craske et al., 2008, 2014), can also help to frame exposures as learning opportunities seeking to test threat expectancies while encoding new memories (i.e., safety learning).

Treatment expectations also seem to predict engagement in ERP, such that patients who have greater expectancy of improvement have greater engagement and thereby better outcomes. This factor might be promoted through education about the potency of ERP (with the caveat that treatment works best with substantial effort), helping patients to develop positive expectancies about their ability to utilize treatment to reduce OCD symptoms.

Develop a Strong Working Alliance Pertaining to Therapy Tasks

The literature reviewed above highlights that having a strong therapeutic working relationship can aid in patient engagement, particularly mutual agreement on therapy tasks. Making sure that patients feel supported by the clinician, while at the same time explicitly agreeing on which tasks will be completed in treatment (both within-sessions and as homework) seems key in this regard (see Chap. 2). Treatment guides (e.g., Abramowitz, 2006) caution against cajoling or coercing patients into doing particular exposures. Rather, disagreements might be resolved by collaboratively revisiting treatment goals. In addition, exposures that are deemed too difficult might be made easier by lowering the intensity of the exposure, or the therapist might volunteer to participate in the exposure to serve as a role model.

Track Patient Engagement in Treatment

Paying attention to treatment engagement is critical to identify when problems with poor engagement arise. The PEAS (Simpson et al. 2010a, b) represents a useful tool to assess completion of between-session therapy tasks. In particular, data suggest that tracking patient engagement in response prevention can be used as an efficient barometer to predict and forecast the likelihood of treatment success (Wheaton et al. 2016a, b). Specifically, by asking patients at each session, "What percent of compulsive rituals have you been able to successfully resist since our last meeting?" clinicians can gauge engagement in ERP and better predict treatment outcome.

Resolve Practical Barriers and Utilize Reminders to Ensure Homework Compliance

In improving engagement with treatment, particularly as pertains to compliance with homework assignments, it is important to develop clear assignments that are achievable and realistic for the patient to complete (e.g., considering work schedules, time commitment, etc.). While assigning homework, a clinician might even ask, "*What barriers to completing these assignments do you anticipate?*" and "*How could we plan to resolve such obstacles?*" For example, a patient may say they have difficulty doing 1 h per day of exposure homework due to a busy work schedule, and the therapist might work with the patient to be creative in designing exposures that could be done at work or during their commute. Many patients find that scheduling their homework at a dedicated time in their calendar makes it easier to remember to complete. In addition, between-session phone calls can be utilized to check in on homework completion, with positive effects (Wheaton & Chen, 2021).

Utilize Motivational Work When Needed

Given the importance of client motivation to successful engagement in ERP, Foa et al. (1983), several strategies have been treatment tested to enhance motivation. In particular, some data suggest motivational interviewing (MI) can increase treatment motivation in conjunction with ERP (Zuckoff et al., 2014; see Chap. 4). MI involves strengthening a person's own motivation and commitment to change through particular attention to the language of change (Miller & Rollnick, 2013). Briefly, in MI, motivational challenges are thought to relate to ambivalence about change, and the therapist uses nonconfrontational questions and reflective listening to invite the patient to talk about why and how they might change (change talk) to resolve ambivalence by eliciting talk in which the patient advocates for change. Simpson et al. (2008) developed a protocol to integrate MI with ERP by developing an MI module to be used in sessions wherein patients were unwilling to engage in exposures or did not complete agreed-upon homework. Specifically, treatment involved a dedication session during the planning phase of treatment to discuss the patients' motivation for treatment, as well as an MI module that could be employed during subsequent ERP sessions when issues of low motivation emerged. Positive results were found in an open pilot trial (Simpson et al., 2008), but a subsequent randomized controlled trial found that ERP+MI was not superior to ERP alone on average (Simpson et al. 2010a, b). One possibility, however, is that this result indicates an MI approach is not necessary for every OCD patient but rather might only be utilized in cases of low motivation.

Case Example

In order to demonstrate some of the issues described above, this chapter presents the case history and treatment course for an individual who presented for ERP at a specialty OCD center and subsequently experienced difficulties with treatment engagement. The patient, Christine (pseudonym), was a 28-year-old woman with OCD symptoms that pertained to fears of making a mistake coupled with checking compulsions. Specifically, she feared that she would accidentally leave her stove turned on, which could cause a catastrophic fire. She would repeatedly go back to check that her stove was turned off before leaving the house to be certain it was safe.

Similarly, she also feared leaving her apartment door unlocked and would repeatedly check to be sure it was locked. At work, Christine reported being bothered by needing to recheck clerical work that she already knew to be correct, while at the same time believing checking and attention to detail helped her to be a model employee. Importantly, however, she acknowledged that at times her compulsive need to check delayed her in completing certain work tasks but still expressed reluctance to reduce this checking owing to the fear of making a mistake. Therefore, she appeared to have some level of ambivalence about treatment and relatively poor expectations for how much ERP would be able to help her.

ERP treatment was delivered in accord with a published ERP manual (Foa et al., 2012) and began with a clinical interview to make a functional assessment of the OCD symptoms. The therapist provided the rationale for ERP by explaining that the anxiety associated with the intrusive doubts would naturally subside (habituate) with time passing, even without giving in to a compulsion. In this way, the patient would be able to break free from using compulsions as a crutch to relieve anxiety and learn to live with intrusive doubts as a normal part of life. The therapist attempted to address the patient's ambivalence about treatment by enhancing her motivation for change by discussing the ways in which OCD symptoms made her life more difficult. Given Christine's low expectations for treatment, the therapist was also careful to spend additional time on the treatment rationale and ensure that there was strong agreement on therapeutic tasks in order to further promote the patient's engagement.

Given the importance of attending to issues of engagement early in treatment, the therapist also made the expectations for therapy clear to the patient by emphasizing the importance of completing between-session assignments (beginning with self-monitoring of rituals). These forms revealed that cumulatively, checking rituals occupied more than 1.5 h of Christine's day. The self-monitoring forms also helped to identify particular environmental triggers for Christine's rituals (e.g., walking by the stove, leaving the apartment, sending emails, and clicking the lock button on her car keys three times to hear the horn beep confirming the doors locked). In the second session, the therapist worked collaboratively with Christine to develop an exposure hierarchy based on these situational cues. For Christine, planned exposure tasks involved leaving her apartment without checking the door to be sure it was locked and the stove to be sure it was off, imaginal exposures to confront the feared scenario of being responsible for a fire, and writing emails without rereading them to check for mistakes. In line with the treatment manual, exposures began during the third session and were assigned thereafter as between-session homework.

Problems with treatment engagement emerged relatively early during the treatment course. The first exposures involved writing emails to friends and family without compulsively checking them for typos as they were being written and similarly refraining from opening her sent mail to check that they had gone through. Christine tolerated these exposure trials well; she reported that they produced only minimal anxiety because her feared consequences of making a mistake in an email to a friend were lower than that to a coworker. However, as exposure difficulty progressed,

Christine began to show poor adherence with exposures, particularly those that had been assigned as homework. For example, Christine was asked to practice locking her car doors without clicking her key fob to hear the car horn confirm they were locked. She reported that she would often give into this ritual even after attempting to resist. Similarly, she reported that she was not able to resist checking her stove and front door lock on leaving her apartment in the morning.

The therapist utilized the Patient E/RP Adherence Scale (PEAS) beginning at treatment session three. As described above, the PEAS quantifies patient effort in exposure practices and overall ritual prevention success, both in session and between sessions. The therapist's scores indicated that Christine had good adherence to in-session exposures, which she was able to conduct with minimal compulsions. However, the therapist noticed that Christine's between-session PEAS scores were significantly lower, as she often would complete only half of assigned exposures. In addition, she was only successful at preventing 25% of her rituals after six sessions of ERP. The therapist identified this underengagement in treatment as posing a potential barrier to treatment and began devoting session time to address the issue.

Specifically, the therapist began each session by checking in on the homework and asking Christine how she felt it had gone. In addition, the therapist made sure to reiterate the rationale for treatment and focused on trying to increase their mutual agreement on therapy tasks. As pertained to ritual prevention, the therapist engaged in a Socratic dialogue with Christine to evaluate the effects of continuing to engage in compulsive rituals on her ability to benefit from treatment as illustrated by the following dialogue:

Therapist: It sounds like it has been difficult to complete the therapy tasks we had aimed for this past week. In particular, it sounds like you've had a hard time resisting those compulsions we were aiming to refrain from engaging in.

Christine: Yes, it has been really much harder than I expected.

Therapist: Let's talk more about this. I want to help you with this difficulty. I think it's important that we go back to the treatment rationale and make sure we are on the same page about why we are incorporating rituals prevention into treatment. Do you remember why the treatment model incorporates ritual prevention?

Christine: I know, I need to get better at it, it just seems like checking the lock takes just a second and sometimes I'd rather just get that relief rather than having to sit with the doubts.

Therapist: The temptation posed by the compulsions is real; they do offer that moment of relief, and that's why we have to work so hard to resist them. Let's try to remember our treatment model though. If we are aiming to show you that those doubts are most likely to be false alarms and that you are capable of living with them, what is the effect of using compulsions to ease doubts?

Christine: Well, I guess I am not showing myself that I can tolerate doubts if I always respond to them.

Therapist: Exactly! Going back to check is robbing you of a learning opportunity to show you that you can live with the doubt. It also strengthens the habit of using compulsions as a way to relieve anxiety.

In this example, the therapist attempts to provide greater rationale for the homework as a way to enhance the therapeutic alliance on therapy tasks, with the aim being to increase adherence. In these conversations, it is important to validate the difficulty of therapy tasks and also to check in with the patient to ensure patient understanding and ensure clarity of homework goals.

In subsequent conversations, it was revealed that some of Christine's difficulty completing her homework exposures was related to practical barriers. Specifically, Christine explained that her workplace was very busy and demanding, and so it was hard for her to budget time during the workday to complete exposures. Moreover, she reported that at times she would forget to complete her exposures, as the assignments would slip her mind when she got busy with work tasks. In evaluating the issue, the therapist identified that using paper and pencil forms to track the exposures was part of the issue, as Christine would sometimes misplace the forms and forget which exposure tasks she was assigned for homework. To enhance her engagement, the therapist worked with Christine to come up with prompts to help Christine remember her therapy tasks. For example, Christine came up with the idea of posting a note at the bottom of her work computer's monitor with a reminder that said "Don't double check!" to help her remember not to engage in checking compulsions when sending emails. In addition, she used her email's "schedule send" function to write emails to herself that would arrive in her inbox at a scheduled time to remind her to complete exposures. For example, she scheduled an email to arrive in her inbox at 8:25 am, just a few minutes before she would be leaving the house, with the subject line reading "remember not to check the locks and purposefully imagine a robbery." Lastly, the therapist also began scheduling brief (<10 min) phone calls to check in with Christine midway through the week to check on progress, provide encouragement, and highlight the importance of completing the therapy homework tasks.

These efforts significantly improved Christine's adherence to her therapy homework, such that by 12 sessions into treatment she was completing 75% of her assigned exposures and resisting more than half of her compulsive rituals (60% response prevention). However, by this time Christine had progressed to near the top of her exposure hierarchy, and she now began to experience reluctance to engage in treatment due to the intensity of facing her greatest fears. Specifically, the exposures during this part of the treatment involved imagining a feared scenario in which she was responsible for harm coming to another person by constructing an imaginal exposure script in which she left her apartment after having forgotten to turn the stove off and a breeze blew a piece of paper into the open flame, causing a catastrophic fire that caused the death of an innocent neighbor. Christine was instructed that she should imagine this scenario vividly, as if it were actually happening, and then would listen to a recording of this feared scenario on a loop tape. Christine still exhibited great reluctance to work on this domain, saying, "I'm honestly not sure I want to change this. I consider myself to be a responsible person, and learning to be okay with the possibility of harming someone else is just something I don't know if I want to do. That makes me feel like I would be an immoral and uncaring person." To enhance her motivation to complete this difficult exposure, the therapist employed a decisional balance discussion. Specifically, the therapist asked questions to explore the potential benefits of not changing ("Maybe there are advantages to not doing anything about your OCD symptoms?"). Although therapists commonly end up advocating for change, this can backfire and put the patient in the position of arguing against change. Thus, this strategy was used to convey acceptance and understanding of the patient's ambivalence, allow for full exploration of reasons not to change, and defuse the potential for discord, before moving on to ask about the potential reasons for change ("What about the other side? What disadvantages of continuing to have OCD really stand out as important?"). Christine identified both positive (i.e., greater confidence that she won't be responsible for harm) and negative (i.e., time lost, potential for running late to appointments and work due to always having to go back and check the stove) aspects of maintaining her checking compulsions. She also identified pros of changing (i.e., greater ease of leaving the house), in addition to potential cons (i.e., exposure would be anxiety provoking). In line with a motivational interviewing approach, the therapist highlighted the pros of making a change as well as the cons of maintaining the status quo through questions, reflections, and selective emphasis (e.g., emphasizing the importance of the ways in which OCD symptoms interfered with Christine's values). Lastly, in line with the inhibitory learning approach to conducting exposures (Craske et al., 2014), the therapist attempted to frame this difficult exposure as a learning opportunity. The therapist asked Christine to reflect on the prior exposures and what she had learned from them. In particular, the therapist framed exposures as a way to "put to the test" fear-based expectancies and posed it as such "In all of the prior exposures you have practiced it seems to me you have surprised yourself by finding that what your OCD expected to happen was not what actually transpired, and that you showed yourself you were capable of withstanding the anxiety that came without it overwhelmed you. What if this would be similar?" Importantly, the therapist waited for Christine to "opt in" and did not force the exposure. Allowing the patient to proactively decide to engage in the exposure thereby enhanced her self-efficacy.

This approach succeeded at enhancing Christine's motivation to complete her most difficult exposures. Christine found that the imagined scenario of being responsible for harming her neighbors became easier to hear with multiple repetitions. Moreover, after practicing this exposure multiple weeks in a row, she observed that *thinking* about her feared scenario did not cause the fear to *materialize* in real life. She also observed that her anxiety subsided on its own, even without giving into checking rituals. She gradually came to understand that the likelihood of being responsible for causing a catastrophe was low, even without checking. In line with the decisional balance discussion referenced above, Christine decided that the minimal risk of being responsible for harm was a risk that was worth taking rather than the certainty of living with bothersome OCD symptoms. By this point, Christine had completed 17 sessions of ERP, which is considered a typical dose. On her post-treatment evaluation, Christine's symptoms had been significantly reduced so that she was spending less than an hour per day experiencing obsessive thoughts and was able to resist more than 90% of her compulsive urges. Christine also considered herself greatly improved. She and the therapist then began relapse prevention planning and concluded treatment.

Conclusion

Treatment with ERP is the recommended form of psychotherapy for OCD and has the potential to substantially improve the lives of individuals with this condition. However, problems with engagement can result in a failure to maximally benefit from this treatment. Limited engagement can manifest as failure to attend sessions and difficulty completing therapy tasks that are assigned as between-session homework, as well as unwillingness to conduct exposures in session. In particular, poor compliance with homework seems to be a robust predictor of less successful treatment. In turn, reduced treatment compliance has been linked to lower treatment motivation, worse expectations for how successful treatment will be, and poorer therapeutic working alliance (particularly the facet of the working alliance pertaining to agreeing on therapy tasks).

As illustrated in the case above, treatment engagement can be enhanced by highlighting the rationale for ERP treatment in particular, which can foster positive treatment expectancies, as well as strengthening agreement on the therapy tasks. In addition, practical barriers to treatment engagement can also be targeted directly in treatment, and motivational enhancement techniques may prove useful in improving treatment engagement. Importantly, there may be myriad reasons why patients have difficulty engaging in ERP treatment, and thus careful, individualized assessment and intervention are needed in order to tailor treatment to each individual.

Clinical Summary Points and Recommendations

- ERP is the recommended form of CBT for OCD and leads to substantial reduction in symptoms for many patients, but problems with patient underengagement can result in premature dropout from or residual symptoms after treatment.
- Improvement with ERP is strongly related to patient engagement in treatment, particularly as it pertains to completion of therapy homework.
- Low treatment engagement has been linked to limited motivation, negative treatment expectancies, and reduced therapeutic working alliance.
- Engagement in ERP can be fostered by enhancing motivation, providing a clear rationale for ERP tasks, and fostering a strong working alliance with patients.

References

Abramowitz, J. S. (2006). *Understanding and treating obsessive-compulsive disorder: A cognitive behavioral approach*. Routledge.

Abramowitz, J. S., Franklin, M. E., Street, G. P., Kozak, M. J., & Foa, E. B. (2000). Effects of comorbid depression on response to treatment for obsessive-compulsive disorder. *Behavior Therapy, 31*(3), 517–528.

Abramowitz, J. S., Franklin, M. E., Zoellner, L. A., & Dibernardo, C. L. (2002). Treatment compliance and outcome in obsessive-compulsive disorder. *Behavior Modification, 26*(4), 447–463.

American Psychiatric Association. (2013). *Diagnostic and statistical manual of mental disorders* (5th ed.). American Psychiatric Publishing.

Andersson, E., Enander, J., Andrén, P., Hedman, E., Ljótsson, B., Hursti, T., & Rück, C. (2012). Internet-based cognitive behaviour therapy for obsessive–compulsive disorder: A randomized controlled trial. *Psychological Medicine, 42*(10), 2193–2203.

Angelakis, I., & Pseftogianni, F. (2021). Association between obsessive-compulsive and related disorders and experiential avoidance: A systematic review and meta-analysis. *Journal of Psychiatric Research, 138*, 228–239.

Anholt, G. E., Aderka, I. M., van Balkom, A. J., Smit, J. H., Hermesh, H., de Haan, E., & van Oppen, P. (2011). The impact of depression on the treatment of obsessive–compulsive disorder: Results from a 5-year follow-up. *Journal of Affective Disorders, 135*(1–3), 201–207.

Anholt, G. E., Aderka, I. M., Van Balkom, A. J. L. M., Smit, J. H., Schruers, K., Van Der Wee, N. J. A., & Van Oppen, P. (2014). Age of onset in obsessive–compulsive disorder: Admixture analysis with a large sample. *Psychological Medicine, 44*(1), 185–194.

Bekker, M. J., Griffiths, K. M., & Barrett, P. M. (2017). Improving accessibility of cognitive behavioural therapy for children and adolescents: Review of evidence and future directions. *Clinical Psychologist, 21*(3), 157–164.

Brantnell, A., Woodford, J., Baraldi, E., van Achterberg, T., & von Essen, L. (2020). Views of implementers and nonimplementers of internet-administered cognitive behavioral therapy for depression and anxiety: Survey of primary care decision makers in Sweden. *Journal of Medical Internet Research, 22*(8), e18033.

Cougle, J. R., Timpano, K. R., Fitch, K. E., & Hawkins, K. A. (2011). Distress tolerance and obsessions: An integrative analysis. *Depression and Anxiety, 28*(10), 906–914.

Craske, M. G., Kircanski, K., Zelikowsky, M., Mystkowski, J., Chowdhury, N., & Baker, A. (2008). Optimizing inhibitory learning during exposure therapy. *Behaviour Research and Therapy, 46*(1), 5–27.

Craske, M. G., Treanor, M., Conway, C. C., Zbozinek, T., & Vervliet, B. (2014). Maximizing exposure therapy: An inhibitory learning approach. *Behaviour Research and Therapy, 58*, 10–23.

De Araujo, L. A., Ito, L. M., & Marks, I. M. (1996). Early compliance and other factors predicting outcome of exposure for obsessive–compulsive disorder. *The British Journal of Psychiatry, 169*(6), 747–752.

Dowling, N., Thomas, N., Blair-West, S., Bousman, C., Yap, K., Smith, D. J., & Ng, C. H. (2016). Intensive residential treatment for obsessive-compulsive disorder: Outcomes and predictors of patient adherence to cognitive-behavioural therapy. *Journal of Obsessive-Compulsive and Related Disorders, 9*, 82–89.

Fawcett, E. J., Power, H., & Fawcett, J. M. (2020). Women are at greater risk of OCD than men: A meta-analytic review of OCD prevalence worldwide. *The Journal of Clinical Psychiatry, 81*(4), 13075.

Foa, E. B., Steketee, G., Grayson, J. B., & Doppelt, H. G. (1983). Treatment of obsessive-compulsives: when do we fail? In: Foa, E.B., & Emmelkamp, P.M.G., (eds). Failures in Behavior Therapy. New York: *John Wiley & Sons*. p 10-34.

Foa, E. B., Yadin, E., & Lichner, T. K. (2012). *Exposure and response (ritual) prevention for obsessive compulsive disorder: Therapist guide*. Oxford University Press.

Goodman, W. K., Price, L. H., Rasmussen, S. A., Mazure, C., Fleischmann, R. L., Hill, C. L., & Charney, D. S. (1989a). The Yale-Brown obsessive compulsive scale: I. Development, use, and reliability. *Archives of General Psychiatry, 46*(11), 1006–1011.

Goodman, W. K., Price, L. H., Rasmussen, S. A., Mazure, C., Delgado, P., Heninger, G. R., & Charney, D. S. (1989b). The Yale-Brown obsessive compulsive scale: II. Validity. *Archives of General Psychiatry, 46*, 1012–1016.

Guy, W. (1976). Clinical Global Impressions. In *ECDEU assessment manual for psychopharmacology, revised (DHEW Publ no ADM 76–338)* (pp. 218–222). National Institute of Mental Health.

Hansen, B., Kvale, G., Hagen, K., Havnen, A., & Öst, L. G. (2018). The Bergen 4-day treatment for OCD: Four years follow-up of concentrated ERP in a clinical mental health setting. *Cognitive Behaviour Therapy*, 1–17.

Hatcher, R. L., & Gillaspy, J. A. (2006). Development and validation of a revised short version of the Working Alliance Inventory. *Psychotherapy research, 16*(1), 12-25.

Hayes, S. C., Wilson, K. W., Gifford, E. V., Follette, V. M., & Strosahl, K. (1996). Experiential avoidance and behavioral disorders: A functional dimensional approach to diagnosis and treatment. *Journal of Consulting and Clinical Psychology, 64*, 1152–1168.

Holdsworth, E., Bowen, E., Brown, S., & Howat, D. (2014). Client engagement in psychotherapeutic treatment and associations with client characteristics, therapist characteristics, and treatment factors. *Clinical Psychology Review, 34*(5), 428–450.

Koran, L., & Simpson, H. (2013). Guideline Watch (March 2013): Practice Guideline for the Treatment of Patients with Obsessive-Compulsive Disorder. In APA Practice Guidelines. *American Psychiatric Publishing*, Inc.

Jacoby, R. J., Berman, N. C., Reese, H. E., Shin, J., Sprich, S., Szymanski, J., & Wilhelm, S. (2019). Disseminating cognitive-behavioral therapy for obsessive compulsive disorder: Comparing in person vs. online training modalities. *Journal of Obsessive-Compulsive and Related Disorders, 23*, 100485.

Knopp, J., Knowles, S., Bee, P., Lovell, K., & Bower, P. (2013). A systematic review of predictors and moderators of response to psychological therapies in OCD: Do we have enough empirical evidence to target treatment? *Clinical Psychology Review, 33*(8), 1067–1081.

Kvale, G., Hansen, B., Björgvinsson, T., Bortveit, T., Hagen, K., Haseth, S., et al. (2018). Successfully treating 90 patients with obsessive compulsive disorder in eight days: The Bergen 4-day treatment. *BMC Psychiatry, 18*(1), 323. https://doi.org/10.1186/s12888-018-1887-4

Launes, G., Hagen, K., Sunde, T., Öst, L. G., Klovning, I., Laukvik, I. L., et al. (2019). A randomized controlled trial of concentrated ERP, self-help and waiting list for obsessive- compulsive disorder: The Bergen 4-day treatment. *Frontiers in Psychology, 10*, 2500. https://doi.org/10.3389/fpsyg.2019.02500

Leeuwerik, T., Cavanagh, K., & Strauss, C. (2019). Patient adherence to cognitive Behavioural therapy for obsessive-compulsive disorder: A systematic review and meta-analysis. *Journal of Anxiety Disorders, 102135.*

Lewin, A. B., Peris, T. S., Bergman, R. L., McCracken, J. T., & Piacentini, J. (2011). The role of treatment expectancy in youth receiving exposure-based CBT for obsessive compulsive disorder. *Behaviour research and therapy, 49*(9), 536–543.

Lundström, L., Flygare, O., Andersson, E., Enander, J., Bottai, M., Ivanov, V. Z., & Rück, C. (2022). Effect of internet-based vs face-to-face cognitive behavioral therapy for adults with obsessive-compulsive disorder: A randomized clinical trial. *JAMA Network Open, 5*(3), e221967.

Maher, M. J., Wang, Y., Zuckoff, A., Wall, M. M., Franklin, M., Foa, E. B., & Simpson, H. B. (2012). Predictors of patient adherence to cognitive-behavioral therapy for obsessive-compulsive disorder. *Psychotherapy and psychosomatics, 81*(2), 124.

Mataix-Cols, D., do Rosario-Campos, M. C., & Leckman, J. F. (2005). A multidimensional model of obsessivecompulsive disorder. *American Journal of Psychiatry, 162*(2), 228–238.

McGuire, J. F., Piacentini, J., Lewin, A. B., Brennan, E. A., Murphy, T. K., & Storch, E. A. (2015). A meta-analysis of cognitive behavior therapy and medication for child obsessive–compulsive

disorder: Moderators of treatment efficacy, response, and remission. *Depression and Anxiety, 32*(8), 580–593.
McKay, D., Abramowitz, J. S., Calamari, J. E., Kyrios, M., Radomsky, A., Sookman, D., ... & Wilhelm, S. (2004). A critical evaluation of obsessive–compulsive disorder subtypes: Symptoms versus mechanisms. *Clinical psychology review, 24*(3), 283–313.
Miller, W. R., & Rollnick, S. (2013). *Motivational interviewing: Helping people change* (3rd ed.). Guilford Press.
Murray, C. J. L., & Lopez, A. D. (1996). *The global burden of disease: A comprehensive assessment of mortality and disability from diseases, injuries and risk factors in 1990 and projected to 2020*. Harvard University Press.
NICE. (2013). *Obsessive-compulsive disorder: Evidence update September 2013*. NICE clinical guideline 31. https://www.nice.org.uk/guidance/cg31/evidence/evidence-update-194847085
Ong, C. W., Clyde, J. W., Bluett, E. J., Levin, M. E., & Twohig, M. P. (2016). Dropout rates in exposure with response prevention for obsessive-compulsive disorder: What do the data really say? *Journal of Anxiety Disorders, 40*, 8–17.
Öst, L. G., Havnen, A., Hansen, B., & Kvale, G. (2015). Cognitive behavioral treatments of obsessive–compulsive disorder. A systematic review and meta-analysis of studies published 1993–2014. *Clinical Psychology Review, 40*, 156–169.
Patel, S. R., & Simpson, H. B. (2010). Patient preferences for obsessive-compulsive disorder treatment. *The Journal of Clinical Psychiatry, 71*(11), 13982.
Patel, S. R., Wheaton, M. G., Andersson, E., Rück, C., Schmidt, A. B., La Lima, C. N., & Simpson, H. B. (2018). Acceptability, feasibility, and effectiveness of internet-based cognitive-behavioral therapy for obsessive-compulsive disorder in New York. *Behavior Therapy, 49*(4), 631–641.
Reese, H. E., Pollard, C. A., Szymanski, J., Berman, N., Crowe, K., Rosenfield, E., & Wilhelm, S. (2016). The behavior therapy training institute for OCD: A preliminary report. *Journal of Obsessive-Compulsive and Related Disorders, 8*, 79–85.
Senter, M. S., Patel, S. R., Dixon, L. B., Myers, R. W., & Simpson, H. B. (2021). Defining and addressing gaps in care for obsessive-compulsive disorder in the United States. *Psychiatric Services, 72*(7), 784–793.
Simpson, H. B., Huppert, J. D., Petkova, E., Foa, E. B., & Liebowitz, M. R. (2006). Response versus remission in obsessive-compulsive disorder. *The Journal of Clinical Psychiatry, 67*(2), 18209.
Simpson, H. B., Zuckoff, A., Page, J. R., Franklin, M. E., & Foa, E. B. (2008). Adding motivational interviewing to exposure and ritual prevention for obsessive–compulsive disorder: An open pilot trial. *Cognitive Behaviour Therapy, 37*, 38–49.
Simpson, H. B., Zuckoff, A. M., Maher, M. J., Page, J. R., Franklin, M. E., Foa, E. B., & Wang, Y. (2010a). Challenges using motivational interviewing as an adjunct to exposure therapy for obsessive-compulsive disorder. *Behaviour Research and Therapy, 48*, 941–948.
Simpson, H. B., Maher, M., Page, J. R., Gibbons, C. J., Franklin, M. E., & Foa, E. B. (2010b). Development of a patient adherence scale for exposure and response prevention therapy. *Behavior Therapy, 41*, 30–37.
Simpson, H. B., Maher, M. J., Wang, Y., Bao, Y., Foa, E. B., & Franklin, M. (2011). Patient adherence predicts outcome from cognitive behavioral therapy in obsessive-compulsive disorder. *Journal of Consulting and Clinical Psychology, 79*, 247.
Simpson, H. B., Marcus, S. M., Zuckoff, A., Franklin, M., & Foa, E. B. (2012). Patient adherence to cognitive-behavioral therapy predicts long-term outcome in obsessive-compulsive disorder. *The Journal of Clinical Psychiatry, 73*(09), 1265–1266.
Simpson, H. B., Foa, E. B., Liebowitz, M. R., Huppert, J. D., Cahill, S., Maher, M. J., & Campeas, R. (2013). Cognitive-behavioral therapy vs risperidone for augmenting serotonin reuptake inhibitors in obsessive-compulsive disorder: A randomized clinical trial. *JAMA Psychiatry, 70*(11), 1190–1199.
Simpson, H. B., Foa, E. B., Wheaton, M. G., Gallagher, T., Gershkovich, M., Schmidt, A. B., & Wang, Y. (2021). Maximizing remission from cognitive-behavioral therapy in medicated adults with obsessive-compulsive disorder. *Behaviour Research and Therapy, 143*, 103890.

Skapinakis, P., Caldwell, D. M., Hollingworth, W., Bryden, P., Fineberg, N. A., Salkovskis, P., & Lewis, G. (2016). Pharmacological and psychotherapeutic interventions for management of obsessive-compulsive disorder in adults: A systematic review and network meta-analysis. *The Lancet Psychiatry, 3*(8), 730–739.

Sookman, D., Phillips, K. A., Anholt, G. E., Bhar, S., Bream, V., Challacombe, F. L., & Veale, D. (2021). Knowledge and competency standards for specialized cognitive behavior therapy for adult obsessive-compulsive disorder. *Psychiatry Research, 303*, 113752.

Stanley, M. A., & Turner, S. M. (1995). Current status of pharmacological and behavioral treatment of obsessive-compulsive disorder. *Behavior Therapy, 26*(1), 163–186.

Tolin, D. F., Frost, R. O., Steketee, G., & Muroff, J. (2015). Cognitive behavioral therapy for hoarding disorder: A meta-analysis. *Depression and Anxiety, 32*(3), 158–166.

Wheaton, M. G., & Chen, S. R. (2021). Homework completion in treating obsessive–compulsive disorder with exposure and ritual prevention: A review of the empirical literature. *Cognitive Therapy and Research, 45*(2), 236–249. https://doi.org/10.1007/s10608-020-10125-0

Wheaton, M. G., & Gallina, E. R. (2019). Using cognitive-behavioral therapy to treat obsessive-compulsive disorder with co-occurring depression. *Journal of Cognitive Psychotherapy, 33*(3), 228–241.

Wheaton, M. G., Gershkovich, M., Gallagher, T., Foa, E. B., & Simpson, H. B. (2018). Behavioral avoidance predicts treatment outcome with exposure and response prevention for obsessive–compulsive disorder. *Depression and anxiety, 35*(3), 256–263.

Wheaton, M. G., Galfalvy, H., Steinman, S. A., Wall, M. M., Foa, E. B., & Simpson, H. B. (2016). Patient adherence and treatment outcome with exposure and response prevention for OCD: Which components of adherence matter and who becomes well? *Behaviour Research and Therapy, 85*, 6–12.

Wheaton, M. G., Carpenter, J. K., Kalanthroff, E., Foa, E. B., & Simpson, H. B. (2016a). Augmenting SRIs for obsessive-compulsive disorder: Patient preference for risperidone does not limit effectiveness of exposure and ritual prevention. *Psychotherapy and Psychosomatics, 85*(5), 314–316.

Whittal, M. L., & McLean, P. D. (1999). CBT for OCD: The rationale, protocol, and challenges. *Cognitive and Behavioral Practice, 6*(4), 383–396.

Zuckoff, A., Balan, I. C., & Simpson, H. B. (2014). Enhancing the effectiveness of exposure and response prevention in the treatment of obsessive compulsive disorder: Exploring a role for motivational interviewing. In H. Arkowitz, W. R. Miller, & S. Rollnick (Eds.), *Motivational interviewing in the treatment of psychological disorders* (2nd ed.). Guilford.

Chapter 15
Posttraumatic Stress Disorder

Stephanie M. Haft and Sheila A. M. Rauch

Background

Trauma-focused cognitive behavioral therapies (TF-CBTs) for PTSD are widely accepted as first-line treatment for PTSD (VA/DOD, 2023). TF-CBTs effectively reduce PTSD symptoms and related psychopathology, including guilt, shame, anger, depression, suicidal ideation, and anxiety (Forbes et al., 2020). TF-CBTs include prolonged exposure (PE; Foa et al., 2019), cognitive processing therapy (CPT; Resick et al., 2017), eye movement desensitization and reprocessing (EMDR; Shapiro, 2018), and written exposure therapy (WET; Sloan & Marx, 2019).

Scope of Problem of Engagement in Treatment Among Those with PTSD

People with PTSD do not initiate treatment for varied reasons. While PTSD begins with the experience of a trauma, it develops and worsens as avoidance of trauma-related internal cues (e.g., thoughts, emotions, memories, body sensations) and external cues (e.g., situations, activities, places, people, objects, smells, conversations) intensifies. Avoidance is a key feature of PTSD and contributes to many of the factors related to low engagement. Epidemiological studies in the United States demonstrate that most people with PTSD never seek treatment (Roberts et al.,

S. M. Haft (✉) · S. A. M. Rauch
Emory University School of Medicine, Atlanta, GA, USA

Joseph Maxwell Cleland Atlanta Veteran Affairs Medical Center, Atlanta, GA, USA
e-mail: stephanie.haft@va.gov; Sheila.a.m.rauch@emory.edu

E. M. Goetter (ed.), *Optimizing Treatment Engagement Processes in CBT for Anxiety and Related Disorders*, CBT: Science Into Practice,
https://doi.org/10.1007/978-3-031-91439-3_15

2011), and those who do may be delayed by an average of 11 years from the time of PTSD onset (Wang et al., 2004). Since obtaining help and engaging in effective treatment require trauma survivors with PTSD to at least disclose the trauma and often involve approaching trauma memories and reminders in various ways, it makes sense that treatment is often delayed and/or avoided entirely.

People with PTSD sometimes do not stay engaged in treatment long enough to receive a full dose. Even when people with PTSD seek treatment, many do not complete what would be considered an effective dose regardless of the type of treatment (Varker et al., 2021). Estimates of dropout prior to completion for TF-CBT for PTSD range from 26 to over 50% (Kehle-Forbes et al., 2016). When focusing on CBT for PTSD, for example, some individuals may not feel ready to approach trauma memories and thus fall back into avoidance patterns after initiating treatment. Indeed, there are consequences of treatment underutilization and dropout for individuals with PTSD. The more someone with PTSD avoids, the more their symptoms worsen and the more their world and sense of community, connection, and belonging is reduced. Avoidance leads to more avoidance in a spiral of reduced quality of life, poorer functioning, and higher societal costs (e.g., $232.2 billion annually in United States; Davis et al., 2022), which further deteriorates social, familial, occupational, and recreational functioning.

Barriers to PTSD Treatment Engagement

Motivational Challenges in the Context of Systemic Barriers

Motivation for treatment waxes and wanes throughout an episode of care. As noted previously, most clients in treatment have lived with PTSD for more than 10 years with significant impact on their social and family context. Their loved ones may interact and care for them based on their PTSD and changing this will alter their relationship dynamics. They may not be working and may receive federal benefits based on their level of PTSD and, thus, have reasonable concerns about what PTSD improvement may mean for their income, e.g., *"What if I get better and my social security stops and then things get worse again?"* Mental health, wellness, vocational, and financial resources for individuals experiencing PTSD and those who have recovered from PTSD are important and necessary. Still, discussing client's motivation to experience symptom relief is an important step to assess readiness for CBTs for PTSD. For those who are motivated for treatment, a lack of mental health providers and an even larger deficit of providers skilled in effective PTSD treatments (Stein et al., 2023) can inhibit treatment engagement.

Cognitive Barriers

A client's belief system may function as either a facilitator or barrier to recovery. If a client believes treatment works, they are likely to stay in treatment and receive benefit. Conversely, if they believe treatment does not work (i.e., does not work for people like them, is inconsistent with their cultural or personal beliefs), they may struggle to stay in treatment long enough to learn if it can work for them. In addition, trauma-related beliefs of self-blame (e.g., *"It's all my fault."*), low self-worth (e.g., *"I'm not deserving to feel better."*), and/or low self-efficacy (e.g., *"If I talk about my trauma, I won't be able to handle it."*) may prevent them from engaging in care. Many clients worry about what will happen after they face trauma-related memories, emotions, body sensations, and thoughts. They may feel like their trauma memory is like a "Pandora's box," and once "released" the memories will wreak havoc in their life and never be contained again. While these beliefs may change once engaged in treatment, they can impact engagement especially early in treatment.

Cultural and Contextual Barriers

Unfortunately, due to colonization, sterilization, unethical withholding of medical treatment (e.g., Tuskegee), slavery, institutionalization, and incarceration, there remain very real and valid mistrusts of medical professionals worldwide. For individuals who do feel safe enough and trust enough to engage in mental health support, there may be shame associated with seeking out support and possible deterrence (or even ostracization) from one's social support network. Help seeking could be inconsistent with someone's personal values and community norms. Assuming that individuals overcome these cultural barriers within their own cultural microcosm, there is a broader perspective to consider. Treatment engagement for a specific trauma may be occurring in the context of a macrocosm of global stressors that are frequent and insidious, e.g., the COVID-19 pandemic, war and ongoing civil unrest, pervasive discrimination and violence, and ethnic genocide. These compounded experiences of trauma can lead many with PTSD to feel treatment may not be relevant or even worthwhile due to the frequency of ongoing threats. In a recent examination of PTSD treatment access worldwide, only 17% of those with a PTSD diagnosis in the past 12 months had received a minimum number of sessions that may indicate adequate therapy with significantly lower rates in low- and middle-income countries (only 4%) (Stein et al., 2023).

Predictors of Loss of Engagement (Dropout) from TF-CBTs

Dropout is a significant problem in PTSD treatment. In effectiveness samples in clinical care, about 38–50% do not complete an adequate episode of care (Schnurr et al., 2022). Most RCTs with PTSD treatments have an approximate dropout rate of at least 20% (Lewis et al., 2020), though few predictors of dropout have been found. Consistent across multiple empirically supported CBTs for PTSD in clinical care, dropout most often occurs between sessions 2 and 4 (e.g., between sessions 2 and 3 in PE; Garcia et al., 2011; after session 3 in CPT; Mott et al., 2014a; and after session 3 in WET; Haft, 2022) leading many to link dropout to initial detailed disclosure of trauma memories. Many studies have examined predictors of dropout across a wide range of possible client characteristics and treatment variables and found no significant contribution of race, gender, ethnicity, assigned sex at birth, marital status, income, employment, education, deployment/service era, co-occurring suicidality, treatment type, type of trauma exposure, time since trauma, and treatment history (Kehle-Forbes et al., 2016; Maglione et al., 2022; Mott et al., 2014a). However, some predictors have been identified. For instance, when clients experience less improvement in symptom reduction (Szafranski et al., 2014) and when clients rate treatment credibility low (Taylor, 2003), they are more likely to drop prior to treatment completion. In addition, across several studies, younger clients were found more likely to dropout prematurely (Garcia et al., 2011; Kehle-Forbes et al., 2016; Maglione et al., 2022), which may be reflective of differences in daily demands, e.g., childcare. Additionally, co-occurring conditions have been associated with higher dropout, including current alcohol and substance use (Bedard-Gilligan et al., 2018) and clinically significant insomnia (Buckheit et al., 2022). More research is needed to examine treatment dropout vs. early response and expand findings to nonveteran samples.

Predictors of Successful Engagement

Engagement is typically defined as treatment initiation, treatment retention, receiving a full dose of treatment, reliably attending treatment sessions, and/or completing within- and between-session activities. In the context of TF-CBT, treatment engagement has been associated with a range of factors, including higher perceived social support (Fivecoat et al., 2023), lower rates of co-occurring insomnia (Buckheit et al., 2022), and lower rates of current drug use (Bedard-Gilligan et al., 2018).

Shared Decision-Making (SDM)

SDM, per Elwyn et al. (2012), is a process that involves introducing choice, describing options, and collaborative decision-making. Clinicians, clients, and support people (e.g., family, friends, caregivers) collaboratively create treatment plans and identify treatment goals, based on client needs, preferences, values, and capabilities. Enhanced engagement may occur through collaborative decision-making (Fortney et al., 2023; VA/DOD, 2023). SDM has been associated with higher rates of treatment initiation (Dwight-Johnson et al., 2001) and treatment adherence (Loh et al., 2007). SDM increases treatment engagement through mechanisms that are particularly relevant for clients experiencing PTSD (Mott et al. 2014a, b). Given that the presentation of multiple treatment options impacts clients' receptivity to TF-CBTs for PTSD (Feeny et al., 2009) and that client perceptions of treatment effectiveness influence client preference for TF-CBTs for PTSD (Angelo et al., 2008), educating clients and shared decision-making can be an important step to enhance treatment planning for individuals receiving a TF-CBT for PTSD (Mott et al. 2014a, b).

Seeing Early Treatment Results

Noticeable and impactful results are possible early on in treatment. Drawn from clinical implications presented by Doane et al. (2010), if clients see decreases in their symptoms, it may bolster important process variables (e.g., therapeutic alliance, confidence in therapeutic approach, motivation) that in turn may increase treatment completion. This is a crucial choice point for clients, as skepticism may be high about whether treatment will be helpful for them, particularly in light of the perceived emotional costs associated with addressing their trauma. Early response often includes sudden gains. *Sudden gains*, or rapid and large decreases in symptoms from one session to the next (Tang & DeRubeis, 1999), have been associated with better outcomes in PE, WET, and CPT (Doane et al., 2010; Sloan et al., 2022). Clients who experience sudden gains may experience increased "buy in" with the treatment model, increased trust in the provider, and engage more (Doane et al., 2010). Seeing early results, including sudden gains, also increases self competence and instills hope. It is also possible that sudden gains may encourage clients to prematurely discontinue trauma-related treatment if they feel they already received full benefit.

Frequency of Sessions

Initial trials of PE for PTSD had twice weekly sessions based on previous work with phobias (Foa et al., 1991), but conventional clinic practice led to the use of weekly models. Recent research suggests that increasing session frequency may increase treatment engagement. *Massed protocols*, also known as *accelerated protocols*, deliver the full treatment dose in a condensed period of time (e.g., 2–4 weeks vs. 8–20 weeks). Frequency of massed treatment protocols vary and have been as brief as 4 days (Goetter et al., 2021) but tend to range from 3 sessions weekly (M/W/F) for 3–4 weeks to 5–7 sessions weekly (M-F or daily) for 2 weeks (Dell et al., 2023; Rauch et al., 2020). As initial treatment effects are typically noticeable after 4–8 sessions (VA/DOD, 2023), massed treatment protocols yield comparable results to weekly sessions in a shortened timeframe, both at treatment completion, 3-month follow-up (Dell et al., 2023), and 6-month follow-up (Peterson et al., 2023). Massed protocols provide fewer opportunities for clients to avoid more timely treatment gains and thus reduce the threat of premature dropout (Ragsdale et al., 2020). With lower drop and accelerated results, providers treat more clients annually, report more meaningful work as they see changes quickly, and may be more resistant to burnout long-term (Haft et al., 2024). Thus, if available and accessible, massed approaches are a worthwhile consideration as a first-line strategy.

Provider/Client Match

Match between a therapist and client may impact treatment engagement and therefore may influence treatment response. Drawn from early examination of patient successes (Whitehorn & Betz, 1954), match refers to congruence of fit between the treating provider and the client who receives care, which can be influenced by a combination of factors (e.g., treatment approach, interpersonal style, demographic variables, values). Although match based on demographic variables (e.g., gender, race, age) and personal characteristics (e.g., religion, values, education) has been weighed heavily as important, it seems to be less impactful on treatment retention and treatment outcome than initially proposed (Sterling et al., 2001). It is important that clients receive adequate explanations about different treatment options, expectations for engagement, and rationale for how the treatments could be beneficial prior to treatment initiation. Further, to optimally engage in CBTs for PTSD, therapists must convey a sense of confidence that the treatment will work *and* genuinely believe that recovery from PTSD is possible. If clinicians experience ambivalence about CBTs for PTSD, that uncertainty can easily be detected by avoidant clients with PTSD who are looking for danger, which may impact client motivation and confidence to engage in treatment overall. Thus, adequate provider training, supervision, and consultation are keys to successful PTSD treatment. For an in-depth conceptual review of therapist–client matching, see Karlsson (2005).

Clinical Considerations That Pertain to Engagement of Those with PTSD

Comorbidity

CBTs for PTSD have been successfully implemented for clients with a range of co-occurring mental health conditions (Forbes et al., 2020). Common comorbid mental health conditions include depressive disorders (including suicidal ideation), anxiety-spectrum disorders, obsessive-compulsive and related disorders, alcohol and substance use disorders, chronic pain, sleep disorders, bipolar disorders, and personality disorders. Given effectiveness of PTSD treatment, it is recommended to prioritize CBT for PTSD rather than delaying PTSD treatment to target co-occurring diagnoses.

Co-occurring Insomnia

For individuals with co-occurring clinical insomnia, it is important to ensure they understand the plan for how their sleep symptoms will be addressed. Of critical importance, if the provider believes sleep may worsen, letting the client know that they need to give treatment a few weeks to impact sleep can also be critical to retention. To maximally benefit during CBT for PTSD, one could consider ensuring clients have a boundary between their "rest" areas and their places to "push" while approaching trauma-related content (i.e., *stimulus control*). Providing brief sleep-related psychoeducation and clear behavioral treatment expectations may facilitate more opportunities for clinical insomnia to reduce during CBTs for PTSD. Having these discussions will be especially important for clients who have an independent sleep disorder (e.g., primary insomnia). Offering directive guidance around practice completion may minimize sleep disruption as clients are less likely to complete exercises at the end of the day, when laying down, or in their bedroom.

Co-occurring Alcohol and Substance Use Difficulties

For individuals with PTSD and co-occurring AUD/SUD, ensuring neither issue is a barrier to intervention for the other disorder is important. Requiring periods of abstinence or loss of either diagnosis will prevent some clients from engaging in PTSD care and may lead to drop if the client has a lapse or relapse. As a provider, there may be medical or safety concerns that need to be addressed due to alcohol and/or substance use. For instance, if someone requires medical detoxification to reduce or stop use, collaborating with a provider with this expertise to ensure this happens safely while planning for a quick transition to a combined PTSD and AUD/SUD protocol or concurrent CBT for PTSD and AUD/SUD can enhance engagement (e.g., to quickly reduce symptoms prior to preexisting habits returning) and potentially better outcomes (VA/DOD, 2023).

Co-occurring Suicidal Ideation (SI) and Suicidal Behaviors (SB)

Treatment engagement for clients with PTSD and suicidality is critical to ensure this particularly vulnerable population has the opportunity for benefit from treatment. Ensuring that clients with nonimminent risk are offered effective PTSD treatment is essential. As previously noted, suicidality is common among those with PTSD and treating PTSD is typically a fundamental part of reducing risk. Providers should engage in appropriate risk assessment and safety planning prior to and throughout the PTSD episode of care. Rather than delaying treatment for a time when risk of suicide is not imminent, initiating a CBT for PTSD while deploying safety planning and ongoing assessment of acute risk for suicide may be the most helpful intervention. Overall, in a context of ongoing assessment and safety planning (as needed) for suicidality, treatment of PTSD symptoms may be protective for individuals with a history of and/or current SI, SB, or suicide attempts.

Co-occurring Obsessive-Compulsive Symptoms

To enhance PTSD treatment for those with comorbid OCD, comprehensive assessment of OCD symptoms (e.g., feared consequences) prior to treatment initiation and ensuring client's understanding of their current symptoms are critical. To maximally benefit, it is fundamental that interventions include a strong exposure component and that there is deliberate learning to build tolerance to uncertainty. Intolerance of uncertainty is a core feature within all presentations of OCD and has been identified as a transdiagnostic risk factor for PTSD (Oglesby et al., 2016) that is associated with overall PTSD severity (Raines et al., 2019). Offering reassurance in certain contexts can be problematic. For instance, providers must be mindful that the exposure focus is on PTSD symptoms if giving reassurance during therapy (e.g., *"You are safe."),* to not reinforce obsessions and compulsions. More effectively, providers can consider offering statements that recognize uncertainty (e.g., *"It's possible. You could pass out while shopping for fruit."*) and promote the client to self-interrupt the habit of compulsions, avoidance, and reassurance seeking. In a related way, providers should clearly differentiate PTSD *reexperiencing* from OCD symptoms of *compulsive reviewing* or *reassurance seeking* as it relates to a trauma experience; if these processes are not distinguished, the PTSD treatment may be undermined while OCD compulsions are reinforced. After agreed upon treatment targets and detailed functional assessment, those with these dual diagnoses can benefit from CBTs for PTSD and exposures can accommodate this comorbidity.

Clinical Strategies for Engaging Clients with PTSD in CBTs

Ensure Buy-In with Specific Motivators Early and Revisit Motivators Throughout Episode of Care

Clients seek mental health treatment for different reasons. To foster engagement and retention, clinicians must understand their client's reasons for seeking treatment prior to initiating a CBT for PTSD. Common motivators include improving quality of life and/or reconnecting with core values, e.g., return to work, be a better parent, and improve sleep. Motivators should be revisited throughout care. Clients often face difficult times in and between therapy sessions, which may make them question *"Is doing treatment even worth it?"* It is natural for clients to question their engagement and experience ambivalence, especially in the context of a provider asking clients to engage in behaviors that they may have never done or have not done in years. In these moments, it can be especially powerful to remind clients of their reasons for investing in treatment. Ensuring continued commitment to treatment can maintain engagement (Mott et al. 2014a, b). Through three steps, a provider can successfully revisit motivators in the context of a client's ambivalence: (1) validate the client's difficulties, (2) incorporate client's primary and specific motivator/s, and (3) give the client the power to choose what comes next. An example of something a therapist might offer is:

> *It makes sense that you're questioning whether it's even worth it to repeat the imaginal exposure, given how upsetting it was yesterday. And, I'm remembering our conversation last week about how important this work is for repairing the relationship with your daughter. But you're right, this is tough work. I'm following your lead here. So where do we go from here?*

Establish a Shared Understanding of the Client's PTSD and Rationale for How the Treatment Works and Revisit the Understanding Throughout the Episode of Care

Due to the nature of PTSD persisting over decades without relief, it can sometimes be challenging for clients to understand how "facing and embracing" trauma memories and associated stimuli facilitates PTSD recovery. One specific strategy to increase insight is to help the client identify strategies they have used to recover without success (e.g., pushing away trauma-related memories, being a workaholic, avoiding the place where it happened, using substances) and noting the difference between these unsuccessful attempts and what they are currently doing in treatment. Through discussion and reflection, the client can begin to see that what they have been doing has been helpful in the short-term but has made them dependent on strategies that do not actually make them safer in the long-term. Throughout treatment, the therapist reminds the client of the "why" they are doing certain activities during the context of therapy (e.g., *"Why am I asking you to visit grocery stores during peak hours?"*). Making the implicit learning of exposures explicit increases their insight, increases motivation to engage in treatment, and facilitates more opportunities for the client to become their own therapist. Establishing a shared understanding of PTSD and the treatment rationale prepares the client for relapse prevention and long-term recovery success.

Use of Metaphors

Metaphors are essential, versatile, and highly effective tools within the therapeutic setting, especially in times of high anxiety and challenge. Metaphors are often utilized to describe particularly complex topics in a language that is digestible for the listener. Their utilization has been explored in cognitive behavioral interventions

(Killick et al., 2016), as well as in the context of understanding PTSD (Foley, 2015), PTSD treatment (Walker et al., 2017), and for increasing personal insights (Törneke, 2017). CBTs for PTSD have all incorporated multiple metaphors in their clinical manuals and materials, (e.g., pool temperature, learning to ride a bike, messy closet, i.e., Foa et al., 2019; Resick et al., 2017). Strategically incorporating culturally salient and individualized metaphors in CBTs for PTSD appears to be a worthwhile clinical strategy to engage clients. For instance, many PE providers use the closet metaphor to describe the overall model of PE. When the client is having trouble with the most difficult parts of the imaginal, the provider can simply reference, *"we are in the back of the closet now"* rather than interrupting the imaginal exposure with reviewing treatment rationale (e.g., why approach the most painful of the memory).

Considerations for Practice Exercises/Homework

Language and word choice for discussing between-session practice exercises can be an unintentional barrier, as many people have pejorative relationships with "homework." Homework tends to be mandated and required by an authority figure, namely a teacher or caregiver. Drawing on suggestions from Garcia et al. (2023), changing the word choice to "practice exercises" is a small way to reduce the power imbalance between the provider and the client and bolster opportunities for collaborative decision-making. Another consideration is the quantity and quality of between-session practice exercises. Some clients are more prepared for paperwork (e.g., readings, journaling, and completing worksheets), while others may prefer more hands-on learning (e.g., in vivo exposures). It is important to ask about client preferences and comfort (i.e., client's reading level, learning disabilities, etc.) with practice exercises. Considering ways to set them up for success to accomplish the practice exercises within their life constraints can enhance engagement and therapeutic momentum. By being judicious about planned practice exercises, providers can help prevent premature treatment dropout due to the "ask" being too great or overwhelming.

Create Behavioral Momentum Through Early Treatment Successes

Client ambivalence may be high at the beginning of treatment. They are often distressed, struggling, and uncertain if the treatment will work (and have likely not had success with previous treatment). Through prioritizing early treatment success, providers can maximize behavioral momentum, early on in treatment and throughout their episode of care. For example, practice exercises that involve a client becoming more behaviorally activated in value-based activities or include facing manageable feared situations (in vivo exposures) will have strong likelihood of success and thus increase motivation for PTSD treatment. Values-based behavioral activation, especially connection-focused (e.g., meeting a friend at a coffee shop) or movement-focused (e.g., going on a 10-min walk outside) activities, provides more opportunities for reinforcing stimuli. By repeating values-based activities as part of CBTs for PTSD, clients may notice an overall mini-boost in their well-being, for example, mood, energy, and connection to loved ones.

Avoidance is costly. By the time people are engaged in treatment, avoidance has likely cost them relationships, time, energy, and money. Taking back these lost parts is another way to increase behavioral momentum early in treatment. For example, through selecting low to moderate level difficulty in vivo exposures, clients can begin facing situations that they have been avoiding. A client who has been restricted to their home after a successful in vivo exposure will likely return home feeling immensely proud of themselves, empowered, hopeful, and confident enough to revisit that situation in the future. Through repetition, clients learn that their anxiety *does not last forever.* For clients with higher PTSD severity or those who cannot identify a lower intensity exposure, consider a therapist-assisted in vivo exercise, where the therapist engages in the in vivo exposure alongside the client (e.g., sitting at dog park *together*). Even when it is accompanied by a therapist, approaching feared situations and other feared stimuli is highly rewarding. Celebrating any attempts to approach (vs. avoid) can enhance engagement. Exercises that clients complete with their therapist can then be scaffolded to encourage independently completed activities.

Assess for Specific Feared Consequences and Reasons for Avoidance

Lastly, to keep clients engaged in CBTs for PTSD, adapt to presenting clinical needs, and use each session to better design the next exposure for this client's needs, treatment should be idiographic. Ensure you are considering the individual culture and context of the client when utilizing these interventions. Each application of CBT for PTSD should be idiographic, meaning that it should be individually personalized to the client. Making assumptions based on identity factors (e.g., gender, nationality, trauma type, religious beliefs, etc.) risks overgeneralization based on stereotypes. For example, when asked *why* they avoid the feeling of sadness, some clients may respond, *"I don't want my family to see me upset. I've burdened my wife with so many things already. She doesn't need another thing to weigh on her."* Therapists must consider the many sources and cultural explanations for avoidance behaviors. Thorough assessment of feared consequences within the client's cultural framework is key. With this information, providers can more skillfully target and prioritize needed treatment exercises.

Case Example

Background Information

Kele, a 38-year-old Indigenous cisgender man and mid-career human rights lawyer, presented for PTSD treatment. At the time of the initial assessment, Kele was in a committed monogamous relationship with his partner, Miguel, a 34-year-old Chicano cisgender man. Kele was a survivor of domestic violence. He endured 2 years of recurrent verbal aggression and physical violence perpetrated by his ex-partner, Chad. Kele sought therapy nearly 3 years following his breakup with Chad due to an increase in PTSD symptoms shortly after moving in with his new partner, Miguel. His course of care, including relevant treatment engagement-enhancing strategies and treatment engagement-interfering barriers, is discussed.

History

During the initial assessment, Kele reported physical and emotional abuse by his ex-partner. He was regularly yelled at and ridiculed for not doing things right. He noted being burned with a lighter on his forearm, threatened with a knife, and pushed into a wall during times of argument. At the time that the domestic violence was occurring, he did not receive any mental health counseling, primarily relying on his loved ones, who encouraged him to leave the relationship. Kele reported that he was afraid that "something worse" would have happened if he left sooner and was especially concerned that Chad might do something to his dog, Roni. At intake, he reportedly had never taken a psychiatric medication but expressed he was open to taking a prescription medication if it was "absolutely necessary." He denied any current alcohol or other drug use. When asked about his primary stressor, he expressed that adjusting to living with his new partner had been especially stressful because of the exacerbation in symptoms.

Identifying an Index Event

He shared that he was reminded of one specific argument more than others, which had become particularly bothersome. During this event, nearly 2 years into the relationship, Roni toileted on a vintage rug in the living room, which infuriated Chad. When Chad moved toward Roni, as he was yelling and threatening her, Kele worried that he was going to hurt her and ran to get in between them. Chad punched Kele several times in his side and told him to "get out of the way." "If you won't discipline your dog, then I will." He kicked Roni once and then grabbed a knife. He continued yelling and made verbal threats toward the dog and Kele if he were to "get in my way." Kele started walking toward Roni and Chad kicked his feet out from under him and started kicking him on the ground. Kele rolled up in a ball as

Chad kicked him over and over and then suddenly stopped and walked out of the room. Kele scooped up Roni and slept with her on the couch. He was in a lot of pain and terrified. During this argument and the days thereafter, Kele was in fear for his dog's life and his own. He moved out to his own apartment 4 months later.

Assessment of PTSD

After the index event was identified, the Clinician Administered PTSD Scale for DSM-5 Revised (CAPS-5-R; Weathers et al., 2018) was utilized to assess PTSD symptoms and severity.

Intrusive Symptoms Shortly after moving in with Miguel, Kele began to experience daily intrusive symptoms, including intrusive visual images (e.g., Chad holding the knife, Roni's face during the argument) and hearing dialogue from this argument, as well as nightmares of being chased with a knife. He reported physiological arousal (e.g., heart racing, chest tightness, sweaty palms, and feeling "hot") when seeing knifes or sharp objects and emotional arousal (e.g., general discomfort and uneasiness) when seeing his current partner, Miguel, in the kitchen.

Avoidance Symptoms Kele endorsed avoidance of internal and external stimuli. In particular, he had been pushing away intrusive violent images and using music as a distraction. After moving in with Miguel, Kele found himself "just agreeing" with Miguel over "small things" (e.g., which type of apple to buy at the grocery store), in fear that it could precipitate an argument. One notable shift was in watching television, as he had been actively avoiding watching lifestyle-based reality TV, as arguments in these shows were activating feelings of anxiety and shame.

Changes in Cognition and Mood Kele described his distress over the former relationship as "baggage" that he was bringing into this new relationship. For example, he endorsed daily guilt about remaining in the relationship and self-blame for not protecting Roni. He also noted uncharacteristic changes in his thinking, e.g., *"I can't protect myself"* and *"If I let someone in emotionally, then they're going to hurt me."*

Hyperarousal Symptoms He described being alert and watchful in multiple safe situations (e.g., when Roni walked around common spaces, when Miguel was near Roni) and endorsed use of safety behaviors (e.g., monitoring Miguel's facial expressions, looking for any gesture that Roni might toilet). These concentration difficulties interfered both during times of leisure (e.g., spending time with Miguel) and during work. For example, he excessively checked his home security cameras to ensure that Roni was "okay" and that Miguel didn't come home early from work. The frequent checking and worries about Roni's safety made completing simple tasks more burdensome and prolonged complex tasks. He slept 4–5 hours nightly with frequent nocturnal awakenings.

Additional Important Clinical Information

In terms of coping, Kele described himself as being very close with his family, extended family, tribal elders, and other community members. He described that throughout his life seeking advice and elder wisdom from his tribal community had been helpful and reinforced Kele's strengths and resilience. It was in discussing his difficulties with his support network that he was encouraged to seek additional mental health support from medical providers.

Treatment

Reasons for Selected Intervention

During the intake assessment, Kele expressed how his PTSD symptoms were interfering in his life. He suspected that other difficulties with his mood and concentration were related to his PTSD symptoms. Together with the provider, they discussed both PE and CPT as providers trained in both models were available. Kele chose PE as it is highly flexible and a robustly effective PTSD treatment that resonated with his personal desire to take his life back. He opted for a massed treatment model (3 sessions weekly) to accelerate recovery and minimize disruption to his life.

Treatment Goals

Kele's primary treatment goals were to reduce his intrusive and hypervigilance symptoms. He also hoped that his sleep and concentration would improve during treatment.

Progression

Per the PE protocol, the first session was largely focused on psychoeducation about PTSD, what to expect during PE treatment, and the treatment rationale. During this session, it became clear that he was experiencing shame and embarrassment about needing treatment and he voiced concerns that treatment might not work for him, citing the fact that he did not know anyone who had seen a psychologist. In response, the therapist discussed what brought him to therapy and his hopes for the future. He identified his mother as his primary motivator, because she often relied on him for caretaking and home-based support. The therapist validated Kele's current difficulties and stressors, while recognizing the uncertainty of possible treatment benefits. The therapist incorporated his primary motivator (e.g., being more present for his mother) and gave him the power to choose what came next in treatment:

You're exactly right. We don't know if this treatment is going to work for you but my experience with others who have been through trauma suggests it will help. You are taking on something new and really riding in brand new territory for your family, which requires bravery and a leap of faith. You've shared with me how important your mom is to you and how people rely on you. I'm really hoping that we can give it our best here—and hopefully pave the way for others behind you to do the same. I do think it's possible for your memories and anxiety to get better. If I didn't believe that to be true, we wouldn't be here. At the end of the day, you're holding the reigns and decide how we move forward. So where do you want to go from here?

In session 2, Kele and his therapist continued psychoeducation about trauma, PTSD, and common reactions to trauma. In vivo exposures were introduced, as well as the rationale for engaging in in vivo exposures (e.g., exposure breaks the habit of avoidance, doing avoided activities gets easier over time, and facing fears would increase his confidence). They discussed what PTSD has "taken" from him and what he wanted to "take back" from PTSD. The therapist was sure to ensure the in vivo exposures were values consistent and meaningful for Kele and intentionally incorporated his extensive support system (e.g., collectivistic considerations, building on Kele's strengths). Together, they identified that Roni's presence often functioned as a safety behavior to increase his safety in certain settings and as an avoidance strategy so that Roni was not left unattended. Some items from his in vivo exposure hierarchy included letting Miguel take Roni on a walk without his supervision, visiting family members while Miguel dog sat for him (1 hour to overnight), watching Miguel cut fruits/vegetables with knife, meeting with his mother (and later tribal elders) to discuss his PTSD recovery, and attending large group community gatherings without Roni. His provider also reminded him that this was in an effort for him to take his power back from his PTSD and from Chad, frankly. Moreover, they reviewed their collective goal to help Kele get back on track as quickly as possible, while the therapist explained that treatment was designed to help him eventually become his own therapist, so he could move forward without continued mental health appointments.

One issue of relevance that arose was a brief exacerbation in intrusive symptoms (nightmares and associated sleep difficulties) following his first imaginal exposure. Although less than 15% of individuals experience a brief exacerbation in symptoms when undergoing PE (Foa et al., 2002), such exacerbations can lead clients to question treatment effectiveness. In this case, Kele's provider offered him an evidence-based perspective, citing that although some people experience brief worsening of PTSD symptoms this does not predict poor treatment outcomes. The therapist reviewed the rationale for exposure and reminded him of his *why* (i.e., his mother). Fortunately, he was still willing to proceed with PE, continue to engage in imaginal exposure during session, and complete his between-session activities.

By session 4 (and less than 2 weeks into treatment), his PCL-5 score had decreased by 10 points to 35 but was still above the clinical threshold on this measure. Specific feedback between sessions 4 and 6 focused on maintaining consistency with practice exercise completion. Kele had a negative relationship with "homework" growing up, where homework felt like a chore. He realized that he was approaching his out of session exercises similarly. So instead of calling those activities homework assignments, the therapist introduced the concept of "practice exercises." Using the intentional language of practice exercises allowed Kele to reframe the exercises not as something he *had* to do but something he could *choose* to do, thus increasing intrinsic motivation and removing unhelpful power dynamics and their associated connotations. Additionally, given his busy work schedule, Kele and his therapist identified challenges in making time for practice exercises. To ensure treatment engagement, Kele was encouraged to schedule the times when he would complete these exercises, just as he would for a briefing or work meeting. By creating these time slots of protected time, he was able to implement the plan with more confidence and better prioritize his out of session practice exercises.

Beginning in session 7, the tone of sessions shifted. His PTSD symptoms had reduced more by this point, and he was noticing large cognitive shifts. The therapist took this opportunity to reinitiate the discussion of *becoming his own therapist* while maintaining important cultural awareness. Initially, Kele was hesitant to engage in treatment in part because of fears of institutionalization or that he would require lifetime mental health support from Western medicine. *Becoming his own therapist* placed the power in his hands. It did not deny or erase the history of exploitation of Western medicine on Indigenous peoples but instead recognized the fact that Indigenous, Native, and First Nation peoples do not need Western medicine to have a full, rich, and meaningful life. Exposure became less about a therapy activity and more a way of an approach to life, that he could integrate with his own values and purpose.

By sessions 8 and 9, his skills in approaching emotions and trauma-related stressors had become truly masterful. Kele and his provider began to apply precision and nuance in *exposure-based living* within the context of exposure to persistent stressors, e.g. hearing prejudicial comments about BIPOC and LGBTQIA+ peoples at work (and in general day-to-day life), concerns about caregiving for his mother, and providing other supports to family members. This is a key factor that therapists must consider when delivering CBT to clients with marginalized identities. In this way, the therapist helped Kele to understand the nuance between avoidance and healthy boundary setting. The therapist was explicit in noting that choosing not to attend an after-hours work function hosted by someone who regularly made derogatory comments toward LGBTQIA+ peoples is not avoidance. Intentional exposure to hostile environments is never in the best interest of one's emotional well-being. In other words, marginalized peoples do not need to repeatedly face verbal aggression (or other types of violence) to learn how to better tolerate it. Limiting exposure to violence (e.g., certain people, places, situations, and social media), when possible, is a choice that they can make, and they can decide if it is in their best interest. It is absolutely appropriate and consistent with evidence-based care for PTSD to distinguish objectively safe exposure targets from those that are truly unsafe. Learning how to set and maintain boundaries and correct boundary violations is a common treatment target that arises in the context of CBTs for PTSD.

At session 10, Kele's PCL-5 had dropped to a 17 (from 45). His imaginal exposure peak subjective units of distress score (SUDS) was 40. He was consistently approaching situations that he was previously avoiding with minimal associated distress. Treatment termination was decided based on measurement-based care approaches as noted in the PE protocol (e.g., clinically significant reductions in PCL-5 score, imaginal exposure SUDS, and in vivo exposure SUDS), clinician observations of treatment change, and Kele's beliefs that he met his treatment goals (along with feelings of confidence and readiness for treatment termination). By session 10, Kele had not only exceeded all these benchmarks, but he also adopted an exposure lifestyle, leading him to approach new situations with ease that were not even on his in vivo exposure hierarchy.

In the final session, they discussed relapse prevention, which included expectations for brief lapses in symptoms and fluctuations over time. Although living a value-based life may spark joy and gratitude in a recovered client's life, clients should be prepared to experience natural fluctuations in stressors. Kele and his therapist discussed the possibility for changes in his symptoms, especially during periods of high stress or if he was to experience additional trauma or discrimination. The therapist conveyed confidence in Kele, reflecting his readiness and affirming his self-knowledge and ability to identify his needs better than anyone else. Upon discharge from therapy, Kele had become his own therapist, reestablished his confidence, reconnected to his internal strengths, and thus had everything he needed to live a value-based life, full of continued growth, meaning, connection, and purpose.

Clinical Summary Points and Recommendations

- Prioritize accelerated protocols to improve engagement and retention.
- Enhance engagement with specific motivators early and revisit motivators throughout the episode of care (e.g., client's values, hopes for the future).
- Maintain engagement with a shared understanding of the client's experience of PTSD, their life and cultural context, and the rationale for how treatment works. Revisit this understanding throughout the episode of care.
- Guide engagement with creative adaptation of therapeutic activities and between-session practice exercises to personally tailor treatment to effectively address treatment targets with fidelity to the evidence-based protocol.

References

Angelo, F. N., Miller, H. E., Zoellner, L. A., & Feeny, N. C. (2008). "I need to talk about it": A qualitative analysis of trauma-exposed women's reasons for treatment choice. *Behavior Therapy, 39*(1), 13–21.

Bedard-Gilligan, M., Garcia, N., Zoellner, L. A., & Feeny, N. C. (2018). Alcohol, cannabis, and other drug use: Engagement and outcome in PTSD treatment. *Psychology of Addictive Behaviors, 32*(3), 277.

Buckheit, K. A., Nolan, J., Possemato, K., Maisto, S., Rosenblum, A., Acosta, M., & Marsch, L. A. (2022). Insomnia predicts treatment engagement and symptom change: A secondary

analysis of a web-based CBT intervention for veterans with PTSD symptoms and hazardous alcohol use. *Translational Behavioral Medicine, 12*(1), ibab118.
Davis, L. L., et al. (2022). The economic burden of posttraumatic stress disorder in the United States from a societal perspective. *Journal of Clinical Psychiatry, 83*(3).
Dell, L., Sbisa, A. M., Forbes, A., O'Donnell, M., Bryant, R., Hodson, S., & Forbes, D. (2023). Effect of massed v. standard prolonged exposure therapy on PTSD in military personnel and veterans: A non-inferiority randomised controlled trial. *Psychological Medicine, 53*(9), 4192–4199.
Doane, L. S., Feeny, N. C., & Zoellner, L. A. (2010). A preliminary investigation of sudden gains in exposure therapy for PTSD. *Behaviour Research and Therapy, 48*(6), 555–560.
Dwight-Johnson, M., Unutzer, J., Sherbourne, C., Tang, L., & Wells, K. B. (2001). Can quality improvement programs for depression in primary care address patient preferences for treatment? *Medical Care*, 934–944.
Elwyn, G., Frosch, D., Thomson, R., Joseph-Williams, N., Lloyd, A., Kinnersley, P., & Barry, M. (2012). Shared decision making: A model for clinical practice. *Journal of General Internal Medicine, 27*, 1361–1367.
Feeny, N. C., Zoellner, L. A., & Kahana, S. Y. (2009). Providing a treatment rationale for PTSD: Does what we say matter? *Behaviour Research and Therapy, 47*(9), 752–760.
Fivecoat, H. C., Lookatch, S. J., Mavandadi, S., McKay, J. R., & Sayers, S. L. (2023). Social factors predict treatment engagement in veterans with PTSD or SUD. *The Journal of Behavioral Health Services & Research, 50*(3), 286–300.
Foa, E. B., Rothbaum, A. O., Hembree, E. A., & Rauch, S. A. M. (2019). *Prolonged exposure therapy for PTSD: Emotional processing of traumatic experiences* (2nd ed.). Oxford University Press.
Foa, E. B., Rothbaum, B. O., Riggs, D. S., & Murdock, T. B. (1991). Treatment of posttraumatic stress disorder in rape victims: A comparison between cognitive-behavioral procedures and counseling. *Journal of Consulting and Clinical Psychology, 59*(5), 715–723. 10.1037//0022-006x.59.5.715.
Foa, E. B., Zoellner, L. A., Feeny, N. C., Hembree, E. A., & Alvarez-Conrad, J. (2002). Does imaginal exposure exacerbate PTSD symptoms? *Journal of Consulting and Clinical Psychology, 70*(4), 1022. 10.1037//0022-006x.70.4.1022.
Foley, P. S. (2015). The metaphors they carry: Exploring how veterans use metaphor to describe experiences of PTSD. *Journal of Poetry Therapy, 28*(2), 129–146.
Forbes, D., Bisson, J. I., Monson, C. M., & Berliner, L. (2020). *Effective treatments for PTSD: Practice guidelines from the International Society for Traumatic Stress Studies* (3rd ed.). The Guilford Press.
Fortney, J. C., Rajan, S., Chen, J. A., Campbell, S. B., Nolan, J. P., Wong, E., & Schnurr, P. P. (2023). A mixed-methods evaluation of why an implementation trial failed to engage veterans with posttraumatic stress disorder in trauma-focused psychotherapy. *Journal of Traumatic Stress*.
Garcia, H. A., Kelley, L. P., Rentz, T. O., & Lee, S. (2011). Pretreatment predictors of dropout from cognitive behavioral therapy for PTSD in Iraq and Afghanistan war veterans. *Psychological Services, 8*(1), 1.
Garcia, N. M., Eiff, A. C., Lopez-Esteban, A., & Zoellner, L. (2023). Cultural considerations for treating PTSD in Latinx sexual assault survivors with prolonged exposure. *Cognitive and Behavioral Practice, 30*(2), 179–194.
Goetter, E. M., Tanev, K. S., Lynch, E., Blackburn, A. M., Mamon, D., Pique, T., & Spencer, T. (2021). An accelerated, weekend-based, prolonged exposure therapy program for veterans and service members with posttraumatic stress disorder. *Journal of Behavioral and Cognitive Therapy, 31*(3), 285–289.
Haft, S. M. (2022). *Determining the effectiveness of virtually-delivered written exposure therapy for treatment of posttraumatic stress symptoms*. Dissertations. 3889. https://scholarworks.wmich.edu/dissertations/3889

Haft, S., Fiskeaux, M., Sprang Jones, K., & Rauch, S. A. M. (2024). *"Intensive delivery of prolonged exposure". Prolonged exposure for PTSD: Innovations to improve access, engagement, and outcomes*. Springer Nature.

Karlsson, R. (2005). Ethnic matching between therapist and client in psychotherapy: An overview of findings, together with methodological and conceptual issues. *Cultural Diversity and Ethnic Minority Psychology, 11*(2), 113–129. https://doi.org/10.1037/1099-9809.11.2.113

Kehle-Forbes, S. M., Meis, L. A., Spoont, M. R., & Polusny, M. A. (2016). Treatment initiation and dropout from prolonged exposure and cognitive processing therapy in a VA outpatient clinic. *Psychological Trauma, 8*(1), 107–114. https://doi.org/10.1037/tra0000065

Killick, S., Curry, V., & Myles, P. (2016). The mighty metaphor: A collection of therapists' favourite metaphors and analogies. *The Cognitive Behaviour Therapist, 9*, E37. https://doi.org/10.1017/S1754470X16000210

Koenen, K. C., Ratanatharathorn, A., Ng, L., McLaughlin, K. A., Bromet, E. J., Stein, D. J., & Kessler, R. (2017). Posttraumatic stress disorder in the world mental health surveys. *Psychological Medicine, 47*(13), 2260–2274.

Lewis, C., Roberts, N. P., Gibson, S., & Bisson, J. I. (2020). Dropout from psychological therapies for post-traumatic stress disorder (PTSD) in adults: Systematic review and meta-analysis. *European Journal of Psychotraumatology, 11*(1), 1709709. https://doi.org/10.1080/20008198.2019.1709709

Loh, A., Leonhart, R., Wills, C. E., Simon, D., & Härter, M. (2007). The impact of patient participation on adherence and clinical outcome in primary care of depression. *Patient Education and Counseling, 65*(1), 69–78.

Maglione, M., Chen, C., Franco, M., Gizaw, M., Shahidinia, N., Baxi, S. M., & RAND CORP SANTA MONICA CA. (2022). *Predictors of PTSD treatment retention and response: A systematic review*. RAND.

Mott, J. M., Mondragon, S., Hundt, N. E., Beason-Smith, M., Grady, R. H., & Teng, E. J. (2014a). Characteristics of US veterans who begin and complete prolonged exposure and cognitive processing therapy for PTSD. *Journal of Traumatic Stress, 27*(3), 265–273.

Mott, J. M., Stanley, M. A., Street, R. L., Jr., Grady, R. H., & Teng, E. J. (2014b). Increasing engagement in evidence-based PTSD treatment through shared decision-making: A pilot study. *Military Medicine, 179*(2), 143–149.

Oglesby, M. E., Boffa, J. W., Short, N. A., Raines, A. M., & Schmidt, N. B. (2016). Intolerance of uncertainty as a predictor of post-traumatic stress symptoms following a traumatic event. *Journal of Anxiety Disorders, 41*, 82–87.

Peterson, A. L., Blount, T. H., Foa, E. B., Brown, L. A., McLean, C. P., Mintz, J., & Keane, T. M. (2023). Massed vs intensive outpatient prolonged exposure for combat-related posttraumatic stress disorder: A randomized clinical trial. *JAMA Network Open, 6*(1), e2249422.

Ragsdale, K. A., Watkins, L. E., Sherrill, A. M., Zwiebach, L., & Rothbaum, B. O. (2020). Advances in PTSD treatment delivery: Evidence base and future directions for intensive outpatient programs. *Current Treatment Options in Psychiatry, 7*(3), 291–300. https://doi.org/10.1007/s40501-020-00219-7

Rauch, S. A., Rothbaum, B. O., Smith, E. R., & Foa, E. B. (2020). *Prolonged exposure for PTSD in intensive outpatient programs (PE-IOP): Therapist guide*. Oxford University Press.

Raines, A. M., Oglesby, M. E., Walton, J. L., True, G., & Franklin, C. L. (2019). Intolerance of uncertainty and DSM-5 PTSD symptoms: Associations among a treatment seeking veteran sample. *Journal of Anxiety Disorders, 62*, 61–67.

Resick, P. A., Monson, C. M., & Chard, K. M. (2017). *Cognitive processing therapy for PTSD: A comprehensive manual*. Guilford Press.

Roberts, A. L., Gilman, S. E., Breslau, J., Breslau, N., & Koenen, K. C. (2011). Race/ethnic differences in exposure to traumatic events, development of post-traumatic stress disorder, and treatment-seeking for post-traumatic stress disorder in the United States. *Psychological Medicine, 41*(1), 71–83. https://doi.org/10.1017/s0033291710000401

Schnurr, P. P., Chard, K. M., Ruzek, J. I., Chow, B. K., Resick, P. A., Foa, E. B., & Shih, M. C. (2022). Comparison of prolonged exposure vs cognitive processing therapy for treatment of posttraumatic stress disorder among US veterans: A randomized clinical trial. *JAMA Network Open, 5*(1), e2136921.

Shapiro, F. (2018). *Eye movement desensitization and reprocessing (EMDR) therapy: Basic principles, protocols, and procedures* (3rd ed.). The Guilford Press.

Sloan, D. M., & Marx, B. P. (2019). *Written exposure therapy for PTSD: A brief treatment approach for mental health professionals*. American Psychological Association Press.

Sloan, D. M., Thompson-Hollands, J., Hayes, A. M., Lee, D. J., Alpert, E., & Marx, B. P. (2022). Sudden gains in two trauma-focused treatments for posttraumatic stress disorder. *Behavior Therapy, 53*(2), 255–266. https://doi.org/10.1016/j.beth.2021.08.003

Stein, D. J., Kazdin, A. E., Munthali, R. J., Hwang, I., Harris, M. G., Alonso, J., et al. (2023). Determinants of effective treatment coverage for posttraumatic stress disorder: Findings from the world mental health surveys. *BMC Psychiatry, 23*, 226. https://doi.org/10.1186/s12888-023-04605-2

Sterling, R. C., Gottheil, E., Weinstein, S. P., & Serota, R. (2001). The effect of therapist/client race-and sex-matching in individual treatment. *Addiction, 96*(7), 1015–1022.

Szafranski, D. D., Gros, D. F., Menefee, D. S., Wanner, J. L., & Norton, P. J. (2014). Predictors of length of stay among OEF/OIF/OND veteran inpatient PTSD treatment noncompleters. *Psychiatry: Interpersonal & Biological Processes, 77*(3), 263–274.

Tang, T. Z., & DeRubeis, R. J. (1999). Sudden gains and critical sessions in cognitive-behavioral therapy for depression. *Journal of Consulting and Clinical Psychology, 67*(6), 894.

Taylor, S. (2003). Outcome predictors for three PTSD treatments: Exposure therapy, EMDR, and relaxation training. *Journal of Cognitive Psychotherapy, 17*(2), 149–162.

Törneke, N. (2017). *Metaphor in practice: A professional's guide to using the science of language in psychotherapy*. Context Press/New Harbinger Publications.

VA/DOD. (2023). *Veterans affairs and department of defense clinical practice guideline for management of post-traumatic stress*.

Varker, T., Jones, K. A., Arjmand, H.-A., Hinton, M., Hiles, S. A., Freijah, I., Forbes, D., Kartal, D., Phelps, A., Bryant, R. A., McFarlane, A., Hopwood, M., & O'Donnell, M. (2021). Dropout from guideline-recommended psychological treatments for posttraumatic stress disorder: A systematic review and meta-analysis. *Journal of Affective Disorders Reports, 4*, 100093. https://doi.org/10.1016/j.jadr.2021.100093

Walker, M. S., Kaimal, G., Gonzaga, A. M., Myers-Coffman, K. A., & DeGraba, T. J. (2017). Active-duty military service members' visual representations of PTSD and TBI in masks. *International Journal of Qualitative Studies on Health and Well-Being, 12*(1), 1267317.

Wang, P. S., Berglund, P. A., Olfson, M., & Kessler, R. C. (2004). Delays in initial treatment contact after first onset of a mental disorder. *Health Services Research, 39*(2), 393–415. https://doi.org/10.1111/j.1475-6773.2004.00234.x

Weathers, F. W., Bovin, M. J., Lee, D. J., Sloan, D. M., Schnurr, P. P., Kaloupek, D. G., & Marx, B. P. (2018). The clinician-administered PTSD scale for DSM–5 (CAPS-5): Development and initial psychometric evaluation in military veterans. *Psychological Assessment, 30*(3), 383.

Whitehorn, J. C., & Betz, B. J. (1954). A study of psychotherapeutic relationships between physicians and schizophrenic patients. *American Journal of Psychiatry, 111*(5), 321–331.

Chapter 16
Youth and Families

Tara J. Shuman and Brent R. Crandal

Background

To initiate treatment, behavioral health clinicians usually have just one door to walk through or one browser or application screen to open. Children, youth, and families, on the other hand, usually have a very different pathway leading to that same treatment encounter. Parents and caregivers may have had their own experiences with mental illness, treatment, or services systems, well before the young person is born (the terms "caregiver" and "parent" will be used throughout this chapter to mean a supportive adult in the young person's life who is responsible for their care and treatment). When a child begins to experience symptoms and impairment from anxiety, caregivers face a behavioral health system that is often foreign and complex. They might not be aware of the several decades of shortages of clinicians in many communities (Thomas et al., 2009), or the differences between a psychiatrist, psychologist, social worker, marriage family therapist, life coach, healer, and so on, and which type of provider they might need, or which ones will work with children and youth. Those who eventually approach behavioral health systems find it roped off and grouped by funding sources, treatment acuities, presenting problems, treatment modalities, and geographical boundaries. Determined to ease their child's distress,

T. J. Shuman (✉)
Clinical PsyD Program, California School of Professional Psychology at Alliant International University, San Diego, CA, USA
e-mail: tshuman@alliant.edu

B. R. Crandal
Department of Psychiatry, University of California, San Diego, La Jolla, CA, USA

The Chadwick Center for Children and Families at Rady Children's Hospital, San Diego, CA, USA
e-mail: bcrandal@rchsd.org

E. M. Goetter (ed.), *Optimizing Treatment Engagement Processes in CBT for Anxiety and Related Disorders*, CBT: Science Into Practice,
https://doi.org/10.1007/978-3-031-91439-3_16

they may encounter inconsistent information from friends, family, and other professionals.

Many children, youth, and families do not have access to crucial information about anxiety and related disorders, such as how common anxiety disorders are among young people. Approximately 7–8% of youth in the United States (Ghandour et al., 2019), Europe (Sacco et al., 2022), and globally (Polanczyk et al., 2015) have anxiety disorders and 15–20% of children will have one in their lifetime (Beesdo et al., 2009). Parents may also be unaware of the different types of anxiety and related disorders a young person could experience—specific phobias, agoraphobia, selective mutism, social anxiety, separation anxiety, generalized anxiety, and panic disorders (Park & Kim, 2020) as well as related anxiety conditions like obsessive-compulsive or posttraumatic stress disorders. They also may be unfamiliar with the early signs of anxiety disorders—more withdrawn behaviors, physiological symptoms like sweating, upset stomach, palpitations especially in unfamiliar settings, more pronounced experiences of negative feelings, and mood.

Perhaps most importantly, parents and their children may not know that anxiety and related mental health conditions are highly treatable, with effective psychotherapies available (Weisz et al., 2023). Specifically, cognitive behavioral therapy (CBT) and CBT-based treatments are the first-line treatment for 6- to 18-year-olds with social, generalized, separation anxiety disorders, specific phobias, and panic disorders, especially for mild to moderate presentations (Walter et al., 2020) as well as for posttraumatic stress disorder (Cohen et al., 2016; Connor et al., 2015). In fact, a 2019 analysis of six decades of research on childhood anxiety disorders pinpointed nine effective CBT interventions which reduced diagnoses across childhood ages and in a variety of treatment settings (Schwartz et al., 2019).

Thus, those first moments of meeting with a therapist are precious. They are hard to come by for parents, they are important, and often they are unfamiliar. Quite the contrary for the therapist who may have met several new clients that week! Therein lies the challenge, and the opportunity. Clinicians who initiate services with empathy, curiosity, and openness to the family's pathway are also inviting engagement into the therapeutic process.

Treatment Engagement for Pediatric Populations

Who contributes to a pediatric client's treatment engagement? If you were to divide a pie for everyone who carried some role in the process, who would get a slice? How large of a slice would they get? In the past, treatment engagement was often conceptualized as a client characteristic, that is to say each client gets the whole pie. If treatment did not progress, the client *was not ready for change*. We did then what we knew how to do, but as a field we have learned better and now do better. One example of this shift is found in Bronfenbrenner's now ubiquitous ecological model (Bronfenbrenner, 1994), cultivating the notion that human development occurs dynamically and reciprocally across the contexts of an individual's environment. In other words, children are nested within systems, such as families, schools, peer groups, and communities, all of which interact and contribute to a child's development. With this conceptualization, who gets a piece of the engagement pie? Certainly, the child, as well as parents, possibly siblings, extended family, teachers, and other care providers. The list continues. Did you serve yourself a slice as well? How large is the therapist's share of responsibility for engagement? How about case managers, psychiatrists, administrative support staff, billing or insurance professionals, systems leaders, or policy makers?

In a seminal article, Becker et al. (2018) summarized 40 years of engagement research in children's mental health services and asserted that treatment engagement is, "…multifaceted, dynamic, and transactional" (p. 2), meaning an individual's commitment to treatment is interactive and constantly changing based on the multiple nested systems involved in the individual's access to and experience with treatment. The authors also emphasized key dimensions of engagement. The REACH framework (Chorpita & Becker, 2022) is an acronym for *Relationship, Expectancy*, *Attendance*, *Clarity*, and *Homework*—five domains contributing to the sum of engagement in child, youth, and family treatment settings.

REACH Framework for Treatment Engagement

Development of the *relationship* between clients and clinicians, i.e., the therapeutic alliance, is immediately developing from the first interaction. Clinicians convey some degree of respect, compassion, openness, humility, and collaboration throughout the relationship. Predictably, this relationship is crucial to the success of treatment (Karver et al., 2018). Well-intentioned enthusiasm for tackling problems is no substitute for compassionate alignment and connection (Patterson & Forgatch, 2001). Clinicians hastily moving into treatment (i.e., teaching and confronting symptoms), excited to help resolve the presenting problems with the evidence-based interventions they are equipped to provide, often find they must not do so at the expense of the relationship that relies on building collaboration (Fjermestad et al., 2021), proving an attitude of support and evocation (Dean et al., 2016) and genuine humility (Mosher et al., 2017). If neglected, these missed opportunities can damage the quality of the relationship, perhaps disproportionately for service recipients whose identities are different from the clinician's (Johansen et al., 2023).

Of course, putting CBT strategies into action is essential for treatment; however, clinicians can promote a treatment process which invites autonomy, growth, and positive treatment outcomes when they are committed to alliance-building behaviors (i.e., collaborating, presenting the treatment model, exploring motivation, attending to experience, praising, and supporting; Fjermestad et al., 2021). Nevertheless, these alliance-building behaviors can be emotionally demanding. They are easily parodied but only effective when genuine. Building a productive relationship for treatment requires intention, a personal commitment, and constant cultivation by the clinician in order to consistently offer opportunities for connection and engagement (Zarzycka et al., 2022).

Expectancy includes the client's and caregiver's attitudes prior to and during treatment. Clients and caregivers develop positive expectations if treatment makes sense to them, if they perceive credibility in the treatment, and if they anticipate improving from treatment. This expectancy can be largely influenced by the clinician's approach: their hopefulness and confidence in care, their beliefs about whether the presenting problems can be resolved, and the opportunities they create for clients to explore questions and concerns about treatment (Chorpita & Becker, 2022).

Attendance is perhaps the most straightforward aspect of treatment engagement from the REACH model, except that for pediatric clients, attendance often relies on participation from supportive others in the client's life. In those cases, attendance includes identifying which individuals are supportive for the client, specifically in ways that will encourage treatment attendance and progress. Perhaps there is an older sibling or extended family member with the time and ability to encourage between-session practice of treatment skills. If so, attendance additionally includes how often and for how long those individuals attend sessions or participate in care coordination outside of sessions.

Clarity has to do with clear roles and responsibilities for the stakeholders involved in treatment as well as the clarity of the treatment processes. Engagement will be more consistent for clinicians who take time to explain responsibilities and the treatment process, aligning expectations about roles and next steps over the course of the client's care.

Finally, *homework* or between-session practice provides the young person and the parents with opportunities to practice skills introduced during treatment sessions (Hudson & Kendall, 2002), facilitates skill integration within other settings (i.e., home and school), and encourages clients to gain greater dexterity and mastery using new skills (Glenn et al., 2013). Homework can be used by clinicians to encourage consistent engagement and regard for the healing process between treatment sessions, reinforcing motivation and commitment to make changes and to assess treatment progress. However, there is wide variability in the use of homework by clinicians. To reinforce engagement and promote treatment progress, homework needs to be developed collaboratively, with empathy and flexibility, to leverage the client's intrinsic motivation and ensure a true fit for the client's life (Cummings et al., 2014).

Facilitators and Barriers to Care

Access to care occurs typically through a consonance of factors. Clinicians can influence many of those, but not all, since (a) many barriers occur prior to the client meeting their clinician and (b) barriers occur in a context that is larger than the individual clinician. In a systematic review, Radez et al. (2021) studied the main themes of barriers/facilitators for youth seeking mental health care, with individual child or adolescent factors being the most common category. This theme included child or adolescent lack of knowledge about mental health care or how to access it, their expectations about clinicians or the effectiveness of services, perceptions about not needing intervention, or biases about engaging in treatment. The second most identified theme was social stigma and embarrassment. Aligned with the REACH model (Chorpita & Becker, 2022), both themes not only emphasize the importance of *expectations* and *clarity* in developing engagement once a client arrives to treatment but also show how embedded these themes can be in the multiple systems that influence a young person (i.e., families, friends/peers, schools, and communities) and how these systems can either encourage or discourage a client from accessing care.

Similarly, Waid and Kelly (2020) assessed key factors for families in accessing appropriate care at the onset of pediatric mental illness. Attitudes toward mental illness, help-seeking, flexibility and availability of needed services, community attitudes and stigma toward mental illness and treatment, and coordination across services systems facilitated the initiation of care. Of note, among these factors clinicians are only secondarily influential in coordination across services systems prior to treatment starting (Crandal et al., 2019). Waid and Kelly suggest interventions to increase access can include family outreach, telehealth and digital health strategies (e.g., coaching or psychoeducation provided through web- or smartphone application-based platforms), and integrated care approaches (e.g., systems of care models coordinated within counties, parishes, states, and across child-serving systems).

Truly, given the broadness of these systems, *it takes a village* to facilitate access to care when young people are experiencing impairment as a result of anxiety. Once treatment starts, however, clinicians can take steps to address attitudes and stigma related to services, reinforcing the help-seeking that led to care, and providing services that are responsive to the specific needs of the client.

Predictors of Engagement, Nonresponse, and Dropout

There are myriad factors that predict treatment engagement, nonresponse, and dropout from psychotherapy for youth with anxiety disorders. Gonzalez et al. (2011) found that anxious youth who dropped out of care (typically later in treatment, i.e., after 6 sessions) in an outpatient setting had higher levels of depressive symptoms at intake, suggesting pretreatment comorbid symptom severity may impact treatment engagement, nonresponse, and attrition rates. However, in their study on CBT for youth with anxiety disorders, Wergeland et al. (2015) found that youth who dropped out of treatment reported similar levels of anxiety and depressive symptoms as those who completed treatment. In a study of trauma-focused CBT (TF-CBT), youth with higher baseline posttraumatic stress symptoms had higher rates of treatment nonresponse (Skar et al., 2022). Additionally, a 2017 study found that anxious youth with a primary social phobia diagnosis and those who had a comorbid mood disorder were more likely not to respond to manualized group CBT than youth without comorbid depression and those who were not diagnosed with social phobia (Lundkvist-Houndoumadi & Thastum, 2017). Taken together, the findings are mixed, but children and adolescents with more complicated symptom presentations may particularly benefit from an ongoing engagement focus throughout the treatment process. Children and youth with comorbid developmental conditions and neurodiversity (autism spectrum disorder, attention deficit hyperactivity disorder, learning disabilities, etc.) will likely benefit from CBT anxiety treatment that is individualized in order to optimize treatment efficacy for the unique needs of the client and family (Delli et al., 2018; Kazzi et al., 2023).

Parental treatment support is pivotal for positive mental health treatment outcomes with children, as parents can reinforce and apply skills learned in therapy in their home. Parental treatment engagement can be impacted by the parent's mental health, their motivation for treatment, and their level of involvement in their child's treatment (Haine-Schlagel et al., 2019). A pilot study conducted with 19 parent–child dyads and 18 child mental health clinicians found that parent's own mental health status contributed to lack of treatment engagement and progress for their children at even greater levels than parental motivation and degree of involvement in the child's treatment (Haine-Schlagel et al., 2019). Another study, specific to individual and group CBT in community clinics for children ages 8–15 years with anxiety disorders, found that high parent self-rated internalizing symptoms predicted their child's dropout from CBT (Wergeland et al., 2015). Both of these studies further indicate that addressing parents' mental health symptoms and level of distress is essential to reduce treatment dropout for their children.

Numerous studies have explored youth demographic factors including race, gender, and age and found that these variables were not significant nor reliable predictors of treatment dropout nor treatment engagement (Gonzalez et al., 2011; Skar et al., 2022; Wergeland et al., 2015). However, in a review of 27 studies of clients 0–20 years old in outpatient mental health treatment, 18 of the 27 studies found that clients with minoritized ethnicities had higher rates of treatment dropout (de Haan et al., 2013) than clients from nonminoritized groups. It was specifically found that during the first few sessions, African American youth clients were at a higher risk of treatment dropout than other clients. The increased dropout risk for African American clients is likely influenced by systemic and individual experiences of racism, lack of multicultural attunement on the part of the clinician, and possibly culturally based systems of coping including religious and spiritual practices that do not align with the treatment provided (de Haan et al., 2013). Attention to the cultural context of the child and family including mental healthcare disparities limiting access to effective care, prior negative experiences in health care, associated mistrust of providers and their settings, and other systemic barriers all need to be considered pretreatment and attended to throughout treatment to optimize engagement.

Specific to TF-CBT, most child demographic factors, including gender and race, are not significant predictors of dropout (Skar et al., 2022; Yasinski et al., 2018). Skar et al. (2022) found that youth 15–18 years old have higher dropout and treatment nonresponse rates than children 6–14 years old. This result highlights the importance of adolescent-specific treatment engagement procedures. Youth may especially benefit from an approach that emphasizes collaboration, finding common ground, exploring subjective experiences, providing praise, and ensures the youth is oriented to treatment, feels respected, understood, valued, and comfortable (e.g., not feeling pushed in a manner that undermines autonomy; Orlowski III et al., 2023).

For evidence-based treatments such as CBT, therapists and researchers need to attend to effective implementation strategies to increase treatment response and prevent dropout among children (Skar et al., 2022). Therapist competency, adherence to treatment manuals, training, and years of experience have predicted treatment engagement and positive outcomes (Podell et al., 2013). Clinicians with more intense training have lower client dropout rates for TF-CBT (Skar et al., 2022). In a study of 183 children aged 8–15 with an anxiety disorder, dropout rates were predicted by low ratings of treatment credibility by both parents and children (Wergeland et al., 2015). Thus, to reduce dropout rates, clinicians should initially focus on psychoeducation about the process of CBT treatment for anxiety (including the importance of attendance and between-session homework), emphasize the expected outcomes, and instill hope that the treatment can be beneficial. Kendall et al. (2023) emphasized the need for individualized and responsive treatment across settings (e.g., schools, home, etc.) with flexibility around treatment pacing and duration, how caregivers are involved, access to therapists, or tailoring skill development materials to encourage engagement in CBT for youth anxiety. The concept of "flexibility within fidelity" referring to adapting and personalizing treatment while still adhering to research supported interventions was discussed as a helpful concept in promoting engagement and positive treatment outcomes.

Engagement with Cultural Humility, Sensitivity to Identity, and Treatment Quality Equity

When implementing CBT for youth with anxiety, as with all clients, it is essential therapists incorporate an understanding of the complexities of clients' identities and lived experiences, especially with BIPOC, LGBTQIA+, and clients from other historically marginalized and underserved groups (Graham et al., 2014). Cultural attunement, cultural competency, and cultural humility demonstrated by the therapist can enhance treatment engagement for anxious youth and their families (Consoli et al., 2018; Tervalon & Murray-Garcia, 1998). Questions regarding racial matching of clients and therapists continue to be explored with inconclusive results; however, what is abundantly clear and backed by research is that therapist cultural understanding is a predictor of treatment engagement (Chu et al., 2023). In Chu et al.' (2023) study of over 1100 youth in school-based therapy, youth's perception of their therapist's cultural understanding was a significant predictor of early treatment engagement regardless of therapist–client racial match. Youth-reported cultural understanding was also positively associated with each of the REACH engagement dimensions, affirming that there is a unique and important contribution of cultural understanding to youth treatment engagement. Youth who feel culturally understood by their therapist may feel more comfortable disclosing information, believe therapy can help their problems, and be more likely to complete therapy activities, which facilitates outcomes (Chu et al., 2023).

Clinicians can promote understanding and convey sensitivity when they attend to the role of cultural norms, values, and beliefs as part of the conceptualization (Consoli et al., 2018). It is essential that clinicians individualize psychoeducation and adapt cognitive restructuring and exposure processes to better reflect the anxiety struggles specific to youth, especially when working with youth from oppressed and underrepresented groups (Graham et al., 2014). It is imperative that clinicians attend to racism-related stressors for minority youth, to prevent potential harm from attempting to restructure valid beliefs regarding discriminatory encounters (Metzger et al., 2021). Metzger et al. (2021) provide specific suggestions for incorporating racial socialization into cognitive coping strategies for minority youth to improve treatment engagement and outcome for African American families. In a study on innovations in CBT with youth, Consoli et al. (2018) urged integration of cultural considerations including cultural humility in treatment to work toward better understanding their youth clients' identities, to deepen the working alliance, better meet the diverse needs of clients, and improve treatment outcomes (Chu et al., 2023). This necessitates therapists and those within the field of psychology to advocate for antiracist and other diversity, equity, inclusion, and belonging policies and practices to engage racially marginalized youth in mental health services (Chu et al., 2023). Clinicians who explore their own biases and guard against assumptions about readiness for treatment or client and family engagement can better avoid the snares which contribute to inequity and exclusion. A clinician with an engagement focus is instead seeking an inclusive, individualized approach to understanding the unique experiences and intersecting identities for each client and their families (see Chaps. 9 and 10).

Strategies to Optimize Treatment Engagement

Across many research studies, several strategies for fostering treatment engagement have been identified. Many of these strategies have been shown to not only improve consistency in the treatment process but also improve the likelihood of successful treatment outcomes.

Early in treatment, specific strategies can be crucial to help launch the treatment episode and prevent early dropout. In a review (Ingoldsby, 2010), four interventions were shown to be effective for initially building engagement in children's mental health: (1) brief engagement-focused discussions, (2) family systems approaches, (3) supporting family coping and resources, and (4) motivational interviewing. In general, these strategies included examining the potential benefits of treatment, exploring family expectations for the process and for outcomes, and addressing foreseeable barriers (such as scheduling, transportation, family stressors, sources of treatment resistance). These discussions were individualized, included multiple family members, continued throughout treatment, and were consistently associated with better engagement throughout the treatment episode.

Becker et al. (2018) distilled specific engagement strategies and assessed how frequently they have been shown to enhance engagement in children's mental health settings. The top strategies used in anxiety treatment included (starting with the most frequently empirically supported strategies): assessment (e.g., gathering information about the child's strengths and needs), psychoeducation (e.g., about roles, expectations, and treatment process), promoting accessibility and reducing barriers to treatment, therapeutic goal setting, homework assignment, therapist monitoring (i.e., of treatment homework, progress, or participation), cultural acknowledgement (e.g., exploring and understanding a client's cultural identity and values), expectation setting (e.g., eliciting belief in growth and hope for change), appointment reminders, rapport building, and reinforcing (i.e., to increase the frequency of desired behaviors). This list provides therapists with a menu of behaviors they may employ to promote engagement.

Particularly in the treatment of anxiety, where therapists are encouraging clients to confront activating, fear-inducing stimuli, these strategies are essential. A client will likely not be willing to engage in exposure-based interventions without the therapist demonstrating compassionate sensitivity or clearly explaining the purpose of the exposure-based activities, i.e., why they are occurring, how they fit in the treatment process, what the client can anticipate they will be asked to do, and most importantly how these activities align with the client's and parent's goals. Of course, a client cannot engage in exposure-based interventions if they do not attend sessions, and attendance-promoting strategies are imperative as well.

Although avoidance is a hallmark symptom of anxiety and often contributes to inconsistent attendance and participation in treatment, there are strategies clinicians and agencies can utilize to mitigate logistical and pragmatic factors that contribute to low mental health service utilization for anxious youth. The use of phone or text message appointment reminders prior to appointments has become standard procedure in medical centers. Mental health clinicians treating children with anxiety may be able to increase attendance rates by sending parents and youth text reminders or leaving a voicemail prior to the appointment. A study conducted at a large medical center found that text messages sent 2 and 3 days prior to a mental health appointment were effective in reducing "no-shows" for both youth and adult mental health visits with a predicted high "no-show" rate (Ulloa-Pérez et al., 2022).

Numerous barriers to attending mental health services have been identified in the literature including limited financial resources, transportation challenges, and not having enough time for treatment (Geffken et al., 2006). The Barriers to Treatment Participation Scale is a parent rating scale for parents of children 3–18 years old aimed to identify barriers that families may experience when their child is in mental health treatment (Kazdin et al., 1997). The measure consists of five subscales including: Stressors and Obstacles that Compete with Treatment, Treatment Demands and Issues, Perceived Relevance of Treatment, Relationship with the

Therapist, and Critical Events. This measure can be administered early in treatment to identify potential barriers to treatment and facilitate a collaborative discussion around possible solutions for these barriers.

Strategies for addressing and overcoming systemic and structural barriers promote treatment engagement by enabling services to be as accessible as possible for clients and their families, thereby optimizing outcomes. While a collaborative discussion will elicit solutions from the family, some examples of clinician- and organizational-level strategies include provision of bus passes and other transportation vouchers (e.g., rideshares, taxis, etc.) to clients with transportation barriers. Within mental health clinics with multidisciplinary teams, social workers have been employed to assist mental health clients with basic needs such as food insecurity and housing through provision of resources which then enable the families to focus more on children's emotional and mental health needs. Some service settings have small snacks available and the client and family are invited to walk with the therapist to choose a snack at the conclusion of a session, as a relationship-building gesture and way to reinforce attendance and participation. Language barriers to CBT treatment for anxiety can be mitigated using in-person translation services provided by trained interpreters or technology-based translation services to increase access for children and families who are unable to meet with a mental health clinician who is proficient in their primary language. An additional pragmatic suggestion to increase CBT treatment engagement for anxious youth is to have coordinated and integrated systems of care for children and adolescents. An example is having a mental health clinician on staff at pediatric and other primary care clinics serving youth, so if anxiety is identified as a primary concern during a medical appointment, the physician can facilitate a warm hand off to a mental health therapist to increase initiation of and engagement in psychotherapy services (Schweitzer et al., 2023).

Engagement Across CBT Treatment Modalities

Various treatment of CBT modalities such as group therapy and modular CBT, as well as school-based treatment present unique treatment engagement considerations and necessitate tailored treatment engagement approaches. Engagement challenges for groups include added concerns about confidentiality, discomfort with vulnerability in a group, shame, and difficulty trusting others with sensitive material (Shuman et al., 2022). Concurrent and parallel TF-CBT treatment groups for youth and their caregivers can provide an engagement-focused approach to treatment. This caregiver group engages caregivers directly in treatment and addresses minimization of trauma impact, assuages feelings of hopelessness and helplessness, and empowers parents to provide support and nurturance for their child which promote treatment engagement (Cohen et al., 2016). In community-based treatment, it is common for clinicians to treat young people who present with multiple social, emotional, and behavioral needs from comorbid conditions across a variety of diagnoses

(Melton et al., 2016). Modular CBT has been implemented widely for treatment of young people with transdiagnostic mental health needs and has been found to be a very efficacious treatment specifically for anxiety disorders (Ewing et al., 2015) while emphasizing responsive and individualized treatment.

School-based CBT treatment for anxiety can improve access to care for students who may not otherwise have the resources to participate in therapy, but parent involvement in school-based services is notoriously challenging (Girio-Herrera et al., 2019). Services are typically provided during school hours and it may not be feasible for parents to get to campus. Participating virtually may be an option for parents but other barriers may arise. In a study of 122 anxious youth receiving school-based mental health services, youth reported that the most frequently encountered barrier was missed schoolwork during the therapy session followed by concerns about stigma and peers being aware of their participation in treatment (Pella et al., 2018). Pella et al. (2018) recommend not having sessions during specific class times and alternating treatment session times to decrease concern about missed school work. The perceived stigma issue is more difficult to address as this is a larger societal issue regarding participating in mental health services and not unique to anxious youth. Concern about seeing a school therapist could be reduced through inclusion of social and emotional education at school and normalizing the need to address mental wellness (Pella et al., 2018). Additionally, modifying CBT protocols, including timing and implementation of exposure interventions, to fit into a typical school schedule (30-min instead of 50-min sessions) may be beneficial to increase engagement in school-based CBT (Kendall et al., 2023).

Telehealth Treatment

In 2020, the unanticipated and rapid onset of the COVID-19 pandemic, and resulting health and safety concerns for clients and therapists, prompted a rapid uptake of virtual sessions, i.e., therapy provided through videoconferencing or phone audio sessions. CBT treatment engagement for anxious youth via telehealth presents both engagement benefits and challenges based on client age and developmental level, severity of symptoms, parent involvement, comorbid diagnoses, and cognitive factors (including limited attention span), to name a few. Participating in a telehealth session may be less stressful for an anxious child than meeting a therapist face-to-face; thus, telehealth could increase treatment engagement for anxious youth who otherwise may not attend treatment or prematurely dropout of treatment (Islam et al., 2023). For many teens, the use of video and devices is familiar and thus more acceptable (Radovic & Badawy, 2020); however, these modalities may reinforce avoidant behaviors if youth choose not to turn on their camera or only show a portion of their face. For socially anxious youth, the expectation to be on camera may serve as an additional stressor, compounding preexisting anxiety and negatively impacting treatment engagement (Islam et al., 2023). There is also a growing evidence base for the use of adjunctive mobile apps for anxious teens to augment CBT treatment (Lu et al., 2021). Clinicians must consider how technology can be optimally leveraged to support and scaffold treatment engagement.

Case Examples

Considerations for Early Treatment A 9-year-old female client presented to treatment with health anxiety and emetophobia precipitated by a vomiting incident on the softball field several months earlier. The client had been in therapy for approximately 2 months with a different therapist utilizing a nonspecific treatment approach and reported this therapy was ineffective in reducing anxiety. The client and mother were worried the new therapist would also be unable to assist them. The client feared she may never have relief from her anxiety and would suffer forever (cognitive distortion). The client's mother was also highly anxious and reported struggling with anxiety her entire life. In order to promote treatment engagement, during the initial assessment session, the therapist met conjointly with the client and her mother and provided a warm, empathic, and supportive presence aimed at helping the client feel understood and building trust that the therapist would be able to assist her in coping with and decreasing her anxiety. The therapist provided validation of the client's and mother's feelings, while also presenting psychoeducation about anxiety and CBT. A treatment plan was collaboratively constructed with the client and the mother. Hope was developed through discussions of the potential for relief including messages of "You will get better," "There is hope, we have a treatment that works," and explanations of the benefits of effective treatment. This therapeutic alliance promoted treatment engagement and through cognitive and behavioral coping skills, the client began to experience reductions in her anxiety symptoms. The client's decrease in symptoms was a powerful reinforcer of treatment engagement as the client and her mother had increased motivation to continue participating in treatment. Early in treatment, instilling hope and fostering a therapeutic alliance with both the child and their parent is essential for initial engagement and to sustain engagement, increasing the likelihood that the child will continue participating in treatment.

A 10-year-old boy with a history of multiple traumas presented to TF-CBT worried he was "going crazy" due to trauma-related reexperiencing symptoms including flashbacks during school. He also feared he was having a heart attack and was "going to die" due to panic symptoms misinterpreted as serious physical health ailments. The therapist provided psychoeducation about anxiety and posttraumatic stress symptoms to normalize his physiological reactions. He was provided information and applied examples regarding the fight/flight/freeze acute stress response to actual and perceived threats to safety. This psychoeducation regarding normal reactions to trauma was comforting and the client realized "I'm not weird or strange to feel these things" and this assuaged his fears which then furthered his treatment engagement. The client's increased understanding of his cognitive and physiological reactions began to reduce self-blame as he worked with his clinician to modify distorted cognitions regarding responsibility for the abuse. In the early phase of treatment, psychoeducation about anxiety including triggers, symptoms, physical sensations, etc., normalizes what the client is experiencing. By teaching youth what is happening in their bodies and minds, they may feel empowered, which increases their engagement or therapeutic "buy-in."

Considerations for Mid-Treatment As treatment progresses, clients move past assessment and treatment planning, and toward coping skill development, shifting the psychoeducation from "What is the problem?" to "What can you do about the problem?" Consider a high school student who noticed an increase in worry, more than he had in the past when he participated in therapy and reported not only feeling anxious but had now begun obsessing about sharp objects when he noticed them. When he saw scissors, letter openers, or knives, he was flooded with worry and a feeling of being unsafe. As a result, he returned to therapy for the first time in 3 years. The therapist presented the cognitive triangle and asked the client if he had seen it before. He had but did not remember it very well. With encouragement the client explained what he remembered, and the therapist genuinely praised the client's memory and willingness to share without remembering every detail. With the client's permission, the therapist shared the cognitive triangle more fully, acknowledging parts the client described, and explored the client's understanding of ways to cope with anxiety, either related to thoughts, feelings, or actions. The client described "box breathing" and "the 3 Cs: catch it, change it, and I don't remember the third one." Again, the therapist genuinely praised the client's understanding of coping skills and asked the client to teach the therapist about box breathing. He was able to, as they practiced the skill and then explored the "3 Cs" together. The therapist listed a few additional coping skills. The therapist explained the reasons for talking about coping skills and emphasized the value for the client (who was a fan of *Avatar: The Last Airbender*) to become not just a "Bender" but a "Master" of the skills by learning how to use the coping skills when no one else is reminding him. Together the client and therapist decided on a homework assignment of the client teaching his father about the cognitive triangle and box breathing. This case stresses the importance of building the relationship, aligning roles and expectations, building upon prior learning, providing clarity for the next treatment steps, and utilization of homework to facilitate coping and enhance mastery and self-efficacy.

In the mid-treatment period, it is crucial to sustain treatment engagement and prevent premature attrition prior to the client achieving and solidifying therapeutic progress. As therapeutic tasks become more challenging and uncomfortable for anxious clients, it may become more difficult to maintain client engagement. Consider a 6-year-old Latina girl who was brought to an outpatient community mental health center by her mother due to an onset of separation anxiety and school refusal. The client was attending kindergarten at a public school in an urban community and was the only child of a single mother who had immigrated to the United States and had an extensive trauma history. The client's separation anxiety and various other fears about her safety often manifested as externalizing behavior problems as the client became increasingly overwhelmed. Once the client arrived at school, she would refuse to exit her mother's car and eventually her mother would pull her out of the car and the client would cry, scream, and cling to her mom. If a school official attempted to separate the client from her mother, she would act aggressively by hitting, kicking, and attempting to bite the staff member. School refusal ensued and the client had numerous absences, with her mother reporting it was too exhausting and upsetting to battle with the client in the mornings to try to get her to school.

Due to the client's age and developmental level, many of the clinic-based CBT interventions were conducted through art, games, and play, which assisted with client engagement as she enjoyed the therapeutic activities. The initial stage of treatment, the majority of which was conducted conjointly with the mother, emphasized psychoeducation, therapist modeling for the mother of how to manage client's anxiety, gradual exposure incorporating a "feelings thermometer," a coping skills toolkit, and developmentally appropriate cognitive restructuring. However, treatment progress stalled when the strategies the mother implemented at home and some of the office-based techniques (e.g., imaginal exposure and separation from the mother during the sessions) were marginally successful with little symptom relief. The therapist modified the treatment plan, aware that additional supports were needed. To provide family support, the mother was referred to another therapist at the agency to provide culturally attuned CBT in Spanish, the mother's native language. This collateral parent therapy addressed acculturation stress and the intergenerational impact of trauma, provided psychoeducation regarding how mom's anxiety increased client's fear of leaving her mother, and taught the mother CBT skills to manage her worries. To optimize efficacy and increase the engagement of the client and her mother, the therapist partnered with the school counselor and client's mom to collaboratively create an exposure hierarchy (fear ladder) and a plan for in vivo exposure to facilitate client's return to regular school attendance. The mother was coached to keep dropoffs brief, offer encouragement, and convey confidence that the client could be successful. On multiple occasions, to continue to promote engagement, the therapist was also present at school in the morning during dropoff, coaching client and mom to use their coping skills and assist them in tolerating distress at manageable levels. This case illustrates the importance of supporting the parent's mental health, remaining culturally attuned, being adaptable when interventions are not initially successful, and partnering with other supports, as clinically indicated, to help the child and family decrease anxiety.

Considerations for Termination and Maintenance In the final stages of treatment, an engagement focus gives way to relapse prevention, with sustainment of healthy behaviors and solidification of growth that has occurred over the course of treatment. Clinicians ensure that the client and family are able to access care in the future if the need arises. Therapists might help align expectations that completing treatment does not equate to perfecting mental health, that setbacks and challenges are common, and returning to treatment is not indicative of failure. While the therapist believes the client and family are equipped to navigate the inevitable turbulence of the future, there is no shame or embarrassment in seeking support again. A relapse prevention plan will include information about signs that would indicate the client may need additional help from a therapist and how to access that help.

Conclusion

CBT is a highly efficacious treatment for youth struggling with anxiety; however, to achieve favorable treatment outcomes and corresponding symptom relief, youth and their caregivers need to access and initiate treatment and then continue to participate in a course of treatment. As this chapter has highlighted, anxiety-focused CBT treatment engagement for pediatric populations is a multifaceted and complex issue. Treatment engagement is influenced by client and family variables, the therapist's clinical and interpersonal skills, and system and community variables. Despite the barriers to care, clinicians can consider the pragmatic strategies offered within to optimize treatment engagement and facilitate more positive outcomes. As clinicians collaborate with clients and their families to elicit engagement, they also expand their client's opportunities to overcome mental health challenges, to heal, to move forward in their lives, and to grow.

Clinical Summary Points and Recommendations

1. To optimize CBT treatment engagement for youth with anxiety and their families, clinicians should attend to the five dimensions of the REACH framework (Chorpita & Becker, 2022): Relationship, Expectancy, Attendance, Clarity, and Homework.
2. Clinicians need to be mindful of steps they can take to increase access to mental health services for youth with anxiety including providing telehealth, school-based mental health services, and outreach to families.
3. Effective CBT treatment for youth with anxiety occurs with primary attention to cultural attunement, cultural competency, and cultural humility to enhance treatment engagement, especially for marginalized and underserved populations.
4. Targeted efforts to include caregivers in treatment are essential for child and adolescent CBT treatment engagement. These efforts need to attend to the specific treatment engagement barriers faced by families.
5. Flexibility with CBT interventions for anxious youth is paramount to treatment engagement and progress as change and symptom reduction do not occur in a one-size-fits-all approach.

References

Becker, K. D., Boustani, M., Gellatly, R., & Chorpita, B. F. (2018). Forty years of engagement research in children's mental health services: Multidimensional measurement and practice elements. *Journal of Clinical Child & Adolescent Psychology, 47*(1), 1–23.

Beesdo, K., Knappe, S., & Pine, D. S. (2009). Anxiety and anxiety disorders in children and adolescents: Developmental issues and implications for DSM-V. *Psychiatric Clinics, 32*(3), 483–524.

Bronfenbrenner, U. (1994). Ecological models of human development. *International encyclopedia of education, 3*(2), 37–43.

Chorpita, B. F., & Becker, K. D. (2022). Dimensions of treatment engagement among youth and caregivers: Structural validity of the REACH framework. *Journal of Consulting and Clinical Psychology, 90*(3), 258–271. https://doi.org/10.1037/ccp0000711

Chu, W., Chorpita, B. F., & Becker, K. D. (2023). Race, racial matching, and cultural understanding as predictors of treatment engagement in youth mental health services. *Psychotherapy Research, 33*(5), 669–682.

Cohen, J. A., Mannarino, A. P., & Deblinger, E. (2016). *Treating trauma and traumatic grief in children and adolescents*. Guilford Publications.

Connor, D. F., Ford, J. D., Arnsten, A. F., & Greene, C. A. (2015). An update on posttraumatic stress disorder in children and adolescents. *Clinical Pediatrics, 54*(6), 517–528.

Consoli, A. J., Blears, K., Bunge, E. L., Mandil, J., Sharma, H., & Whaling, K. M. (2018). Integrating culture, pedagogy, and humor in CBT with anxious and depressed youth. *Practice Innovations, 3*(2), 138–151. https://doi.org/10.1037/pri0000069

Crandal, B. R., Martin, J. K., Hazen, A. L., & Rolls Reutz, J. A. (2019). Measuring collaboration across children's behavioral health and child welfare systems. *Psychological Services, 16*(1), 111.

Cummings, C. M., Kazantzis, N., & Kendall, P. C. (2014). Facilitating homework and generalization of skills to the real world. In *Evidence-based CBT for anxiety and depression in children and adolescents: A competencies-based approach* (pp. 141–155). Monash University.

de Haan, A. M., Boon, A. E., De Jong, J. T., Hoeve, M., & Vermeiren, R. R. (2013). A meta-analytic review on treatment dropout in child and adolescent outpatient mental health care. *Clinical Psychology Review, 33*(5), 698–711.

Dean, S., Britt, E., Bell, E., Stanley, J., & Collings, S. (2016). Motivational interviewing to enhance adolescent mental health treatment engagement: A randomized clinical trial. *Psychological Medicine, 46*(9), 1961–1969.

Delli, C. K. S., Polychronopoulou, S. A., Kolaitis, G. A., & Antoniou, A. S. G. (2018). Review of interventions for the management of anxiety symptoms in children with ASD. *Neuroscience & Biobehavioral Reviews, 95*, 449–463.

Ewing, D. L., Monsen, J. J., Thompson, E. J., Cartwright-Hatton, S., & Field, A. (2015). A meta-analysis of transdiagnostic cognitive behavioural therapy in the treatment of child and young person anxiety disorders. *Behavioural and Cognitive Psychotherapy, 43*(5), 562–577.

Fjermestad, K. W., Føreland, Ø., Oppedal, S. B., Sørensen, J. S., Vognild, Y. H., Gjestad, R., Ost, L., Bjaastad, J., Shiek, S., & Wergeland, G. J. (2021). Therapist alliance-building behaviors, alliance, and outcomes in cognitive behavioral treatment for youth anxiety disorders. *Journal of Clinical Child & Adolescent Psychology, 50*(2), 229–242.

Geffken, G. R., Keeley, M. L., Kellison, I., Storch, E. A., & Rodrigue, J. R. (2006). Parental adherence to child psychologists' recommendations from psychological testing. *Professional Psychology: Research and Practice, 37*(5), 499–505. https://doi.org/10.1037/0735-7028.37.5.499

Ghandour, R. M., Sherman, L. J., Vladutiu, C. J., Ali, M. M., Lynch, S. E., Bitsko, R. H., & Blumberg, S. J. (2019). Prevalence and treatment of depression, anxiety, and conduct problems in US children. *The Journal of Pediatrics, 206*, 256–267.

Girio-Herrera, E., Ehrlich, C. J., Danzi, B. A., & La Greca, A. M. (2019). Lessons learned about barriers to implementing school-based interventions for adolescents: Ideas for enhancing future research and clinical projects. *Cognitive and Behavioral Practice, 26*(3), 466–477. https://doi.org/10.1016/j.cbpra.2018.11.004

Glenn, D., Golinelli, D., Rose, R. D., Roy-Byrne, P., Stein, M. B., Sullivan, G., & Craske, M. G. (2013). Who gets the most out of cognitive behavioral therapy for anxiety disorders? The role of treatment dose and patient engagement. *Journal of Consulting and Clinical Psychology, 81*(4), 639.

Gonzalez, A., Weersing, V. R., Warnick, E. M., Scahill, L. D., & Woolston, J. L. (2011). Predictors of treatment attrition among an outpatient clinic sample of youths with clinically significant anxiety. *Administration and Policy in Mental Health and Mental Health Services Research, 38*, 356–367.

Graham, J. R., Sorenson, S., & Hayes-Skelton, S. A. (2014). Enhancing the cultural sensitivity of cognitive behavioral interventions for anxiety in diverse populations. *The Behavior Therapist, 37*(5), 101–108.

Haine-Schlagel, R., Dickson, K. S., Shapiro, A. F., May, G. C., & Cheng, P. (2019). Parent mental health problems and motivation as predictors of their engagement in community-based child mental health services. *Children and Youth Services Review, 104*, 104370.

Hudson, J. L., & Kendall, P. C. (2002). Showing you can do it: Homework in therapy for children and adolescents with anxiety disorders. *Journal of Clinical Psychology, 58*(5), 525–534.

Ingoldsby, E. M. (2010). Review of interventions to improve family engagement and retention in parent and child mental health programs. *Journal of Child and Family Studies, 19*, 629–645.

Islam, S., Sanchez, A. L., McDermott, C. L., Clapp, D., Worley, J., & Becker-Haimes, E. M. (2023). To proceed via telehealth or not? Considerations for pediatric anxiety and related disorders beyond COVID-19. *Cognitive and Behavioral Practice*. https://doi.org/10.1016/j.cbpra.2023.01.004

Johansen, K., Saran, I., Cho, E., Weisz, J., & Price, A. M. A. (2023). *Examining racial and ethnic differences in youth psychotherapy treatment engagement and outcomes*. https://osf.io/preprints/osf/v9cdb

Karver, M. S., De Nadai, A. S., Monahan, M., & Shirk, S. R. (2018). Meta-analysis of the prospective relation between alliance and outcome in child and adolescent psychotherapy. *Psychotherapy, 55*(4), 341–355. https://doi.org/10.1037/pst0000176

Kazdin, A. E., Holland, L., Crowley, M., & Breton, S. (1997). Barriers to treatment participation scale: Evaluation and validation in the context of child outpatient treatment. *Journal of Child Psychology and Psychiatry, 38*(8), 1051–1062.

Kazzi, C., Campbell, L., & Porter, M. (2023). Psychological therapies for anxiety in autistic individuals with co-occurring intellectual developmental disorder: A systematic review. *Review Journal of Autism and Developmental Disorders*, 1–17.

Kendall, P. C., Ney, J. S., Maxwell, C. A., Lehrbach, K. R., Jakubovic, R. J., McKnight, D. S., & Friedman, A. L. (2023). Adapting CBT for youth anxiety: Flexibility, within fidelity, in different settings. *Frontiers in Psychiatry, 14*, 194.

Lu, C., Chu, W., Madden, S., Parmanto, B., & Silk, J. S. (2021). Adolescent perspectives on how an adjunctive mobile app for social anxiety treatment impacts treatment engagement in telehealth group therapy. *Social Sciences, 10*(10), 397.

Lundkvist-Houndoumadi, I., & Thastum, M. (2017). Anxious children and adolescents non responding to CBT: Clinical predictors and families' experiences of therapy. *Clinical Psychology & Psychotherapy, 24*(1), 82–93.

Melton, T. H., Croarkin, P. E., Strawn, J. R., & Mcclintock, S. M. (2016). Comorbid anxiety and depressive symptoms in children and adolescents: A systematic review and analysis. *Journal of Psychiatric Practice, 22*(2), 84.

Metzger, I. W., Anderson, R. E., Are, F., & Ritchwood, T. (2021). Healing interpersonal and racial trauma: Integrating racial socialization into trauma-focused cognitive behavioral therapy for African American youth. *Child Maltreatment, 26*(1), 17–27.

Mosher, D. K., Hook, J. N., Captari, L. E., Davis, D. E., DeBlaere, C., & Owen, J. (2017). Cultural humility: A therapeutic framework for engaging diverse clients. *Practice Innovations, 2*(4), 221.

Orlowski, E. W., III, Bender, A. M., & Karver, M. S. (2023). A systematic review and meta-analysis of clinician behaviors and characteristics related to alliance building with youth clients. *Clinical Psychology Review, 102273.*

Park, S. C., & Kim, Y. K. (2020). Anxiety disorders in the DSM-5: Changes, controversies, and future directions. In *Anxiety Disorders: Rethinking and Understanding Recent Discoveries* (pp. 187–196).

Patterson, G. R., & Forgatch, M. S. (2001). Therapist behavior as a determinant for client non-compliance: A paradox for the behavior modifier. In C. E. Hill (Ed.), *Helping skills: The empirical foundation* (pp. 271–283). American Psychological Association. https://doi.org/10.1037/10412-016

Pella, J. E., Ginsburg, G. S., Casline, E., Pikulski, P. J., & Drake, K. L. (2018). Children's perceptions of barriers to session attendance in school-based treatment for anxiety. *School Mental Health, 10*(4), 417–427.

Podell, J. L., Kendall, P. C., Gosch, E. A., Compton, S. N., March, J. S., Albano, A.-M., Rynn, M. A., Walkup, J. T., Sherrill, J. T., Ginsburg, G. S., Keeton, C. P., Birmaher, B., & Piacentini, J. C. (2013). Therapist factors and outcomes in CBT for anxiety in youth. *Professional Psychology: Research and Practice, 44*(2), 89–98. https://doi.org/10.1037/a0031700

Polanczyk, G. V., Salum, G. A., Sugaya, L. S., Caye, A., & Rohde, L. A. (2015). Annual research review: A meta-analysis of the worldwide prevalence of mental disorders in children and adolescents. *Journal of Child Psychology and Psychiatry, 56*(3), 345–365.

Radez, J., Reardon, T., Creswell, C., Lawrence, P. J., Evdoka-Burton, G., & Waite, P. (2021). Why do children and adolescents (not) seek and access professional help for their mental health problems? A systematic review of quantitative and qualitative studies. *European Child & Adolescent Psychiatry, 30*(2), 183–211. https://doi.org/10.1007/s00787-019-01469-4

Radovic, A., & Badawy, S. M. (2020). Technology use for adolescent health and wellness. *Pediatrics, 145*(Supplement_2), S186–S194.

Sacco, R., Camilleri, N., Eberhardt, J., Umla-Runge, K., & Newbury-Birch, D. (2022). A systematic review and meta-analysis on the prevalence of mental disorders among children and adolescents in Europe. *European Child & Adolescent Psychiatry*, 1–18.

Schwartz, C., Barican, J., Yung, D., Zheng, Y., & Waddell, C. (2019). Six decades of preventing and treating childhood anxiety disorders: A systematic review and meta-analysis to inform policy and practice. *BMJ Mental Health, 22*, 103–110.

Schweitzer, J., Bird, A., Bowers, H., Carr-Lee, N., Gibney, J., Schellinger, K., Holt, J. R., Adams, D. P., Hensler, D. J., & Hollenbach, K. (2023). Developing an innovative pediatric integrated mental health care program: Interdisciplinary team successes and challenges. *Frontiers in Psychiatry, 14*. https://doi.org/10.3389/fpsyt.2023.1252037

Shuman, T., Johnson, K., Lively Cookson, L., & Gilbert, N. (2022). Creative interventions for preparing and disclosing trauma narratives in group therapy for child sexual abuse. *Journal of Child Sexual Abuse, 31*(1), 127–146. https://doi.org/10.1080/10538712.2020.1801931

Skar, A. M. S., Braathu, N., Jensen, T. K., & Ormhaug, S. M. (2022). Predictors of nonresponse and drop-out among children and adolescents receiving TF-CBT: Investigation of client-, therapist-, and implementation factors. *BMC Health Services Research, 22*(1), 1–13. https://doi.org/10.1186/s12913-022-08497-y

Tervalon, M., & Murray-Garcia, J. (1998). Cultural humility versus cultural competence: A critical distinction in defining physician training outcomes in multicultural education. *Journal of Health Care for the Poor and Underserved, 9*(2), 117–125.

Thomas, K. C., Ellis, A. R., Konrad, T. R., Holzer, C. E., & Morrissey, J. P. (2009). County-level estimates of mental health professional shortage in the United States. *Psychiatric Services, 60*(10), 1323–1328.

Ulloa-Pérez, E., Blasi, P. R., Westbrook, E. O., Lozano, P., Coleman, K. F., & Coley, R. Y. (2022). Pragmatic randomized study of targeted text message reminders to reduce missed clinic visits. *The Permanente Journal, 26*(1), 64–72.

Waid, J., & Kelly, M. (2020). Supporting family engagement with child and adolescent mental health services: A scoping review. *Health & Social Care in the Community, 28*(5), 1333–1342.

Walter, H. J., Bukstein, O. G., Abright, A. R., Keable, H., Ramtekkar, U., Ripperger-Suhler, J., & Rockhill, C. (2020). Clinical practice guideline for the assessment and treatment of children and adolescents with anxiety disorders. *Journal of the American Academy of Child & Adolescent Psychiatry, 59*(10), 1107–1124.

Weisz, J. R., Venturo-Conerly, K. E., Fitzpatrick, O. M., Frederick, J. A., & Ng, M. Y. (2023). What four decades of meta-analysis have taught us about youth psychotherapy and the science of research synthesis. *Annual Review of Clinical Psychology, 19*, 79–105.

Wergeland, G. J. H., Fjermestad, K. W., Marin, C. E., Haugland, B. S. M., Silverman, W. K., Öst, L. G., Havik, O. E., & Heiervang, E. R. (2015). Predictors of dropout from community clinic child CBT for anxiety disorders. *Journal of Anxiety Disorders, 31*, 1–10.

Yasinski, C., Hayes, A. M., Alpert, E., McCauley, T., Ready, C. B., Webb, C., & Deblinger, E. (2018). Treatment processes and demographic variables as predictors of dropout from trauma-focused cognitive behavioral therapy (TF-CBT) for youth. *Behaviour Research and Therapy, 107*, 10–18.

Zarzycka, B., Jankowski, T., & Krasiczyńska, B. (2022). Therapeutic relationship and professional burnout in psychotherapists: A structural equation model approach. *Clinical Psychology & Psychotherapy, 29*(1), 250–259.

Chapter 17
Older Adults

Steven R. Thorp, Charlotte S. Zell, Kelly Colón, Katarzyna Modzelewska, Carolyn B. Allard, and Natalie M. Rice-Thorp

Background

Approximately one in five people across the globe will be aged 65 or older by 2050 (Roberts et al., 2018). There are many stressors typical with increasing age, including significant health and lifestyle changes that impact well-being (Thorp et al., 2011). Older adults may experience physical and cognitive decline, social isolation, role transition, and the loss of loved ones (Hill, 2011; Thorp, 2022). Older adulthood also poses an increased likelihood of suicide, and the Baby Boomer cohort (born between 1946 and 1964) has higher rates of suicide than any other living generational cohort (Tisdale, 2022). However, older adults may have reduced income due to disability or retirement status (Wuthrich & Frei, 2015), and those on fixed income may not view treatment as a necessary expense.

Although less common than in younger adult populations, disorders involving anxiety symptoms (e.g., social anxiety disorder, posttraumatic stress disorder [PTSD], and obsessive-compulsive disorder [OCD]) are common in older adults and are more than twice as prevalent as mood disorders (Gum et al., 2009). Older and younger adults appear to prefer psychotherapy to medications (Gum et al., 2006; Jaeger et al., 2010). One type of psychotherapy, cognitive-behavioral therapy (CBT), has been shown in thousands of empirical studies to reduce symptom severity across psychological disorders (Beck, 2021).

S. R. Thorp (✉) · C. S. Zell · K. Colón · K. Modzelewska · C. B. Allard
California School of Professional Psychology, Alliant International University, San Diego, CA, USA
e-mail: steven.thorp@alliant.edu; cszell@uh.edu; kcolon@alliant.edu; kmodzelewska@alliant.edu; carolyn.allard@alliant.edu

N. M. Rice-Thorp
Private Practice, San Diego, CA, USA

E. M. Goetter (ed.), *Optimizing Treatment Engagement Processes in CBT for Anxiety and Related Disorders*, CBT: Science Into Practice,
https://doi.org/10.1007/978-3-031-91439-3_17

CBT involves the monitoring and changing of thoughts and actions to reduce symptom severity. In recent years, there has been an increased focus on culturally responsive CBT that addresses the challenges faced by individuals from diverse backgrounds (Beck, 2021; Iwamasa & Hays, 2019). One facet of diversity that is relatively neglected in the empirical literature is older adulthood (Dinnen et al., 2015; Thorp et al., 2009). There is evidence that CBTs have provided relief for older adults impacted by a variety of anxiety disorders, such as PTSD and OCD (Barlow, 2021; Gould et al., 2012; Hall et al., 2016; Thorp et al., 2019). Aspects of CBT may be particularly well-suited to older adults, including the consistency and learning-based focus of components in every session (e.g., check-in, agenda setting, homework review, summary of discussions, and a multimedia approach to enhance learning and memory). Anxious older adults may have difficulties engaging in CBTs, however (Woodhead et al., 2013; Wuthrich & Frei, 2015).

Symptoms of Anxiety, PTSD, and OCD

There is a dearth of literature examining older adults' phenomenology, presentation, and treatment with regard to anxiety-based disorders (Brenes, 2006; Thorp et al., 2009). The hallmark of anxiety disorders is excessive fear or worry that interferes with daily activities and functioning. Anticipation of future threats that may be difficult to control may lead to avoidance behaviors. Older adults may have different sources of anxiety than those of younger adults due to the increasing likelihood of physical or cognitive decline, as well as bereavement and loss of social support.

Symptom presentations may also differ between younger and older adults. Older adults report less worry in comparison to younger adults (Brenes, 2006). Some symptoms, such as "excessive" anxiety, may be harder to detect in older adults (Mohlman et al., 2012). Older adults may be reluctant to acknowledge or unable to recognize mental health symptoms due to lack of awareness and terminology and perceived stigma (Cook et al., 2017). Recognizing the effects of aging on clinical presentations for anxiety and other disorders (e.g., mood disorders), the Advisory Committee to the Lifespan Disorders Work Group (Mohlman et al., 2012) generated eight recommendations to inform the evolution of the DSM, including greater inclusion of older adults in clinical trials and clearer guidance about assessing anxiety and avoidance in older adults, especially in the context of medical and cognitive impairments.

Other updates ultimately reflected in the DSM-5 and its subsequent text revision included moving PTSD from the anxiety disorders section into the trauma and stressor-related disorders section due to the recognition that it shares elements of both anxiety and mood disorders while also comprising unique features (American Psychiatric Association, 2013). Compared to younger adults, older adults report less exposure to potentially traumatic events (PTE) and lower rates of PTSD (Cook et al., 2017). Older adults might not connect current symptoms to traumatic events decades in the past, which may result in a different experience and expression of PTSD symptoms relative to younger adults (Thorp et al., 2011). OCD was similarly moved from anxiety disorders to its own section in DSM-5. The symptoms of OCD do not appear to differ between older and younger adults, though the content of obsessions may be different. However, older adults may report higher levels of pathological doubt, related to checking and reassurance-seeking behaviors, than younger adults (Jazi & Ashghar-Ali, 2020).

Prevalence of Anxiety Disorders, PTSD, and OCD in Older Adults

Many epidemiological studies about anxiety exclude adults over a certain age, have a young cutoff for what is considered "older adulthood," or do not report detailed analyses based on age (Thorp et al., 2009). In general, anxiety and related disorders appear to be common in older adults, though less prevalent than in younger adult populations. A meta-analysis of epidemiological studies using diagnostic criteria from 1980 to 2013 (Witlox et al., 2021) estimated the 12-month prevalence of specific phobia at 6.0%, PTSD at 2.9%, generalized anxiety disorder (GAD) at 3.0%, social anxiety disorder at 1.7%, agoraphobia at 1.5%, panic disorder at 1.3%, and OCD at 1.1% among adults aged 55 or older. The authors reported that subthreshold anxiety can still be functionally impairing and was even more common in older adults than the full syndromes, particularly for panic, specific phobia, and generalized anxiety.

Lower estimated prevalence rates in older compared to younger adults may be due to the insufficiency of traditional diagnostic tools, which were designed primarily for younger populations and do not account for differences in symptom expression and reporting in older adults (Thorp et al., 2011). Few studies have examined the 12-month prevalence of anxiety disorders in older adults using DSM-5 criteria, and those that do use standard adult diagnostic tools. Those studies estimate the prevalence of GAD at about 3.5% and PTSD at 2.2% in older samples (Nilsson et al., 2019; Rhee et al., 2019). Overall, reliable and up-to-date prevalence data on anxiety and other mental disorders in older adults is lacking; more research is needed using age-specific DSM-5 diagnostic instruments to better inform care and facilitate targeted treatment engagement efforts. More accurate data on prevalence rates can help further guide research on potential barriers to care in the older population.

Potential Barriers to Care

Stigma and Inexperience with Mental Health Services

Older adults may be less familiar with psychological assessments, treatments, and terminology than younger adults and thus may be less comfortable pursuing mental health services (Thorp et al., 2009). Clinicians should seek to minimize psychological jargon and be mindful of assumptions and potential sources of stigma to optimize receptivity and engagement. For example, older combat veterans may report feeling "stressed out" or "on guard" as opposed to feeling afraid. Older clients may describe feeling "blue" or "down" as opposed to sad or depressed. They might also prefer more empowering terminology such as "survivor" versus "victim" and "older person" versus "elderly" (Avers et al., 2011). Regarding assignments by therapists between sessions, older adults may respond more to terms such as "practice," "activities," and "challenges" as opposed to "homework" (Thorp, 2022).

Older adults may underutilize mental health services due to a belief that it is normal to be anxious and depressed in old age (Wuthrich & Frei, 2015). Symptoms may have begun long ago, before there was much public knowledge or terminology for them, such that older adults do not recognize them as something for which they could get treatment. As discussed earlier, older adults may report anxiety somatically to their primary care physicians, which may not be recognized as part of a condition that mental health treatment could address. Even if symptoms were to be recognized, there are many older generations who have a salient culture of self-reliance, which also serves as a barrier to treatment (Wuthrich & Frei, 2015).

People often assume that older adults have higher levels of stigma related to mental health. The limited evidence, however, suggests the opposite. Older adults appear to have the lowest levels of stigma and the most positive attitudes toward help-seeking (Mackenzie et al., 2019). However, in older but not younger patients, greater perceived stigma was associated with a greater likelihood of premature treatment discontinuation, and those patients did not seek care elsewhere (Sirey et al., 2001). Addressing stigma early in treatment may thus be particularly important.

Poor Physical Health and Mobility

Older adults may experience health and mobility problems that make attending therapy sessions more difficult. Clinicians working with older adults can improve the accessibility of their office space by offering CBT remotely via videoconferencing, which evidence suggests is equivalent in efficacy to in-person therapy (e.g., Liu et al., 2019). Physical health problems could also make it challenging for older clients to engage in behavioral interventions. In such cases, clinicians can collaboratively modify behavioral experiments with older clients while examining maladaptive thoughts about their physical impairments or fear of falling that may prevent them from participating in activities (Evans, 2007; Liu et al., 2018; Mohlman et al., 2012). Collaboration with clients' other healthcare providers may also be helpful throughout this process.

Technological Challenges

Although technology can provide more access to some clients, it is not without barriers itself. Operating smartphones may prove challenging for older adults with decreased fine motor skills. Smartphone performance is negatively correlated with age (Martin et al., 2019). In addition, technology-related anxiety—technophobia—can lead to avoidance, embarrassment, and diminished perceptions of abilities related to electronic devices and telehealth (Mohlman et al., 2022).

Potential Adaptations to Promote Engagement

Integration of Services

There is evidence that collaborative care models, in which mental health and physical health services are integrated, greatly improve access to preferred treatments (Gum et al., 2006). Older adults may have scheduling flexibility if they are retired, but when mental health and physical health treatment settings are colocated and adjacent appointments are created, attendance is maximized (Thorp, 2022). Providing resources for reliable transportation can also facilitate health care (Thorp et al., 2009).

Optimizing the Therapeutic Alliance

Older adults are often in the midst of difficult life transitions, including the loss of important relationships and aspects of personal identity. The therapist may thus provide a critical source of relational and personal stability (Secker et al., 2004). A strong therapeutic alliance is positively associated with treatment completion and adherence in the general adult population (Buchholz & Abramowitz, 2020). It may be particularly important among older adults. The process of learning about the principles and methods of CBT can take longer in older adults, who may lack familiarity with cognitive behavioral concepts and have greater deficits in cognition or memory (Secker et al., 2004). In the beginning of therapy, therefore, improvements in symptoms and motivation to participate in CBT among older adults may be primarily driven by the therapeutic relationship.

For older adults with spiritual or religious identities, the incorporation of spirituality into CBT can lead to anxiety and depressive symptom relief earlier in treatment (Paukert et al., 2009). This may have important implications for alliance, attrition, and adherence. Early improvement may motivate older adults to stay in treatment and engage more deeply in the therapeutic process. Therapists can potentially mitigate age-related challenges associated with fluid intelligence by incorporating familiar religious beliefs, practices, and metaphors into otherwise novel cognitive behavioral frameworks and skills (such as cognitive restructuring; Paukert et al., 2009). For nonreligious clients, integration of familiar cultural beliefs and practices may be similarly helpful.

Social Support

Social support is associated with greater treatment satisfaction and perceived effectiveness among older adults (Lippens & Mackenzie, 2011). A study found that older adults with more pretreatment social support and improvement in social support during CBT treatment experienced greater improvements in self-reported quality of life (LaRocca & Scogin, 2015). In another study, older adults with greater emotional social support were more likely to complete the recommended sessions of CBT (Vásquez et al., 2021). Loved ones should be included in treatment when indicated (Thorp et al., 2011).

Clinical Strategies for Engaging Adults in CBT

Pretreatment Considerations

Advertising and Language

To reach more older adults, targeted outreach should emphasize how CBT can help with overall well-being, functioning, and health issues, as well as connections with loved ones, finding and engaging in pleasant activities, and navigating general issues of aging and loss. Incorporating images of older clients in advertising may increase the perceived relevance of CBT. In a study on marketing evidence-based treatments for PTSD to veterans (Kehle-Forbes et al., 2022), female participants assumed that the treatments were only for men if women were not portrayed in educational videos. Older adults may make similar assumptions when materials do not depict clients in their age group.

Needs and preferences should also be considered. Diminished vision and hearing are correlated with age (Thorp et al., 2009, 2011), and as such, larger, bolded font is preferred among older adults and should therefore be used on informational materials (Price et al., 2016), which should be provided in print as well as online. Many older adults appreciate being addressed formally (e.g., Mr. X, Ms. Y, Dr. Z), at least initially.

Scheduling

Memory may be a vulnerability for some older adults, potentially exacerbated by their psychiatric symptoms (Schuitevoerder et al., 2013). Coles et al. (2004) found that only 15% of individuals inquiring about treatment for social anxiety eventually started treatment at their clinic, and the authors noted that encouragement, addressing financial concerns directly, and having an inclusive approach could potentially increase attendance. Automated phone call or text reminders may make it less likely that potential clients will "no show." At the end of each session, staff can provide clients with business cards with the appointment date and time and stickers to apply to calendars. Staff can also assist with entering smartphone reminders, if indicated.

Motivation for Treatment

Motivational interviewing (MI) is a therapeutic skill that has the potential to increase an individual's motivation, engagement, and commitment. MI utilizes collaborative conversations and questions to elicit intrinsic motivation (Serdarevic & Lemke, 2013). Treatment initiation, engagement, and outcomes all appear to be positively influenced by MI (Marker & Norton, 2018; Randall & McNeil, 2017; Westra et al., 2016). However, for this intervention to be effectively applied with older adults, it is important to understand the factors that motivate this population to seek therapy. Among older adults, the top factors that motivated treatment initiation were health concerns, family issues, mental health symptoms, positive therapy experiences observed in others, and the belief that therapy would be helpful (Woodhead et al., 2013). One study directly compared the treatment goals of older and younger adults and found that older adults were less focused on personal growth and more focused on well-being, functioning, navigating physical losses, and coping with aging (Sittler et al., 2022). Similarly, handling health issues and age-related losses were top concerns for older adults participating in a trial of CBT (Vathke et al., 2022). Together, this research suggests that common challenges in late life are important treatment motivators for older adults, regardless of their specific diagnoses or symptoms. This data should inform targeted advertising of CBT and early interactions by clinicians and office staff to increase access and engagement in treatment by older adults.

The Office Setting

In a study on perceptions of psychotherapy, waiting rooms that included older adults, spacious, very well-lit waiting rooms with positive distractions in the room (e.g., older adult magazines) and different types of seating (to promote agency), as well as nature-themed decor, improved the contentedness of clients (Noble & Devlin, 2021). Spaciousness also helps to accommodate wheelchairs, canes, and other mobility devices. Clinicians should also consider the perceived privacy of information and the noise level in the room. If televisions are used in waiting rooms, they should be tuned to neutral, welcoming channels (e.g., home and garden) with subtitles on. Ambient noise may make it more difficult to hear, with or without hearing aids.

The Assessment Process

Common assessment methods include diagnostic interviews, intake interviews, and questionnaires. Providing feedback to clients about assessments is critical for validating symptoms and client concerns as well as educating clients (Barlow, 2021). It is important to include trauma histories as part of intake interviews for older adults, as traumatic events that occurred many years ago may not be salient without direct questioning (Thorp et al., 2011). Obtaining releases of information to interview collateral informants, such as loved ones, can greatly enhance the assessment process with any individual who may have memory issues (Thorp et al., 2011).

Clients with physical disabilities may benefit from a modification to typical questionnaire administration, such as reading questions and responses aloud, allowing for pointing or eye movement responses, inclusion of multiple-choice materials, and pantomiming instructions (Caplan & Shechter, 1995). Older adult clients may be assessed for cognitive decline, if indicated, to help identify if compensatory techniques would be helpful in the therapy setting (Evans, 2007). Printed assessment materials should be in large, bold font (Caplan & Shechter, 1995; Thorp et al., 2011), and interviewers should ensure that their lips are visible to the client, when possible, to facilitate communication if there is hearing impairment. Screening questionnaires can be used to flag potential safety issues such as abuse or suicide risk.

Self-monitoring is commonly used in CBT: It typically involves the client tracking thoughts, behaviors, and emotions daily or weekly (such as thought or activity records; Barlow, 2021). Therapists can instill in clients the ability to self-monitor and identify their symptoms and help them be aware of the context in which the symptoms occur. Clients can also be shown graphs that show the trajectory of symptom change over time and how to interpret scores in a personal way.

Psychoeducation About Treatment

In the general population, the credibility of a treatment is one of the strongest predictors of treatment preference (Zoellner et al., 2019), and clients who agree with rationales for CBT appear to improve more quickly and have better outcomes than those who do not (Zoellner et al., 2003). Low perceived effectiveness is associated with increased risk of dropping out of treatment among older adults (Lippens & Mackenzie, 2011). Hundt et al. (2013) found that compared to enhanced usual care for older individuals with GAD, CBT resulted in greater treatment satisfaction, which was related to treatment credibility and adherence. This suggests that older patients who follow the therapist's recommendations and believe CBT will work are more likely to be satisfied with and be engaged in the treatment. Therapists are therefore advised to follow CBT best practices and spend time openly and clearly providing psychoeducation about the treatment rationale, content, and expectations, using the learning methods most appropriate to their older clients.

Optimizing Engagement During Treatment

CBT therapists can utilize multidisciplinary collaboration to help clients become engaged. In CBT with older adults, harnessing social support is often an explicit goal. Developing social networks for those with limited supports should be considered a priority, and including a loved one in treatment may facilitate treatment (Thorp et al., 2011). Older adults with anxiety may also require a longer, modified course of CBT (Wetherell et al., 2013).

To help consolidate new learning among older adult clients with varying degrees of memory, cognitive, and physical abilities, the CBT therapist can turn to different strategies, including summarizing information, presenting the same information in multiple ways (including audio and visual tools such as a whiteboard or videos), and providing note-taking materials to clients (Evans, 2007). They might consider behavioral strategies such as activity scheduling and graded exposure if there has been little response to more abstract cognitive restructuring (Chand & Grossberg, 2013). In addition, Cognitive Symptom Management and Rehabilitation Therapy (CogSMART) provides strategies for clients with cognitive limitations, including reminders/alarms, utilization of a daily calendar, creating to-do lists, prioritizing tasks, and linking tasks (Lindamer et al., 2022). Learning and memory can be improved through strategies such as writing things down, paraphrasing, repetition, association, chunking, categorizing, and using acronyms, rhymes, visual imagery, and name-learning strategies.

Psychoeducation About Physical Activity

Psychoeducation about physical activity, coupled with validation about concerns relating to them, can enhance engagement. CBT for anxiety often includes behavioral activation—pleasant activities assigned between therapy sessions, often involving some form of physical activity. These activities typically coincide with client goals of improved physical, cognitive, or emotional functioning because physical activity is correlated with all of these areas of functioning (McPhee et al., 2016). Paluska and Schwenk (2000) noted that physical exercise reduced anxiety levels and that it may be a valuable addition to treatments for anxiety in older adults. Moreover, physical activity is associated with decreased stress, burnout, and anxiety symptoms in older adults (Martínez-Moreno et al., 2020; Paluska & Schwenk, 2000). Yet, fear of falling is also common among older adults and can reduce balance, activity levels, and social performance. CBT significantly reduces fear of falling and improves balance (Liu et al., 2018). As such, clinicians may need to consider such interventions for fear of falling alongside interventions that promote physical activity.

Psychoeducation About Homework

Assigning tasks between session assignments is an intrinsic part of CBT, and strong reinforcement of task completion (e.g., praise) is particularly important early in treatment. Barlow (2021) notes that psychoeducation should be used to provide a rationale about the importance of completing practice assignments. CBT therapists can discuss how completion of assignments is under the client's control, as much as session attendance, and it is a factor that will likely hasten and optimize the client's benefits from treatment. Though it varies across individuals, older adults may have greater respect for authority than younger adults, which may facilitate task adherence (Thorp, 2022).

Exposure Therapy

Clinicians endorse using other treatment techniques significantly more than exposure therapy for older anxious adults due to concerns about the safety and tolerability of exposure for that population (Chen et al., 2022). This is unfortunate because exposure therapy is one of the most powerful interventions for anxiety disorders (Barlow, 2021), and older adults respond to it well (Thorp et al., 2011; Thorp, 2022). Not surprisingly, given its effectiveness, adults appear to prefer exposure therapy over other forms of psychotherapy, and fear related to the perceived difficulty of exposure therapy was not found to be a significant factor in treatment preference (Jaeger et al., 2010). Therapists working with older adults with anxiety and related disorders should therefore offer this gold standard treatment, which can include in vivo exposure (to situations or stimuli in daily life), imaginal exposure (to memories or imagined events), and interoceptive exposure (to physiological sensations), and response prevention, depending on the source of the anxiety.

Formats of CBT

Individual (one-on-one) and group therapy modalities each have distinct advantages for engaging older adults. Individual therapy allows for adaptation of style and topics to the unique challenges and preferences of each older adult. Group therapy offers older adults unique opportunities to improve social connectedness and interpersonal skills while receiving social support and understanding from others facing age-related difficulties and losses (Wetherell et al., 2003). Couples and family CBT work particularly well for improving social functioning (Barlow, 2021).

Wetherell et al. (2013) noted that older adults with GAD do not seem to respond as well as younger adults to traditional (first wave) CBT. The authors proposed that age-related factors may be responsible for the delayed and less robust treatment response among older adults. Wetherell et al. (2011) proposed utilizing acceptance and commitment therapy (ACT) for this specific population, where the aim is to reduce efforts to control private experiences and instead increase engagement in meaningful and valued life activities. This approach includes mindfulness techniques designed to foster nonjudgmental awareness of experience, such as noticing thoughts without perseveration or avoidance of the thought content.

In recent years, there has been growing interest in, and empirical support for, transdiagnostic or "unified" treatments. These approaches recognize that common diagnoses share many common elements that go beyond DSM formulations, many clients have comorbid mental health problems, and many CBT protocols for specific disorders share common techniques (Lopez et al., 2019). These approaches offer the advantage of reducing training requirements that are necessary with multiple single-disorder treatments, reducing the cost and storage of multiple treatment manuals, and allowing clients with common characteristics to be treated together. Though studies in older adults are needed, Barlow (2021) notes that one such approach, the Unified Protocol, works particularly well with anxiety disorders and shows outcomes similar to single-disorder protocols but with fewer treatment dropouts.

Videoconferencing CBT is an effective form of treatment for anxiety, particularly for those with transportation and mobility problems, and both clients and therapists are satisfied with it (Backhaus et al., 2012; Goetter et al., 2022). This appears to apply to older adults as well (Egede et al., 2015). Older and younger adults have about the same rate of interest and use of other mobile health applications (Erbes et al., 2014). Older adults can benefit from the many different options this format can provide, like accessing additional instructional videos and interactive tutorials and complementary interventions as needed (e.g., learning emotion regulation to reduce frustration and better engage with CBT and other interventions; Mohlman et al., 2022).

If technology is involved in treatment, however, it is important for CBT therapists to be repetitive and multimodal in teaching their clients to use the different tools and slow the pace to increase client comfort as needed. Validation of client concerns, practicing with written instructions, reminding the client they can learn about the technology as a "team," and using humor about any glitches can be helpful (Thorp et al., 2015). Providers can demonstrate the use of tech tools such as calendar reminders, taking notes using a note-taking app or audio recording, and completing electronic assessments (Erbes et al., 2014; Lindamer et al., 2022).

End-of-Treatment Issues

The standard termination procedure in CBT includes a review of treatment goals and progress made. The therapist typically joins the client in identifying their strengths and areas of growth while setting them up for a realistic and hopeful future. It may be more important with older adults to be explicit about future expectations regarding symptoms (e.g., some symptoms may reappear during times of stress, but they can use the tools they have gained to resolve them again). Older adults may benefit from written materials at the planned final session to help consolidate learning, as well as automated text or phone call reminders and check-ins to enhance continued practice of learned skills. Some clinical trials of CBT for anxiety disorders and PTSD have found that treatment gains in older adults are lost by the follow-up assessments (Thorp et al., 2019; Wetherell et al., 2013). Given that they may not maintain treatment gains as well as younger adults, older adults may require more focus on relapse prevention and booster sessions. Relapse prevention involves a discussion of likely future stressors and how to utilize learned skills and resources to address those situations. Booster sessions are additional, occasional sessions of CBT, scheduled to allow clients to practice skills independently before returning for feedback and guidance.

Case Example

Consider the following case example. The client (we will call her "Alejandra Cruz") was seen in a private practice in a collaborative care model. Her therapist, who is the practice owner, chose an office near providers from related disciplines (e.g., primary care, psychiatry, social work, pharmacy) to facilitate access and holistic collaborative client care. Upon noticing characteristic anxiety symptoms, Ms. Cruz' primary care physician provided her with a referral card with large font and with her permission contacted the therapist's office to arrange a same day appointment. Ms.

Cruz meanwhile reviewed the therapist's website from the link (printed on the referral card) using a tablet provided to her. Staff from the physician's office familiar to Ms. Cruz escorted her to the therapy waiting room and introduced her to the person at the front desk. Ms. Cruz was reassured by this "warm handoff" from a trusted provider to a new one and felt less stigma about mental health treatment since the care was provided adjacent to her normal medical clinic. In the waiting room, she saw many plants and a poster on the wall depicting an older couple playing with children on a beach. She saw AARP magazines on a coffee table and friendly looking books about CBT on a bookshelf. She recognized the waiting room from the website, which had also mentioned how the therapists specialized in helping adults navigate problems during later life, and it showed a photo of an older woman who looked like herself. The front desk person directed Ms. Cruz back to meet with the client care coordinator; this is the clinic's first point of contact to provide and receive information with all potential clients in person or on the phone. Ms. Cruz appreciated that the doorways and walkways in the clinic were wide enough for her wheelchair and that all doors had automated opening mechanisms.

Identifying and Background Information

The client care coordinator smiled at Ms. Cruz and offered water or coffee and asked if there was anything else he could do to make her comfortable. Ms. Cruz noticed a pamphlet on his desk that said, "Getting Your Life Back with CBT." It showed a smiling woman of color in a colorful kitchen, surrounded by food and her family. The coordinator asked her for demographic information. He learned that she was a 76-year-old, heterosexual, retired, cisgender Latina, and that she was widowed after 52 years of marriage 2 years ago. She and her husband had three children and seven grandchildren, but she now lived alone. She had a high school education but received poor grades.

The coordinator asked Ms. Cruz what brought her in today. She described what she had shared with her physician. Since her husband had passed, she withdrew from social engagements, had unexpected panic attacks (which she called "out of the blue feelings of dread"), and had trouble sleeping. She said she had alienated her two grown sons with what they called her "relentless need for hand-holding," and she was estranged from their families. She remained close to her daughter and her daughter's children. The coordinator validated Ms. Cruz's frustration and desire for change, and he smiled as he said, "I'm happy to tell you that you've come to the right place. We can work out a plan that fits your finances, and we have free parking. Most importantly, we help people just like you feel better within just a few months." He set an initial appointment for her with the therapist, gave her an appointment sticker, and offered to give her a reminder call, which Ms. Cruz accepted.

Relevant Symptoms and Treatment Process Variables

During the intake appointment, the therapist helped Ms. Cruz fill out some questionnaires, which were offered in her choice of paper-and-pencil or digital format, in large font, and completed a psychodiagnostics interview to obtain Ms. Cruz' history (including any experiences with traumatic events), and current chief complaints and presenting problems. This determined that Ms. Cruz met criteria for social anxiety disorder, panic disorder with agoraphobia, and OCD (with repeated checking behaviors, particularly of her stove and door locks; hours of Internet research about potential personal and world problems and reassurance-seeking behavior). Her insomnia had worsened in recent months, and she reported some minor forgetfulness. She had never before tried psychotherapy.

Contextual and Individual Factors Important to Case Conceptualization

Ms. Cruz was still mobile due to her wheelchair, but her movement was slow and would limit some activities. She lived alone, which increased her sense of loneliness and exacerbated her need for reassurance about daily tasks. She was on a fixed income, which limited her flexibility to manage unexpected expenses such as international travel or extravagant leisure activities. She has fallen and injured herself twice in the past year. As a resident of the United States, she did not have universal healthcare coverage, but she was covered for up to 20 outpatient psychotherapy sessions via Medicare.

Case Conceptualization Grounded in CBT Principles

CBT is based on the notion that the frequency and severity of unwanted emotions can be improved by changing actions and thoughts. Ms. Cruz lives alone and avoids social gatherings. Although English was her second language, she is comfortable speaking it. However, there are times when she does not feel welcome by others because of her Latinx appearance. She is not physically active, and she could not name an activity that gives her pleasure. She disclosed several recurring negative thoughts, such as "I just can't do anything right anymore," "I am a burden to everyone," and "There's no point in going out anymore, since my husband died. I'll never be loved again." The therapist determined that her lack of activity, particularly social behaviors, keeps her from eliciting reinforcement in the environment. Her avoidance is negatively reinforced because she feels temporary relief from anxiety when she declines invitations. The therapist posited that this reinforced isolation and inactivity, coupled with her maladaptive thoughts, perpetuated her anxiety and related problems.

Matching Techniques to the Case Conceptualization

Based on this comorbid presentation, the therapist determined that the Unified Protocol would be a good fit for Ms. Cruz because this transdiagnostic approach is particularly good at retaining clients with multiple anxiety diagnoses, is seen as credible by clients, and has good maintenance of treatment gains (Barlow, 2021). The therapist gave Ms. Cruz an overview of the treatment, including the empirical evidence supporting the intervention. He normalized her symptoms, validated her, and smiled to encourage her. He shared his plan to see her for 16 weekly 1-hour one-on-one sessions to help her re-engage with the activities and people she enjoys and help her to have more helpful thoughts about herself and the world. Ms. Cruz agreed to start the treatment. The therapist offered her videoconferencing CBT in case that was more convenient, but she chose in-person meetings. The therapist asked her to track her activities for the next week on an hourly basis and asked her to write down her thoughts during times of strong emotion for homework, though he called it "at home assignments" to avoid connotations with schoolwork.

In the first and second sessions, the therapist helped her set goals and enhance motivation for the treatment and taught her how to notice and understand her emotional experiences. With her permission, he included her daughter in the first few sessions so that she would be aware of the treatment plan and could provide support and assistance in implementing it as needed. In subsequent sessions, they discussed and practiced mindful emotion awareness, cognitive flexibility, countering emotional behaviors, understanding and confronting physical sensations, and exposure. Throughout the treatment, the therapist taught Ms. Cruz to utilize technology to set reminders, help facilitate practice, and access written and video resources consistent with the principles of CogSMART. He asked her to practice behavioral activation, including physical exercise and social meetings, that Ms. Cruz approached in the graduated manner of her choosing. Exposure included learning she could tolerate the distress and uncertainty she experienced when refraining from checking and reassurance-seeking behaviors to ultimately alleviate her OCD symptoms. In the final planned session, they focused on recognizing accomplishments and looking to the future. They added two booster sessions, 2 and 4 weeks following the last session, to ease the ending of treatment and to enhance retention and generalizability of her new skills and independence. Throughout treatment, the therapist administered brief questionnaires to track progress. By the end of treatment, Ms. Cruz reported less social anxiety, fewer panic attacks, better sleep, and fewer checking behaviors. She had renewed friendships and her relationship with her sons and their children. She had gone on two dates. She was invited to return if her symptoms worsened substantially. She left with a smile and said, "I'm back to my old self!"

Clinical Summary Points and Recommendations

CBT with anxious older adults can be enhanced by:

- Integrating CBT with multidisciplinary services.
- Optimizing therapeutic alliance and motivation for treatment.
- Ensuring that treatment addresses social support, physical activity, and spirituality and religion, if indicated.
- Providing advertising and a treatment environment that are welcoming and that represent older adults.
- Including psychoeducation about assessment and treatment procedures, including helping older adults who are new to the process understand the rationale for those procedures.
- Tailoring the format of CBT to best fit each client, including the client's comfort level with technology.

References

American Psychiatric Association. (2013). *Diagnostic and statistical manual of mental disorders* (5th ed.). APA. https://doi.org/10.1176/appi.books.9780890425596

Avers, D., Brown, M., Chui, K. K., Wong, R., & Lusardi, M. M. (2011). Use of the term "elderly". *Journal of Geriatric Physical Therapy, 34*(4), 153–154. https://doi.org/10.1519/jpt.0b013e31823ab7ec

Backhaus, A., Agha, Z., Maglione, M. L., Repp, A., Ross, B., Zuest, D., Rice-Thorp, N. M., Lohr, J., & Thorp, S. R. (2012). Videoconferencing psychotherapy: A systematic review. *Psychological Services, 9*(2), 111–131. https://doi.org/10.1037/a0027924

Barlow, D. H. (2021). *Clinical handbook of psychological disorders: A step-by-step treatment manual* (6th ed.). Guilford Press.

Beck, J. S. (2021). *Cognitive behavior therapy: Basics and beyond* (3rd ed.). Guilford Press.

Brenes, G. A. (2006). Age differences in the presentation of anxiety. *Aging & Mental Health, 10*(3), 298–302. https://doi.org/10.1080/13607860500409898

Buchholz, J. L., & Abramowitz, J. S. (2020). The therapeutic alliance in exposure therapy for anxiety-related disorders: A critical review. *Journal of Anxiety Disorders, 70*, 102194. https://doi.org/10.1016/j.janxdis.2020.102194

Caplan, B., & Shechter, J. (1995). The role of nonstandard neuropsychological assessment in rehabilitation: History, rationale, and examples. In *Psychological assessment in medical rehabilitation* (pp. 359–391). American Psychological Association. https://doi.org/10.1037/10175-009

Chand, S., & Grossberg, G. (2013). How to adapt cognitive-behavioral therapy for older adults. *Current Psychiatry, 12*(3), 10–15.

Chen, J. T. H., Wuthrich, V. M., & Zagic, D. (2022). Practitioners' use of exposure therapy in older adults with anxiety disorders. *Australian Psychologist, 57*(6), 332–337. https://doi.org/10.1080/00050067.2022.2134757

Coles, M. E., Turk, C. L., Jindra, L., & Heimberg, R. G. (2004). The path from initial inquiry to initiation of treatment for social anxiety disorder in an anxiety disorders specialty clinic. *Journal of Anxiety Disorders, 18*(3), 371–383. https://doi.org/10.1016/S0887-6185(02)00259-1

Cook, J. M., McCarthy, E., & Thorp, S. R. (2017). Older adults with PTSD: Brief state of research and evidence-based psychotherapy case illustration. *American Journal of Geriatric Psychiatry, 25*(5), 522–530. https://doi.org/10.1016/j.jagp.2016.12.016

Dinnen, S., Simiola, V., & Cook, J. M. (2015). Post-traumatic stress disorder in older adults: A systematic review of the psychotherapy treatment literature. *Aging and Mental Health, 19*, 144–150. https://doi.org/10.1080/13607863.2014.920299

Egede, L. E., Acierno, R., Knapp, R. G., Lejuez, C., Hernandez-Tejada, M., Payne, E. H., & Frueh, B. C. (2015). Psychotherapy for depression in older veterans via telemedicine: A randomised, open-label, non-inferiority trial. *The Lancet Psychiatry, 2*(8), 693–701. https://doi.org/10.1016/S2215-0366(15)00122-4

Erbes, C. R., Stinson, R., Kuhn, E., Polusny, M., Urban, J., Hoffman, J., Ruzek, J. I., Stepnowsky, C., & Thorp, S. R. (2014). Access, utilization, and interest in mHealth applications among veterans receiving outpatient care for PTSD. *Military Medicine, 179*(11), 1218–1222. https://doi.org/10.7205/MILMED-D-14-00014

Evans, C. (2007). Cognitive–behavioural therapy with older people. *Advances in Psychiatric Treatment, 13*(2), 111–118. https://doi.org/10.1192/apt.bp.106.003020

Goetter, E. M., Iaccarino, M. A., Tanev, K. S., Furbish, K. E., Xu, B., & Faust, K. A. (2022). Telemental health uptake in an outpatient clinic for veterans during the COVID-19 pandemic. *Professional Psychology: Research & Practice, 53*, 151–159. https://doi.org/10.1037/pro0000437

Gould, R. L., Coulson, M. C., & Howard, R. J. (2012). Efficacy of cognitive behavioral therapy for anxiety disorders in older people: A meta-analysis and meta-regression of randomized controlled trials. *Journal of the American Geriatrics Society, 60*(2), 218–229. https://doi.org/10.1111/j.1532-5415.2011.03824.x

Gum, A. M., Arean, P. A., Hunkeler, E., Tang, L., Katon, W., Hitchcock, P., et al. (2006). Depression treatment preferences in older primary care patients. *Gerontologist, 46*, 14–22. https://doi.org/10.1093/geront/46.1.14

Gum, A. M., King-Kallimanis, B., & Kohn, R. (2009). Prevalence of mood, anxiety, and substance-abuse disorders for older Americans in the National Comorbidity Survey Replication. *American Journal of Geriatric Psychiatry, 17*, 769–781. https://doi.org/10.1097/JGP.0b013e3181ad4f5a

Hall, J., Kellett, S., Berrios, R., Bains, M. K., & Scott, S. (2016). Efficacy of cognitive behavioral therapy for generalized anxiety disorder in older adults: Systematic review, meta-analysis, and meta-regression. *The American Journal of Geriatric Psychiatry, 24*(11), 1063–1073. https://doi.org/10.1016/j.jagp.2016.06.006

Hill, R. A. (2011). A positive aging framework for guiding geropsychology interventions. *Behavior Therapy, 42*(1), 66–77. https://doi.org/10.1016/j.beth.2010.04.006

Hundt, N. E., Armento, M. E., Porter, B., Cully, J. A., Kunik, M. E., & Stanley, M. (2013). Predictors of treatment satisfaction among older adults with anxiety in a primary care psychology program. *Evaluation and Program Planning, 37*, 58–63. https://doi.org/10.1016/j.evalprogplan.2013.01.003

Iwamasa, G. Y., & Hays, P. A. (Eds.). (2019). *Culturally responsive cognitive behavior therapy: Practice and supervision* (2nd ed.). American Psychological Association.

Jaeger, J. A., Echiverri, A., Zoellner, L. A., Post, L., & Feeny, N. C. (2010). Factors associated with choice of exposure therapy for PTSD. *International Journal of Behavioral Consultation & Therapy, 5*(3/4), 294–310. https://doi.org/10.1037/h0100890

Jazi, A. N., & Ashghar-Ali, A. A. (2020). Obsessive-compulsive disorder in older adults: A comprehensive literature review. *Journal of Psychiatric Practice, 26*(3), 175–184. https://doi.org/10.1097/PRA.0000000000000463

Kehle-Forbes, S. M., Gerould, H., Polusny, M. A., Sayer, N. A., & Partin, M. R. (2022). "It leaves me very skeptical" messaging in marketing prolonged exposure and cognitive processing therapy to veterans with PTSD. *Psychological Trauma: Theory, Research, Practice, and Policy, 14*(5), 849–852. https://doi.org/10.1037/tra0000550

LaRocca, M. A., & Scogin, F. R. (2015). The effect of social support on quality of life in older adults receiving cognitive behavioral therapy. *Clinical Gerontologist, 38*(2), 131–148. https://doi.org/10.1080/07317115.2014.990598

Lindamer, L., Almklov, E., Pittman, J. O. E., Shi, S., Maye, J., Jak, A., Twamley, E., & Rabin, B. (2022). Multi-method study of the implementation of cognitive symptom management and rehabilitation training (CogSMART) in real-world settings. *BMC Health Services Research, 22*(1), 1542. https://doi.org/10.1186/s12913-022-08941-z

Lippens, T., & Mackenzie, C. S. (2011). Treatment satisfaction, perceived treatment effectiveness, and dropout among older users of mental health services. *Journal of Clinical Psychology, 67*(12), 1197–1209. https://doi.org/10.1002/jclp.20842

Liu, L., Thorp, S. R., Moreno, L., Wells, S. Y., Glassman, L. H., Busch, A. C., Zamora, T., Rodgers, C. S., Allard, C. B., Morland, L. A., & Agha, Z. (2019). Videoconferencing psychotherapy for veterans with PTSD: Results from a randomized controlled non-inferiority trial. *Journal of Telemedicine and Telecare, 26*(9), 507–519. https://doi.org/10.1177/1357633X19853947

Liu, T.-W., Ng, G. Y. F., Chung, R. C. K., & Ng, S. S. M. (2018). Cognitive behavioural therapy for fear of falling and balance among older people: A systematic review and meta-analysis. *Age and Ageing, 47*, 520–527. https://doi.org/10.1093/ageing/afy010

Lopez, M. E., Thorp, S. R., Dekker, M., Noorollah, A., Zerbi, G., Payne, L. A., Meier, E., & Stoddard, J. (2019). The unified protocol for anxiety and depression with comorbid borderline personality disorder: A single case design clinical series. *The Cognitive Behaviour Therapist, 12*, e37. https://doi.org/10.1017/S1754470X19000254

Mackenzie, C. S., Heath, P. J., Vogel, D. L., & Chekay, R. (2019). Age differences in public stigma, self-stigma, and attitudes toward seeking help: A moderated mediation model. *Journal of Clinical Psychology, 75*(12), 2259–2272. https://doi.org/10.1002/jclp.22845

Marker, I., & Norton, P. J. (2018). The efficacy of incorporating motivational interviewing to cognitive behavior therapy for anxiety disorders: A review and meta-analysis. *Clinical Psychology Review, 62*, 1–10. https://doi.org/10.1016/j.cpr.2018.04.004

Martin, K. J., Lauderdale, S. A., Thorp, S., & Mohlman, J. (2019). Psychometric properties of the older adult technophobia scale and the smartphone challenge task. *Innovating Aging, 3*(S1). https://doi.org/10.1093/geroni/igz038.1195

Martínez-Moreno, A., Ibáñez-Pérez, R. J., Cavas-García, F., & F., & Cano-Noguera, F. (2020). The influence of physical activity, anxiety, resilience and engagement on the optimism of older adults. *International Journal of Environmental Research and Public Health, 17*(21), 82–84. https://doi.org/10.3390/ijerph17218284

McPhee, J. S., French, D. P., Jackson, D. A., Nazroo, J., Pendleton, N., & Degens, H. (2016). Physical activity in older age: Perspectives for healthy ageing and frailty. *Biogerontology, 17*(3), 567–580. https://doi.org/10.1007/s10522-016-9641-0

Mohlman, J., Bryant, C., Lenze, E. J., Stanley, M. A., Gum, A., Flint, A., Beekman, A. T. F., Wetherell, J. L., Thorp, S. R., & Craske, M. G. (2012). Improving recognition of late life anxiety disorders in diagnostic and statistical manual of mental disorders, fifth edition: Observations and recommendations of the Advisory Committee to the Lifespan Disorders Work Group. *International Journal of Geriatric Psychiatry, 27*, 549–556. https://doi.org/10.1002/gps.2752

Mohlman, J., Tsang, W., Magee, S. A., Dalokay, L., & Basch, C. (2022). Which variant of anxiety is associated with smartphone expertise in community dwelling older adults? *Clinical Gerontologist, 45*(2), 403–413. https://doi.org/10.1080/07317115.2021.2013382

Nilsson, J., Sigström, R., Östling, S., Waern, M., & Skoog, I. (2019). Changes in the expression of worries, anxiety, and generalized anxiety disorder with increasing age: A population study of 70 to 85-year-olds. *International Journal of Geriatric Psychiatry, 34*(2), 249–257. https://doi.org/10.1002/gps.5012

Noble, L., & Devlin, A. S. (2021). Perceptions of psychotherapy waiting rooms: Design recommendations. *HERD: Health Environments Research & Design Journal, 14*(3), 140–154. https://doi.org/10.1177/19375867211001885

Paluska, S. A., & Schwenk, T. L. (2000). Physical activity and mental health: Current concepts. *Sports Medicine (Auckland, N.Z.), 29*(3), 167–180. https://doi.org/10.2165/00007256-200029030-00003

Paukert, A. L., Phillips, L., Cully, J. A., Loboprabhu, S. M., Lomax, J. W., & Stanley, M. A. (2009). Integration of religion into cognitive-behavioral therapy for geriatric anxiety and depression. *Journal of Psychiatric Practice, 15*(2), 103–112. https://doi.org/10.1097/01.pra.0000348363.88676.4d

Price, J. N., McElroy, K., & Martin, N. G. (2016). The role of font size and font style in younger and older adults' predicted and actual recall performance. *Aging Neuropsychology and Cognition, 23*(3), 366–388. https://doi.org/10.1080/13825585.2015.1102194

Randall, C. L., & McNeil, D. W. (2017). Motivational interviewing as an adjunct to cognitive behavior therapy for anxiety disorders: A critical review of the literature. *Cognitive and Behavioral Practice, 24*(3), 296–311. https://doi.org/10.1016/j.cbpra.2016.05.003

Rhee, T. G., Barry, L. C., Kuchel, G. A., Steffens, D. C., & Wilkinson, S. T. (2019). Associations of adverse childhood experiences with past-year DSM-5 psychiatric and substance use disorders in older adults. *Journal of the American Geriatrics Society, 67*(10), 2085–2093. https://doi.org/10.1111/jgs.16032

Roberts, A. W., Ogunwole, S. U., Blakeslee, L., & Rabe, M. A. (2018). The population 65 years and older in the United States: 2016. *American Community Survey Reports*, ACS-38, U.S. Census Bureau. Retrieved from https://www.census.gov/content/dam/Census/library/publications/2018/acs/ACS-38.pdf.

Schuitevoerder, S., Rosen, J. W., Twamley, E. W., Ayers, C. R., Sones, H., Lohr, J. B., Goetter, E. M., Fonzo, G. A., Holloway, K. J., & Thorp, S. R. (2013). A meta-analysis of cognitive functioning in older adults with PTSD. *Journal of Anxiety Disorders, 27*, 550–558. https://doi.org/10.1016/j.janxdis.2013.01.001

Secker, D. L., Kazantzis, N., & Pachana, N. A. (2004). Cognitive behavior therapy for older adults: Practical guidelines for adapting therapy structure. *Journal of Rational-Emotive & Cognitive-Behavior Therapy, 22*, 93–109. https://doi.org/10.1023/B:JORE.0000025440.38005.7e

Serdarevic, M., & Lemke, S. (2013). Motivational interviewing with the older adult. *The International Journal of Mental Health Promotion, 15*, 240–249. https://doi.org/10.1080/14623730.2013.862362

Sirey, J. A., Bruce, M. L., Alexopoulos, G. S., Perlick, D. A., Raue, P., Friedman, S. J., & Meyers, B. S. (2001). Perceived stigma as a predictor of treatment discontinuation in young and older outpatients with depression. *American Journal of Psychiatry, 158*(3), 479–481. https://doi.org/10.1176/appi.ajp.158.3.479

Sittler, M. C., Lechner-Meichsner, F., Wilz, G., & Kessler, E. M. (2022). Does age matter? Initial treatment goals of older adults with major depression in outpatient cognitive behavioral therapy. *Clinical Psychology & Psychotherapy, 29*(2), 554–566. https://doi.org/10.1002/cpp.2646

Thorp, S. R. (2022). Prolonged exposure therapy with an older adult: An extended case example. *Cognitive and Behavioral Practice, 29*, 161–174. https://doi.org/10.1016/j.cbpra.2020.04.002

Thorp, S. R., Ayers, C. R., Nuevo, R., Stoddard, J. A., Sorrell, J. T., & Wetherell, J. L. (2009). Meta-analysis comparing different behavioral treatments for late-life anxiety. *American Journal of Geriatric Psychiatry, 17*, 105–115. https://doi.org/10.1097/JGP.0b013e31818b3f73

Thorp, S. R., Sones, H. M., & Cook, J. M. (2011). Posttraumatic stress disorder among older adults. In K. H. Sorocco & S. Lauderdale (Eds.), *Cognitive behavior therapy with older adults: Innovations across care settings* (pp. 189–217). Springer Publishing Company.

Thorp, S. R., Wells, S. Y., Williams, K., Walter, K., Moreno, L., Butler, E., & Glassman, L. (2015). The informed consent process for therapeutic communication in clinical videoconferencing. In P. W. Tuerk & P. Shore (Eds.), *Behavioral telehealth series: Clinical video conferencing in telehealth: Program development and practice* (pp. 133–166). Springer International. https://doi.org/10.1007/978-3-319-08765-8_7

Thorp, S. R., Glassman, L. H., Wells, S. Y., Walter, K. H., Gebhardt, H., Twamley, E., Golshan, S., Pittman, J., Penski, K., Allard, C., Morland, L. A., & Wetherell, J. (2019). A randomized controlled trial of prolonged exposure therapy versus relaxation training for older veterans with military-related PTSD. *Journal of Anxiety Disorders, 64*, 45–44. https://doi.org/10.1016/j.janxdis.2019.02.003

Tisdale, W. III (2022, September 28). *Suicide warning signs and prevention strategies for older adults*. Substance Abuse and Mental Health Services Administration. https://www.samhsa.gov/blog/suicide-warning-signs-prevention-strategies-older-adults

Vásquez, E., O'Malley, I., Cruz-Gonzalez, M., Velásquez, E., & Alegría, M. (2021). The impact of social support on treatment participation and completion in a disability prevention intervention for older adults. *Journal of Aging and Health, 33*(7–8), 557–564. https://doi.org/10.1177/0898264321999897

Vathke, C., Kessler, E. M., Gellert, P., O'Sullivan, J. L., & Lech, S. (2022). Motivation and psychotherapy in older adults with care needs and depression. *GeroPsych, 36*(2), 49–62. https://doi.org/10.1024/1662-9647/a000305

Westra, H. A., Constantino, M. J., & Antony, M. M. (2016). Integrating motivational interviewing with cognitive-behavioral therapy for severe generalized anxiety disorder: An allegiance-controlled randomized clinical trial. *Journal of Consulting and Clinical Psychology, 84*(9), 768–782. https://doi.org/10.1037/ccp0000098

Wetherell, J. L., Kim, D. S., Lindamer, L. A., Thorp, S. R., Hawthorne, W., Kim, K., Hough, R. L., Garcia, P., & Jeste, D. V. (2007). Anxiety disorders in a public mental health system: Clinical characteristics and service use patterns. *Journal of Affective Disorders, 104*(1–3), 179–183. https://doi.org/10.1016/j.jad.2007.02.02

Wetherell, J. L., Afari, N., Ayers, C. R., Stoddard, J. A., Ruberg, J., Sorrell, J. T., Liu, L., Petkus, A. J., Thorp, S. R., Kraft, A., & Patterson, T. L. (2011). Acceptance and commitment therapy for generalized anxiety disorder in older adults: A preliminary report. *Behavior Therapy, 42*(1), 127–134. https://doi.org/10.1016/j.beth.2010.07.002

Wetherell, J. L., Petkus, A. J., Thorp, S. R., Stein, M. B., Chavira, D. A., Campbell-Sills, L., Craske, M. G., Sherbourne, C., Bystritsky, A., Sullivan, G., & Roy-Byrne, P. (2013). Age differences in treatment response to a collaborative care intervention for anxiety disorders. *The British Journal of Psychiatry: the Journal of Mental Science, 203*(1), 65–72. https://doi.org/10.1192/bjp.bp.112.118547

Witlox, M., Garnefski, N., Kraaij, V., Simou, M., Dusseldorp, E., Bohlmeijer, E., & Spinhoven, P. (2021). Prevalence of anxiety disorders and subthreshold anxiety throughout later life: Systematic review and meta-analysis. *Psychology and Aging, 36*(2), 268–287. https://doi.org/10.1037/pag0000529

Woodhead, E. L., Ivan, I. I., & Emery, E. E. (2013). Impact of older adults' experience with psychotherapy on treatment engagement. *Clinical Gerontologist, 36*(3), 260–273. https://doi.org/10.1080/07317115.2013.767869

Wuthrich, V. M., & Frei, J. (2015). Barriers to treatment for older adults seeking psychological therapy. *International Psychogeriatrics, 27*(7), 1227–1236. https://doi.org/10.1017/S1041610215000241

Zoellner, L. A., Feeny, N. C., Cochran, B. N., & Pruitt, L. D. (2003). Treatment choice for PTSD. *Behaviour Research and Therapy, 41*(8), 879–886. https://doi.org/10.1016/s0005-7967(02)00100-6

Zoellner, L. A., Roy-Byrne, P., Mavissakalian, M., & Feeny, N. C. (2019). Doubly randomized preference trial of prolonged exposure versus sertraline for treatment of PTSD. *American Journal of Psychiatry, 176*(4), 287–296. https://doi.org/10.1176/appi.ajp.2018.17090995

Index

E. M. Goetter (ed.), *Optimizing Treatment Engagement Processes in CBT for Anxiety and Related Disorders*, CBT: Science Into Practice,
https://doi.org/10.1007/978-3-031-91439-3

MIX
Papier aus verantwortungsvollen Quellen
Paper from responsible sources
FSC® C105338

If you have any concerns about our products,
you can contact us on
ProductSafety@springernature.com

In case Publisher is established outside the EU,
the EU authorized representative is:
Springer Nature Customer Service Center GmbH
Europaplatz 3, 69115 Heidelberg, Germany

Printed by Libri Plureos GmbH
in Hamburg, Germany